Fodor's® 99

Montréal & Québec City

The complete guide, thoroughly up-to-date

Packed with details that will make your trip

The must-see sights, off and on the beaten path

What to see, what to skip

Mix-and-match vacation itineraries

City strolls, countryside adventures

Smart lodging and dining options

Essential local dos and taboos

Transportation tips, distances, and directions

Key contacts, savvy travel tips

When to go, what to pack

Clear, accurate, easy-to-use maps

Excerpted from *Fodor's Canada '99*

Fodor's Travel Publications, Inc.
New York • Toronto • London • Sydney • Auckland
www.fodors.com

Fodor's Montréal & Québec City

EDITOR: Linda Cabasin

Editorial Contributors: David Brown, Susan Brown, Helga Loverseed, Helayne Schiff, M. T. Schwartzman (Gold Guide editor), Elizabeth Thompson, Paul Waters

Editorial Production: Stacey Kulig

Maps: David Lindroth, *cartographer*; Robert Blake, Steven Amsterdam, *map editors*

Design: Fabrizio La Rocca, *creative director*; Guido Caroti, *associate art director*; Jolie Novak, *photo editor*

Production/Manufacturing: Mike Costa

Cover Photograph: Bob Krist

Copyright

ISBN 0-679-00161-1

Special Sales

Fodor's Travel Publications are available at special discounts for bulk purchases for sales promotions or premiums. Special editions, including personalized covers, excerpts of existing guides, and corporate imprints, can be created in large quantities for special needs. For more information, contact your local bookseller or write to Special Markets, Fodor's Travel Publications, 201 East 50th Street, New York, NY 10022. Inquiries from Canada should be directed to your local Canadian bookseller or sent to Random House of Canada, Ltd., Marketing Department, 2775 Matheson Boulevard East, Mississauga, Ontario L4W 4P7. Inquiries from the United Kingdom should be sent to Fodor's Travel Publications, 20 Vauxhall Bridge Road, London SW1V 2SA, England.

PRINTED IN THE UNITED STATES OF AMERICA

10 9 8 7 6 5 4 3 2 1

ON THE ROAD WITH FODOR'S

WHEN I PLAN A VACATION, the first thing I do is cast around among my friends and colleagues to find someone who's just been where I'm going. That's because there's no substitute for a recommendation from a good friend who knows your tastes, your budget, and your circumstances, someone who's just been there. Unfortunately, such friends are few and far between. So it's nice to know that there's Fodor's *Montréal & Québec City '99.*

In the first place, this book won't stay home when you hit the road. It will accompany you every step of the way, steering you away from wrong turns and wrong choices and never expecting a thing in return. It includes a wonderful, full-color map from Rand McNally, the world's largest commercial mapmaker. Most important of all, it's written and assiduously updated by the kind of people you *would* hit up for travel tips if you knew them. They're as choosy as your pickiest friend, except they've probably seen a lot more of Montréal and Québec City. In these pages, they don't send you chasing down every town and sight but instead have selected the best ones, the ones that are worthy of your time and money. To make it easy for you to put it all together in the time you have, they've created short, medium, and long itineraries and, in cities, neighborhood walks that you can mix and match in a snap. Just tear out the map at the perforation, and join us on the road in Montréal and Québec City.

About Our Writers

Our success in helping to make your trip the best of all possible vacations is a credit to the hard work of our extraordinary writers.

Helga Loverseed, a well-traveled freelance journalist and photographer based in Magog in the Eastern Townships, shared her insights on Québec province. She also writes columns for the Montréal *Gazette* and the Chicago *Sun-Times.*

Elizabeth Thompson, a Québec City–based reporter, returned to the city after her family left it for Montréal nearly 150 years ago. She covers the provincial government and delights in exploring the city (her Fodor's beat) with her husband and daughter.

Paul Waters, travel editor of the *Gazette* in Montréal, is the expert who updated the Montréal chapter. He's passionate about everything in his city, whether it's the latest restaurant or the city's lovely churches.

Connections

We're pleased that the American Society of Travel Agents continues to endorse Fodor's as its guidebook of choice. ASTA is the world's largest and most influential travel trade association, operating in more than 170 countries, with 27,000 members pledged to adhere to a strict code of ethics reflecting the Society's motto, "Integrity in Travel." ASTA shares Fodor's devotion to providing smart, honest travel information and advice to travelers, and we've long recommended that our readers—even those who have guidebooks and traveling friends—consult ASTA member agents for the experience and professionalism they bring to your vacation planning.

On Fodor's Web site (www.fodors.com), check out the new Resource Center, an online companion to the Gold Guide section of this book, complete with useful hot links to related sites. In our forums, you can also get lively advice from other travelers and more great tips from Fodor's experts worldwide.

How to Use This Book

Organization

Up front is the **Gold Guide,** an easy-to-use section arranged alphabetically by topic. Under each listing you'll find tips and information that will help you accomplish what you need to in Canada. You'll also find addresses and telephone numbers of organizations and companies that offer destination-related services and detailed information and publications.

The first chapter in the guide, Destination: Montréal and Québec City, helps get you in the mood for your trip. New and Noteworthy cues you in on trends and happenings, What's Where gets you oriented, Pleasures and Pastimes describes the activities and sights that make Québec unique, Fodor's Choice showcases our top picks, and Festivals and Seasonal Events alerts you to special events you'll want to seek out.

Both city chapters begin with an Exploring section subdivided by neighborhood; each section recommends a walking or driving tour and lists sights in alphabetical order. The regional chapter is divided by geographical area; within each area, towns are covered in logical geographical order, and attractive stretches of road and minor points of interest between them are indicated by designation *En Route*. Throughout, Off the Beaten Path sights appear after the places from which they are most easily accessible. And within town sections, all restaurants and lodgings are grouped together.

To help you decide what to visit in the time you have, chapters begin with our recommended itineraries. You can mix and match those from several chapters to create a complete vacation. The A to Z section that ends all chapters covers getting there and getting around. It also provides helpful contacts and resources.

Icons and Symbols

★ Our special recommendations
✕ Restaurant
🏨 Lodging establishment
✕🏨 Lodging establishment whose restaurant warrants a special trip
⛺ Campgrounds
🦆 Good for kids (rubber duck)
☞ Sends you to another section of the guide for more information
✉ Address
☎ Telephone number
⏲ Opening and closing times
🎟 Admission prices (those we give apply to adults; substantially reduced fees are almost always available for children, students, and senior citizens)

Numbers in white and black circles ③❸ that appear on the maps, in the margins, and within the tours correspond to one another.

Currency

Unless otherwise stated, all prices, including dining and lodging, are given in Canadian dollars. The exchange rate at press time (fall 1998) is about US$1 to C$1.38, and £1 to C$2.35.

Dining and Lodging

The restaurants and lodgings we list are the cream of the crop in each price range. Price charts appear in the Pleasures and Pastimes section that follows the chapter introduction or, in city chapters, at the start of the dining and lodging sections.

Hotel Facilities

We always list the facilities that are available—but we don't specify whether you'll be charged extra to use them: When pricing accommodations, always ask what's included. Assume that all rooms have private baths unless noted otherwise. In addition, when you book a room, be sure to mention if you have a disability or are traveling with children, if you prefer a private bath or a certain type of bed, or if you have specific dietary needs or other concerns.

Assume that hotels operate on the **European Plan** (EP, with no meals) unless we specify that they use the **Continental Plan** (CP, with a Continental breakfast daily), **Modified American Plan** (MAP, with breakfast and dinner daily), or the **American Plan** (AP, with all meals).

Restaurant Reservations and Dress Codes

Reservations are always a good idea; we mention them only when they're essential or are not accepted. Book as far ahead as you can, and reconfirm as soon as you arrive. Unless otherwise noted, the restaurants listed are open daily for lunch and dinner. We mention dress only when men are required to wear a jacket or a jacket and tie. Look for an overview of local dining-out habits in the Pleasures and Pastimes section that follows the chapter introduction and in city chapter dining sections.

Credit Cards

The following abbreviations are used: **AE,** American Express; **D,** Discover **DC,** Diners Club; **MC,** MasterCard; and **V,** Visa.

Don't Forget to Write

You can use this book in the confidence that all prices and opening times are based on information supplied to us at press time; Fodor's cannot accept responsibility for any errors. Time inevitably brings change, so always confirm information when it matters—especially if you're making a detour to visit a specific place.

Were the restaurants we recommended as described? Did our hotel picks exceed your expectations? Did you find a museum we recommended a waste of time? Keeping a travel guide fresh and up-to-date is a big job, and we welcome your feedback, positive *and* negative. If you have complaints, we'll look into them and revise our entries when the facts warrant it. If you've discovered a special place that we haven't included, we'll pass the information along to our correspondents and have them check it out. So send us your thoughts via e-mail at editors@fodors.com (specifying the name of the book on the subject line) or on paper in care of the Montréal and Québec City editor at Fodor's, 201 East 50th Street, New York, NY 10022. In the meantime, have a wonderful trip!

Karen Cure
Editorial Director

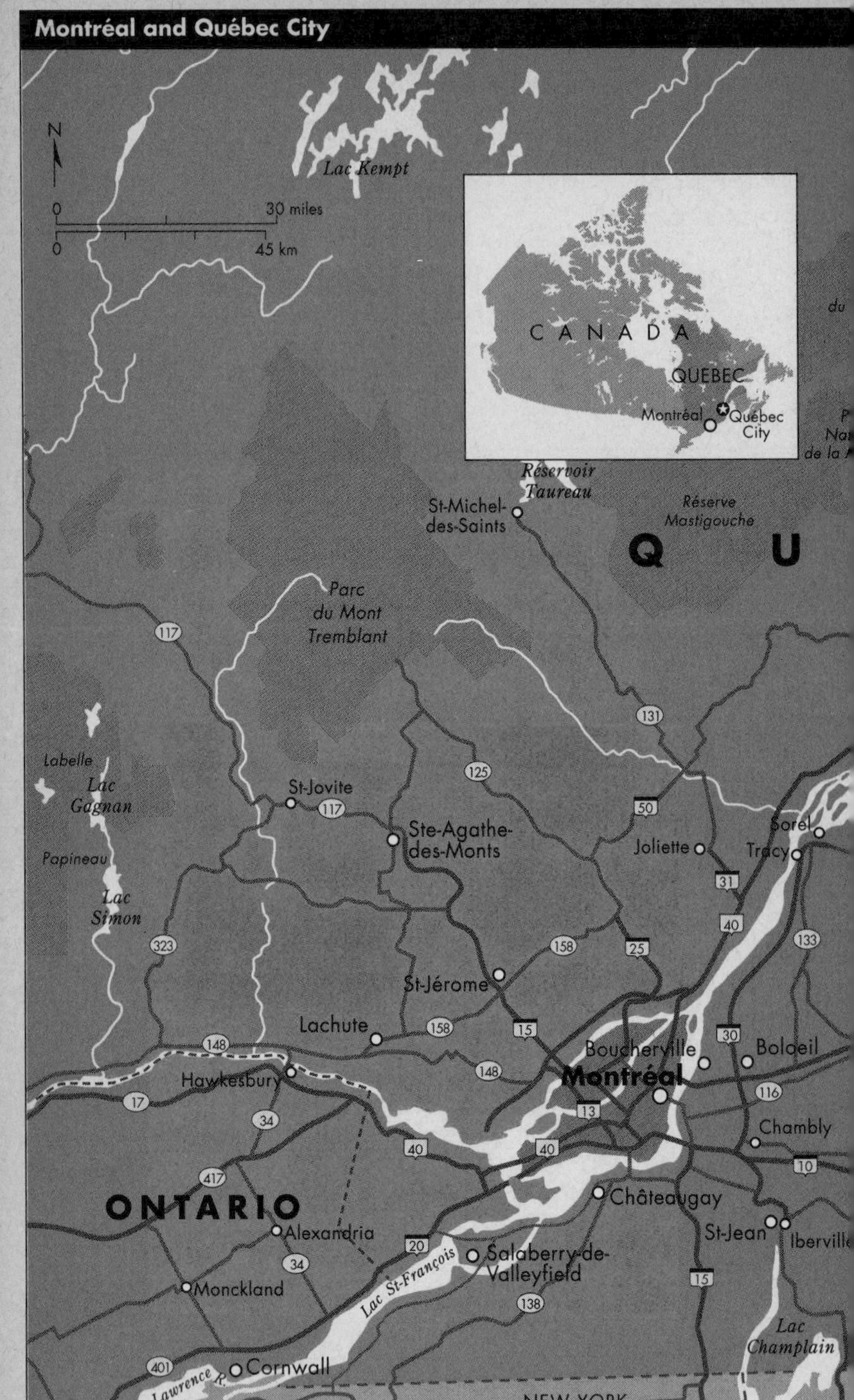
Montréal and Québec City
Lac Kempt
N
0
30 miles
0
45 km
CANADA
QUEBEC
Montréal
Québec City
Réservoir Taureau
St-Michel-des-Saints
Réserve Mastigouche
Q
U
Parc du Mont Tremblant
117
131
125
Labelle
Lac Gagnan
St-Jovite
117
Ste-Agathe-des-Monts
50
Joliette
Sorel
Tracy
Papineau
Lac Simon
31
40
323
158
25
133
St-Jérome
Lachute
158
15
30
148
Boucherville
Boloeil
Hawkesbury
148
Montréal
116
17
34
13
Chambly
40
40
10
417
Châteaugay
ONTARIO
St-Jean
Iberville
Alexandria
20
Salaberry-de-Valleyfield
34
Lac St-François
15
Monckland
138
Lac Champlain
401
Cornwall
St. Lawrence R.
NEW YORK

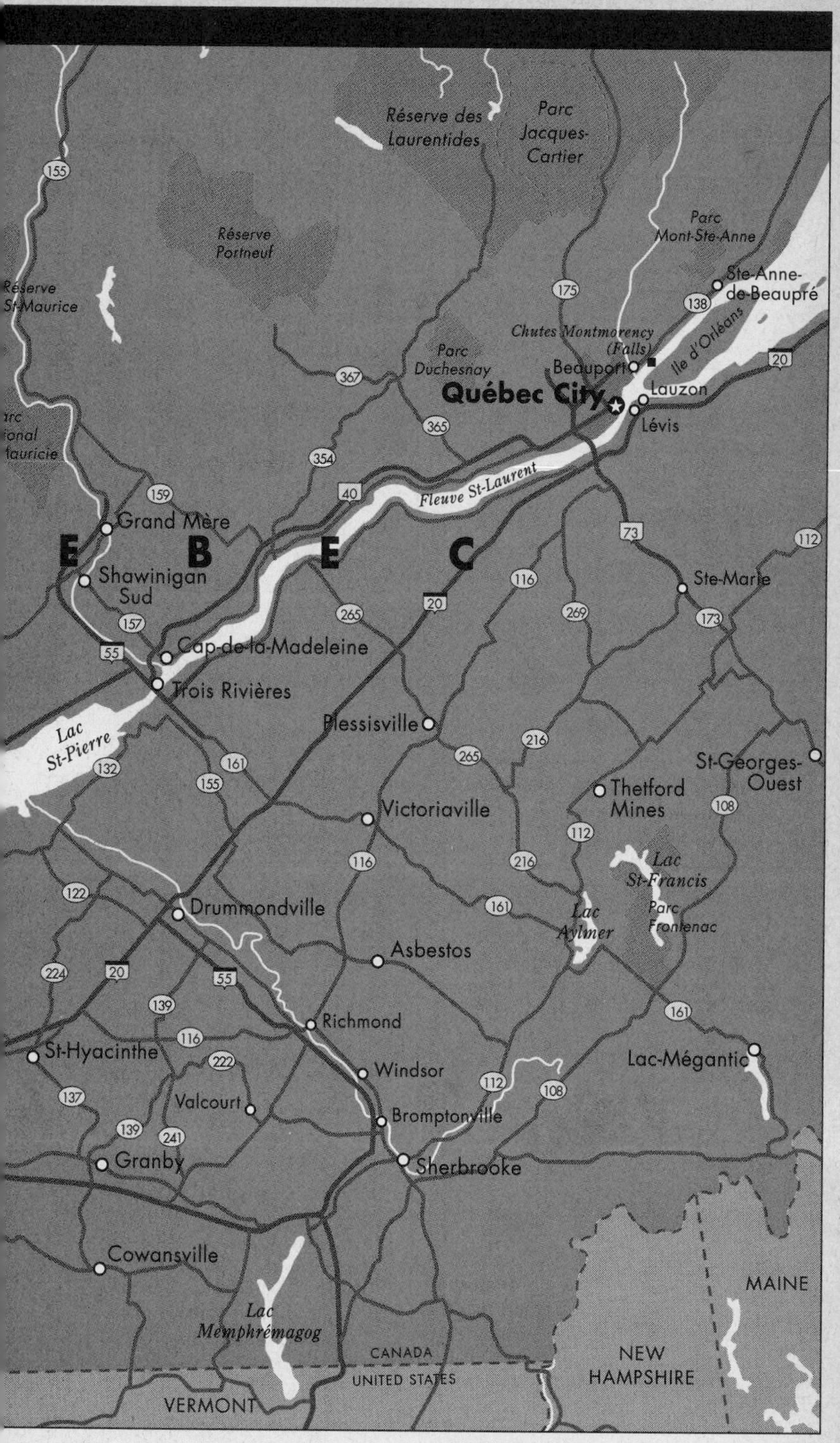

Réserve des Laurentides
Parc Jacques-Cartier
Réserve Portneuf
Réserve St-Maurice
Parc Mont-Ste-Anne
Ste-Anne-de-Beaupré
Chutes Montmorency (Falls)
Ile d'Orléans
Parc Duchesnay
Beauport
Québec City
Lauzon
Lévis
Fleuve St-Laurent
Grand Mère
Shawinigan Sud
E B E C
Ste-Marie
Cap-de-la-Madeleine
Trois Rivières
Lac St-Pierre
Plessisville
St-Georges-Ouest
Thetford Mines
Victoriaville
Lac St-Francis
Parc Frontenac
Lac Aylmer
Drummondville
Asbestos
Richmond
St-Hyacinthe
Lac-Mégantic
Windsor
Valcourt
Bromptonville
Granby
Sherbrooke
Cowansville
MAINE
Lac Memphrémagog
CANADA
UNITED STATES
NEW HAMPSHIRE
VERMONT

SMART TRAVEL TIPS A TO Z

Basic Information on Traveling in Montréal & Québec City, Savvy Tips to Make Your Trip a Breeze, and Companies and Organizations to Contact

AIR TRAVEL

BOOKING YOUR FLIGHT

Price is just one factor to consider when booking a flight: Frequency of service and even a carrier's safety record are often just as important. Major airlines offer the greatest number of departures. Smaller airlines—including regional and no-frills airlines—usually have a limited number of flights daily. On the other hand, so-called low-cost airlines usually are cheaper, and their fares impose fewer restrictions, such as advance-purchase requirements. Safety-wise, low-cost carriers as a group have a good history—about equal to that of major carriers.

When you book, **look for nonstop flights** and **remember that "direct" flights stop at least once.** Try to **avoid connecting flights,** which require a change of plane. Two airlines may jointly operate a connecting flight, so ask if your airline operates every segment—you may find that your carrier flies you only part of the way. International flights on a country's flag carrier are almost always nonstop; U.S. airlines often fly direct.

CARRIERS

When flying internationally, you must usually choose between a domestic carrier, the national flag carrier of the country you are visiting, and a foreign carrier from a third country. You may, for example, choose to fly Air Canada to Canada. National flag carriers have the greatest number of nonstops. Domestic carriers may have better connections to your home town and serve a greater number of gateway cities. Third-party carriers may have a price advantage.

Within Canada, regularly scheduled flights to every major city and to most smaller cities are available on Air Canada or Canadian Airlines International, the two major domestic carriers, or the domestic carriers associated with them. The smaller airlines can also be contacted through their parent carrier's toll-free numbers or at local numbers within each of the many cities they serve.

You should check with the regional tourist agencies for charter companies and with the District Controller of Air Services in the territorial (and provincial) capitals for the locations of air bases that allow private flights and for regulations. Private pilots should obtain information from the Canada Map Office.

➤ MAJOR AIRLINES: **Air Canada** (☎ 800/776–3000) to Montréal, Québec City. **American** (☎ 800/433–7300) to Montréal, Québec City. **Continental** (☎ 800/525–0280) to Montréal. **Delta** (☎ 800/221–1212) to Montréal, Québec City. **Northwest** (☎ 800/225–2525) to Montréal, Québec City. **United** (☎ 800/241–6522) to Montréal. **US Airways** (☎ 800/428–4322) to Montréal.

➤ SMALLER AIRLINES: **Canadian** (☎ 800/426–7000).

➤ FROM THE U.K.: **Air Canada** (☎ 0990/247–226). **British Airways** (☎ 0345/222–111).

➤ WITHIN CANADA: **Air Alliance** (☎ 514/393–3333). **Air Canada** (☎ 800/776–3000). **Canadian Airlines International** (☎ 800/426–7000). **Inter–Canadien** (☎ 514/847–2211). **Canada 3000 Airlines** (☎ 416/259–1118) flies between many major Canadian cities and may offer lower rates.

➤ INFORMATION FOR PRIVATE PILOTS: The **Canada Map Office** (✉ 130 Bentley Ave., Nepean, ON K1A 0E9, ☎ 800/465–6277) has the "Canada Flight Supplement" (lists of airports with Canada Customs services) as well as aeronautical charts.

CHECK IN & BOARDING

Airlines routinely overbook planes, assuming that not everyone with a ticket will show up, but sometimes everyone does. When that happens, airlines ask for volunteers to give up their seats. In return these volunteers usually get a certificate for a free flight and are rebooked on the next flight out. If there are not enough volunteers, the airline must choose who will be denied boarding. The first to get bumped are passengers who checked in late and those flying on discounted tickets, so **get to the gate and check in as early as possible,** especially during peak periods.

Although the trend on international flights is to drop reconfirmation requirements, many airlines still ask you to reconfirm each leg of your international itinerary. Failure to do so may result in your reservation being canceled.

Always **bring a government-issued photo ID to the airport.** You will be asked to show it before you are allowed to check in.

CONSOLIDATORS

Consolidators buy tickets for scheduled international flights at reduced rates from the airlines, then sell them at prices that beat the best fare available directly from the airlines, usually without restrictions. Sometimes you can even get your money back if you need to return the ticket. Carefully read the fine print detailing penalties for changes and cancellations, and **confirm your consolidator reservation with the airline.**

➤ CONSOLIDATORS: Cheap Tickets (☎ 800/377–1000). Discount Travel Network (☎ 800/576–1600). Unitravel (☎ 800/325–2222). Up & Away Travel (☎ 212/889–2345). World Travel Network (☎ 800/409–6753).

CUTTING COSTS

The least-expensive airfares to Montréal and Québec City are priced for round-trip travel and usually must be purchased in advance. It's smart to **call a number of airlines, and when you are quoted a good price, book it on the spot**—the same fare may not be available the next day. Airlines generally allow you to change your return date for a fee. If you don't use your ticket, you can apply the cost toward the purchase of a new ticket, again for a small charge. However, most low-fare tickets are nonrefundable. To get the lowest airfare, **check different routings.** Compare prices of flights to and from different airports if your destination or home city has more than one gateway. Also price off-peak flights.

Travel agents, especially those who specialize in finding the lowest fares (☞ Discounts & Deals, *below*), can be especially helpful when booking a plane ticket. When you're quoted a price, **ask your agent if the price is likely to get any lower.** Good agents know the seasonal fluctuations of airfares and can usually anticipate a sale or fare war. However, waiting can be risky: The fare could go *up* as seats become scarce, and you may wait so long that your preferred flight sells out. A wait-and-see strategy works best if your plans are flexible.

FLYING TIMES

Flying time to Montréal is 1½ hours from New York, 2 hours from Chicago, 6 hours from Los Angeles, 6½ hours from London.

HOW TO COMPLAIN

If your baggage goes astray or your flight goes awry, complain right away. Most carriers require that you **file a claim immediately.**

➤ AIRLINE COMPLAINTS: U.S. Department of Transportation Aviation Consumer Protection Division (✉ C-75, Room 4107, Washington, DC 20590, ☎ 202/366–2220). Federal Aviation Administration Consumer Hotline (☎ 800/322–7873).

AIRPORTS

Montréal's **Dorval International Airport** handles all scheduled flights foreign and domestic and some charter operations; **Mirabel International** handles most charter traffic. Québec City's smaller **Jean Lesage International Airport** serves mostly domestic traffic and a few international flights.

For further information about using these airports, *see* Arriving and Departing *in* the A to Z section at the end of Chapters 2 and 3; and Customs & Duties, *below*.

➤ AIRPORT INFORMATION: In Montréal, **Dorval Airport** (☎ 514/633–3105). **Jean Lesage International Airport** (☎ 418/640–2600). **Mirabel International** (☎ 514/476–3010).

BUS TRAVEL

The bus is an essential form of transportation in Canada, including Québec, especially if you want to visit out-of-the-way towns that do not have airports or rail lines.

➤ BUS COMPANIES: **Greyhound** (✉ 877 Greyhound Way, Calgary, AB T3C 3V8, ☎ 800/661–8747 in Canada or 800/231–2222 in the U.S.). **Voyageur** (✉ 505 E. Boulevard Maisonneuve, Montréal, Québec H2L 1Y4, ☎ 514/842–2281). In the United Kingdom, contact **Greyhound International** (✉ Sussex House, London Rd., E. Grinstead, East Sussex RHI9 1LD, UK, ☎ 01342/317317).

➤ FROM THE U.S.: **Greyhound** (☎ 800/231–2222).

BUSINESS HOURS

BANKS

Most banks are open Monday–Thursday 10–3 and Friday 10–5 or 6. Some banks are open longer hours and also on Saturday morning. All banks are closed on national holidays.

SHOPS

Stores, shops, and supermarkets are usually open Monday–Saturday 9–6, although in major cities supermarkets are often open from 7:30 AM to 9 PM. Blue laws are in effect in much of Canada, but a growing number of provinces have stores with limited Sunday hours, usually noon–5 (shops in areas highly frequented by tourists are usually open on Sunday). Retail stores are generally open on Thursday and Friday evenings, most shopping malls until 9 PM. Drugstores in major cities are often open until 11 PM, and convenience stores are often open 24 hours a day, seven days a week.

CAR RENTAL

Rates in Montréal begin at $14 a day and $75 a week for an economy car with air-conditioning, a manual transmission, and 100 free km (62 mi). This does not include tax on car rentals, which is 15%.

➤ MAJOR AGENCIES: **Alamo** (☎ 800/327–9633, 0800/272–2000 in the U.K.). **Avis** (☎ 800/331–1212, 800/879–2847 in Canada, 008/225–533 in Australia). **Budget** (☎ 800/527–0700, 0800/181181 in the U.K.). **Dollar** (☎ 800/800–4000; 0990/565656 in the U.K., where it is known as Eurodollar). **Hertz** (☎ 800/654–3131, 800/263–0600 in Canada, 0345/555888 in the U.K., 03/9222–2523 in Australia, 03/358–6777 in New Zealand). **National InterRent** (☎ 800/227–7368; 0345/222525 in the U.K., where it is known as Europcar InterRent).

CUTTING COSTS

To get the best deal, **book through a travel agent who is willing to shop around.** When pricing cars, **ask about the location of the rental lot.** Some off-airport locations offer lower rates, and their lots are only minutes from the terminal via complimentary shuttle. Remember to ask about required deposits, cancellation penalties, and drop-off charges if you're planning to pick up the car in one city and leave it in another.

INSURANCE

When driving a rented car you are generally responsible for any damage to or loss of the vehicle. You also are liable for any property damage or personal injury that you may cause while driving. Before you rent, **see what coverage you already have** under your personal auto-insurance policy and credit cards.

REQUIREMENTS

In Canada your own driver's license is acceptable.

SURCHARGES

Before you pick up a car in one city and leave it in another, **ask about drop-off charges or one-way service fees,** which can be substantial. Note, too, that some rental agencies charge extra if you return the car before the time specified in your contract. To avoid a hefty refueling fee, **fill the tank just before you turn in the car,** but be aware that gas stations near the rental outlet may overcharge.

CAR TRAVEL

Canada's highway system is excellent. It includes the Trans-Canada Highway (which uses several different numbers), the longest highway in the world, which runs about 8,000 km/5,000 mi from Victoria, British Columbia, to St. John's, Newfoundland, using ferries to bridge coastal waters at each end. North of the population centers, roads become fewer and less developed.

AUTO CLUBS

➤ IN AUSTRALIA: **Australian Automobile Association** (☎ 06/247–7311).

➤ IN CANADA: **Canadian Automobile Association** (CAA; ☎ 613/247–0117).

➤ IN NEW ZEALAND: **New Zealand Automobile Association** (☎ 09/377–4660).

➤ IN THE U.K.: **Automobile Association** (AA; ☎ 0990/500–600), **Royal Automobile Club** (RAC; ☎ 0990/722–722 for membership, 0345/121–345 for insurance).

➤ IN THE U.S.: **American Automobile Association** (☎ 800/564–6222).

FROM THE U.S.

Drivers must carry owner registration and proof of insurance coverage, which is compulsory in Canada. The Canadian Non-Resident Inter-Provincial Motor Vehicle Liability Insurance Card, available from any U.S. insurance company, is accepted as evidence of financial responsibility in Canada. The minimum liability coverage in Canada is $200,000, except in Québec, where the minimum is $50,000. If you are driving a car that is not registered in your name, carry a letter from the owner that authorizes your use of the vehicle.

The U.S. Interstate Highway System leads directly into Canada: I–91 and I–89 from Vermont to Québec; I–87 from New York to Québec. Most of these connections hook up with the miles. There are many smaller highway crossings between the two countries as well.

GASOLINE

Gasoline costs from 44¢ to 63¢ a liter. (There are 3.8 liters in a U.S. gallon.) Distances are always shown in kilometers, and gasoline is always sold in liters.

ROAD CONDITIONS

The A to Z sections of each chapter have information about road conditions.

RULES OF THE ROAD

By law, you are required to wear seat belts (and use infant seats). Some provinces have a statutory requirement to drive with vehicle headlights on for extended periods after dawn and before sunset. Right turns on red are not permitted in Québec.

Speed limits are usually within the 90–100 kph (50–60 mph) range outside the cities.

CHILDREN & TRAVEL

CHILDREN IN MONTREAL & QUÉBEC CITY

Travelers crossing the border with children should **carry identification for them** similar to that required by adults (i.e., passport or birth certificate). Children traveling with one parent or other adult should **bring letter of permission** from the other parent, parents, or legal guardian. Divorced parents with shared custody rights should **carry legal documents establishing their status.**

Most hotels in Canada allow children under a certain age to stay in their parents' room at no extra charge, but others charge them as extra adults; be sure to **ask about the cutoff age for children's discounts.**

FLYING

If your children are two or older, **ask about children's airfares.** As a general rule, infants under two not occupying a seat fly at greatly reduced fares or even for free.

When booking, **ask about carry-on allowances for those traveling with infants.** In general, for babies charged lowed one carry-on bag and a collapsible stroller, which may have to be checked; you may be limited to less if the flight is full.

Experts agree that it's a good idea to use safety seats aloft for children weighing less than 40 pounds. Airlines, however, can set their own policies: U.S. carriers allow FAA-approved models but usually require that you buy a ticket, even if your child would otherwise ride free, since the seats must be strapped into regular seats. It's important to **check your airline's policy about using safety seats during takeoff and landing.** Safety seats cannot obstruct the movement of other passengers in the row, so get an appropriate seat assignment as early as possible.

When making your reservation, **request children's meals or a free-standing bassinet** if you need them; the latter are available only to those seated at the bulkhead, where there's enough legroom. Remember, however, that bulkhead seats may not have their own overhead bins, and there's no storage space in front of you—a major inconvenience.

CONSUMER PROTECTION

Whenever possible, **pay with a major credit card** so you can cancel payment or get reimbursed if there's a problem, provided that you can provide documentation. This is the best way to pay, whether you're buying travel arrangements before your trip or shopping at your destination.

If you're buying a package or tour, always **consider travel insurance** that includes default coverage (☞ Insurance, *below*).

➤ LOCAL BBBS: **Council of Better Business Bureaus** (✉ 4200 Wilson Blvd., Suite 800, Arlington, VA 22203, ☎ 703/276–0100, FAX 703/525–8277).

CUSTOMS & DUTIES

When shopping, **keep receipts** for all of your purchases. Upon reentering the country, **be ready to show customs officials what you've bought.** If you feel a duty is incorrect, appeal the assessment. If you object to the way your clearance was handled, get the inspector's badge number. In either case, first ask to see a supervisor, then write to the appropriate authorities, beginning with the port director at your point of entry.

U.S. Customs and Immigration has preclearance services at the international airport in Montréal. This allows U.S.-bound air passengers to depart their airplane directly on arrival at their U.S. destination without further inspection and delays.

IN CANADA

American and British visitors may bring in the following items duty-free: 200 cigarettes, 50 cigars, and 14 ounces of tobacco; 1 bottle (1.1 liters or 40 imperial ounces) of liquor or wine, or 24 355-milliliter (12-ounce) bottles or cans of beer for personal consumption. Any alcohol and tobacco products in excess of these amounts is subject to duty, provincial fees, and taxes. You can also bring in gifts up to the value of $60 (Canadian) per gift. A deposit is sometimes required for trailers (refunded upon return). Cats and dogs must have a certificate issued by a licensed veterinarian that clearly identifies the animal and certifies that it has been vaccinated against rabies during the preceding 36 months. Seeing-eye dogs are allowed into Canada without restriction. Plant material must be declared and inspected. There may be restrictions on some live plants, bulbs, and seeds. With certain restrictions or prohibitions on some fruits and vegetables, visitors may bring food with them for their own use, providing the quantity is consistent with the duration of the visit.

Canada's firearms laws are significantly stricter than the U.S.'s. All handguns and semiautomatic and fully automatic weapons are prohibited and cannot be brought into the country. Sporting rifles and shotguns may be imported provided they are to be used for sporting, hunting, or competition while in Canada. All firearms must be declared to Canada Customs at the first point of entry. Failure to declare firearms will result in their seizure, and criminal charges may be made.

IN AUSTRALIA

Australia residents who are 18 or older may bring back $A400 worth of souvenirs and gifts (including jewelry), 250 cigarettes or 250 grams of tobacco, and 1,125 ml of alcohol (including wine, beer, and spirits). Residents under 18 may bring back $A200 worth of goods.

➤ INFORMATION: **Australian Customs Service** (Regional Director, ✉ Box 8, Sydney, NSW 2001, ☎ 02/9213–2000, FAX 02/9213–4000).

IN NEW ZEALAND

Homeward-bound residents with goods to declare must present themselves for inspection. If you're 17 or older, you may bring back $700 worth of souvenirs and gifts. Your duty-free allowance also includes 4.5 liters of wine or beer; one 1,125-milliliter bottle of spirits; and either 200 cigarettes, 250 grams of tobacco, 50 cigars, or a combo of all three up to 250 grams.

➤ INFORMATION: **New Zealand Customs** (✉ Custom House, 50 Anzac Ave., Box 29, Auckland, New Zealand, ☎ 09/359–6655 or 09/309–2978).

IN THE U.K.

From countries outside the EU, including Canada, you may import, duty-free, 200 cigarettes or 50 cigars; 1 liter of spirits or 2 liters of fortified or sparkling wine or liqueurs; 2 liters of still table wine; 60 milliliters of perfume; 250 milliliters of toilet water; plus £136 worth of other goods, including gifts and souvenirs.

➤ INFORMATION: **HM Customs and Excise** (✉ Dorset House, Stamford St., London SE1 9NG, ☎ 0171/202–4227).

IN THE U.S.

U.S. residents may bring home $400 worth of foreign goods duty-free if they've been out of the country for at least 48 hours (and if they haven't used the $400 allowance or any part of it in the past 30 days).

U.S. residents 21 and older may bring back 1 liter of alcohol duty-free. In addition, regardless of your age, you are allowed 200 cigarettes and 100 non-Cuban cigars. Antiques, which the U.S. Customs Service defines as objects more than 100 years old, enter duty-free, as do original works of art done entirely by hand, including paintings, drawings, and sculptures.

You may also send packages home duty-free: up to $200 worth of goods for personal use, with a limit of one parcel per addressee per day (and no alcohol or tobacco products or perfume worth more than $5); label the package PERSONAL USE, and attach a list of its contents and their retail value. Do not label the package UNSOLICITED GIFT, or your duty-free exemption will drop to $100. Mailed items do not affect your duty-free allowance on your return.

➤ INFORMATION: **U.S. Customs Service** (Inquiries, ✉ Box 7407, Washington, DC 20044, ☎ 202/927–6724; complaints, ✉ Office of Regulations and Rulings, 1301 Constitution Ave. NW, Washington, DC 20229; registration of equipment, ✉ Resource Management, 1301 Constitution Ave. NW, Washington DC 20229, ☎ 202/927–0540).

DISABILITIES & ACCESSIBILITY

ACCESS IN MONTREAL & QUÉBEC CITY

➤ LOCAL RESOURCES: **Canadian Paraplegic Association National Office** (✉ 1101 Prince of Wales Dr., Ottawa, ON K2C 3W7, ☎ 613/723–1033) provides information about touring in Canada.

MAKING RESERVATIONS

When discussing accessibility with an operator or reservations agent, **ask hard questions.** Are there any stairs, inside *or* out? Are there grab bars next to the toilet *and* in the shower/tub? How wide is the doorway to the room? To the bathroom? For the most extensive facilities meeting the latest legal specifications, **opt for newer accommodations,** which are more likely to have been designed with access in mind. Be sure to **discuss your needs before booking.**

TRANSPORTATION

➤ COMPLAINTS: **Disability Rights Section** (✉ U.S. Department of Justice, Civil Rights Division, Box

66738, Washington, DC 20035–6738, ☏ 202/514–0301 or 800/514–0301, TTY 202/514–0383 or 800/514–0383, FAX 202/307–1198) for general complaints. **Aviation Consumer Protection Division** (☞ Air Travel, *above*) for airline-related problems. **Civil Rights Office** (✉ U.S. Department of Transportation, Departmental Office of Civil Rights, S-30, 400 7th St. SW, Room 10215, Washington, DC 20590, ☏ 202/366–4648, FAX 202/366–9371) for problems with surface transportation. In Canada, contact the **Canadian Disability Rights Council** (✉ 428 Portage Ave., Suite 208, Winnipeg, MN R3C 0E2, ☏ 204/943–4787). Contact the Director, **Accessible Transportation Directorate** (☏ 819/997–6828), to file a complaint about transportation obstacles at Canadian airports (including flights), railroads, or ferries.

TRAVEL AGENCIES & TOUR OPERATORS

As a whole, the travel industry has become more aware of the needs of travelers with disabilities. In the U.S., the Americans with Disabilities Act requires that travel firms serve the needs of all travelers. Note, though, that some agencies and operators specialize in making travel arrangements for people with disabilities.

➤ TRAVELERS WITH MOBILITY PROBLEMS: **Access Adventures** (✉ 206 Chestnut Ridge Rd., Rochester, NY 14624, ☏ 716/889–9096), run by a former physical-rehabilitation counselor. **Accessible Journeys** (✉ 35 W. Sellers Ave., Ridley Park, PA 19078, ☏ 610/521–0339 or 800/846–4537, FAX 610/521–6959), for escorted tours exclusively for travelers with mobility impairments. **CareVacations** (✉ 5019 49th Ave., Suite 102, Leduc, AB T9E 6T5, ☏ 403/986–6404, 800/648–1116 in Canada) has group tours and is especially helpful with cruise vacations. **Flying Wheels Travel** (✉ 143 W. Bridge St., Box 382, Owatonna, MN 55060, ☏ 507/451–5005 or 800/535–6790, FAX 507/451–1685), a travel agency specializing in customized tours and itineraries worldwide. **Hinsdale Travel Service** (✉ 201 E. Ogden Ave., Suite 100, Hinsdale, IL 60521, ☏ 630/325–1335), a travel agency that benefits from the advice of wheelchair traveler Janice Perkins. **Twin Peaks Press** (✉ Box 129, Vancouver, WA 98666, ☏ 360/694–2462 or 800/637–2256) publishes a directory listing more than 300 travel agencies specializing in helping travelers with disabilities.

➤ TRAVELERS WITH DEVELOPMENTAL DISABILITIES: **Sprout** (✉ 893 Amsterdam Ave., New York, NY 10025, ☏ 212/222–9575 or 888/222–9575, FAX 212/222–9768).

DISCOUNTS & DEALS

Be a smart shopper and **compare all your options** before making any choice. A plane ticket bought with a promotional coupon may not be cheaper than the least expensive fare from a discount ticket agency. For high-price travel purchases, such as packages or tours, keep in mind that what you get is just as important as what you save.

CREDIT-CARD BENEFITS

When you use your credit card to make travel purchases you may get free travel-accident insurance, collision-damage insurance, and medical or legal assistance, depending on the card and the bank that issued it. American Express, MasterCard, and Visa provide one or more of these services, so **get a copy of your credit card's travel-benefits policy.** If you are a member of an auto club, always **ask hotel and car-rental reservations agents about auto-club discounts.** Some clubs offer discounts on tours, cruises, and admission to attractions.

DISCOUNT RESERVATIONS

To save money, **look into discount-reservations services** with toll-free numbers, which use their buying power to get a better price on hotels, airline tickets, even car rentals. When booking a room, always **call the hotel's local toll-free number** (if one is available) rather than the central reservations number—you'll often get a better price. Always ask about special packages or corporate rates.

When shopping for the best deal on hotels and car rentals, **look for guaranteed exchange rates,** which protect you against a falling dollar. With your rate locked in, you won't pay more, even if the price goes up in the local currency.

➤ AIRLINE TICKETS: ☎ 800/FLY-4-LESS. ☎ 800/FLY-ASAP.

➤ HOTEL ROOMS: RMC Travel (☎ 800/245-5738). Steigenberger Reservation Service (☎ 800/223-5652).

PACKAGE DEALS

Packages and guided tours can save you money, but don't confuse the two. When you buy a package, your travel remains independent, just as though you had planned and booked the trip yourself. Fly-drive packages, which combine airfare and car rental, are often a good deal.

ELECTRICITY

Canada, like the United States, uses 110-volt, 60-cycle electric power.

EMERGENCIES

Emergency information is given in the A to Z section at the end of each chapter.

GAY & LESBIAN TRAVEL

➤ GAY- AND LESBIAN-FRIENDLY TRAVEL AGENCIES: Corniche Travel (✉ 8721 Sunset Blvd., Suite 200, West Hollywood, CA 90069, ☎ 310/854-6000 or 800/429-8747, FAX 310/659-7441). Islanders Kennedy Travel (✉ 183 W. 10th St., New York, NY 10014, ☎ 212/242-3222 or 800/988-1181, FAX 212/929-8530). Now Voyager (✉ 4406 18th St., San Francisco, CA 94114, ☎ 415/626-1169 or 800/255-6951, FAX 415/626-8626). Yellowbrick Road (✉ 1500 W. Balmoral Ave., Chicago, IL 60640, ☎ 773/561-1800 or 800/642-2488, FAX 773/561-4497). Skylink Travel and Tour (✉ 3577 Moorland Ave., Santa Rosa, CA 95407, ☎ 707/585-8355 or 800/225-5759, FAX 707/584-5637), serving lesbian travelers.

HEALTH

MEDICAL PLANS

No one plans to get sick while traveling, but it happens, so **consider signing up with a medical-assistance company.** Members get doctor referrals, emergency evacuation or repatriation, 24-hour telephone hot lines for medical consultation, cash for emergencies, and other personal and legal assistance. Coverage varies by plan, so **review benefits carefully.**

➤ MEDICAL-ASSISTANCE COMPANIES: International SOS Assistance (✉ 8 Neshaminy Interplex, Suite 207, Trevose, PA 19053, ☎ 215/245-4707 or 800/523-6586, FAX 215/244-9617; ✉ 12 Chemin Riant-bosson, 1217 Meyrin 1, Geneva, Switzerland, ☎ 4122/785-6464, FAX 4122/785-6424; ✉ 10 Anson Rd., 14-07/08 International Plaza, Singapore, 079903, ☎ 65/226-3936, FAX 65/226-3937).

HOLIDAYS

Canadian national holidays for 1999 are as follows: New Year's Day, Good Friday (April 2), Easter Monday (April 5), Victoria Day (May 17), Canada Day (July 1), Labor Day (September 6), Thanksgiving (October 11), Remembrance Day (November 11), Christmas, and Boxing Day (December 26).

Québec's provincial holiday is St. Jean Baptiste Day (June 24).

INSURANCE

Travel insurance is the best way to **protect yourself against financial loss.** The most useful plan is a comprehensive policy that includes coverage for trip cancellation and interruption, default, trip delay, and medical expenses (with a waiver for preexisting conditions).

Without insurance, you will lose all or most of your money if you cancel your trip, regardless of the reason. Default insurance covers you if your tour operator, airline, or cruise line goes out of business. Trip-delay covers unforeseen expenses that you may incur due to bad weather or mechanical delays. It's important to **compare the fine print regarding trip-delay coverage when comparing policies.**

For overseas travel, one of the most important components of travel insurance is its medical coverage. Supplemental health insurance will pick up the cost of your medical bills should you get sick or injured while traveling. U.S. residents should note that Medicare generally does not cover health-care costs outside the United States, nor do many privately issued policies. Residents of the United Kingdom can buy an annual travel-insurance policy valid for most vacations taken during the year in which the coverage is purchased. If you are pregnant or have a pre-existing condition, make sure you're covered. British citizens should buy extra medical coverage when traveling overseas, according to the Association of British Insurers. Australian travelers should buy travel insurance, including extra medical coverage, whenever they go abroad, according to the Insurance Council of Australia.

Always **buy travel insurance directly from the insurance company**; if you buy it from a cruise line, airline, or tour operator that goes out of business, you probably will not be covered for the agency or operator's default, a major risk. Before you make any purchase, **review your existing health and home-owner's policies** to find out whether they cover expenses incurred while traveling.

➤ TRAVEL INSURERS: In the U.S., **Access America** (✉ 6600 W. Broad St., Richmond, VA 23230, ☎ 804/285–3300 or 800/284–8300). **Travel Guard International** (✉ 1145 Clark St., Stevens Point, WI 54481, ☎ 715/345–0505 or 800/826–1300). In Canada, **Mutual of Omaha** (✉ Travel Division, 500 University Ave., Toronto, ON M5G 1V8, ☎ 416/598–4083, 800/268–8825 in Canada).

➤ INSURANCE INFORMATION: In the U.K., **Association of British Insurers** (✉ 51 Gresham St., London EC2V 7HQ, ☎ 0171/600–3333). In Australia, the **Insurance Council of Australia** (☎ 613/9614–1077, FAX 613/9614–7924).

LANGUAGE

Canada's two official languages are English and French. Though English is widely spoken, it is useful to **learn a few French phrases.** Canadian French has many distinctive words and expressions, but it's no more different from the language of France than North American English is from the language of Great Britain.

LODGING

Aside from the quaint hotels of Québec, Canada's range of accommodations more closely resembles that of the United States than of Europe. In the cities you'll have a choice of luxury hotels, moderately priced modern properties, and smaller older hotels with perhaps fewer conveniences but more charm. Options in smaller towns and in the country include large, full-service resorts; small, privately owned hotels; roadside motels; and bed-and-breakfasts.

There is no national government rating system for hotels, but many provinces rate their accommodations. Québec restructured its rating system during 1998; ratings are listed in the province's official Web site (☞ Web Sites, *below*). The ratings will also be in printed visitor literature in 1999.

Expect accommodations to cost more in summer than in the off-season (except for places such as ski resorts, where winter is high season). When making reservations, **ask about special deals and packages.** Big-city hotels that cater to business travelers often offer weekend packages, and many city hotels offer rooms at up to 50% off in winter. If you're planning to visit a major city or resort area in high season, **book well in advance.** Also be aware of any special events or festivals that may coincide with your visit and fill every room for miles around. For resorts and lodges, consider the winter ski-season high as well and plan accordingly.

B&BS

Bed-and-breakfasts can be found in both the country and the cities. For assistance in booking these, **contact the provincial tourist board,** which either has a listing of B&Bs or can refer you to an association that will help you secure reservations. Room quality varies from house to house as well, so you can **ask to see a room before making a choice.**

HOME EXCHANGES

If you would like to exchange your home for someone else's, **join a home-**

exchange organization, which will send you its updated listings of available exchanges for a year and will include your own listing in at least one of them. It's up to you to make specific arrangements.

➤ EXCHANGE CLUBS: HomeLink International (✉ Box 650, Key West, FL 33041, ☎ 305/294–7766 or 800/638–3841, FAX 305/294–1148; $83 per year).

HOSTELS

No matter what your age, you can **save on lodging costs by staying at hostels.** In some 5,000 locations in more than 70 countries around the world, Hostelling International (HI), the umbrella group for a number of national youth hostel associations, offers single-sex, dorm-style beds and, at many hostels, "couples" rooms and family accommodations. Membership in any HI national hostel association, open to travelers of all ages, allows you to stay in HI-affiliated hostels at member rates (one-year membership is about $25 for adults; hostels run about $10–$25 per night). Members also have priority if the hostel is full; they're eligible for discounts around the world, even on rail and bus travel in some countries.

➤ HOSTEL ORGANIZATIONS: Hostelling International—American Youth Hostels (✉ 733 15th St. NW, Suite 840, Washington, DC 20005, ☎ 202/783–6161, FAX 202/783–6171). Hostelling International—Canada (✉ 400-205 Catherine St., Ottawa, ONK2P 1C3, ☎ 613/237–7884, FAX 613/237–7868). Youth Hostel Association of England and Wales (✉ Trevelyan House, 8 St. Stephen's Hill, St. Albans, Hertfordshire AL1 2DY, ☎ 01727/855215 or 01727/845047, FAX 01727/844126; membership in the U.S. $25, in Canada C$26.75, in the U.K. £9.30).

HOTELS

➤ HOTEL CHAINS: Best Western International (☎ 800/528–1234, 0181/541–0033 in the U.K.), Canadian Pacific Hotels & Resorts (☎ 800/441–1414, 0800/898852 in the U.K.), Choice Hotels International (☎ 800/424–6423, 0800/444–4444 in the U.K.), Days Inns (☎ 800/329–7466, 01483/440470 in the U.K.), Delta Hotels (☎ 800/877–1133, 0171/937–8033 in the U.K.), Four Seasons Hotels (☎ 800/332–3442, 0800/526648 in the U.K.), Hilton Hotels (☎ 800/445–8667), Holiday Inns (☎ 800/465–4329, 0800/897121 in the U.K.), Hyatt Hotels (☎ 800/223–1234, 0171/580–8197 in the U.K.), Inter-Continental (☎ 800/327–0200), Marriott Hotels and Resorts (☎ 800/228–9290, 0800/282811 in the U.K.), Novotel Hotels (☎ 800/668–6835), Radisson Hotels (☎ 800/333–3333, 0800/891999 in the U.K.), Ramada (☎ 800/228–2828, 0181/688–1418 in the U.K.), Relais & Châteaux (☎ 212/856–0115), Sheraton (☎ 800/325–3535, 0800/353535 in the U.K.), Travelodge (☎ 800/255–3050, 0345/404040 in the U.K.), and Westin Hotels (☎ 800/228–3000, 0171/408–0636 in the U.K.).

MAIL

In Québec you can **buy stamps at the post office or from automatic vending machines** in most hotel lobbies, railway stations, airports, bus terminals, many retail outlets, and some newsstands. If you're sending mail to Québec, **be sure to include the postal code** (six letters and numbers). You should also **include the two-letter abbreviation for the province:** PQ.

POSTAL RATES

Within Canada, postcards and letters up to 30 grams cost 45¢; between 31 grams and 50 grams, the cost is 71¢ and between 51 grams and 100 grams the cost is 90¢. Letters and postcards to the United States cost 52¢ for up to 30 grams, 77¢ for between 31 and 50 grams, and $1.17 for up to 100 grams. Prices include GST (Goods and Services Tax).

International mail and postcards run 90¢ for up to 20 grams, $1.37 for between 21 and 50 grams, and $2.25 for between 51 and 100 grams.

RECEIVING MAIL

Visitors may have mail sent to them c/o General Delivery in the town they are visiting, for pickup in person within 15 days, after which it will be returned to the sender.

MONEY

CREDIT & DEBIT CARDS

Should you use a credit card or a debit card when traveling? Both have benefits. A credit card allows you to delay payment and gives you certain rights as a consumer (☞ Consumer Protection, *above*). A debit card, also known as a check card, deducts funds directly from your checking account and helps you stay within your budget.

Otherwise, the two types of plastic are virtually the same. Both will get you cash advances at ATMs worldwide if your card is properly programmed with your personal identification number (PIN). (For use in Canada, your PIN must be four digits long.) Both offer excellent, wholesale exchange rates, and both protect you against unauthorized use if the card is lost or stolen. Your liability is limited to $50, as long as you report the card missing.

➤ ATM LOCATIONS: **Cirrus** (☎ 800/424–7787). **Plus** (☎ 800/843–7587) for locations in the U.S. and Canada, or visit your local bank.

➤ REPORTING LOST CARDS: **American Express** (☎ 800/528–4000). **Diners Club** (☎ 800/234–6377). **Discover** (☎ 800/347–2683). **MasterCard** (☎ 800/307–7309). **Visa** (☎ 800/336–8472).

CURRENCY

American money is accepted in much of Canada (especially in communities near the border). However, to get the most favorable exchange rate, **exchange at least some of your money into Canadian funds at a bank or other financial institution.** Traveler's checks (some are available in Canadian dollars) and major U.S. credit cards are accepted in most areas.

The units of currency in Canada are the Canadian dollar (C$) and the cent, in almost the same denominations as U.S. currency ($5, $10, $20, 1¢, 5¢, 10¢, 25¢, etc.). The $1 and $2 bill are no longer used; they have been replaced by $1 and $2 coins (known as a "loonie," because of the loon that appears on the coin, and a "toonie," respectively). At press time the exchange rate was US$1 to C$1.38 and £1 to C$2.35.

EXCHANGING MONEY

For the most favorable rates, **change money through banks.** Although fees charged for ATM transactions may be higher abroad than at home, Cirrus and Plus exchange rates are excellent, because they are based on wholesale rates offered by major banks. You won't do as well at exchange booths in airports or rail and bus stations, in hotels, in restaurants, or in stores, although you may find their hours convenient. To avoid lines at airport exchange booths, **get a bit of local currency before you leave home.**

➤ EXCHANGE SERVICES: **Chase *Currency to Go*** (☎ 800/935–9935; 935–9935 in NY, NJ, and CT). **International Currency Express** (☎ 888/842–0880 on the East Coast, 888/278–6628 on the West Coast). **Thomas Cook Currency Services** (☎ 800/287–7362 for telephone orders and retail locations).

TRAVELER'S CHECKS

Do you need traveler's checks? It depends on where you're headed. If you're going to rural areas and small towns, go with cash; traveler's checks are best used in cities. Lost or stolen checks can usually be replaced within 24 hours. To ensure a speedy refund, **buy your own traveler's checks**—don't let someone else pay for them: Irregularities like this can cause delays. The person who bought the checks should make the call to request a refund.

OUTDOOR ACTIVITIES & SPORTS

BICYCLING

➤ ASSOCIATION: **Canadian Cycling Association** (✉ 1600 James Naismith Dr., Gloucester, ON K1B 5N4, ☎ 613/748–5629).

CANOEING AND KAYAKING

Provincial tourist offices can be of assistance, especially in locating an outfitter to suit your needs.

➤ ASSOCIATION: **Canadian Recreational Canoeing Association** (✉ 5–1029 Hyde Park Rd., London, ON N0M 1Z0, ☎ 519/473–2109).

CLIMBING/MOUNTAINEERING

➤ ASSOCIATION: **Alpine Club of Canada** (✉ Box 2040, Canmore, AB T0L 0M0, ☎ 403/678–3200).

GOLF

➤ ASSOCIATION: **Royal Canadian Golf Association** (✉ 1333 Dorval Dr., Oakville, ON L6J 4Z3, ☎ 905/849–9700).

SCUBA DIVING

➤ ASSOCIATION: **Canadian Amateur Diving Association** (✉ 1600 James Naismith Dr., Suite 705, Gloucester, ON K1B 5N4, ☎ 613/748–5631).

TENNIS

➤ ASSOCIATION: **Tennis Canada** (✉ 3111 Steeles Ave. W, Downsview, ON M3J 3H2, ☎ 416/665–9777).

PACKING

LUGGAGE

How many carry-on bags you can bring with you is up to the airline. Most allow two, but the limit is often reduced to one on certain flights. Gate agents will take excess baggage—including bags they deem oversize—from you as you board and add it to checked luggage. To avoid this situation, make sure that everything you carry aboard will fit under your seat. Also, get to the gate early, and request a seat at the back of the plane; you'll board first, while the overhead bins are still empty. Since big, bulky baggage attracts the attention of gate agents and flight attendants on a busy flight, make sure your carry-on is really a carry-on.

If you are flying internationally, note that baggage allowances may be determined not by piece but by weight—generally 88 pounds (40 kilograms) in first class, 66 pounds (30 kilograms) in business class, and 44 pounds (20 kilograms) in economy.

Airline liability for baggage is limited to $1,250 per person on flights within the United States. On international flights it amounts to $9.07 per pound or $20 per kilogram for checked baggage (roughly $640 per 70-pound bag) and $400 per passenger for unchecked baggage. You can buy additional coverage at check-in for about $10 per $1,000 of coverage, but it excludes a rather extensive list of items, shown on your airline ticket.

Before departure, **itemize your bags' contents** and their worth, and label the bags with your name, address, and phone number. (If you use your home address, cover it so that potential thieves can't see it readily.) Inside each bag, **pack a copy of your itinerary.** At check-in, **make sure that each bag is correctly tagged** with the destination airport's three-letter code. If your bags arrive damaged or fail to arrive at all, file a written report with the airline before leaving the airport.

PACKING LIST

How you pack will depend on when you go and what you plan to do. In winter, **bring layers,** the best defense against Canada's cold winters; a hat, scarf, and gloves are essential. For summer travel, **select loose-fitting natural-fiber clothes**; bring a wool sweater and light jacket. For Montréal and Québec City, pack both casual clothes for day touring and more formal wear for evenings out.

In your carry-on luggage **bring an extra pair of eyeglasses or contact lenses** and **enough of any medication you take** to last the entire trip. You may also want your doctor to write a spare prescription using the drug's generic name, since brand names may vary from country to country. **Never put prescription drugs or valuables in luggage to be checked.** To avoid customs delays, carry medications in their original packaging. And don't forget to copy down and carry addresses of offices that handle refunds of lost traveler's checks.

PASSPORTS & VISAS

When traveling internationally, **carry a passport even if you don't need one** (it's always the best form of ID) and **make two photocopies of the data page** (one for someone at home and another for you, carried separately from your passport). If you lose your passport, promptly call the nearest embassy or consulate and the local police.

ENTERING CANADA

Citizens and legal residents of the United States do not need a passport or a visa to enter Canada, but proof of citizenship (a birth certificate or valid passport) and photo identification will be requested. Naturalized U.S. citizens should carry their naturalization certificate or other evidence of citizenship. Permanent legal residents of the U.S. should carry their "green card." U.S. residents entering Canada from a third country must have a valid passport, naturalization certificate, or green card.

Citizens of the United Kingdom need only a valid passport to enter Canada for stays of up to six months.

PASSPORT OFFICES

➤ AUSTRALIAN CITIZENS: **Australian Passport Office** (☎ 13/1232).

➤ NEW ZEALAND CITIZENS: **New Zealand Passport Office** (☎ 04/494–0700 for information on how to apply, 0800/727–776 for information on applications already submitted).

➤ U.K. CITIZENS: **London Passport Office** (☎ 0990/21010), for fees and documentation requirements and to request an emergency passport.

SENIOR-CITIZEN TRAVEL

To qualify for age-related discounts, **mention your senior-citizen status up front** when booking hotel reservations and before you're seated in restaurants. Note that discounts may be limited to certain menus, days, or hours. When renting a car, **ask about promotional car-rental discounts,** which can be cheaper than senior-citizen rates.

➤ EDUCATIONAL PROGRAMS: **Elderhostel** (✉ 75 Federal St., 3rd floor, Boston, MA 02110, ☎ 617/426–8056).

STUDENT TRAVEL

Persons under 18 years of age who are not accompanied by their parents should **bring a letter from a parent or guardian** giving them permission to travel to Canada.

TRAVEL AGENCIES

To save money, **look into deals available through student-oriented travel agencies.** To qualify you'll need a bona fide student ID card. Members of international student groups are also eligible.

➤ STUDENT IDS & SERVICES: **Council on International Educational Exchange** (CIEE; ✉ 205 E. 42nd St., 14th floor, New York, NY 10017, ☎ 212/822–2600 or 888/268–6245, FAX 212/822–2699), for mail orders only, in the United States. **Travel CUTS** (✉ 187 College St., Toronto, ON M5T 1P7, ☎ 416/979–2406 or 800/667–2887) in Canada.

➤ STUDENT TOURS: **Contiki Holidays** (✉ 300 Plaza Alicante, Suite 900, Garden Grove, CA 92840, ☎ 714/740–0808 or 800/266–8454, FAX 714/740–2034).

TAXES

A goods and services tax of 7% (GST) applies on virtually every transaction in Canada except for the purchase of basic groceries.

In addition to the GST, the province of Québec levies a sales tax of 7.5% on most items purchased in shops, on restaurant meals, and on hotel rooms.

PROVINCIAL TAX REFUNDS

Québec offers a sales-tax rebate system similar to the federal one. For provincial tax refunds, **call the provincial toll-free visitor information line for details** (☞ Visitor Information, *below*).

GST REFUNDS

You can **get a GST refund on purchases taken out of the country and on short-term accommodations** (but not on food, drink, tobacco, car or motor-home rentals, or transportation); rebate forms, which must be submitted within 60 days of leaving Canada, may be obtained from certain retailers, duty-free shops, customs officials, or from Revenue Canada. Instant cash rebates up to a maximum of $500 are provided by some duty-free shops when leaving Canada, and most provinces do not tax goods that are shipped directly by the vendor to the purchaser's home. Always **save your original receipts** from stores and hotels, and **be sure the name and address of the establishment is shown on the receipt.** Original receipts are not returned. The total amount of GST on each receipt must be at least $50.

➤ INFORMATION: **Revenue Canada** (✉ Visitor Rebate Program, Summerside Tax Centre, Summerside, PE C1N 6C6, ☎ 902/432–5608 or 800/668–4748 in Canada).

TELEPHONES

COUNTRY CODES

The country code for Canada is 1.

DIRECTORY & OPERATOR INFORMATION

For operator assistance, dial "0." For directory assistance in Canada, dial the area code followed by 555–1212; dial 1 before the area code if the area code is not the same as the one you are calling from.

INTERNATIONAL CALLS

International calls can be direct-dialed from most phones. If you're dialing Canada from the United States, dial 1 plus the area code and telephone number. If you're dialing the United States from Canada, dial 1 plus the area code and telephone number.

LOCAL CALLS

For local calls, simply dial the number. No area code is needed.

LONG-DISTANCE CALLS

To dial another province or an area of the same province that has a different area code, dial 1 followed by the area code and number.

Competitive long-distance carriers make calling within the United States and Canada relatively convenient and let you avoid hotel surcharges. By dialing an 800 number, you can get connected to the long-distance company of your choice.

➤ LONG-DISTANCE CARRIERS: **AT&T** (☎ 800/225–5288). **MCI** (☎ 800/888–8000). **Sprint** (☎ 800/366–2255).

PUBLIC PHONES

Pay telephones take coins, and charge phones are found in many locations, including airports and some shopping malls. These phones can be used to charge a call to a telephone company card, your home, or the party you are calling.

TIPPING

Tips and service charges are not usually added to a bill in Canada. In general, tip 15% of the total bill. This goes for waiters, waitresses, barbers and hairdressers, and taxi drivers. Porters and doormen should get about $1 a bag (or more in a luxury hotel). For maid service, $1 a day is sufficient ($2 in luxury hotels).

TOUR OPERATORS

Buying a prepackaged tour or independent vacation can make your trip less expensive and more hassle-free. Because everything is prearranged, you'll spend less time planning.

Operators that handle several hundred thousand travelers per year can use their purchasing power to give you a good price. Their high volume may also indicate financial stability. But some small companies provide more personalized service; because they tend to specialize, they may be more knowledgeable about an area.

BOOKING WITH AN AGENT

Travel agents are excellent resources. In fact, large operators accept bookings made only through travel agents. But it's a good idea to **collect brochures from several agencies,** because some agents' suggestions may be influenced by relationships with tour and package firms that reward them for volume sales. If you have a special interest, **find an agent with expertise in that area**; ASTA (☞ Travel Agencies, *below*) has a database of specialists worldwide.

Make sure your travel agent knows the accommodations and other services. Ask about the hotel's location, room size, beds, and whether it has a pool, room service, or programs for children, if you care about these. Has your agent been there in person or sent others you can contact?

Do some homework on your own, too: Local tourism boards can provide information about lesser-known and small-niche operators.

BUYER BEWARE

Each year consumers are stranded or lose their money when tour operators—even very large ones with excellent reputations—go out of business. So **check out the operator.** Find out how long the company has been in business, and ask several travel agents about its reputation. If the package or tour you are considering is priced lower than in your wildest dreams, **be skeptical.** Try to **book with a company that has a consumer-protection program.** If the operator has such a program, you'll find information about it in the company's brochure. If an operator does not offer some kind of consumer protection, then ask for references from satisfied customers.

In the U.S., members of the National Tour Association and United States Tour Operators Association are required to set aside funds to cover your payments and travel arrangements in case the company defaults. It's also a good idea to choose a company that participates in the American Society of Travel Agent's Tour Operator Program (TOP). This gives you a forum if there are any disputes between you and your tour operator; ASTA will act as mediator.

➤ TOUR-OPERATOR RECOMMENDATIONS: **American Society of Travel Agents** (☞ Travel Agencies, *below*). **National Tour Association** (NTA; ✉ 546 E. Main St., Lexington, KY 40508, ☎ 606/226–4444 or 800/755–8687). **United States Tour Operators Association** (USTOA; ✉ 342 Madison Ave., Suite 1522, New York, NY 10173, ☎ 212/599–6599 or 800/468–7862, FAX 212/599–6744).

COSTS

The more your package or tour includes, the better you can predict the ultimate cost of your vacation. Make sure you know what is covered, and **beware of hidden costs.** Are taxes, tips, and service charges included? Transfers and baggage handling? Entertainment and excursions?

Prices for packages and tours are usually quoted per person, based on two sharing a room. If traveling solo, you may be required to pay the full double-occupancy rate. Some operators eliminate this surcharge if you agree to be matched with a roommate of the same sex.

GROUP TOURS

Among companies that sell tours to Canada, the following have a proven reputation and offer plenty of options. The classifications used below represent different price categories. The key difference is usually in accommodations, which run from budget to better, and better-yet to best.

➤ DELUXE: **Globus** (✉ 5301 S. Federal Circle, Littleton, CO 80123-2980, ☎ 303/797–2800 or 800/221–0090, FAX 303/347–2080). **Maupintour** (✉ 1515 St. Andrews Dr., Lawrence, KS 66047, ☎ 785/843–1211 or 800/255–4266, FAX 785/843–8351). **Tauck Tours** (✉ Box 5027, 276 Post Rd. W, Westport, CT 06881-5027, ☎ 203/226–6911 or 800/468–2825, FAX 203/221–6866).

➤ FIRST-CLASS: **Brendan Tours** (✉ 15137 Califa St., Van Nuys, CA 91411, ☎ 818/785–9696 or 800/421–8446, FAX 818/902–9876). **Caravan Tours** (✉ 401 N. Michigan Ave., Chicago, IL 60611, ☎ 312/321–9800 or 800/227–2826, FAX 312/321–9845). **Collette Tours** (✉ 162 Middle St., Pawtucket, RI 02860, ☎ 401/728–3805 or 800/340–5158, FAX 401/728–4745). **Gadabout Tours** (✉ 700 E. Tahquitz Canyon Way, Palm Springs, CA 92262–6767, ☎ 619/325–5556 or 800/952–5068). **Mayflower Tours** (✉ Box 490, 1225 Warren Ave., Downers Grove, IL 60515, ☎ 708/960–3430 or 800/323–7064). **Trafalgar Tours** (✉ 11 E. 26th St., New York, NY 10010, ☎ 212/689–8977 or 800/854–0103, FAX 800/457–6644).

➤ BUDGET: **Cosmos** (☞ Globus, *above*).

PACKAGES

Like group tours, independent vacation packages are available from major tour operators and airlines. The companies listed below offer packages in a broad price range.

➤ AIR/HOTEL: **Air Canada's Canada** (☎ 800/774–8993). **American Airlines Vacations** (☎ 800/321–2121). **Continental Vacations** (☎ 800/634–5555). **Delta Vacations** (☎ 800/872–7786). **Northwest WorldVacations** (☎ 800/754–8599). **US Airways Vacations** (☎ 800/455–0123).

➤ AIR/HOTEL/CAR: **Air Canada's Canada** (☞ Air/Hotel, *above*). American Airlines Vacations (☞ Air/Hotel, *above*). **Delta Vacations** (☞ Air/Hotel, *above*).

➤ FROM THE U.K.: **British Airways Holidays** (✉ Astral Towers, Betts Way, London Rd., Crawley, West Sussex RH10 2XA, ☎ 01293/723191).

THEME TRIPS

The companies listed below provide multiday tours in Montréal or Québec City. Additional local or regionally based companies that have different-length trips with these themes are listed in each chapter, either with information about the town or in the A to Z section that concludes the chapter.

➤ BICYCLING: **Backroads** (✉ 801 Cedar St., Berkeley, CA 94710-1800, ☎ 510/527–1555 or 800/462–2848, FAX 510/527–1444).

➤ HORSEBACK RIDING: **Equitour Worldwide Riding Holidays** (✉ Box 807, Dubois, WY 82513, ☎ 307/455–3363 or 800/545–0019, FAX 307/455–2354).

➤ LEARNING: **Smithsonian Study Tours and Seminars** (✉ 1100 Jefferson Dr. SW, Room 3045, MRC 702, Washington, DC 20560, ☎ 202/357–4700, FAX 202/633–9250).

➤ SPAS: **Spa-Finders** (✉ 91 5th Ave., No. 301, New York, NY 10003-3039, ☎ 212/924–6800 or 800/255–7727).

➤ WALKING/HIKING: **Backroads** (☞ Bicycling, *above*). **New England Hiking Holidays** (✉ Box 1648, North Conway, NH 03860, ☎ 603/356–9696 or 800/869–0949).

TRAIN TRAVEL

Amtrak currently has service from New York to Montréal, providing connections between Amtrak's U.S.-wide network and VIA Rail's Canadian routes. Via Rail connects Montréal with Canada's major cities, including Quebec City, Toronto, and Vancouver.

➤ INFORMATION: **Amtrak** (☎ 800/872–7245). **VIA Rail Canada** (☎ 800/561–3949 or 800/361–5390 in Quebec Province. In the U.K., **Long-Haul Leisurail** (✉ Box 113, Peterborough, PE3 8HY UK, ☎ 01733/335599) represents VIA Rail.

DISCOUNT PASSES

If you're planning to travel a lot by train, **look into the Canrailpass.** It allows 12 days of coach-class travel within a 30-day period; sleeping cars are available, but they sell out very early and must be reserved at least a month in advance during the high season (June 1–mid-October), when the pass is C$569 for adults age 25–60, C$499 for travelers under 25 or over 60. Low-season rates (October 16–May 31) are C$369 for adults and C$339 for youths and senior citizens. The pass is not valid during the Christmas period (December 15–January 5). For more information and reservations, contact a travel agent in the U.S. or Long-Haul Leisurail in the United Kingdom (☞ *above*).

Train travelers can **check out the new 30-day North American Rail Pass** offered by Amtrak and Via Rail. It allows unlimited coach/economy travel in the U.S. and Canada. You must indicate the itinerary when purchasing the pass. The cost is $645 June 1–October 15, $450 at other times.

TRAVEL AGENCIES

A good travel agent puts your needs first. Look for an agency that has been in business at least five years, emphasizes customer service, and has someone on staff who specializes in your destination. In addition, **make sure the agency belongs to a professional trade organization,** such as ASTA in the United States. (If your travel agency is also acting as your tour operator, ☞ Buyer Beware in Tour Operators, *above*).

➤ LOCAL AGENT REFERRALS: **American Society of Travel Agents** (ASTA, ☎ 800/965–2782 for 24-hr hot line, FAX 703/684–8319). **Association of British Travel Agents** (✉ 55–57 Newman St., London W1P 4AH, ☎ 0171/637–2444, FAX 0171/637–0713). **Association of Canadian Travel Agents** (✉ Suite 201, 1729 Bank St., Ottawa, ON K1V 7Z5, ☎ 613/521–0474, FAX 613/521–0805). **Australian Federation of Travel Agents** (☎ 02/9264–3299). **Travel**

Agents' Association of New Zealand (☎ 04/499–0104).

VISITOR INFORMATION

TOURIST INFORMATION

➤ PROVINCIAL TOURIST OFFICE: in Québec, **Tourisme Québec** (✉ C.P. 979, Montréal, Québec H3C 2W3, ☎ 800/363–7777).

➤ IN THE U.K.: **Visit Canada Center** (✉ 62–65 Trafalgar Sq., London, WC2 5DY UK, ☎ 0891/715–000). Calls to the Visit Canada Center cost 50p per minute peak rate and 45p per minute cheap rate. **Québec Tourism** (✉ 59 Pall Mall, London SW1Y 5JH UK, ☎ 0990/561705 or 0171/930–8314).

WEB SITES

Do **check out the World Wide Web** when you're planning. You'll find everything from up-to-date weather forecasts to virtual tours of famous cities. Fodor's Web site, www.fodors.com, is a great place to start. There are also many sites with information specifically on Québec, a few of which follow.

➤ CANADIAN WEB SITES: For Parks Canada: **parkscanada.pch.gc.ca** has information about national parks throughout the country. For the Province of Québec: **www.tourisme.gouv.qc.ca**, the province's offical site, covers all areas; it also lists special packages. For Montréal: **www.tourism-montreal.org** is the city's official tourism site, with information about everything from festivals and museums to lodging and the weather. For Québec City: **www.quebec-region.cuq.qc.ca** covers the city and surrounding area, but its lists of sights, lodgings, and restaurants are not annotated. It also has a calendar of events.

WHEN TO GO

Québec has hot, steamy summers and severe winters, with snow lasting from mid-December to mid-March. Winter is celebrated with major carnivals in Montréal and Québec City; the Laurentians, near Montréal, and several other areas have excellent skiing. Summer is the season for many festivals. The whole of eastern Canada enjoys blooming springs and brilliant autumns.

➤ FORECASTS: **Weather Channel Connection** (☎ 900/932–8437), 95¢ per minute from a Touch-Tone phone.

CLIMATE

The following are average daily maximum and minimum temperatures.

MONTRÉAL

Jan.	23F	- 5C	May	65F	18C	Sept.	68F	20C
	9	-13		48	9		53	12
Feb.	25F	- 4C	June	74F	23C	Oct.	57F	14C
	12	-11		58	14		43	6
Mar.	36F	2C	July	79F	26C	Nov.	42F	6C
	23	- 5		63	17		32	0
Apr.	52F	11C	Aug.	76F	24C	Dec.	27F	- 3C
	36	2		61	16		16	- 9

QUÉBEC CITY

Jan.	20F	- 7C	May	62F	17C	Sept.	66F	19C
	6	-14		43	6		49	9
Feb.	23F	- 5C	June	72F	22C	Oct.	53F	12C
	8	-13		53	12		39	4
Mar.	33F	1C	July	78F	26C	Nov.	39F	4C
	19	- 7		58	14		28	- 2
Apr.	47F	8C	Aug.	75F	24C	Dec.	24F	- 4C
	32	0		56	13		12	-11

1 Destination: Montréal and Québec City

FRANCOPHONES IN THE NEW WORLD

QUÉBEC IS the largest and oldest of Canada's provinces, covering 600,000 square miles of land and waterways, one-sixth of Canada's land. Of Québec's 6,627,000 inhabitants, 5,300,000 are French-speaking, 81.3% of the French-speaking population of Canada. Although Montréal and Québec City are linked by their history and culture, no two cities could be more different.

History buffs and romantics will want to roam the winding cobblestone streets of Québec City, the capital of the province. Its French colonial history is evident in its architecture, silver-spired churches, and grand cathedrals. In Montréal the Old World meets the New with French bistros and postmodern skyscrapers vying for the limelight. Québec may be the center of the province's government, but Montréal is the business center. Much like New York City, Montréal has attracted a large immigrant population. Its ethnic diversity can be seen in its wide range of restaurants and enclaves. It is not only considered the Canadian center for book publishing, the film industry, and architecture and design; it is also considered the unrivaled bagel capital of Canada.

Québec History

Montréal's and Québec City's histories are inextricably linked. Montréal sits on the site that was called Hochelaga by the Indians who lived there. Québec City was known as Stadacona. In 1534 Jacques Cartier, a young sea captain setting out to find a passage to China, instead came upon Canada and changed the course of events in that region forever. He returned in the following year seeking gold. But this time he found a wide river, sailed down it, and arrived at Stadacona, an Indian village. He admired the location of the village perched on the cliffs overlooking a *kebec,* the Algonquin word for a narrowing of the waters. He continued along to Hochelaga, which eventually became Montréal. More than 1,000 surprised Iroquois greeted the Frenchman. It would take two centuries of fierce battles before the French made peace with the Iroquois people. Perhaps the violent meeting of the French explorers and the Canadian natives discouraged the French, because no more exploring was done until 1608, when Samuel de Champlain established a French settlement at Stadacona.

Throughout the 17th century, the French opened up Canada and some of what became the United States, using both Montréal and Québec City as convenient trading posts and strategic military locations. They discovered and mapped a vast area stretching from Hudson Bay to the Gulf of Mexico. *Coureurs de bois* (fur traders), missionaries, and explorers staked out this immense new territory.

During this time, France tamed and populated its new colonies across the ocean with the firm hand of *seigneurs,* aristocrats to whom the king distributed land. In turn, the seigneurs swore loyalty to the king, served in the military, maintained manor houses, ceded land to tenant farmers, and established courts to settle local grievances. Seigneuries were close knit, with sons and fathers able to establish farms within the same territory. In addition, the Roman Catholic Church's influence was strong in these communities. Priests and nuns acted as doctors, educators, and overseers of business arrangements among the farmers and between French-speaking traders and English-speaking merchants. An important doctrine of the church in Québec was *survivance,* the survival of the French people and their culture. Couples were told to have large families, and they did. Ten to 12 children in a family was the norm, not the exception.

The Seven Years' War between England and France marked the second half of the 18th century. In 1756, France sent the commander Louis-Joseph, Marquis de Montcalm, to secure the frontier of New France and consolidate the new territory of Louisiana. Although Montcalm, leading a French and Indian expedition, was able to secure the Ohio Valley, turn Lake

Ontario into a French waterway, and secure Fort Carillon (now Ticonderoga) on Lake Champlain, the tides began to turn in 1759 with the arrival of a large British fleet to the shores of Québec City, commanded by James Wolfe.

After bombarding the city for several weeks, Wolfe and his 4,000 men decided the fate of Canada in a vicious battle that lasted 20 minutes. The British won, but both leaders were mortally wounded. Today, in Québec City's Governors Park, there is a unique memorial to these two army men—the only statue in the world commemorating both victor and vanquished of the same battle. A year later the French regained the city of Québec, but they were soon forced to withdraw when English ships arrived with supplies and reinforcements. The French were driven back to Montréal, where a large British army defeated them in 1760. In 1763, the Treaty of Paris ceded Canada to Britain. France preferred to give up the new country to preserve its sugar islands, which it believed were of greater value. At that time, all the French civil administrators, as well as the principal landowners and businessmen, returned to France. Of the leaders of New France, only the Roman Catholic clergy remained, and they became more important to the peasant farmers than ever before.

Québec's trouble was in no way over with the Treaty of Paris. In 1774, the British Parliament passed the Québec Act. It extended Québec's borders, hemming in the northernmost of the independence-minded British colonies to the south. The Roman Catholic Church's authority and the seigneurial landlord system were maintained under the act, leaving traditional Québecois life fairly intact. But the American colonists were furious with the passing of the Québec Act and hoped to incite a revolt in Québec against British rule. After the American War of Independence broke out in 1775, Generals Richard Montgomery and Benedict Arnold led American troops that took over Montréal and set up headquarters in the Château de Ramezay, home of the British governor (and now a museum). The Americans then attempted to capture Québec City, but they had misunderstood the Catholic Royalist heritage of the Canadians. Québecois did not share the Americans' love of independence and republicanism. Rather than incite a revolt, the Americans managed to draw the Canadians and British together. The Canadians stood with the British in Québec City to fight off the invasions. Montgomery died in the attack and Arnold fled. The following year, British forces arrived and recaptured Montréal.

The Creation of Upper and Lower Canada

A number of British and American settlers left Albany in New York and settled in Montréal. They began to press the authorities, as did other British colonists west of the Ottawa River, to introduce representative government.

The British responded with the Constitutional Act of 1791, which divided Québec into two provinces, Upper and Lower Canada, west and east of the Ottawa. The act provided for nominated legislative councils and elected assemblies, like those that had existed in the English colonies. The first election was held the following year.

Elected government was a novelty to the French Canadians, who had never known democracy and had been shielded from the French Revolution of 1789. But democracy suited them well, and before long there was a rising demand for more rights. Heading the movement for greater rights was Louis Joseph Papineau, who was also leader of the French-speaking majority in the legislative assembly. He demanded that the English *château clique,* which made up the governor's council, should be subject to elections as the assembly was. In 1834, he and his associates issued a long list of grievances, "The 92 Resolutions." Papineau lost the support of many of his own associates, and that of the leaders of the church. The British responded with their own "10 resolutions" and refused elections to the council. That same year crops failed and unemployment spread. General unrest led to clashes between the English and young French *Patriotes* in Montréal. Soon a general insurrection broke out. Patriote irregulars fought British troops at St. Charles and St. Eustache near Montréal.

In spite of bad feelings, the upheavals led to major legislative changes in 1841. England passed the Act of Union, which produced a united Canada. Québec was now known as Canada East, while Upper Canada became Canada West. Each sent an equal number of representatives to the elected assembly; the governor was not responsible to the assembly, but rather to the Colonial Office in London. This continued to bridle both English and French members of the assembly.

The Growth of Montréal

Toward the end of the 1700s, the fur trade declined so much that Montréal almost faced economic disaster. But in Europe the demand for lumber increased, and Québec had lots of it. As a result, Montréal became the major trading center in British North America, helped by the fact that New York and New England had seceded from Britain.

Then the flood of immigration from Britain started, so much so that by the mid-1800s, Montréal was transformed into a predominantly English city. About 100,000 Irish immigrants came to work in Montréal's flour mills, breweries, and shipyards, which had sprung up on the shores of the river and the Lachine Canal, begun in 1821. By 1861, working-class Irish made up a third of Montréal's population. Within the next 80 years, Polish, Hungarian, Italian, Chinese, Ukrainian, Greek, Armenian, Spanish, Czech, Japanese, German, and Portuguese immigrants, escaping from poverty and political hardships, arrived by the thousands, seeking freedom in the New World. By 1867, more than a half million immigrants had arrived from Europe, pushing Canada's population to more than 2 million. The demand for union came from all the provinces of British North America to increase trade and economic prosperity, to increase their military strength in case of attack from the United States, to create a government capable of securing and developing the Northwest (the vast lands west of Canada West), and to make possible the building of a railway that would contribute to the realization of all these ambitions.

The Dominion of Canada was created on July 1, 1867, by an act of the British Parliament, known as the British North America (BNA) Act. It divided the province of Canada into Québec and Ontario and brought in Nova Scotia and New Brunswick. Manitoba joined in 1870, British Columbia in 1871, Prince Edward Island in 1873, Alberta and Saskatchewan in 1905, and Newfoundland in 1949. The BNA Act also enshrined French as an official language. The province of Québec, like the other provinces, was given far-reaching responsibilities in social and civil affairs.

The Conscription Crisis

The entente between the French and the English in Canada was viable until World War I strained it. At the outbreak of the war, the two groups felt equally supportive of the two European motherlands. Many volunteered, and a totally French regiment, the Royal 22nd, was created. But two things ended the camaraderie.

On the battlefields of Europe, Canadians, along with Australians, formed the shock troops of the British Empire and died horribly, by the thousands. More than 60,000 Canadians died in the war, a huge loss for a country of 7.5 million. In 1915, Ontario passed Regulation 17, severely restricting the use of French in its schools. It translated into an anti-French stand and created open hostility. The flow of French Canadians into the army became a trickle. Then Prime Minister Robert Borden ordered the conscription of childless males to reinforce the ailing Canadian corps. A wider conscription law loomed in Ottawa, resulting in an outcry in Québec led by nationalist, journalist, and politician Henry Bourassa (grandson of patriot Louis Joseph Papineau). The nationalists claimed that conscription was a device to diminish the French-speaking population. When, in 1917, conscription did become law, Québec was ideologically isolated from the rest of Canada.

The crisis led to the formation of the Union Nationale provincial party in 1936, initially a reformist party. Under its leader Maurice Duplessis, it held control until 1960 and was characterized by lavish patronage, strong-arm methods, fights with Ottawa, and nationalistic sloganeering. Duplessis believed that to survive, Québecois should remain true to their traditions. Duplessis deterred industrial expansion in Québec, which went to Ontario, and slowed the growth of reformist ideas until his death and the flowering of the Quiet Revolution.

The Quiet Revolution

The population of Québec had grown to 6 million, but the province had fallen economically and politically behind Canada's English majority. Under Duplessis and the Union Nationale party, French-language schools and universities were supervised by the church and offered courses in the humanities rather than in science and economics. Francophones (French-speaking Québeckers) were denied any chance of real business education unless they attended English institutions. As a result, few of them held top positions in industry or finance. On a general cultural basis, the country overwhelmingly reflected Anglo-Saxon attitudes rather than an Anglo-French mixture.

In 1960 the Liberal Party under Jean Lesage swept to power. Though initially occupied with social reform, it soon turned to economic matters. In 1962, Lesage's minister of natural resources, René Lévesque, called for the nationalization of most of the electricity industry, which up to then had been in private hands. This was the first step toward economic independence for Québec. The financiers of Montréal's St. James Street, the heart of the business district, opposed it, but ordinary Québecois were enthusiastic. In 1965, Lévesque's ministry established a provincial mining company to explore and develop the province's mineral resources.

Meanwhile U.S. capital poured into Québec, as it did everywhere else in Canada. With it came American cultural influence, which increased Québecois' expectations of a high standard of living. English-speaking citizens remained in firm control of the large national corporations headquartered in Montréal. Indeed it became clear that they had no intention of handing power over to the French. Few Francophones were promoted to executive status. Successive provincial governments became increasingly irritated by the lack of progress.

The discontent led to a dramatic radicalization of Québec politics. A new separatist movement arose that hoped to make Québec a distinct state by breaking away from the rest of the country. The most extreme faction of the movement was the Front de Libération du Québec (FLQ). It backed its demands with bombs and arson, culminating in the kidnapping and murder of Québec Cabinet Minister Pierre Laporte in October 1970.

The federal government in Ottawa, under Prime Minister Pierre Elliott Trudeau, himself a French-speaking Québecois, imposed the War Measures Act. This permitted the police to break up civil disorders and arrest hundreds of suspects and led to the arrest of the murderers of Laporte.

The political crisis calmed down, but it left behind vibrations that affected all of the country. The federal government redoubled its efforts to correct the worst grievances of the French Canadians. Federal funds flowed into French schools outside Québec to support French-Canadian culture in the other provinces. French Canadians were appointed to senior positions in the government and crown corporations. The federal government dramatically increased its bilingual services to the population.

In Québec from the mid-1970s, the Liberal government and then the Parti Québecois, elected in 1976 and headed by René Lévesque (who had left the Liberal party in 1967 and helped found the Parti Québecois), replaced the English language with the French language in Québec's economic life. In 1974, French was adopted as the official language of Québec. This promoted French-language instruction in the schools and made French the language of business and government. The Parti Québecois followed up in 1977 with the Charter of the French Language, which established deadlines and fines to help enforce the program to make French the chief language in all areas of Québec life. The charter brought French into the workplace; it also accelerated a trend for English companies to relocate their headquarters outside Québec, particularly in and near Toronto. The provincial government is working to attract new investment to Québec to replace those lost jobs and revenues.

The Parti Québecois proposed to go further by taking Québec out of the confederation, provided that economic ties with the rest of Canada could be maintained. Leaders in the other provinces announced that such a scheme would not be acceptable. A referendum was held in 1980 for the authority to negotiate a sovereignty association with the rest of Canada. Québec voters rejected the proposal by a wide margin. In 1985, the Parti Québecois government was defeated at the polls by the Liberal Party, headed by Robert Bourassa.

Bourassa was committed to keeping Québec within Canada until the collapse of the Meech-Lake Accord, a three-year attempt to integrate Québec into the Canadian constitution, in 1990. Bourassa then vowed to put the interests of the province before those of the country, even if this meant separation. The Québec Bélanger-Campeau commission, set up to study the future of Québec in Canada, concluded that the province should be recognized as a "sovereign state," although it would remain part of the Canadian Federation given certain conditions. However, the federal and provincial governments did not reach an agreement. In a 1995 referendum, Québecois decided by a narrow margin to remain in the Federation.

The People of Québec

Although French is the official language of Québec, Québec also has a large English-speaking population (676,000), particularly in Montréal, the Ottawa Valley, and the Eastern Townships. They are descendants of those English, Irish, and Scots who landed here after the conquest of New France, and of immigrants from other nations whose main language is English. English-speaking Montréalers founded and financed a variety of such great institutions as universities, museums, hospitals, orchestras, and social agencies, as well as a number of national and multinational corporations in the worlds of banking and finance, transportation, natural resources, and distilled spirits.

Half a million immigrants from Europe, Asia, Latin America, and the Caribbean also live in Québec. People from 80 different countries have made their new homes in the province. In proportion to its population, this land, along with the rest of Canada, has welcomed the greatest number of fugitives from political and economic unrest over the past 20 years. Between 1968 and 1982, for example, 60,000 immigrants arrived from Czechoslovakia, Haiti, Uganda, Lebanon, Chile, and Southeast Asia. A much larger wave of immigrants—from Italy, Greece, and Eastern Europe—had arrived following World War II.

The native people of Québec number more than 40,000. Nearly 30,000 of Québec's Amerindians live in villages within reserved territories in various parts of Québec, where they have exclusive fishing and hunting rights. The Inuit people (Eskimo) number over 5,000 and live in villages scattered along the shores of James Bay, Hudson Bay, Hudson Strait, and Ungava Bay. They have abandoned their igloos for prefabricated houses, but they still make their living by trapping and hunting.

The French Canadians of Québec, often called Latins of the North, have an ever-sparkling joie de vivre, especially at the more than 400 festivals and carnivals they celebrate each year. Even the long winter does not dampen their good spirits. The largest festival splash is on June 24, which was originally the Feast of Saint John the Baptist. Now it is called La Fête Nationale (National Day). Everyone celebrates the long weekend by building roaring bonfires and dancing in the streets.

February brings Québec City's Winter Carnival, an 11-day-long noisy and exciting party. Chicoutimi also has a winter carnival in which residents of the city celebrate and dress up in period costumes. In September international canoe races are held in Mauricie, and in August an international swim gets under way across Lac-Saint-Jean. Trois-Rivières celebrates the summer with automobile races through its streets, and Valleyfield is the scene of international regattas.

NEW AND NOTEWORTHY

You may be visiting Montréal or Québec City for any number of reasons—to shop, to experience the area's French heritage, or to attend a festival. Whatever you're planning to do, this year your dollar will go further in Canada, even with higher Canadian taxes. Following the trend of the past few years, the exchange rate (summer 1998) is about US$1 to C$1.38, and £1 to C$2.35.

The transformed **Tremblant,** the Laurentians ski resort at Mont-Tremblant, north of Montréal, has been drawing rave reviews and crowds of skiers and snowboarders. A pedestrian-only village that recalls old Québec City and a new water recreation complex add to the fun. Grosse Ile, east of **Québec City,** has been turned into a national park where visitors can learn about the hardships faced by early immigrants to Canada, particularly the Irish who were fleeing the potato famine in the mid-19th century. Many buildings erected when Grosse Ile served as a quarantine station have been restored.

WHAT'S WHERE

Québec is probably what all North America would have been like if the French rather than the English had won the Seven Years' War. This eastern province is set apart by its strong French heritage. French in Québec is more than the language of love—it's the language of law, business, politics, culture, and of more than 80% of the people.

The province's historic capital, **Québec City,** has one of the the beautiful natural settings in North America, perched on a cliff above a narrow point in the St. Lawrence River. Vieux-Québec, the old fortified city, is a World Heritage Site. The island city of **Montréal** is the second-largest French-speaking city in the world. Vieux-Montréal holds 17th-century buildings, and grand churches and museums throughout Montréal offer insight into its long history. But this is a modern city, with an abundance of fine dining, good shopping, and vibrant nightlife. Defining the land outside the cities are innumerable lakes, streams, and rivers; farmlands and villages; great mountains, such as the Laurentians with their ski resorts, and deep forests; and a rugged coastline along the Gulf of St. Lawrence.

PLEASURES AND PASTIMES

Dining

Canadian fine dining really began in Québec, where eating out in a good restaurant with a good bottle of wine has long been a traditional part of life. Montréal can claim many superb restaurants that serve both classic and innovative French cuisine. The city's varied population has also made it rich in ethnic restaurants from delis to Asian eateries. Québec City has a narrower range of choices, but good French and Québécois fare are available, and some fine new restaurants have opened recently. In the countryside a number of inns, including some in the Eastern Townships, provide food that can compete with any served in the cities for freshness and creativity. Hearty meat pies, pâtés, and creative uses of maple syrup are traditional specialties throughout the province. When you're in Québec, do as the locals do and order the table d'hóte, a several-course package deal that is often cheaper and may give you a chance to sample some special dishes.

French Heritage

To visit Québec is to encounter more than 450 years of French civilization in North America. The well-preserved streets of Vieux-Montréal and the Upper and Lower Towns of Québec City hold centuries-old buildings filled with history. Churches such as the Basilique Notre-Dame-de-Québec in Québec City, the Basilique Notre-Dame-de-Montréal in Montréal, and the Basilique Ste-Anne-de-Beaupré in Ste-Anne-de-Beaupré tell part of the story. Excellent museums, including the Musée d'Archéologie Pointe-à-Callière in Montréal and the Musée de la Civilisation and the Musée de Québec in Québec City, add further insight. But history is alive in Québec: in the language, the people, and the arts. Whether you're sitting in a café, walking through a beautiful botanical garden, or just strolling the city streets at night, you'll enter a different culture.

The Great Outdoors

Most Canadians live in towns and cities within 325 km (200 mi) of the American border, but the country has a splendid backyard to play in. Even major cities like Montréal and Québec City are just a few hours' drive from a wilderness full of rivers, lakes, and mountains, and lovely rural areas are even closer. It's easy to combine a visit to Québec's cities with a side trip to the countryside. The Laurentian Mountains, with the revitalized Mont-Tremblant ski resort, are just an hour north of Montréal, and the hills and lakes of the bucolic Eastern Townships lie to the city's southeast. The Ile d'Orléans, just 15 minutes from Québec City, embodies the traditional lifestyle of rural Québec and is well worth exploring. The lovely villages, mountains, and waterfalls of the Charlevoix stretch along the north shore of the St. Lawrence River from Ste-Anne-de-Beaupré to the Saguenay River.

Shopping

Distinctively Canadian items include furs and fashions from Montréal, wood carvings from rural Québec, and antiques (the best are in Montréal). The weak Canadian dollar has made shopping even more appealing.

ANTIQUES➢ On the whole, prices for antiques are lower in Canada than in the United States. Shops along Montréal's rue Sherbrooke Ouest stock everything from ancient maps to fine crystal; stores along rue Notre-Dame Ouest and rue Amherst sell antiques from Napoléonic-period furniture to 1950s bric-a-brac.

MAPLE SYRUP➢ Eastern Canada is famous for its sugar maples. The trees are tapped in early spring, and the sap is collected in buckets to be boiled into maple syrup. This natural confection is sold all year. You can also buy maple taffy, candy, and even liqueur. Avoid the tourist shops and department stores; for the best prices, stop at farm stands and markets.

NATIVE CANADIAN ART➢ Interest has grown in the highly collectible art and sculpture of the Inuit, usually rendered in soapstone. For the best price and a guarantee of authenticity, purchase Inuit and other native crafts in the province where they originate. Many styles are now attributed to certain tribes and are mass-produced for sale in galleries and shops miles away from their regions of origin. At the very top galleries you can be assured of getting pieces done by individual artists, though the prices will be higher than in the provinces of origin. The Canadian government has registered the symbol of an igloo as a mark of a work's authenticity. Be sure this Canadian government sticker or tag is attached before you make your purchase.

FODOR'S CHOICE

No two people will agree on what makes a perfect vacation, but it's fun and helpful to know what others think. We hope you'll have a chance to experience some of Fodor's Choices yourself in Canada. For detailed information about each entry, refer to the appropriate chapter.

Historic Sites

★ **Basilique Notre-Dame-de-Montréal, Montréal.** The enormous (3,800-seat) neo-Gothic church, opened in 1829, has a medieval-style interior with stained-glass windows; a star-studded, vaulted blue ceiling; and pine and walnut carving.

★ **Basilique Ste-Anne-de-Beaupré, outside Québec City.** The monumental church is an important shrine that draws hordes of pilgrims. According to local legend, St. Anne was responsible over the years for saving voyagers from shipwrecks; she is also believed to have healing powers.

★ **Plains of Abraham, Québec City.** The site of the famous 1759 battle between the French and the British that decided the fate of New France is now part of a large park overlooking the St. Lawrence River.

★ **Vieux-Québec, Québec City.** The old town is small and dense, steeped in four centuries of history and French tradition. Immaculately preserved as the only fortified city in North America, it is a UNESCO World Heritage Site.

Restaurants

★ **Toqué, Montréal.** At the most fashionable and the most zany restaurant in town, the menu depends on what the two chefs found fresh that day and on which way their ever-creative spirit moves them. *$$$$*

★ **Mediterraneo, Montréal.** The eclectic food at this handsome establishment is a big hit with trendy locals. *$$$–$$$$*

★ **Bazou, Montréal.** Bring your own bottle of wine to this eatery, whose name means "jalopy." The car theme appears in dishes such as rabbit cooked in a "Mustang sauce" of cream, white wine, and mushrooms. *$$–$$$*

★ **Laurie Raphaël, Québec City.** This local hot spot offers boldly creative recipes that mix classic French cuisine with the flavors of the world. *$$$$*

★ **L'Echaudé, Québec City.** Duck confit is one of the choices at a chic bistro between the financial and antiques districts. *$$–$$$$*

★ **L'Eau à la Bouche, Ste-Adèle, Québec.** At this Bavarian-style property you'll find a superb marriage of nouvelle cuisine and traditional Québec cooking in such dishes as roast veal in a cognac and Roquefort sauce. *$$$$*

Hotels

★ **Loews Hôtel Vogue, Montréal.** Behind the hotel's facade of polished rose granite are elegant rooms that promise rest in the busy heart of downtown. *$$$$*

★ **Ritz-Carlton Kempinski, Montréal.** Edwardian style, modern amenities, and careful service are hallmarks of one of the city's finest luxury hotels. *$$$$*

★ **Auberge du Vieux-Port, Montréal.** In an 1880s building in Vieux-Montréal, the inn overlooks the Vieux-Port and has tall windows and massive exposed beams. *$$–$$$*

★ **Auberge Hatley, North Hatley.** The guest rooms of this 1903 country manor near Lake Massawippi are charmingly decorated, and the restaurant serves superb regional cuisine. *$$$$*

★ **Château Frontenac, Québec City.** Its history and architecture make this hotel overlooking the St. Lawrence one of the city's most recognizable landmarks. *$$$$*

★ **Hôtel Loews Le Concorde, Québec City.** The rooms in this tall concrete hotel on Grande Allée have fine views of Battlefields Park and the St. Lawrence River. *$$$–$$$$*

FESTIVALS AND SEASONAL EVENTS

Québec has always been able to find a reason to party. Québec City celebrates one of the world's most brutal winters with a carnival that has parades of majorettes and teams who race boats across an ice-choked river. Throughout the province, the rest of the year is full of festivals celebrating jazz, international folklore, film, classical music, fireworks, comedy, and hot-air balloons. Contact local or provincial tourist boards for more information about these and other festivals.

WINTER

FEBRUARY➢ ***La Fête des Neiges*** is festive Winter Carnival in Montréal. **Winter Carnival** in Québec City is an 11-day festival of winter-sports competitions, ice-sculpture contests, and parades.

SPRING

MARCH–APRIL➢ **Sugaring-off parties** celebrate the maple syrup season. The many commercial enterprises in the area have tours of the process. A number of sugar shacks serve hearty meals at which you can sample the maple syrup.

SUMMER

JUNE➢ Some of the world's best drivers compete in the **Player's Grand Prix** in Montréal. In June and July, the **International Fireworks Competition** takes place every Saturday and Sunday evening in Montréal, when teams from around the world launch fireworks from Ile Ste-Hélène. Québec City hops with the **International Jazz Festival.** Beauport hosts the **International Children's Folklore Festival.**

JULY➢ The **Festival International de Jazz de Montréal** draws more than 2,000 musicians from all over the world for this 11-day series. **Québec International Summer Festival** offers entertainment in the streets and parks of old Québec City. Montréal's 12-day **Juste pour Rire** (Just for Laughs) comedy festival features comics from around the world, in French and English. At **Festival Orford** (through August), international artists perform classical and chamber music in in Orford in the Eastern Townships. **Matinée Ltd. International** spotlights the best male tennis players in Montréal.

AUGUST➢ Montréal hosts a **World Film Festival** that showcases international stars and directors; it continues into early September. **St-Jean-sur-Richelieu's Hot Air Balloon Festival** is the largest gathering of hot-air balloons in Canada.

AUTUMN

SEPTEMBER➢ **Québec International Film Festival** screens films from around the world in Québec City. The **Gatineau Hot Air Balloon Festival** brings together hot-air balloons from across Canada, the United States, and Europe.

OCTOBER➢ The **Festival of Colors** celebrates foliage throughout the province.

2 Montréal

Traces of this island city's long history are found everywhere, from the 17th-century buildings in Vieux-Montréal to grand churches and verdant parks such as Mont-Royal. But Montréal, with its atmosphere of romantic elegance, is also full of very modern pleasures: fine dining, whether you want French cuisine or any kind of ethnic fare; good shopping for everything from antiques to high fashion; and nightlife, arts events, and festivals that provide diversions year-round.

By Paul and Julie Waters

MONTRÉAL IS CANADA'S most romantic metropolis, an island city that seems to favor grace and elegance over order and even prosperity; a city full of music, art, and joie de vivre. It is rather like the European capital Vienna—past its peak of power and glory, perhaps, but still a vibrant and beautiful place full of memories, dreams, and festivals.

That's not to say Montréal is ready to fade away. It may not be so young anymore—it celebrated its 350th birthday in 1992—but it remains Québec's largest city and an important port and financial center. Its office towers are full of young Québécois entrepreneurs, members of a new breed who are ready and eager to take on the world.

Montréal is the only French-speaking metropolis in North America and the second-largest French-speaking city in the world, but it's a tolerant place that over the years has made room for millions of immigrants who speak dozens of languages. Today about 15% of the 3.1 million people who live in the metropolitan area claim English as their mother tongue, and another 15% claim a language that's neither English nor French. The city's gentle tolerance has won recognition: Several times it has been voted one of the world's most livable cities.

The city's grace, however, has been sorely tested. Since 1976, Montréal has twice weathered the election of a separatist provincial government, a law banning all languages but French on virtually all public signs and billboards, and four referendums on the future of Québec and Canada. The latest chapter in this long constitutional drama was the cliffhanger referendum on Québec independence on October 30, 1995. In that showdown Québécois voters chose to remain part of Canada but by the thinnest of possible margins. More than 98% of eligible voters participated, and the final province-wide result was 49.42% in favor of independence and 50.58% against. In fact 60% of the province's Francophones voted in favor of establishing an independent Québec. But Montréal, where most of the province's Anglophones and immigrants live, bucked the separatist trend and voted nearly 70% against independence. The drama has since cooled. The separatist Parti-Québécois controls the provincial government, but it has switched its focus to the flagging economy, and its leader, Lucien Bouchard, has tried to steer clear of arguments about language.

In spite of uncertainty about the future, most Montrealers still delight in their city, which has weathered all these storms with aplomb. It is, after all, a city that's used to turmoil. It was founded by the French, conquered by the British, and occupied by the Americans. It has a long history of reconciling contradictions and even today is a city of contrasts. The glass office tower of La Maison des Coopérants, for example, soars above a Gothic-style Anglican cathedral that squats gracefully in its shadow. The neo-Gothic facade of the Basilique Notre-Dame-de-Montréal glares across Place d'Armes at the pagan temple that is the head office of the Bank of Montréal. And while pilgrims still climb the steps to the Oratoire St-Joseph on their knees on one side of the mountain, thousands of their fellow Catholics line up to get into the very chic Casino de Montréal on the other side—certainly not what the earnest French settlers who founded Montréal envisioned when they landed on the island in May 1642.

Those 54 pious men and women under the leadership of Paul de Chomedey, Sieur de Maisonneuve, hoped to do nothing less than create a new Christian society. They named their settlement Ville-Marie in honor of the mother of Christ and set out to convert the natives.

Those early years were marked by the heroism of two women—Jeanne Mance, a French noblewoman who arrived with de Maisonneuve, and Marguerite Bourgeoys, who came 11 years later. Jeanne Mance, working alone, established the Hôpital Hôtel-Dieu de St-Joseph, still one of the city's major hospitals. In 1659 she invited members of a French order of nuns to help her in her efforts. That order, the Religieuses Hospitalières de St-Joseph, now has its motherhouse in Montréal and is the oldest nursing group in the Americas. Marguerite Bourgeoys, with Jeanne Mance's help, established the colony's first school and taught both French and native children how to read and write. Bourgeoys founded the Congrégation de Notre Dame, a teaching order that still has schools in Montréal, across Canada, and around the world. She was canonized a saint by the Roman Catholic Church in 1982.

Piety wasn't the settlement's only raison d'être, however. Ville-Marie was ideally located to be a commercial success as well. It was at the confluence of two major transportation routes—the St. Lawrence and Ottawa rivers—and fur trappers used the town as a staging point for their expeditions. But the city's religious roots were never forgotten. Until 1854, long after the French lost possession of the city, the island of Montréal remained the property of the Sulpicians, an aristocratic order of French priests. The Sulpicians were responsible for administering the colony and for recruiting colonists. They still run the Basilique Notre-Dame-de-Montréal and are still responsible for training priests for the Roman Catholic archdiocese.

The French regime in Canada ended with the Seven Years' War—what Americans call the French and Indian Wars. British troops took Québec City in 1759, and Montréal fell less than a year later. The Treaty of Paris ceded all New France to Britain in 1763, and soon English and Scottish settlers poured into Montréal to take advantage of the city's geography and economic potential. By 1832 Montréal was a leading colonial capital of business, finance, and transportation and had grown far beyond the walls of the old settlement. Much of that business and financial leadership has since moved to Toronto, the upstream rival Montrealers love to hate.

Pleasures and Pastimes

Dining

Montrealers are passionate about food. They love to dine on classic dishes in restaurants like Les Halles and the Beaver Club, or swoon over culinary innovations in places like Toqué and Mediterraneo, but they can get equally passionate about humbler fare. They'll argue with some heat about where to get the juiciest smoked meat (the city's beloved version of corned beef), the crispiest barbecued chicken, and the soggiest *stimés* (steamed hot dogs). You'll find great French food here but also cuisines from around the world; the city's restaurants represent more than 75 ethnic groups.

Faith and History

Reminders of the city's long history are found everywhere, including in its churches. Some buildings in Vieux-Montréal date to the 17th century. Other parts of the city are full of wonderful examples of Victorian architecture. Museums like the Musée McCord de l'Histoire Canadienne, the Musée d'Archéologie de la Pointe-à-Callière, and the Stewart Museum in the Old Fort on Ile Ste-Hélène attest to the city's fascination with its past.

Montréal's two most popular attractions are monuments dedicated to a Jewish couple who lived 2,000 years ago—the oratory dedicated to

Montréal

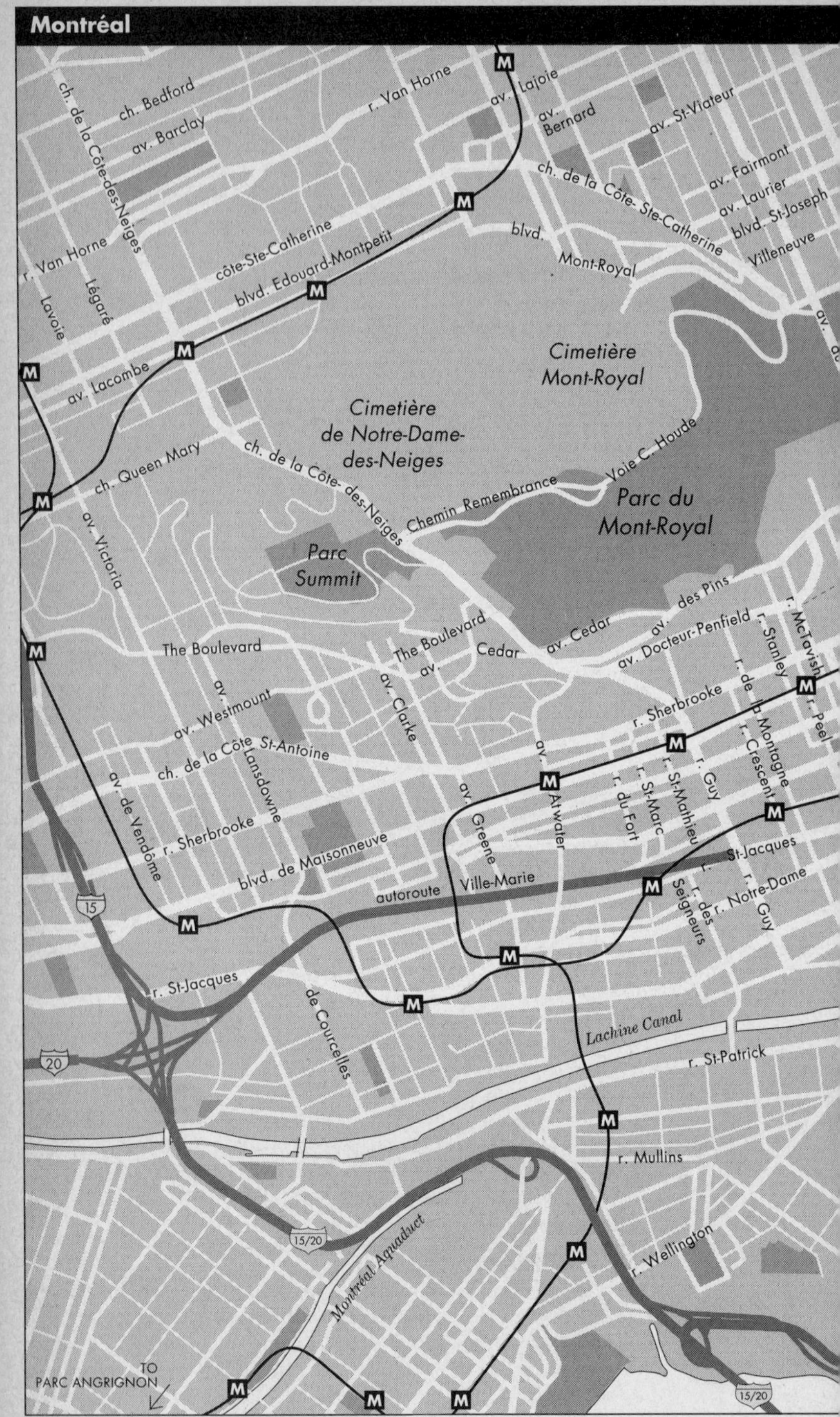

ch. Bedford
av. Barclay
ch. de la Côte-des-Neiges
r. Van Horne
av. Lajoie
av. Bernard
av. St-Viateur
ch. de la Côte- Ste-Catherine
av. Fairmont
av. Laurier
blvd. St-Joseph
Villeneuve
blvd. Mont-Royal
côte-Ste-Catherine
blvd. Edouard-Montpetit
r. Van Horne
Lavoie
Légaré
av. Lacombe
Cimetière Mont-Royal
Cimetière de Notre-Dame-des-Neiges
ch. Queen Mary
ch. de la Côte-des-Neiges
Voie C. Houde
Chemin Remembrance
Parc du Mont-Royal
av. Victoria
Parc Summit
av. des Pins
av. Cedar
av. Docteur-Penfield
r. McTavish
r. Stanley
The Boulevard
The Boulevard
av. Cedar
av. Clarke
r. Sherbrooke
r. de la Montagne
r. Peel
av. Westmount
av. Lansdowne
ch. de la Côte St-Antoine
av. Atwater
r. Guy
r. Crescent
r. St-Mathieu
r. St-Marc
r. du-Fort
av. de Vendôme
r. Sherbrooke
av. Greene
blvd. de Maisonneuve
autoroute Ville-Marie
r. St-Jacques
r. des Seigneurs
r. Notre-Dame
r. Guy
15
r. St-Jacques
de Courcelles
Lachine Canal
r. St-Patrick
20
r. Mullins
15/20
Montréal Aqueduct
r. Wellington
TO PARC ANGRIGNON
15/20

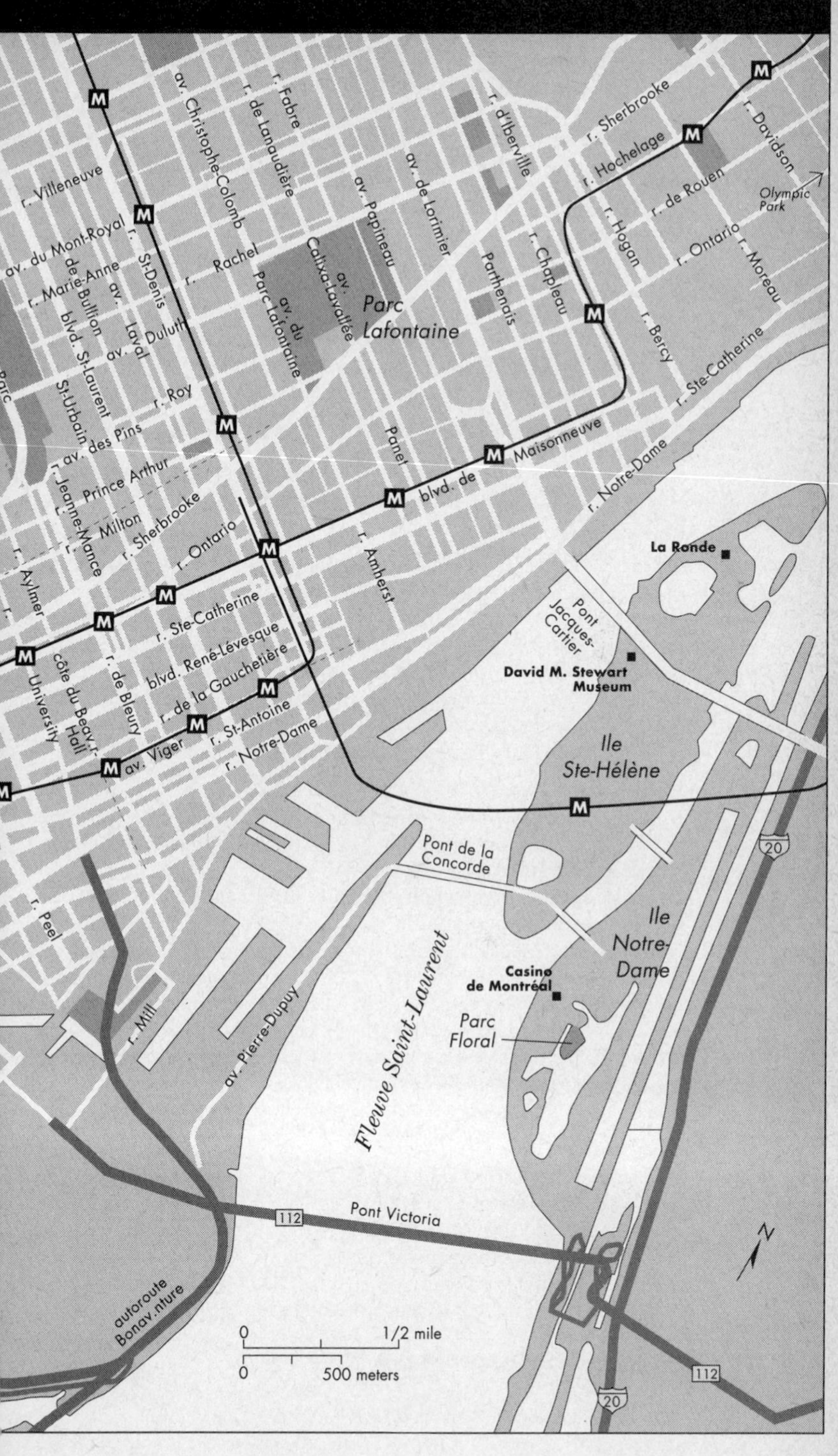

r. Villeneuve
av. du Mont-Royal
r. Marie-Anne
de Bullion
blvd. St-Laurent
av. Laval
r. St-Denis
av. Duluth
av. Christophe-Colomb
r. de Lanaudière
r. Fabre
r. Rachel
av. du Parc Lafontaine
av. Calixa-Lavallée
av. Papineau
av. de Lorimier
Parc Lafontaine
Parthenais
r. Chapleau
r. d'Iberville
r. Sherbrooke
r. Hochelage
r. de Rouen
r. Davidson
Olympic Park
r. Hogan
r. Ontario
r. Moreau
r. Bercy
r. Ste-Catherine
r. Roy
St-Urbain
av. des Pins
Prince Arthur
r. Jeanne-Mance
r. Milton
r. Sherbrooke
r. Ontario
Panet
blvd. de Maisonneuve
r. Notre-Dame
r. Amherst
r. Aylmer
r. Ste-Catherine
blvd. René-Lévesque
r. de la Gauchetière
r. de Bleury
côte du Beaver Hall
University
r. St-Antoine
r. Notre-Dame
av. Viger
La Ronde
Pont Jacques-Cartier
David M. Stewart Museum
Ile Ste-Hélène
Pont de la Concorde
Ile Notre-Dame
r. Peel
Casino de Montréal
Parc Floral
r. Mill
av. Pierre-Dupuy
Fleuve Saint-Laurent
20
112
Pont Victoria
N
autoroute Bonaventure
0
1/2 mile
0
500 meters
112
20

St. Joseph on the north side of Mont-Royal and the Basilique Notre-Dame-de-Montréal dedicated to his wife in the old city. These are just two of dozens of beautiful churches built in the days when the Québécois were among the most devout adherents to the Roman Catholic Church. Other gems of ecclesiastical architecture are St. Patrick's Basilica and the Chapelle Notre-Dame-de-Lourdes. Even parish churches in working-class neighborhoods are as grand as some cathedrals.

Festivals

Summer and fall are just one long succession of festivals that begin in late June with a 10-day Festival International de Jazz, when as many as a million fans descend on the city to hear more than 1,000 musicians, including giants like guitarist John Scofield and tenor saxophonist Joe Lovano. In August there's the World Film Festival and the lively Just for Laughs Comedy Festival in the Vieux-Port area. Other festivals celebrate beer, alternative films, French-language music and song from around the world, and international cuisine. Every Saturday in June and every Sunday in July the skies over the city waterfront erupt in color and flame as fireworks teams from around the world vie for prizes in the International Fireworks Competition.

Lodging

On the island of Montréal alone there are rooms available in every type of accommodation, from world-class luxury hotels to youth hostels, from student dormitories to budget executive motels. The Ritz-Carlton Kempinski has been setting standards of luxury since 1912, and the nearby Westin Mont-Royal is one of the best modern luxury hotels in the country. But the city also offers more intimate charm, at the Château Versailles on rue Sherbrooke, for example, or the tiny Auberge les Passants du Sans Soucy in the heart of Vieux-Montréal.

Nightlife

Montréal's reputation as a fun place to visit for a night on the town dates at least to Prohibition days, when hordes of thirsty Americans would flood the city every weekend to eat, drink, and be merry. The city has dozens of dance clubs, bistros, and jazz clubs, not to mention hundreds of bars where you can go to argue about sports, politics, and religion until the early hours of the morning. Much of the action takes place along rue St-Denis and adjacent streets in the eastern part of the city or rues Bishop, Crescent, and de la Montagne in the downtown area. The night scene is constantly shifting—last year's hot spot can quickly become this year's dive. The best and easiest way to figure out what's in is to stroll down rue St-Denis or rue Bishop at about 10:30 and look for the place with the longest lineup and the rudest doorman.

Shopping

The development of the Underground City has made shopping a year-round sport in Montréal. That vast complex linked by underground passageways and the Métro includes two major department stores, at least a dozen huge shopping malls, and more than 1,000 boutiques. Add to this Montréal's status as one of the fur capitals of the world, and you have a city that was born to be shopped.

EXPLORING MONTRÉAL

The Ile de Montréal is an island in the St. Lawrence River, 51 km (32 mi) long and 14 km (9 mi) wide. The only rise in the landscape is the 764-ft-high Mont-Royal, which gave the island its name and which residents call simply "the mountain." The city of Montréal is the oldest and by far the largest of the 24 municipalities on the island, which together make up the Communauté Urbaine de Montréal (the Montréal Urban Community), the regional government that runs, among other things, the police department and the transit system. There is a belt of off-island suburbs on the South Shore of the St. Lawrence, and just to the north across the narrow Rivière-des Prairies, on an island of its own, is Laval, a suburb that has grown to be the second-largest city in the province. But the countryside is never far away. The pastoral Eastern Townships, first settled by Loyalists fleeing the American Revolution, are less than an hour's drive away, and the Laurentians, an all-season playground full of lakes and ski hills, are even closer.

For a good overview of the city, head for the lookout at the Chalet du Mont-Royal. You can drive most of the way, park, and walk ½ km (¼ mi) or hike all the way up from chemin de la Côte-des-Neiges or avenue des Pins. If you look directly out—southeast—from the belvedere, at the foot of the hill will be the McGill University campus and, surrounding it, the skyscrapers of downtown Montréal. Just beyond, along the banks of the river, are the stone houses of Vieux-Montréal. Hugging the South Shore on the other side of the river are the Iles Ste-Hélène and Notre-Dame, sites of La Ronde amusement park, the Biosphere, the Casino de Montréal, acres of parkland, and the Lac de l'Ile Notre-Dame public beach—all popular excursions. To the east are rue St-Denis and the Quartier Latin, with its rows of French and ethnic restaurants, bistros, chess hangouts, designer boutiques, antiques shops, and art galleries. Even farther east you can see the flying-saucer-shape Olympic Stadium with its leaning tower.

Montréal is easy to explore. Streets, subways, and bus lines are clearly marked. The city is divided by a grid of streets roughly aligned east–west and north–south. (This grid is tilted about 40 degrees off—to the left of—true north, so west is actually southwest and so on.) North–south street numbers begin at the St. Lawrence River and increase as you head north. East–west street numbers begin at boulevard St-Laurent, which divides Montréal into east and west halves. The city is not so large that seasoned walkers can't see all the districts around the base of Mont-Royal on foot. Nearly everything else is easily accessible by the city's quiet, clean, and very safe bus and Métro (subway) system. If you're planning to visit a number of museums, look into the city's museum pass (☞ Contacts and Resources *in* Montréal A to Z, *below*).

Numbers in the text correspond to numbers in the margin and on the Vieux-Montréal, Downtown Montréal (Centre-Ville) and Golden Square Mile, Quartier Latin and Parc du Mont-Royal, and Olympic Park and Botanical Garden maps.

Great Itineraries

Getting any real feel for this bilingual, multicultural city takes some time. An ideal stay would be seven days, but you should spend at least three days walking and soaking up the atmosphere. That's enough time to visit Mont-Royal, explore Vieux-Montréal, do some shopping, and perhaps visit the Parc Olympique. It also includes enough nights for an evening of bar-hopping on rue St-Denis or rue Crescent and another for a long, luxurious dinner at one of the city's excellent restaurants.

IF YOU HAVE 3 DAYS

Any visit to Montréal should start with Mont-Royal, Montréal's most enduring symbol. Afterward wander down to avenue des Pins and then through McGill University to downtown. Make an effort to stop at the Musée des Beaux-Arts and St. Patrick's Basilica. Day 2 should be spent exploring Vieux-Montréal, with special emphasis on the Basilique Notre-Dame-de-Montréal and the Musée d'Archéologie Pointe-à-Callière. On Day 3 you can either visit the Parc Olympique (recommended for children) or stroll through the Quartier Latin.

IF YOU HAVE 5 DAYS

Once again start with a visit to Parc du Mont-Royal, but instead of going downtown after you've viewed the city from the Chalet du Mont-Royal, visit the Oratoire St-Joseph. You should still have enough time to visit the Musée des Beaux-Arts before dinner. That will leave time on Day 2 to get in more shopping as you explore downtown, with perhaps a visit to the Centre Canadien d'Architecture. Spend all of Day 3 in Vieux-Montréal, and on Day 4 stroll through the Quartier Latin. On Day 5, visit the Parc Olympique and then do one of three things: visit the islands, take a ride on the Lachine Rapids, or revisit some of the sights you missed in Vieux-Montréal or downtown.

IF YOU HAVE 7 DAYS

A week will give you enough time to do the five-day itinerary, expanding your Vieux-Montréal explorations to two days and adding a shopping spree on rue Chabanel and a visit to the Casino de Montréal.

Vieux-Montréal

When Montréal's first European settlers arrived by river in 1642 they stopped to build their houses just below the treacherous Lachine Rapids that blocked the way upstream. They picked a site near an old Iroquois settlement on the bank of the river nearest Mont-Royal. In the mid-17th century Montréal consisted of a handful of wood houses clustered around a pair of stone buildings, all flimsily fortified by a wood stockade. For almost three centuries this district—bounded by rues Berri and McGill on the east and west, rue St-Jacques on the north, and the river to the south—was the financial and political heart of the city. Government buildings, the largest church, the stock exchange, the main market, and the port were here. The narrow but relatively straight streets were cobblestone and lined with solid, occasionally elegant houses, office buildings, and warehouses—also made of stone. A thick stone wall with four gates protected the city against native people and marauding European powers. Montréal quickly grew past the bounds of its fortifications, however, and by World War I the center of the city had moved toward Mont-Royal. The new heart of Montréal became Dominion Square (now Square Dorchester). For the next two decades Vieux-Montréal (Old Montréal), as it became known, was gradually abandoned, the warehouses and offices emptied. In 1962 the city began studying ways to revitalize Vieux-Montréal, and a decade of renovations and restorations began.

Today Vieux-Montréal is a center of cultural life and municipal government. Most of the summer activities revolve around Place Jacques-Cartier, which becomes a pedestrian mall with street performers and outdoor cafés, and the Vieux-Port, one of the city's most popular recreation grounds. The Orchestre Symphonique de Montréal performs summer concerts at Basilique Notre-Dame-de-Montréal, which has one of the finest organs in North America, and English-language plays are staged in the Centaur Theatre in the old stock-exchange building. This district has six museums devoted to history, religion, and the arts.

A Good Walk

Take the Métro to the Square-Victoria Station and follow the signs to the **Centre de Commerce Mondial de Montréal** ①, one of the city's more appealing enclosed spaces, with a fountain and frequent art exhibits. Exit on the east side of the complex and turn right on rue St-Pierre, walk south to **rue St-Jacques,** and turn left. Walking east, you'll see the Victorian office buildings of the country's former financial center. This area can seem tomblike on weekends when the business and legal offices close down, but things get livelier closer to the waterfront.

Stop at **Place d'Armes** ②, a square that was the site of battles with the Iroquois in the 1600s and later became the center of Montréal's Haute-Ville, or Upper Town. There are calèches at the south end of the square; the north side is dominated by the **Bank of Montréal** ③, an impressive building with Corinthian columns. The **Basilique Notre-Dame-de-Montréal** ④, one of the most beautiful churches in North America, dominates the south end of Place d'Armes. The low, more retiring stone building behind a wall to the west of the basilica is the **Vieux Séminaire** ⑤, Montréal's oldest building. Unlike the basilica, it is closed to the public. To the east of the basilica is **rue St-Sulpice,** one of the first streets in Montréal, and catercorner from it is the Art Deco Aldred Building. Next to that is Montréal's first skyscraper, a nine-story red-stone tower built by the now defunct Québec Bank in 1888. One block farther east on rue Notre-Dame, just past boulevard St-Laurent, on the left, rises the black-glass-sheathed **Palais de Justice** (1971), or courthouse. The large domed building at 155 rue Notre-Dame Est is the **Vieux Palais de Justice** ⑥ (1857). Across the street, at 160 rue Notre-Dame Est, is the Maison de la Sauvegarde, one of the city's oldest houses. The Old Courthouse abuts the small **Place Vauquelin** ⑦, named after an 18th-century naval hero. North of this square is Champs-de-Mars, a former military parade ground and now a public park crisscrossed by archaeologists' trenches. The ornate building on the east side of Place Vauquelin is the Second Empire–style **Hôtel de Ville** ⑧, or City Hall, built in 1878.

You are in a perfect spot to explore **Place Jacques-Cartier** ⑨, the square that is the heart of Vieux-Montréal. At the western corner of rue Notre-Dame is the **Office des Congrès et du Tourisme du Grand Montréal** ⑩. Both sides of the square are lined with two- and three-story stone buildings that were originally homes or hotels. In summer the one-block **rue St-Amable** ⑪ near the bottom of the square becomes a marketplace.

Retrace your steps to the north end of Place Jacques-Cartier and continue east on rue Notre-Dame. On the right, at the corner of rue St-Claude, is **Château Ramezay** ⑫, built as the residence of the 11th governor of Montréal, Claude de Ramezay, and now a museum. Continue east to rue Berri. On the corner are two houses from the mid-19th century that have been transformed into the **Musée Georges-Étienne Cartier** ⑬, a museum honoring one of the leading figures in founding the Canadian federation in 1867.

When you come out of the museum, walk south on rue Berri to rue St-Paul and then start walking west again toward the center of the city. The first street on your right is rue Bonsecours, one of the oldest in the city. On the corner is the charming Maison du Calvet, now a restaurant and small bed-and-breakfast. Opposite it is the small but beautiful **Chapelle Notre-Dame-de-Bonsecours** ⑭, built by St. Marguerite Bourgeoys, Montréal's first schoolteacher. The long, domed building to the west of the chapel is the **Marché Bonsecours** ⑮, a public market transformed into a cultural center with exhibits on Montréal.

The fashionable 20 blocks of **rue St-Paul** are lined with restaurants, shops, and nightclubs. In an old stone building on rue St-Paul Ouest is an exhibit that focuses on the very new: **Cité des Arts et des Nouvelles Technologies** ⑯ is devoted to exploring cyberspace. Eight blocks

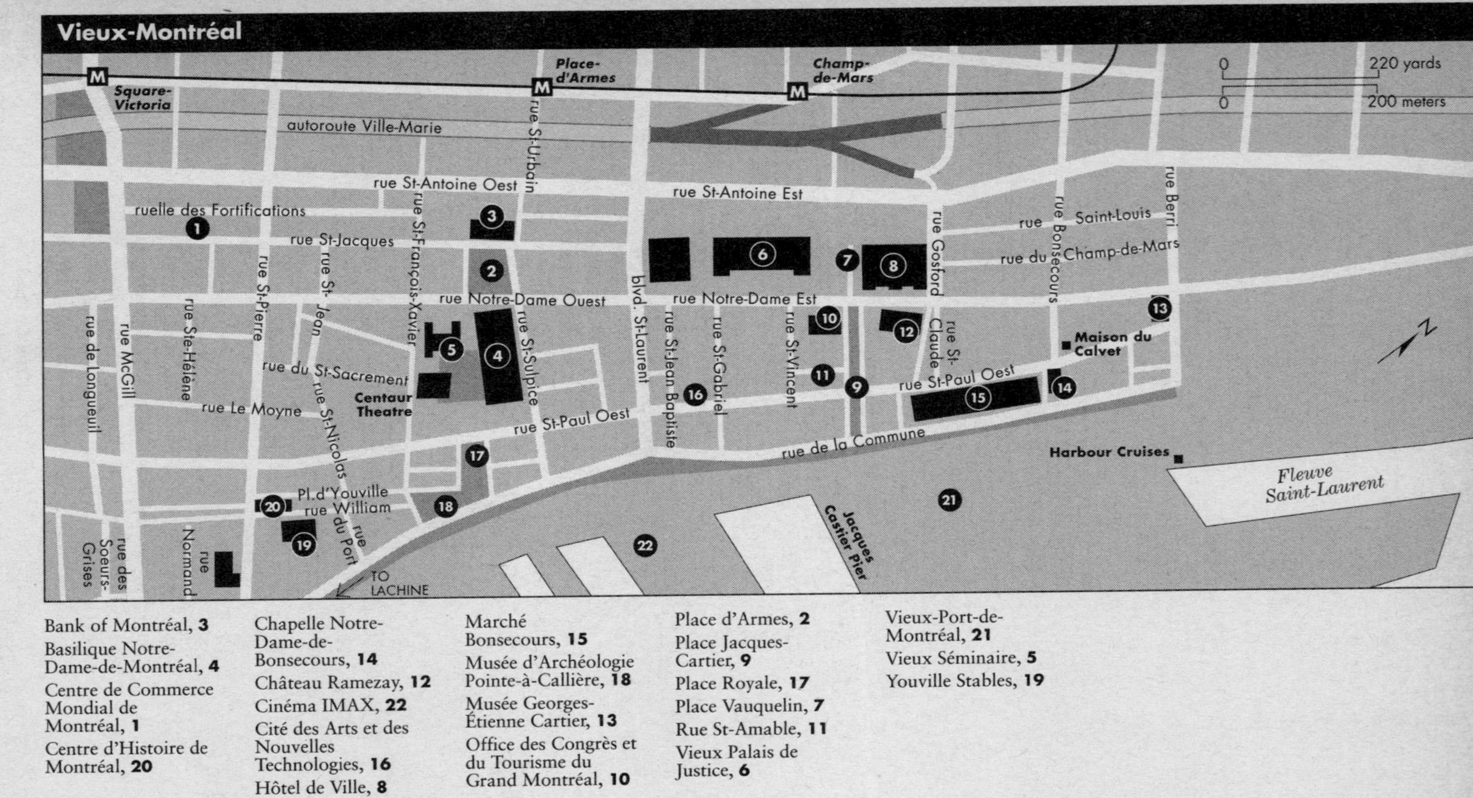

Bank of Montréal, **3**
Basilique Notre-Dame-de-Montréal, **4**
Centre de Commerce Mondial de Montréal, **1**
Centre d'Histoire de Montréal, **20**
Chapelle Notre-Dame-de-Bonsecours, **14**
Château Ramezay, **12**
Cinéma IMAX, **22**
Cité des Arts et des Nouvelles Technologies, **16**
Hôtel de Ville, **8**
Marché Bonsecours, **15**
Musée d'Archéologie Pointe-à-Callière, **18**
Musée Georges-Étienne Cartier, **13**
Office des Congrès et du Tourisme du Grand Montréal, **10**
Place d'Armes, **2**
Place Jacques-Cartier, **9**
Place Royale, **17**
Place Vauquelin, **7**
Rue St-Amable, **11**
Vieux Palais de Justice, **6**
Vieux-Port-de-Montréal, **21**
Vieux Séminaire, **5**
Youville Stables, **19**

west of Place Jacques-Cartier, rue St-Paul leads to **Place Royale** ⑰, the oldest public square in Montréal. Behind the Old Customs House on the square is **Pointe-à-Callière,** a small park that commemorates the settlers' first landing, and the **Musée d'Archéologie Pointe-à-Callière** ⑱, Montréal's dazzling museum of history and archaeology. A 1½-block walk down rue William takes you to the **Youville Stables** ⑲ on the left. These low stone buildings enclosing a garden now house offices, shops, and a restaurant.

Across rue William from the stables is the old fire station that houses the **Centre d'Histoire de Montréal** ⑳, a museum that chronicles the day-to-day life of Montrealers throughout the years. Now walk back east on rue William and turn right down rue du Port to rue de la Commune. Across the street is the **Vieux-Port-de-Montréal** ㉑, a pleasant and popular waterfront park that makes a fitting close to any walk in Vieux-Montréal. If you have time, you can arrange for a harbor excursion or a daring ride on the Lachine Rapids. The Vieux-Port is also home to the **Cinéma IMAX** ㉒, which shows films on a seven-story screen. The impact can be more terrifying than the rapids.

TIMING

If you walk briskly and don't stop, you could get through this route in under an hour. A more realistic and leisurely pace would take about 90 minutes—still without stopping—longer in winter when the streets are icy. Comfortable shoes are a must for the cobblestone streets. The Basilique Notre-Dame is one of Montréal's most famous landmarks and deserves at least a 45-minute visit; Château Ramezay deserves the same. Pointe-à-Callière could keep an enthusiastic history buff occupied for a whole day, but give it at least two hours. If you're visiting any museums, check ahead for seasonal hours.

Sights to See

❸ **Bank of Montréal.** The head office of Canada's oldest chartered bank is a neoclassical building with Corinthian columns, built in 1847 and remodeled by the renowned architectural firm McKim, Mead & White in 1905. It has a one-room museum that recounts the early history of banking in Canada. ✉ *119 rue St-Jacques Ouest.* *Museum free.* ⏲ *Weekdays 10–4.*

★ ❹ **Basilique Notre-Dame-de-Montréal** (Notre-Dame Basilica). The first church called Notre-Dame was a bark-covered structure built in 1642. Three times it was torn down and rebuilt, each time larger and more ornate. The present church is an enormous (3,800-seat) neo-Gothic structure that opened in 1829. Its architect was an American Protestant named James O'Donnell, who converted to Catholicism during construction and is buried in the church crypt. The twin towers are 228 ft high, and the western one holds one of North America's largest bells. The interior is neo-Gothic, with stained-glass windows, pine and walnut carvings, and a vaulted blue ceiling studded with thousands of 24-carat gold stars. With more than 7,000 pipes, the pipe organ is one of the largest on the continent. If you just want to hear the organ roar, drop in for the 11 AM solemn Mass on Sunday and pay special attention to the recessional. Behind the main altar is the **Sacré-Coeur Chapel,** destroyed by fire in 1978 and rebuilt in five different styles. The chapel is often called the Wedding Chapel because of the hundreds of Montrealers who get married in it every year. When pop star Céline Dion married her manager in 1994, however, the lavish and elaborate ceremony was in the main church. Also in the back of the church is a small museum of religious paintings and historical objects. Please note: Notre-Dame is an active house of worship and visitors should dress accordingly. Also, it is advisable to plan your visit around the daily 12:15 PM Mass in the chapel and the 5 PM Mass in the main church. ✉ *116 rue Notre-Dame Ouest,* ☎ *514/849–1070 basilica, 514/842–2925 museum.* 🎫 *Basilica donation requested, tour free, museum $1.* ⏲ *Basilica Labor Day–June 24, daily 8:30–6, and June 25–Labor Day, daily 8:30–8. Guided tour (except Sun. morning) May–June 24, daily 9–4; June 25–Labor Day, daily 8:30–4:30. Museum weekends 9:30–4:30.*

1 **Centre de Commerce Mondial de Montréal** (Montréal World Trade Center). This is one of the nicest enclosed spaces in Montréal, with a fountain, frequent art exhibits, and Montréal's own chunk of the Berlin Wall, complete with colorful graffiti. The center covers a block of the rundown ruelle des Fortifications, a narrow lane that marks the place where the city walls stood. Developers glassed it in and sandblasted and restored 11 of the 19th-century buildings that lined it. It's home to the Hôtel Inter-Continental Montréal (☞ Lodging, *below*) and some boutiques and restaurants. ✉ *747 Sq. Victoria. Métro: Square-Victoria Station and follow signs.*

20 **Centre d'Histoire de Montréal.** Video games, soundtracks, and more than 300 artifacts re-create the day-to-day life of the ordinary men and women who have lived in Montréal, from precolonial to modern times. Some of the most touching exhibits depict family life in Montréal's working-class tenements in the 20th century. ✉ *335 Pl. d'Youville,* ☎ *514/872–3207.* 🎫 *$4.50.* ⏲ *Tues.–Sun. 10–5.*

14 **Chapelle Notre-Dame-de-Bonsecours.** St. Marguerite Bourgeoys dedicated this chapel to the Virgin Mary in 1657. It became known as a sailor's church, and small wood models of sailing ships hang from the ceiling. It reopened in 1998 after a major renovation project that, among other things, revealed several priceless murals that had been hidden behind glued-on paintings. The attached Musée Marguerite Bourgeoys explores the life of the saint and the history of Montréal, with an emphasis on education. You can climb to the rather precarious bell tower (beware of the slippery metal steps in winter) for a fine view of the Vieux-Port. ✉ *400 rue St-Paul Est,* ☎ *514/282–8670.* 🎫 *Museum $5.* ⏲ *Tues.–Sun., May 1–Oct. 31, 10–4:30; Nov. 1–mid-Jan. and mid-Mar.–Apr. 30, 11–3. Chapel open May 1–Oct. 31, daily 10–6, Nov. 1–mid-Jan. and mid-Mar.–Apr. 30, daily 11–6. The museum is closed mid-Jan.–mid-Mar. and the chapel opens only from 4:30 PM to 6 PM.*

12 **Château Ramezay.** This elegant colonial building was the residence of the 11th governor of Montréal, Claude de Ramezay. In 1775–76 it served as headquarters for American troops seeking to conquer Canada; Benjamin Franklin stayed here during that winter occupation. The château became a museum of city and provincial history in 1895, and it has been restored to the style of Governor de Ramezay's day. Château Ramezay is built on the lines of a Norman castle, with squat stone turrets and graceful, wood-paneled rooms. Of particular interest is the Salon Nantes, with its 18th-century carved paneling by French architect Germain Boffrand. ✉ *280 rue Notre-Dame Est,* ☎ *514/861–3708.* 🎫 *$5.* ⏲ *June–Sept., daily 10–6; Oct.–May, Tues.–Sun. 10–4:30.*

NEED A BREAK?

In summer few places are lovelier and livelier than **Place Jacques-Cartier.** You could stop at a *terasse* (sidewalk café) for a beer or a coffee or just sit on a bench amid the flower vendors and listen to the street musicians or watch a juggler. If you're peckish, there are several snack bars and ice-cream stands. If you're really daring, you could try *poutine,* Québec's contribution to junk-food culture. It consists of french fries covered with cheese curds and smothered in gravy—an acquired taste.

22 **Cinéma IMAX.** Nausea and vertigo are some of the more negative things people experience the first time they see an IMAX film roar at them from a seven-story screen. Wonder and excitement are among the more positive. The films—most under an hour long—are decidedly educational. It's best to reserve ahead. ✉ *Vieux-Port, Shed No. 7,* ☎ *514/790–1245.* 🎫 *$11.75.* ⊙ *Tues.–Sun. from 9:45* AM.

16 **Cité des Arts et des Nouvelles Technologies.** The center, dedicated to art and modern technology, has revolving exhibits that explore virtual reality, interactive art, computer animation, and other wonders of the cyber universe. In the electronic café you can have coffee and a sandwich and plug into the Internet on one of 40 computers. ✉ *85 rue St-Paul Ouest,* ☎ *514/849–1612.* 🎫 *$11.75.* ⊙ *Sun.–Thurs. 10–6, Fri.–Sat. 10–9; call for show times.*

8 **Hôtel de Ville.** Montréal's ornate City Hall was built in 1878 in the Second Empire style. On July 24, 1967, President Charles de Gaulle of France stood on the central balcony here and made his famous "*Vive le Québec libre*" speech. There are no tours, but the main hall is used for occasional exhibitions. ✉ *275 rue Notre-Dame Est.*

15 **Marché Bonsecours.** Built in 1845, this domed building was for years Montréal's main produce, meat, and fish market. It now houses municipal offices and a cultural center with exhibits on Montréal. ✉ *350 rue St-Paul Est.*

★ 18 **Musée d'Archéologie Pointe-à-Callière.** Here you can get to the very foundations of New France. This museum in the ☞ **Pointe-à-Callière** park was built around the excavated remains of structures dating to Montréal's beginnings, including the city's first Catholic cemetery. It's a labyrinth of stone walls and corridors, illuminated by spotlights and holograms of figures from the past. An audiovisual show gives a historical overview of the area. It also has an excellent gift shop, full of interesting books on Montréal's history, as well as pictures and reproductions of old maps, engravings, and other artifacts. ✉ *350 Pl. Royale,* ☎ *514/872–9150.* 🎫 *$8.* ⊙ *June 24–Labor Day, Tues.–Sun. 10–8; Sept. 6–June 23, Tues.–Fri. 10–5, Sun. 11–5.*

13 **Musée George-Étienne Cartier.** This museum, which honors one of the architects of the 1867 Canadian federation, comprises two houses. The west house was the Cartiers' home in 1862 and has been meticulously restored to the style of that period, with plush Victorian furniture. The house on the east focuses on the political career of one of the most important French-Canadian statesmen of his day. Costumed guides act out the roles of the Cartiers' friends and servants. From mid-November to mid-December the Cartiers' home is festooned with Victorian decorations. ✉ *458 rue Notre-Dame Est,* ☎ *514/283–2282.* 🎫 *$3.25.* ⊙ *Late May–Labor Day, daily 10–6; Labor Day–mid-May, Wed.–Sun. 10–noon and 1–5.*

10 **Office des Congrès et du Tourisme du Grand Montréal.** This small building (1811) was the site of the old Silver Dollar Saloon, so named because there were 350 silver dollars nailed to the floor. Today it's one of two visitor information offices operated by Info-Touriste; the other is at 1001 square Dorchester. The staff can answer travel questions, and guides to the city and brochures on attractions and hotels are available. ✉ *174 rue Notre-Dame Est,* ☎ *514/873–2015.*

Palais de Justice. Built in 1971, this black glass building is the main courthouse for the judicial district of Montréal. Criminal law in Canada falls under federal jurisdiction and is based on British common law, but civil law is a provincial matter and Québec's is based on France's

Napoleonic Code, which governs all the minutiae of private life—from setting up a company and negotiating a mortgage to drawing up a marriage contract and registering the names of children. Lawyers and judges in Québec courts wear the same elaborate gowns as their British counterparts, but not the wigs. This building is not open for tours. ✉ *1 rue Notre-Dame Est.*

❷ **Place d'Armes.** Montréal's founder, Paul de Chomedy, slew an Iroquois chief in a battle here in 1644 and was wounded in return. His statue stands in a fountain in the middle of the square. Tunnels beneath the square protected the colonists from the winter weather and provided an escape route; unfortunately they are too small and dangerous to visit. ✉ *Bordered by rues Notre-Dame Ouest and St-Jacques.*

★ ❾ **Place Jacques-Cartier.** This two-block-long square, at the heart of Vieux-Montréal, opened in 1804 as a municipal market, and every summer it is transformed into a flower market. The 1809 monument at the top of the square celebrates Lord Nelson's victory over Napoléon Bonaparte's French navy at Trafalgar. It was built not by patriotic British residents of Montréal but by the Sulpician priests, who didn't have much love for the Corsican emperor either. ✉ *Bordered by rues Notre-Dame Est and de la Commune.*

⓱ **Place Royale.** The oldest public square in Montréal served as a public market during the French regime and later became a Victorian garden. The severely beautiful neoclassical Vielle Douane (Old Customs House) on its south side serves as the gift shop for the ☞ **Musée d'Archéologie Pointe-à-Callière.**

❼ **Place Vauquelin.** The statue in this little square is of Admiral Jacques Vauquelin, a naval hero of the French regime.

Pointe-à-Callière. This small park commemorates the settlers' first landing. A small stream used to flow into the St. Lawrence here, and it was on the point of land between the two waters that the colonists landed their four boats on May 17, 1642. The settlement was almost washed away the next Christmas by a flood. When it was spared, Paul de Chomedey, Sieur de Maisonneuve, placed a cross on top of Mont-Royal as thanks to God. ✉ *Bordered by rues de la Commune and William.*

⓫ **Rue St-Amable.** A one-block lane near Place Jacques-Cartier is a summer marketplace for local jewelers, artists, and craftspeople.

Rue St-Jacques. This was once the financial heart, not just of Montréal but of Canada. As you walk here, note the fine decorative stone flourishes—grapevines, nymphs, angels, and goddesses—on the Victorian office buildings.

Rue St-Paul. The most fashionable street in Vieux-Montréal, rue St-Paul is lined with restaurants, shops filled with Québécois handicrafts, and nightclubs for almost 20 blocks.

Rue St-Sulpice. This is one of the oldest streets in Montréal. A plaque on the eastern side marks the spot where Jeanne Mance built Hôpital Hôtel-Dieu, the city's first hospital, in 1644.

❻ **Vieux Palais de Justice.** The old courthouse, a domed building in the Classical Revival style, was built in 1857. It once housed the civil courts but is now a warren of city offices. ✉ *155 rue Notre-Dame Est.*

㉑ **Vieux-Port-de-Montréal.** Today the port is a recreational area rather than the heart and soul of the city's commercial life. Its docks are too small and its channels too shallow for modern megaships, and only a few freighters and cruise ships use it. However, the area is a popular waterfront park with a promenade, snack bars, and the ☞ **Cinéma IMAX.** In summer, you can rent bicycles and in-line skates, and in winter you can skate on a giant outdoor rink. A new science center is planned to open in January 2000. The port also marks the start of one of the city's most popular bicycle paths. Every weekend hundreds of Montrealers follow the route of the old Lachine Canal (built in 1825 to bypass the Lachine Rapids and rendered obsolete by the St. Lawrence Seaway) to Parc René-Lévesque in Lachine, a narrow spit of land jutting into Lac St-Louis.

5 **Vieux Séminaire.** Montréal's oldest building is considered the finest, most elegant example of 17th-century Québec architecture. It was built in 1685 as a headquarters for the Sulpician priests who owned the island of Montréal until 1854, and it is still a residence for the Sulpicians who administer the basilica. The clock on the roof over the main doorway is the oldest (pre-1701) public timepiece in North America. Behind the seminary building is a garden, which is unfortunately closed to the public, as is the seminary itself. ✉ *116 rue Notre-Dame Ouest, behind wall west of Basilique Notre-Dame-de-Montréal.*

19 **Youville Stables.** These low stone buildings enclosing a garden were originally built as warehouses in 1825 (they never were stables). They now house offices, shops, and Gibby's restaurant (☞ Dining, *below*). ✉ *298 Pl. d'Youville.*

Downtown

On the surface Montréal's downtown, or *centre-ville,* is much like the downtown core of many other major cities—full of life and noisy traffic, its streets lined with department stores, boutiques, bars, restaurants, strip clubs, amusement arcades, and bookstores. But, in fact, much of the area's activity goes on beneath the surface, in Montréal's Cité Souterrain (Underground City). Development of this unique endeavor began in 1966 when the Métro opened. Now it includes (at last count) seven hotels, 1,500 offices, 30 movie theaters, more than 1,600 boutiques, 200 restaurants, three universities, two colleges, two train stations, a skating rink, 40 banks, a bus terminal, an art museum, a complex of concert halls, the home ice of the Montréal Canadiens, and a church. All this is linked by Métro lines and more than 30 km (19 mi) of well-lit, boutique-lined passages that protect shoppers and workers from the hardships of winter and the heat of summer. A traveler arriving by train could book into a fine hotel and spend a week shopping, dining, and going to a long list of movies, plays, concerts, sports events, and discos, without once stepping outside.

A Good Walk

The start of this walk is designed for moles—it's all underground—but it will give you an idea of the extent of the Underground City. Start at the McGill Métro station, one of the central points in the Underground City. It's linked to a half dozen office towers and two of the "Big Three" department stores, Eaton (the city's biggest) and La Baie (the other is Ogilvy). Passages also link the station to such major shopping malls as Le Centre Eaton, Les Promenades de la Cathédrale, and Place Montreal Trust.

Follow the signs from the station through Eaton's bargain basement to Le Centre Eaton and then descend yet another floor to the tunnel that leads to **Place Ville-Marie** ㉓. The mall complex underneath this cruciform skyscraper was the first link in the Underground City. From here head south via the passageways toward **Le Reine Elizabeth** ㉔, or

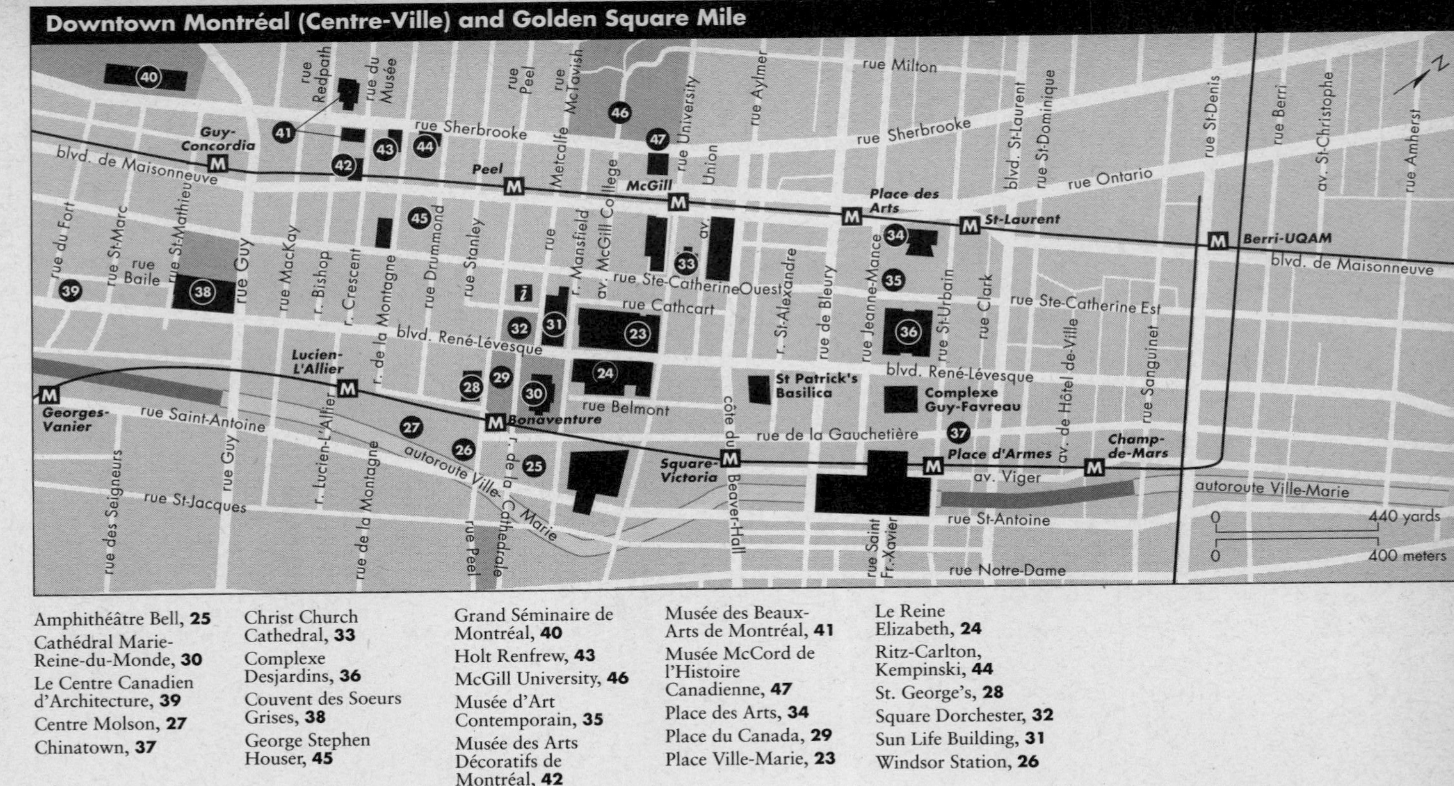

Amphithéâtre Bell, **25**
Cathédral Marie-Reine-du-Monde, **30**
Le Centre Canadien d'Architecture, **39**
Centre Molson, **27**
Chinatown, **37**
Christ Church Cathedral, **33**
Complexe Desjardins, **36**
Couvent des Soeurs Grises, **38**
George Stephen Houser, **45**
Grand Séminaire de Montréal, **40**
Holt Renfrew, **43**
McGill University, **46**
Musée d'Art Contemporain, **35**
Musée des Arts Décoratifs de Montréal, **42**
Musée des Beaux-Arts de Montréal, **41**
Musée McCord de l'Histoire Canadienne, **47**
Place des Arts, **34**
Place du Canada, **29**
Place Ville-Marie, **23**
Le Reine Elizabeth, **24**
Ritz-Carlton, Kempinski, **44**
St. George's, **28**
Square Dorchester, **32**
Sun Life Building, **31**
Windsor Station, **26**

Queen Elizabeth, hotel, which straddles the entrance to the Gare Centrale (Central Station). Walk through the station and follow the signs marked MÉTRO/PLACE BONAVENTURE until you see a sign for Le 1000 rue de la Gauchetière, a skyscraper that's home to the **Amphithéâtre Bell** ㉕, an indoor ice rink. Return to the tunnels and follow signs to the Bonaventure Métro station and then to the Canadian Pacific Railway Company's **Windsor Station** ㉖, with its massive stone exterior and steel-and-glass roof. The rail station and the Place Bonaventure Métro station below it are all linked to **Centre Molson** ㉗, the home of the Montréal Canadiens.

By now you'll be ready for some fresh air. You'll have covered 10 city blocks and visited two train stations, a couple of malls, a major hotel, an office tower, and the city's most important sports shrine without once emerging from cover. Exit the Underground City at the north end of Windsor Station and cross rue de la Gauchetière to **St. George's** ㉘, the prettiest Anglican church in the city. Just to the east across rue Peel is **Place du Canada** ㉙, a park with a statue of Sir John A. Macdonald, Canada's first prime minister. Cross the park and rue de la Cathédrale to **Cathédrale Marie-Reine-du-Monde** ㉚, which is modeled after St. Peter's Basilica in Rome. People sometimes call the gray granite building across boulevard René-Lévesque from the cathedral the Wedding Cake, because it rises in tiers of decreasing size and has lots of columns, but its real name is the **Sun Life Building** ㉛. The park that faces the Sun Life Building just north of boulevard René-Lévesque is **Square Dorchester** ㉜, for many years the heart of Montréal. Backtrack across the park to rue Peel and walk north to rue Ste-Catherine. This intersection is regarded by many as the heart of downtown.

Turn right and walk east along rue Ste-Catherine, pausing briefly to admire the view at the corner of avenue McGill College. Look north up this broad boulevard and you can see the Victorian-era buildings of the McGill University campus with Mont-Royal looming in the background. The grim-looking gray castle high on the slopes to the right is the Royal Victoria Hospital. One block more brings you to the Eaton department store, where this whole adventure started, and next to that is **Christ Church Cathedral** ㉝ (1859), the main church of the Anglican diocese of Montréal.

You can end your stroll here or continue six blocks farther east on rue Ste-Catherine to **Place des Arts** ㉞, Montréal's main theater complex. The **Musée d'Art Contemporain** ㉟, the city's modern art museum, is also part of the complex. While still in Place des Arts, follow the signs to the **Complexe Desjardins** ㊱, an office building, hotel, and mall along the lines of Place Ville-Marie (☞ *above*). The next development south is the Complexe Guy-Favreau, a huge federal office building named after the Canadian minister of justice in the early '60s. If you continue in a straight line, you will hit the Palais de Congrès, Montréal's convention centre, above the Place d'Armes Métro stop. But if you take a left out of Guy-Favreau onto rue de la Gauchetière, you will be in **Chinatown** ㊲, a relief after all that enclosed retail space.

TIMING

Just to walk this route briskly will take a minimum of an hour, even on a fine day. The Musée d'Art Contemporain is worthy of at least two hours by itself, so plan on a half-day.

Sights to See

25 **Amphithéâtre Bell.** Skating is a passion in Montréal, and you can do it year-round in this indoor ice rink on the ground floor of a skyscraper. The rink is bathed in natural light and surrounded by cafés, a food court,

and a winter garden. It's open to skaters of all levels of experience; skate rentals and lockers are available. There are also skating lessons, Saturday- and Sunday-night disco skating, and scheduled ice shows. To find the rink once you're inside the building, remember the French word for skating rink is *patinoire.* ✉ *1000 rue de la Gauchetière,* ☎ *514/395–0555.* 🎫 *$5, skate rental $4.* ⏲ *Sun.–Thurs. 11:30 AM–9PM, Fri. 11:30 AM–10 PM, Sat. 11:30–7 for all ages; Sat. 7 PM–10 PM for those 16 and older, Sat. 10–11 for those under 12.*

30 **Cathédrale Marie-Reine-du-Monde** (Mary Queen of the World Cathedral). Seat of the Roman Catholic archbishop of Montréal, this church (1894) is modeled after St. Peter's Basilica in Rome. Victor Bourgeau, the same architect who did the interior of Notre-Dame in Vieux-Montréal, thought the idea of the cathedral's design terrible but completed it after the original architect proved incompetent. Inside there is even a canopy over the altar that is a miniature copy of Bernini's baldachin in St. Peter's. ✉ *1085 rue de la Cathédral; through main doors on blvd. René-Lévesque.*

27 **Centre Molson.** This arena is the new (1996) home of the Montréal Canadiens, the hockey team hometown fans call simply *les Glorieux.* The brown-brick building replaces the old Forum that had been the Canadiens' home since 1917. The name refers to the Molson family, who established Montréal's first brewery in the 18th century and whose company, Molson-O'Keefe, owns the hockey team. ✉ *1260 rue de la Gauchetière Ouest,* ☎ *514/932–2582, 514/925–5656 for tours.* 🎫 *Tour $7.* ⏲ *Tour in English at 11 and 2, in French at 10:30 and 1:30.*

37 **Chinatown.** The Chinese first came to Montréal in large numbers after 1880, following the construction of the transcontinental railroad. They settled in an 18-block area between boulevard René-Lévesque and avenue Viger to the north and south, and near rues Hôtel de Ville and Bleury on the west and east, an area now full of restaurants, food stores, and gift shops. If you have enough energy, stroll south on rue St-Urbain for a block to rue St-Antoine. A half block east is **Steve's Music Store** (✉ 51 rue St-Antoine Ouest, ☎ 514/878–2216), a shabby warren of five storefronts jammed with just about everything you need to be a rock star except talent. Sooner or later every musician and wannabe musician in the city wanders through it.

NEED A BREAK?

Pho Bang New York (✉ 970 blvd. St-Laurent, ☎ 514/954-2032) is a small Vietnamese restaurant on the edge of Chinatown that specializes in traditional noodle soups served in bowls big enough to bathe a small dog. And it's cheap, too—for less than $5, you get soup, a plate of crispy vegetables, and a small pot of tea. The restaurant does not accept credit cards.

33 **Christ Church Cathedral.** This is the main church (1859) of the Anglican diocese of Montréal. In early 1988 the diocese leased the land and air rights to a consortium of developers. The consortium then built **La Maison des Coopérants,** a 34-story office tower behind the cathedral, and a huge retail complex, **Les Promenades de la Cathédrale,** under it. The church has a quiet graceful interior and frequent organ recitals and concerts. ✉ *535 rue Ste-Catherine Ouest.* ⏲ *Daily 8–6.*

36 **Complexe Desjardins.** The large galleria space in this boutique-rich mall is the scene of all types of performances, from lectures on Japanese massage techniques to pop music. ✉ *Bordered by rues Ste-Catherine, Jeanne-Mance, and St-Urbain and blvd. René-Lévesque.*

35 **Musée d'Art Contemporain.** The museum's large permanent collection of modern art represents works by Québécois, Canadian, and international artists in every medium. Its more than 5,000 works reflect all the major movements, but it focuses on the works of Québec artists. It has, for example, 72 paintings, 32 works on paper, and a sculpture by Paul-Émile Borduas, one of Canada's most important artists. The museum often has weekend programs, with many child-oriented activities, and almost all are free. The hours for guided tours vary. ✉ *175 rue Ste-Catherine Ouest,* ☎ *514/847–6226.* *$6; Wed. evening free.* *Tues. and Thurs.–Sun. 11–6, Wed. 11–9.*

34 **Place des Arts.** The Place des Arts theater is a government-subsidized complex of five very modern theaters. Guided tours of the halls and backstage are available for groups of at least 15. ✉ *175 rue Ste-Catherine Ouest,* ☎ *514/842–2112 for tickets, 514/285–4270 for information, 514/285–4275 for guided tours.*

29 **Place du Canada.** This park has a statue of Sir John A. Macdonald, Canada's first prime minister. In October 1995 the park was the site of a huge rally for Canadian unity that drew more than 300,000 participants from across the country. That patriotic demonstration was at least partly responsible for preserving a slim victory for the pro-unity forces in the subsequent referendum on independence for Québec. At the south end of Place du Canada is **Le Marriott Château Champlain** (☞ Lodging, *below*), known as the Cheese Grater because of its rows and rows of half-moon-shape windows. ✉ *Bordered by blvd. René-Lévesque and rue de la Gauchetière.*

23 **Place Ville-Marie.** This cross-shape 1962 office tower was Montréal's first modern skyscraper; the mall complex underneath it was the first link in the Underground City. ✉ *Bordered by blvd. René-Lévesque and rues Mansfield, Cathcart, and University.*

NEED A BREAK? The once grim passageways at the back of Central Station just below the escalators leading to Place Ville-Marie now house a trendy food court, **Les Halles de la Gare.** The food includes some of the city's best bread and pastries, salads, and sandwiches made with fresh terrines and pâtés. If it's nice out, you can take your snack up the escalator to the mall under Place Ville-Marie and then up the stairs in the middle of its food court to the terrace, a wide area with a fine view.

24 **Le Reine Elizabeth.** One of the city's major hotels (☞ Lodging, *below*) straddles the **Gare Centrale** (Central Station), where most trains from the United States and the rest of Canada arrive. ✉ *900 blvd. René-Lévesque,* ☎ *514/861–3511.*

28 **St. George's.** A jewel of neo-Gothic architecture, the prettiest Anglican church in the city was built in 1872. St. George's dimly reverent interior has a beamed wooden ceiling, a richly carved choir screen, and some fine stained-glass windows. ✉ *1101 rue Stanley.*

OFF THE BEATEN PATH **ST. PATRICK'S BASILICA** – A gem of church architecture rarely visited by tourists, this 1847 church is one of the purest examples of the Gothic Revival style in Canada. It is to Montréal's English-speaking Catholics what the Basilique Notre-Dame is to the city's French-speaking Catholics. The church's colors are soft, and the vaulted ceiling over the sanctuary glows with green and gold mosaics. The old pulpit has panels depicting the Apostles, and a huge lamp decorated with six 6-ft-high angels hangs over the main altar. The church is just three blocks west of Place Ville-Marie. ✉ *460 blvd. René-Lévesque Ouest,* ☎ *514/866-7379.* *Daily 8:30–6.*

32 **Square Dorchester.** Until 1870 a Catholic burial ground occupied this downtown park, and there are still bodies buried beneath the grass. The statuary includes a monument to the Boer War and statues of Scottish poet Robert Burns and Sir Wilfrid Laurier, Canada's first French-speaking prime minister. ✉ *Bordered by rues Peel, Metcalfe, and McTavish.*

31 **Sun Life Building.** At one time this was the largest building in the British Commonwealth. During World War II much of England's financial reserves and national treasures were stored in Sun Life's vaults. ✉ *1155 rue Metcalfe.*

26 **Windsor Station.** This magnificent building with its massive stone exterior and steel-and-glass roof was once the eastern passenger terminus for the Canadian Pacific Railway, Canada's first transcontinental link. Alas, today it is a trainless shell. ✉ *1100 rue de la Gauchetière.*

Golden Square Mile

As Montréal grew in confidence and economic might in the 19th century, the city's prosperous merchant class moved north, building lavish stone homes on the slopes of Mont-Royal. In fact, at the turn of the century, the people who lived here—mostly of Scottish descent—controlled 70% of the country's wealth. Their baronial homes and handsome churches—Protestant, of course—covered the mountain north of rue Sherbrooke roughly between avenue Côte-des-Neiges and rue University.

Humbler residents south of rue Sherbrooke referred to the area simply as the Square Mile, a name immortalized in novelist Hugh MacLennan's *Two Solitudes*. The Square Mile was eventually gilded by newspaper columnist Al Palmer in the 1950s, long after its golden age had passed. Real Square Milers like actor Christopher Plummer still bridle at the extra adjective. Many of the area's palatial homes have been leveled to make way for high-rises and office towers, but it is still studded with architectural gems, and rue Sherbrooke is still the city's most elegant street.

This walk takes in much of the Square Mile along with an area named Shaughnessy Village to the southwest, bounded roughly by rues Atwater and Guy to the west and east and rue Sherbrooke and boulevard René-Lévesque to the north and south. The village takes its name from the very lush Shaughnessy Mansion on boulevard René-Lévesque, a house that would fit in quite comfortably up the hill in the Square Mile. But while most of the Shaughnessy family's 19th-century neighbors were well-off businesspeople and professionals who lived in elegantly comfortable homes, they certainly weren't wealthy enough to make it into the Square Mile.

A Good Walk

This walk starts at the Guy–Concordia Métro station at the rue Guy exit. The statue just north of the station on the little triangular slice of land in the middle of boulevard de Maisonneuve portrays Norman Bethune, a McGill University–trained doctor from Gravenhurst, Ontario, who served with the Loyalists in the Spanish civil war and died in China in 1939 while serving with Mao's Red Army. Walk south to rue Ste-Catherine and turn right. The long building on the south side of the street used to be a car dealership and bowling alley until it was transformed into the Faubourg Ste-Catherine, an enclosed market selling specialty foods, pastries, bagels, and ethnic lunches.

At rue St-Mathieu, turn left and head south. The huge gray building on the left side of the street is **Couvent des Soeurs Grises** ㊳, the motherhouse of an order of nuns founded by St. Marguerite d'Youville, Canada's first native-born saint. Across from the convent, turn right down rue Baile and into the heart of Shaugnessy Village, named for a family mansion that now forms part of **Le Centre Canadien d'Architecture** ㊴. Many of the area's town houses and mansions were torn down during the philistine '60s to make way for boxy high-rises, but a few remain. Note, for example, the fine row of stone town houses just across rue Baile from Le Centre Canadien d'Architecture.

Turn right on rue Fort and walk north four blocks to rue Sherbrooke. On the north side of the street you will see a complex of fine neoclassical buildings in a shady garden. This is the **Grand Séminaire de Montréal** ㊵, which trains priests for Montréal's Roman Catholic parishes. The two stone towers on the property are among the oldest buildings on the island. In 1928, the anticlerical Freemasons built their windowless and grandly Greek Masonic Temple right across the street at Number 1859.

Walk east along stately rue Sherbrooke past rows of exclusive shops and galleries housed in old town houses to the **Musée des Beaux-Arts de Montréal** ㊶ at the corner of rues Sherbrooke and du Musée. This houses the city's main art collection, which includes works from around the world. Right behind it is the **Musée des Arts Décoratifs de Montréal** ㊷, with its fine collection of furniture, hangings, and decorations. Farther east on rue Sherbrooke is the small and exclusive **Holt Renfrew** ㊸ department store, perhaps the city's fanciest, at the corner of rue de la Montagne. **Rue de la Montagne** and **rues Crescent and Bishop,** the two streets just west of it, are filled with trendy restaurants, shops, and bars. One block farther east on the south side of rue Sherbrooke at rue Drummond stands the **Ritz-Carlton Kempinski** ㊹, the grande dame of Montréal hotels. Right across from the Ritz is Le Château (1926), a huge, copper-roofed apartment building that looks somewhat like a cross between a French Renaissance château and a Scots castle. It is one of the few samples of gracious living left west of rue Atwater. Others worth looking at are the Corby House (⊠ 1201 rue Sherbrooke Ouest) and the Maison Louis-Joseph Forget next door (⊠ 1195 rue Sherbrooke Ouest). One of the area's most magnificent homes, however, is on rue Drummond just south of Sherbrooke. The **George Stephen House** ㊺ was built for the founder of the Canadian Pacifice Railway and is now the Mount Stephen Club, a private gathering place for Montréal business leaders.

The campus of **McGill University** ㊻ is on the north side of rue Sherbrooke just three blocks east of the Ritz-Carlton. Opposite its main gates is the Banque Commerciale Italienne (⊠888 rue Sherbrooke Ouest), housed in a beautiful neo-Elizabethan house built in 1906 for Dr. William Alexander Molson, a scion of Montréal's most famous brewing family. A block farther east is the **Musée McCord de l'Histoire Canadienne** ㊼, one of the best history museums in Canada.

TIMING

To walk this route briskly will take a minimum of 90 minutes, but the area is rich in places—the Musée des Beaux-Arts, the Musée des Art Décoratifs, the Musée McCord de l'Histoire Canadienne, the Musée d'Art Contemporain, the Couvent des Soeurs Grises—that all deserve longer visits. It's easy to spend a day or more here.

Sights to See

39 **Le Centre Canadien d'Architecture** (Canadian Center for Architecture). The center's rotating exhibits on the history and philosophy of architecture are displayed in an ultramodern building and tend to be a bit

academic. The attached Shaughnessy Mansion, with its paneled conservatory and vast reception rooms, is worth a look; so is the amusing sculpture garden across the street. ✉ *1920 rue Baile,* ☎ *514/939-7000.* 🎫 *$5.* ⏲ *Wed. and Fri. 11–6, Thurs. 11–8, weekends 11–5.*

38 **Couvent des Soeurs Grises.** *Soeurs grises* translates as "gray nuns," but the name has nothing to do with the color of the good sisters' habits. Their founder, St. Marguerite d'Youville (1701–71), started looking after the city's down-and-outs after her unhappy marriage to a whiskey trader ended in widowhood. Her late husband's profession and the condition of many of her clients earned her and her colleagues the sobriquet "soeurs grises," which is slang for tipsy nuns. The order ran a public hospital, opened the city's first nursing schools, and operated shelters for abandoned children. They still administer hospitals, shelters for battered women, halfway houses, and nursing homes. The order moved to this vast, graystone convent in 1874. Highlights are the beautiful Romanesque Revival chapel that was restored in 1996, the church crypt where many of the pioneer members are buried, and a small museum containing mementos of the saint's life—her books, the knife and fork she used at boarding school, a re-creation of her simple room—as well as artifacts of the order's history. ✉ *1185 rue St-Mathieu,* ☎ *514/937-9501.* 🎫 *Free.* ⏲ *Wed.–Sun. 1:30–4:30.*

45 **George Stephen House.** Scottish-born George Stephen, founder of the Canadian Pacific Railway, spent $600,000 to build this impressive home in 1883—an almost unimaginable sum at the time. He imported artisans from all over the world to panel its ceilings with Cuban mahogany, Indian lemon tree, and English oak and to decorate its walls with marble, onyx, and gold. The house is a private club now, but most Sundays, visitors can drop in for a guided tour or, if they reserve ahead, a sumptuous brunch ($25) of braised duck or roast beef served to the accompaniment of live music. ✉ *1440 rue Drummond,* ☎ *514/849-7338 for information on guided tours and brunches. Closed to public mid-July–Aug. and over Christmas.*

40 **Grand Séminaire de Montréal.** The Montréal Roman Catholic archdiocese trains its priests here in buildings that date to 1860. Two squat towers in the gardens date to the 17th century, and it was in one of these that St. Marguerite Bourgeoys set up her first school for native girls. The towers, among the oldest buildings on the island, are visible from the street; a little area just by the gates has three plaques that explain the towers and their history in French. The seminary is private, but you can go to Mass at 10:30 on Sunday morning from September through June in the lovely neoclassical chapel. ✉ *2065 rue Sherbrooke Ouest.*

43 **Holt Renfrew.** This is perhaps the city's fanciest department store (☞ Shopping, *below*). ✉ *1300 rue Sherbrooke Ouest,* ☎ *514/842-5111.*

46 **McGill University.** James McGill, a wealthy Scottish fur trader, bequeathed the money and the land for this institution, which opened in 1828 and is perhaps the finest English-language university in the nation. The student body numbers 15,000, and the university is best known for its medical and engineering schools. Most of the campus buildings are fine examples of Victorian architecture. ✉ *845 rue Sherbrooke Ouest.*

NEED A BREAK? The **McGill University campus** is an island of green in a sea of traffic and skyscrapers. On a fine day you can sit on the grass in the shade of a 100-year-old tree and just let the world drift by.

42 **Musée des Arts Décoratifs de Montréal.** Homey things like coffeepots and chairs—some of them wildly stylish—are displayed in an ultra-

modern setting. The museum is attached to the ☞ Musée des Beaux-Arts by a glass atrium. ✉ *2200 rue Crescent,* ☎ *514/284–1242.* 🎫 *$4.* ⏲ *Tues. and Thurs.–Sun. 11–6, Wed. 11–9.*

41 **Musée des Beaux-Arts de Montréal** (Museum of Fine Arts). The oldest museum in the country was founded by a group of English-speaking Montrealers in 1860. The art collection is housed in two buildings—the older Benaiah-Gibb Pavilion on the north side of rue Sherbrooke and the glittering glass-fronted Pavilion Jean-Noël-Desmarais right across the street. The two buildings are connected by underground tunnels and hold a large collection of European and North American fine and decorative art; ancient treasures from Europe, the Near East, Asia, Africa, and America; art from Québec and Canada; and Native American and Eskimo artifacts. The museum is particularly strong in 19th-century works and has one of the finest collections of Canadian paintings, prints, and drawings. It also has a gift shop, an art-book store, a restaurant, a cafeteria, and a gallery from which you can buy or rent paintings by local artists. ✉ *1380 rue Sherbrooke Ouest,* ☎ *514/285–1600.* 🎫 *Permanent collection free, special exhibitions $10.* ⏲ *Tues. and Thurs.–Sun. 11–6, Wed. 11–9.*

47 **Musée McCord de l'Histoire Canadienne.** A grand, eclectic attic of a museum, the McCord documents the life of ordinary Canadians, using costumes and textiles, decorative arts, paintings, prints and drawings, and the 450,000-print-and-negative Notman Photographic Archives, which highlights 19th-century life in Montréal. The McCord is the only museum in Canada with a permanent costume gallery. There are guided tours (call for times), a reading room and documentation center, a gift shop and bookstore, and a café. ✉ *690 rue Sherbrooke Ouest,* ☎ *514/398–7100.* 🎫 *$7.* ⏲ *Tues.–Wed. and Fri. 10–6, Thurs. 10–9, weekends 10–5. Closed Mon. except statutory holidays.*

44 **Ritz-Carlton Kempinski.** The grande dame of Montréal hotels (☞ Lodging, *below*) has been in business since 1912. ✉ *1228 rue Sherbrooke Ouest,* ☎ *514/842–4212.*

Rues de la Montagne, Crescent, and **Bishop.** Today dozens of trendy bars, restaurants, and bistros are ensconced in the old row houses that line these streets between boulevard René-Lévesque and rue Sherbrooke. This area once formed the playing fields of the Montréal Lacrosse and Cricket Grounds. Later it became an exclusive suburb lined with millionaires' row houses.

Quartier Latin

Early in this century, rue St-Denis cut through a bourgeois neighborhood of large, comfortable residences. The Université de Montréal was established here in 1893, and the students and academics who moved into the area dubbed it the Quartier Latin, or Latin Quarter. The university eventually moved to a larger campus on the north side of Mont-Royal, and the area went into decline. It revived in the early 1970s, largely as a result of the 1969 opening of the Université du Québec à Montréal and the launch of the International Jazz Festival in the summer of 1980. Plateau Mont-Royal, the trendy neighborhood just north of the Quartier Latin, shared in this revival. Residents are now a mix of immigrants, working-class Francophones, and young professionals eager to find a home they can renovate close to the city center. The Quartier Latin and Plateau Mont-Royal are home to rows of French and ethnic restaurants, charming bistros, coffee shops, designer boutiques, antiques shops, and art galleries. When night falls, these streets are always full of omnilingual hordes—young and not so young, rich and poor, established and still studying.

Many of the older residences in this area have graceful wrought-iron balconies and twisting staircases that are typical of Montréal. They were built that way for practical reasons. The buildings are what Montrealers call duplexes or triplexes, that is, two or three residences stacked on top of each other. To save interior space, the stairs to reach the upper floors were put outside. The stairs and balconies are treacherous in winter, but in summer they are often full of families and couples, gossiping, picnicking, and partying. If Montrealers tell you they spend the summer in Balconville, they mean they don't have the money or the time to leave town and won't get any farther than their balcony.

A Good Walk

Begin at the Berri-UQAM Métro stop. The "UQAM" in the subway name is pronounced "oo-kam" by local Francophones and "you-kwam" by local Anglophones. It refers to the **Université du Québec à Montréal** ㊽, whose drab brick campus fills up much of three city blocks between rues Sanguinet and Berri. A few splendid fragments of the old Église St-Jacques poke up amid this modern dreck. A more substantial religious monument that has survived intact right in UQAM's resolutely secularist heart is the ornate **Chapelle Notre-Dame-de-Lourdes** ㊾, on rue Ste-Catherine.

Just west of rue St-Denis you find the **Cinémathèque Québécoise** ㊿, which houses one of the largest cinematic reference libraries in the world. Around the corner and a half block north on rue St-Denis stands the 2,500-seat **Théâtre St-Denis** (51), the city's second-largest auditorium. On the next block north is the **Bibliothèque Nationale du Québec,** which houses Québec's official archives.

Turn left on Sherbrooke and left again on boulevard St-Laurent for the **Musée Juste pour Rire** (52), the world's first museum of humor. Backtrack east on rue Sherbrooke, turn left on rue St-Denis, and walk north to **Square St-Louis** (53), a lovely green space.

The stretch of **rue Prince Arthur** (54), beginning at the western end of Square St-Louis and continuing several blocks west, is a center of youth culture. When you reach **boulevard St-Laurent** (55), take a right and stroll north through Montréal's ethnic diversity. This area was still partly rural in the mid-19th century, with lots of fresh air, which made it healthier than overcrowded Vieux-Montréal. So in 1861 the Hôpital Hôtel-Dieu, the hospital Jeanne Mance founded in the 17th century, moved into a new building at what is now the corner of avenue des Pins and rue St-Urbain, just a block west of boulevard St-Laurent. Hôtel-Dieu, one of the city's major hospitals, is still there, and right next to it is the **Musée des Hospitalières de l'Hôtel-Dieu** (56), which gives a remarkable picture of the early days of colonization.

Merchants are attempting to re-create rue Prince Arthur on **rue Duluth** (57). Turn right and walk four blocks east to rue St-Denis, where you will find Greek and Vietnamese restaurants and boutiques and art galleries. Walk east another nine blocks and you come to **Parc Lafontaine,** the smallest of Montréal's three major parks.

After exploring the park's 100 acres, walk south to rue Sherbrooke Est and then turn right and walk west on rues Sherbrooke and Cherrier to the Sherbrooke Métro station to complete the walk. Or head west to explore Parc du Mont-Royal (☞ *below*).

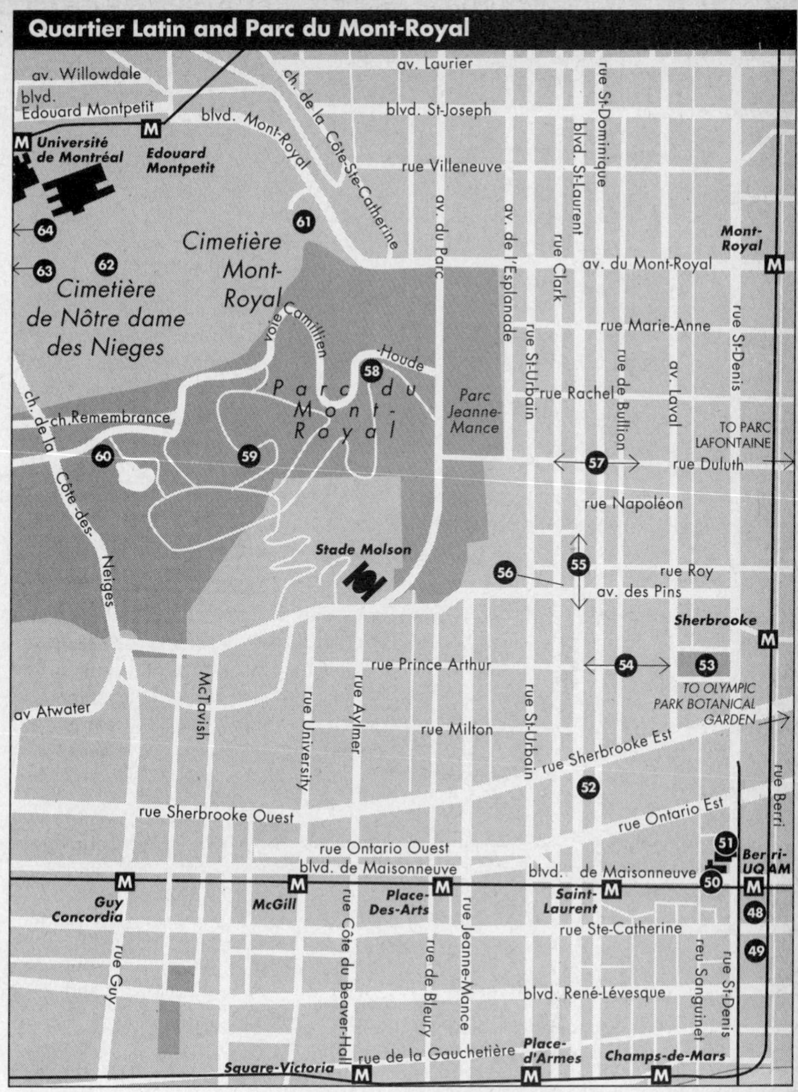

Boulevard St-Laurent, **55**

Chalet du Mont-Royal, **59**

Chapelle Notre-Dame-de-Lourdes, **49**

Cimetière Mont-Royal, **61**

Cimetière Notre-Dame-des-Neiges, **62**

Cinémathèque Québécoise, **50**

Collège Notre Dame, **64**

Lac aux Castors, **60**

Musée des Hospitalières de l'Hôtel-Dieu, **56**

Musée Juste pour Rire, **52**

Obsérvatoire de l'Est, **58**

Oratoire St-Joseph, **63**

Rue Duluth, **57**

Rue Prince Arthur, **54**

Square St-Louis, **53**

Théâtre St-Denis, **51**

Université du Québec à Montréal, **48**

TIMING

This is a comfortable afternoon walk, lasting perhaps two hours, longer if you linger for an hour or so in the Musée des Hospitalières and spend some time shopping. There's a bit of a climb from boulevard de Maisonneuve to rue Sherbrooke.

Sights to See

Bibliothèque Nationale du Québec. This Beaux-Arts library built in 1915 houses Québec's official archives. ✉ *1700 rue St-Denis,* ☎ *514/873–1100.* ⏲ *Tues.–Sat. 9–5.*

55 **Boulevard St-Laurent.** Depending on how you look at it, this street divides the city into east and west or it's where East and West meet. After the first electric tramway was installed on boulevard St-Laurent, working-class families began to move in. In the 1880s the first of many waves of Jewish immigrants escaping pogroms in eastern Europe arrived. They called the street the Main, as in "Main Street." The Jews were followed by Greeks, Eastern Europeans, Portuguese, and, most recently, Latin Americans. The 10 blocks north of rue Sherbrooke are filled with delis, junk stores, restaurants, luncheonettes, and clothing stores, as well as fashionable boutiques, bistros, cafés, bars, nightclubs, bookstores, and galleries. The block between rues Roy and Napoléon is particularly rich in delights.

49 **Chapelle Notre-Dame-de-Lourdes.** This tiny Roman Catholic chapel is one of the most ornate pieces of religious architecture in the city. It was built in 1876 and decorated with brightly colored murals by artist Napoléon Bourassa, who lived nearby. The chapel is a mixture of Roman and Byzantine styles, and the beautifully restored interior is a must-see, despite the panhandlers that cluster at its doors and the somewhat eccentric devotees it attracts. ✉ *430 rue Ste-Catherine Est.* ⏲ *Daily 8–5.*

50 **Cinémathèque Québécoise.** This museum and repertory movie house is one of Montréal's great bargains. For $4 you can visit the permanent exhibition on the history of filmmaking equipment and see two movies. Expansion in 1997 added two exhibition rooms and a TV documentary center. ✉ *335 blvd. de Maisonneuve Est,* ☎ *514/842–9763.* 💳 *$3.* ⏲ *Tues.–Sun. 11–9.*

OFF THE BEATEN PATH

ÉGLISE DE LA VISITATION DE LA BIENHEUREUSE VIERGE MARIE – Far to the north on the banks of Rivière des Prairies is the oldest extant church on the island of Montréal, the Church of the Visitation of the Blessed Virgin Mary. Its stone walls were raised in the 1750s, and the beautifully proportioned Palladian front was added in 1850. The task of decorating lasted from 1764 until 1837, with simply stunning results. The altar and the pulpit are as ornate as wedding cakes and as delicate as starlight. Mid-afternoon is the best time to visit, when the light in the church is soft and subtle. The church's most notable treasure is a rendering of the Visitation attributed to Pierre Mignard, a painter in the 17th-century court of Louis XIV. The church is a 15-minute walk from the Henri Bourassa Métro station, but the trek is worth it. Parkland surrounds the church, and the nearby Iles de la Visitation (reachable by footbridge) make a delightful walk. ✉ *1847 blvd. Gouin Est,* ☎ *514/388-4050.* ⏲ *Daily 10–6.*

56 **Musée des Hospitalières de l'Hôtel-Dieu.** More than just a fascinating and sometimes chilling exhibit on the history of medicine and nursing, this museum captures the spirit of an age. France in the 17th century was consumed with religious fervor, and aristocratic men and women often built hospitals, schools, and churches in distant lands. The nuns

of the Religieuses Hospitalières de St-Joseph who came to Montréal in the mid-17th century to help Jeanne Mance run the Hôpital Hôtel-Dieu were good examples of this fervor, and much of their spirit is evident in the letters, books, and religious artifacts displayed here. Pay special attention to the beautiful wooden stairway in the museum's entrance hall. ✉ *201 av. des Pins Ouest,* ☎ *514/849–2919.* 🎫 *$5.* ⏲ *Mid-June–mid-Oct., Tues.–Fri. 10–5, weekends 1–5; mid-Oct.–mid-June, Wed.–Sun. 1–5.*

NEED A BREAK? **Café Santropol** (✉ 3990 rue St-Urbain, ☎ 514/842–3110) serves hearty soups, cake, salads, and unusual high-rise sandwiches garnished with fruit (the Jeanne Mance mixes pineapples and chives in cream cheese). The atmosphere is homey, with a molded tin ceiling and a little *terasse* out back. One percent of the profits go to charity, and the staff runs a meals-on-wheels program. Credit cards are not accepted.

---

52 **Musée Juste pour Rire** (Just for Laughs Museum). This is the first museum in the world to be dedicated to laughter. Its multimedia exhibits explore and celebrate humor by drawing visitors into their plots. Some of the visiting exhibits have a serious side, too. There is a large collection of humor videos, a cabaret where budding comics can test their material, and a restaurant where you can watch old tapes while you eat. ✉ *2111 blvd. St-Laurent,* ☎ *514/845–2322.* 🎫 *$9.95.* ⏲ *Tues.–Sun. 1–8.*

Parc Lafontaine. Montréal's two main cultures are reflected in the layout of this very popular park: The eastern half is pure French, with paths, gardens, and lawns laid out in geometric shapes; the western half is very English, with meandering paths and irregularly shaped ponds that follow the natural contours of the land. In summer there are two artificial lakes where you can enjoy paddleboats, bowling greens, tennis courts, and an open-air theater with free arts events. In winter the two artificial lakes form a large skating rink. ✉ *3933 av. Parc Lafontaine,* ☎ *514/872–6211.* ⏲ *Daily 9 AM–10 PM.*

57 **Rue Duluth.** Modest little ethnic restaurants with outdoor terraces have sprouted along the street, along with crafts boutiques and a few shops selling collectibles such as cookie jars and bottles.

54 **Rue Prince Arthur.** In the 1960s the young people who moved to the neighborhood transformed this street into a small hippie bazaar of clothing, leather, and smoke shops. It remains a center of youth culture, although it's now much tamer and more commercial. The city turned the blocks between avenue Laval and boulevard St-Laurent into a pedestrian mall. Hippie shops have metamorphosed into inexpensive Greek, Vietnamese, Italian, Polish, and Chinese restaurants and little neighborhood bars. ✉ *Beginning at western end of Sq. St-Louis and stretching a few blocks west.*

53 **Square St-Louis.** This graceful square has a fountain, benches, and trees and is surrounded by 19th-century homes built in the large, comfortable style of the Second Empire. Originally a reservoir, these blocks became a park in 1879 and attracted upper-middle-class families and artists. French-Canadian poets were among the most famous creative people to occupy the houses back then, and the neighborhood is now home to painters, filmmakers, musicians, and writers. On the wall of 336 Square St-Louis you can see—and read, if your French is good—a long poem by Michel Bujold. ✉ *Bordered by av. Laval and rue St-Denis.*

51 **Théâtre St-Denis.** This is the second-largest auditorium in Montréal (after Salle Wilfrid Pelletier in Place des Arts). Sarah Bernhardt and many

other famous actors have graced its stage. ✉ *1594 rue St-Denis,* ☎ *514/849–4211.*

48 **Université du Québec à Montréal.** Part of a network of provincial campuses set up by the provincial government in 1969, UQAM is housed in a series of massive, modern brick buildings that clog much of the three city blocks bordered by rues Sanguinet and Berri and boulevards de Maisonneuve and René-Lévesque. The splendid fragments of Gothic grandeur sprouting up among the modern brick hulks like flowers in a swamp are all that's left of Église St-Jacques.

Parc du Mont-Royal

Parc du Mont-Royal is 494 acres of forest and paths in the heart of the city. Frederick Law Olmsted, the architect of New York's Central Park, designed this park. He believed that communion with nature could cure body and soul, and the park follows the natural topography and accentuates its features, in the English style. You can jog, cycle, stroll the miles of paths, or just scan the horizon from one of two lookouts. Horse-drawn transport is popular year-round: sleigh rides in winter and calèche rides in summer. On the eastern side of the hill stands the 100-ft steel cross that is the symbol of the city. Not far away from the park and perched on a neighboring crest of the same mountain is the Oratoire St-Joseph, a shrine that draws millions of visitors and pilgrims every year.

A Good Walk

Begin by taking the Métro's Orange Line to the Mont-Royal station and transfer to Bus 11 (be sure to get a transfer—*correspondance* in French—from a machine before you get on the Métro). The No. 11 drives right through the park on the Voie Camillien Houde. Get off at the **Obsérvatoire de l'Est** 58, a lookout. Climb the stone staircase at the end of the parking lot and follow the trails to the **Chalet du Mont-Royal** 59, a baronial building with a terrace that overlooks downtown Montréal. The next stop is **Lac aux Castors** 60, and there are at least three ways to get to this lake. You can take the long way and walk down the steep flight of stairs at the east end of the terrace and then turn right to follow the gravel road that circles the mountain. The shortest way is to leave the terrace at the west end and follow the crowds along the road. The middle way is to leave at the east end, but then to turn off the main road and follow one of the shaded paths that lead through the woods and along the southern ridge of the mountain.

Across chemin Remembrance from Lac aux Castors is what looks like one vast cemetery. It is in fact two cemeteries—one Protestant and the other Catholic. The **Cimetière Mont-Royal** 61 is toward the east in a little valley that cuts off the noise of the city; it is the final resting place of Anna Leonowens, the real-life heroine of *The King and I.* The yellow-brick buildings and tower on the north side of the mountain beyond the cemetery belong to the Université de Montréal, the second-largest French-language university in the world, with nearly 60,000 students. If you're now humming "Getting to Know You," you'll probably change your tune to Canada's national anthem when you enter the **Cimetière Notre-Dame-des-Neiges** 62, as the song's composer, Calixa Lavallée, is buried here.

Wander northwest through the two cemeteries, and you will eventually emerge on chemin Queen Mary on the edge of a decidedly lively area of street vendors, ethnic restaurants, and boutiques. Walk west on Queen Mary across chemin Côte-des-Neiges, and you come to Montréal's most grandiose religious monument, the **Oratoire St-**

Joseph ㉝. Across the street is the ivy-covered **Collège Notre Dame** ㉞, where the oratory's founder, Brother André, worked as a porter. After visiting the church, retrace your steps to chemin Côte-des-Neiges and walk to the Côte-des-Neiges station to catch the Métro.

TIMING
Allot the better part of a day for this tour, longer if you plan on catching some rays or ice-skating in the park.

Sights to See

★ 59 **Chalet du Mont-Royal.** The view here overlooks downtown Montréal. In the distance you can see Mont-Royal's sister mountains—Mont St-Bruno, Mont St-Hilaire, and Mont St-Grégoire. These isolated peaks—called the Montérégies, or Mountains of the King—rise quite dramatically from flat surrounding countryside. Be sure to take a look inside the chalet, especially at the murals that depict scenes from Canadian history. There's a snack bar in the back. ⏲ *Daily 9–5.*

61 **Cimetière Mont-Royal.** This cemetery was established in 1852 by the Anglican, Presbyterian, Unitarian, and Baptist churches and was laid out like a landscaped garden with monuments that are genuine works of art. The cemetery's most famous permanent guest is Anna Leonowens, who was governess to the children of the King of Siam and the real-life model for the heroine of the musical *The King and I.* There are no tours of the cemetery. ✉ *1297 chemin de la Forêt,* ☎ *514/279–7375.*

62 **Cimetière Notre-Dame-des-Neiges.** The largest Catholic graveyard in the city is the final resting place of hundreds of prominent artists, poets, intellectuals, politicians, and clerics. Among them is Calixa Lavallée, who wrote "O Canada." Many of the monuments and mausoleums—scattered along 55 km (34 mi) of paths and roadways—are the work of leading artists. There are no tours of the cemetery, but a book at the reception gates lists graves and their location. ✉ *4601 chemin Côte-des-Neiges,* ☎ *514/735–1361.*

64 **Collège Notre Dame.** Brother André, founder of the Oratoire St-Joseph, worked as a porter here. It's still an important private school and one of the few in the city that still accept boarders. Its students these days, however, include girls, a situation that would have shocked Brother André. ✉ *3791chemin Queen Mary.*

60 **Lac aux Castors.** Beaver Lake was reclaimed from boggy ground and so violates Olmsted's purist vision of a natural environment. But children like to float boats on it in summer, and it makes a fine skating rink in winter. ✉ *Off chemin Remembrance.*

58 **Obsérvatoire de l'Est.** This lookout gives a spectacular view of the east end of the city and the St. Lawrence River.

63 **Oratoire St-Joseph.** St. Joseph's Oratory, a huge domed church perched high on a ridge of Mont-Royal, is the largest shrine in the world dedicated to the earthly father of Jesus. It is the result of the persistence of a remarkable little man named Brother André, who was a porter in the school that his religious order ran. He dreamed of building a shrine dedicated to St. Joseph—Canada's patron saint—and began in 1904 by building a little chapel. Miraculous cures were reported and attributed to St. Joseph's intercession, and Brother André's project caught the imagination of Montréal. The result is one of the most important shrines in North America. The oratory dome is one of the biggest in the world, and the church has a magnificent setting. It's also home to Les Petits Chanteurs de Mont-Royal, the city's finest boys' choir. But alas, the interior is oppressive and drab. There's a more modest and quite undistinguished crypt church at the bottom of the structure, and right be-

hind it is a room that glitters with hundreds of votive candles lit in honor of St. Joseph. The walls are festooned with crutches discarded by the cured. Right behind that is the simple tomb of Brother André, who was beatified in 1982. Brother André's heart is displayed in a glass case upstairs in a small museum depicting events in his life. From early December through February the oratory has a display of crèches (nativity scenes) from all over the world. High on the mountain beside the main church is a beautiful garden, commemorating the Passion of Christ with life-size representations of the 14 traditional Stations of the Cross. Carillon, choral, and organ concerts are held weekly at the oratory during the summer. To visit the church you can either climb the more than 300 steps to the front door (many pilgrims do so on their knees, pausing to pray at each step) or you can take the shuttle bus that runs from the front gate. ✉ *3800 chemin Queen Mary, near Côte-des-Neiges Métro station,* ☎ *514/733–8211.* ⏲ *Sept.–May, daily 6 AM–9:30 PM; June–Aug., daily 6 AM–10:30 PM.*

Olympic Park and Botanical Garden

The Parc Olympique (Olympic Park) and the Jardin Botanique (Botanical Garden) are in the east end of the city. You can reach them via the Pie-IX or Viau Métro station (the latter is nearer the stadium entrance). The giant, mollusk-shape Stade Olympique and the leaning tower that supports the stadium's roof dominate the skyline of the eastern end of the city. But the area has more to recommend it than just the stadium complex; there's the city's world-class botanical garden, the world's largest museum dedicated to bugs, and Parc Maisonneuve. For guided tours of the Olympic complex, *see* Tour Olympique, *below*.

A Good Walk

Start with a ride on the Métro's Green Line and get off at the Viau station, which is only a few steps from the main entrance to the 70,000-seat **Stade Olympique** (65), a stadium built for the 1976 summer games. A trip to the top of the **Tour Olympique** (66), the world's tallest tilting structure, can give you a view up to 80 km (50 mi) on a clear day. The six pools of the **Centre Aquatique** (67) are under the tower.

Right next to the tower is the **Biodôme** (68), where you can explore both a rain forest and an arctic landscape. Continuing your back-to-nature experience, cross rue Sherbrooke to the north of the park (or take the free shuttle bus) to reach the **Jardin Botanique** (69), a botanical garden that is the second-largest attraction of its kind in the world. It includes the **Insectarium** (70) and the 5-acre **Montréal-Shanghai Lac de Rêve** (71), an elegant Ming-style garden.

After you've looked at the flowers, return to boulevard Pie-IX, which runs along the western border of the gardens. The name of this traffic artery (and the adjoining Métro station) puzzles thousands of visitors every year. The street is named for the 19th-century pope Pius IX, or Pie IX in French. It's pronounced Pee-neuf, however, which isn't at all how it looks from an English-speaker's standpoint.

TIMING

To see all the sights at a leisurely pace, you'll need a full day.

Sights to See

68 **Biodôme.** Not everyone thought it was a great idea to change an Olympic bicycle-racing stadium into a natural-history exhibit, but the result is one of the city's most popular attractions. It combines four ecosystems—the boreal forest, tropical forest, polar world, and St. Lawrence River—under one climate-controlled dome. You follow protected pathways through each environment, observing flora and fauna

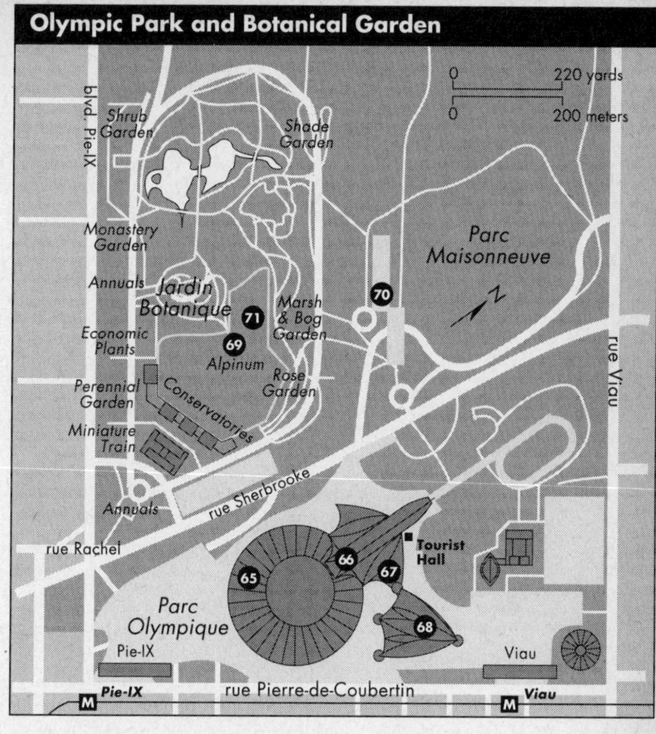

of each ecosystem. A word of warning: The tropical forest really is tropical. If you want to stay comfortable, dress in layers. ✉ *4777 av. Pierre-de-Coubertin,* ☎ *514/868–3000.* 🎫 *$9.50.* ⏲ *Daily 9–5.*

67 **Centre Aquatique.** Olympic swimmers competed here in 1976, but anyone can use the six swimming pools now. ✉ *4141 av. Pierre-de-Coubertin,* ☎ *514/252–4622.* 🎫 *$3.30.* ⏲ *Opens weekdays at 6 AM; closes at 10 PM Mon., 7 PM Tues. and Thurs., 9 PM Wed., 5 PM Fri.; weekends 1–4.*

70 **Insectarium.** A bug-shape building in the ☞ **Jardin Botanique** houses more than 250,000 insect specimens. Most are mounted, but the rainbow flies free in the butterfly room, and there are ant and bee exhibits, too. In February you can taste such delicacies as deep-fried bumblebees.

★ 69 **Jardin Botanique.** This botanical garden, with 181 acres of gardens in summer and 10 exhibition greenhouses open all year, is the second-largest attraction of its kind in the world (after England's Kew Gardens). The garden was founded in 1931 and has more than 26,000 species of plants. The poisonous-plant garden is a favorite. Traditional tea ceremonies are held in the Japanese Garden, which also has one of the best bonsai collections in the West. Other highlights are the ☞ **Insectarium** and the ☞ **Montréal-Shanghai Lac de Rêve.** ✉ *4101 rue Sherbrooke Est,* ☎ *514/872–1400.* 🎫 *May–Oct. $8.75, Nov.–Apr. $6.50, combined ticket for Biodôme and Jardin Botanique $14.75.* ⏲ *Weekdays 9–4, weekends 9–8 (Insectarium closes at 5). Metro: Pie-IX.*

71 **Montréal-Shanghai Lac de Rêve.** These 5 acres in the ☞ **Jardin Botanique** are the largest Ming-style Chinese garden outside Asia, with seven elegant pavilions and a 30-ft rockery built around a reflecting pool.

65 **Stade Olympique.** The stadium, built for the 1976 summer games, is beautiful to look at but not very practical. It's hard to heat, and the

retractable fabric roof, supported by the tower, has never worked properly. Nevertheless, it's home to the Expos of baseball's National League and is used for events like Montréal's annual car show. ✉ *4141 av. Pierre-de-Coubertin,* ☎ *514/252–8687.*

66 **Tour Olympique.** A trip to the top of this tower, the world's tallest tilting structure, is very popular; a two-level cable car can whisk 90 people up the exterior of the 890-ft tower. On a clear day you can see up to 80 km (50 mi) from the tower-top observatory. Daily guided tours of the Olympic complex leave from the **Tourist Hall** (☎ 514/252–8687) in the base of the tower. Tours at 12:40 and 3:40 are in English and the ones at 11 and 2 are in French; cost is $5.25. A tower ride costs $9, a tour plus tower ride is $12; call 514/252–4141, ext. 5246, to arrange the tour plus tower ride.

The Islands

Expo '67—the world fair staged to celebrate the centennial of the Canadian federation—was the biggest party in Montréal's history, and it marked a defining moment in the city's evolution as a modern metropolis. That party was held on two islands in the middle of the St. Lawrence River—Ile Ste-Hélène, which was formed by nature, and Ile Notre-Dame, which was created by humans out of the stone rubble excavated for Montréal's Métro. The two islands are still a playground—the Parc des Iles has a major amusement park, acres of flower gardens, a beach with clean filtered water, and the Casino de Montréal. There's history, too, at the Old Fort, where soldiers in colonial uniforms display the military skills of ancient wars. In winter you can skate on the old Olympic rowing basin or slide down iced trails on an inner tube. Call for more information on activities and attractions at **Parc des Iles** (☎ 514/872–6222).

A Good Walk

Start at the Ile Ste-Hélène station on the Métro's Yellow Line. The first thing you'll see when you emerge will be the huge geodesic dome that houses **Biosphere,** an environmental exhibition center. From the Biosphere walk to the northern shore and then east through the Parc des Iles to the **Old Fort,** now a museum of colonial life and a parade ground. Just east of the Old Fort past the Pont Jacques-Cartier (Jacques Cartier Bridge) is **La Ronde,** an amusement park.

Now cross over to the island's southern shore and walk back along the waterfront to the Cosmos Footbridge, which leads to Ile Notre-Dame. On the way you'll pass the Hélène de Champlain restaurant (☞ Dining, *below*), which probably has the prettiest setting of any restaurant in Montréal, and the military cemetery of the British garrison stationed on Ile Ste-Hélène from 1828 to 1870.

Ile Notre-Dame is laced by a network of canals and ponds, and the grounds are brilliant with flower gardens left from the 1980 Floralies Internationales flower show. Most of the Expo '67 buildings are gone, the victims of time and weather. One that has remained, however, is the fanciful French Pavilion. It and the neighboring Québec Pavilion have been turned into the **Casino de Montréal.** A five-minute walk west of the casino is the Lac de l'Ile Notre-Dame, site of **Plage de l'Ile Notre-Dame,** Montréal's only beach. In mid-June Ile Notre-Dame is the site of the Player's Grand Prix du Canada, a top Formula 1 international auto race at the **Circuit Gilles Villeneuve.**

After your walk you can either return to the Métro or walk back to the city via the Pont de la Concorde and the Parc de la Cité du Havre to Vieux-Montréal. If you walk, you'll see **Habitat '67,** an irregular pile of prefabricated concrete blocks that was built as an experiment in housing for Expo.

TIMING

This is a comfortable two-hour stroll, but the Biosphere and the Old Fort (try to time your visit to coincide with a drill display by the colonial troops of the Fraser Highlanders and the Compagnie Franche de la Marine, ☞ *below*) deserve at least an hour each, and you should leave another half hour to admire the flowers. Children will want to spend a whole day at La Ronde, but in summer the best time to go is in the evening when it's cooler. Try to visit the casino during a weekday when the crowds are at their thinnest.

Sights to See

Biosphere. An environmental center in the huge geodesic dome designed by Buckminster Fuller as the American Pavilion at Expo '67 successfully brings fun to an earnest project—heightening awareness of the St. Lawrence River system and its problems. ✉ *Ile St-Hélène,* ☎ *514/496–8300.* 🎫 *$6.50.* ⏲ *June–Sept., daily 10–5; Oct.–May, Tues.–Sun. 10–5.*

★ **Casino de Montréal.** This spectacular building was built as the French Pavilion for Expo '67, Montréal's world fair. It's now one of the biggest gambling palaces in the world (☞ Nightlife and the Arts, *below*). ✉ *Ile Notre-Dame.*

Circuit Gilles Villeneuve. All the big names in motor sports gather at this track every summer for the Player's Grand Prix, one of the racing season's most important Formula 1 events. One of the hottest stars these days is Québécois driver Jacques Villeneuve, who won the world championship in 1997. The track is named for his father, Gilles, who was killed in a racing crash in Belgium in 1982. ✉ *Ile Notre-Dame.*

Habitat '67. This private apartment complex, a pile of concrete blocks that resembles an updated version of a Hopi cliff dwelling, was designed by Moshe Safdie and built as an experiment in housing for Expo. ✉ *Av. Pierre-Dupuy.*

Old Fort. In summer the grassy parade square of this fine stone fort comes alive with the crackle of colonial musket fire. The French are represented by the Compagnie Franche de la Marine and the British by the kilted 78th Fraser Highlanders, one of the regiments that participated in the conquest of Québec in 1759. The fort itself, built to protect Montréal from American invasion, is now the David M. Stewart Museum at the Fort, which tells the story of colonial life in Montréal through displays of old firearms, maps, and uniforms. The two companies of colonial soldiers raise the flag every day at 11, practice their maneuvers at 1, put on a combined display of precision drilling and musket fire at 2:30, and lower the flag at 5. Children can participate. ✉ *Ile Ste-Hélène,* ☎ *514/861–6701.* 🎫 *$5.* ⏲ *Summer, Wed.–Mon. 10–6; winter, Wed.–Mon. 10–5.*

Plage de l'Ile Notre-Dame. This strip of sand is often filled to capacity in summer. The swimming beach is an oasis, with clear, filtered lake water and an inviting stretch of lawn and trees. Lifeguards are on duty, a shop rents swimming and boating paraphernalia, and there are picnic areas and a restaurant. 🎫 *$3.* ⏲ *Daily.*

La Ronde. A world-class amusement park has Ferris wheels, boat rides, simulator-style rides, and the second-highest roller coaster in the world. It is also the site of the popular Benson & Hedges International Fireworks Competition, which takes place every weekend in June and July. ✉ *Ile Ste-Hélène,* ☎ *514/872–6222.* 🎫 *$24.75; grounds only (no* *rides) $13. ⏲ May, weekends 10–9; June 1–20, daily 10–9; June 21–Sept. 2, daily 11–11; fireworks June–July, weekends, 10 PM–midnight.*

DINING

Montréal has more than 4,500 restaurants of every price range, representing dozens of ethnic groups. When you dine out, you can, of course, order à la carte, choosing each course yourself. But be sure to look for the table d'hôte, a two- to four-course package deal. It's usually cheaper, often offers interesting special dishes, and may also take less time to prepare. If you want to splurge with your time and money, indulge yourself with the *menu de dégustation,* a five- to seven-course dinner executed by the chef. It generally includes soup, salad, fish, sherbet (to refresh the taste buds), a meat dish, dessert, and coffee or tea. At the city's finest restaurants, such a meal for two, along with a good bottle of wine, can cost more than $200 and last four hours; it's worth every cent and every second.

A word about language: Menus in many restaurants are bilingual, but some are in French only. If you don't understand what a dish is, don't be shy about asking; a good server will be delighted to explain. If you feel brave enough to order in French, remember that in French an entrée is an appetizer and what English-speakers call an entrée is a *plat principal,* or main dish.

CATEGORY	COST*
$$$$	over $40
$$$	$30–$40
$$	$20–$30
$	under $20

**per person, in Canadian dollars, excluding tax (combined GST of 7% and provincial tax of 7.5% on all meals), service, and drinks*

Canadian

$ ✕ **Chez Clo.** Deep in east-end Montréal, where seldom is heard an English word, lies that rarest of the city's culinary finds—authentic Québécois food. A meal could start with a bowl of the best pea soup in the city, followed by a slab of *tourtière* (meat pie), mounds of mashed potatoes, carrots and turnips, and a bowl of gravy on the side. Desserts include bread pudding and several flavors of *renversées* (upside-down cakes). But the specialty is *pudding au chomeur* (literally, pudding for the unemployed), a kind of shortcake smothered in a thick brown-sugar sauce. The service is noisy and friendly and the clientele mostly local. ✉ *3199 rue Ontario Est,* ☎ *514/522–5348. No credit cards.*

Chinese

$$–$$$$ ✕ **Piment Rouge.** High ceilings, crystal chandeliers, and floor-to-ceiling windows serve as an elegant Edwardian backdrop for excellent Szechuan and northern Chinese food. Starters include beef and banana rolls and sliced kidneys in hot sauce. Crispy shrimp with honeyed walnuts, shredded lamb in spiced sauce, and steamed fish in ginger are among the main dishes. Servings are generous, and prices are high. ✉ *Le Windsor, 1170 rue Peel,* ☎ *514/866–7816. AE, D, DC, MC, V.*

$$–$$$ ✕ **Zen.** This very fine modern restaurant specializes in "Zen fusion": Asian dishes combining styles from China, Thailand, Indonesia, and Malaysia are all presented with artistic flair. For $27 try the "Zen Experience," picking as many items as you want from a menu of more than 40 magnificently prepared Szechuan items. ✉ *Le Westin Mont-*

Royal, 1050 rue Sherbrooke Ouest, ☏ *514/499–0801. Reservations essential. AE, DC, MC, V.*

$–$$ ✕ **Bon Blé Riz.** The food in this little restaurant is flamboyantly Chinese, but the prices are as modest as its unpretentious decor. Shrimp sizzled with onion, green pepper, and carrot, and finely chopped lamb served with celery and bamboo shoots in a peppery anise-flavored sauce are some of the intriguing dishes. The Beijing-style dumplings are good starters. ✉ *1437 rue St-Laurent,* ☏ *514/844–1447. AE, MC, V.*

$–$$ ✕ **Maison Kam Fung.** This bright, airy restaurant serves the most reliable dim sum lunch in Chinatown. Every day from 10 to 3, waiters push a parade of trolleys through the restaurant, carting treats like firm dumplings stuffed with pork and chicken, stir-fried squid, and delicate pastry envelopes filled with shrimp. ✉ *1008 rue Clark,* ☏ *514/878–2888. Reservations not accepted for dim sum. AE, MC, V.*

Continental

$$–$$$$ ★ ✕ **Nuances.** The main restaurant at the Casino de Montréal (☞ The Islands *in* Exploring Montréal, *above*) on Ile Notre-Dame is simply stunning. Diners sit amid rosewood paneling and have a magnificent view of the city. You might start with sautéed duck foie gras with exotic fruits and progress to lightly grilled red tuna with vegetables marinated in balsamic vinegar and olive oil. Even dishes that have been approved by the Québec Heart and Stroke Foundation sound exciting, like the saddle of rabbit pot-au-feu served with mushrooms. ✉ *1 av. de Casino,* ☏ *514/392–2708. Reservations essential. AE, DC, MC, V. No lunch.*

$ ✕ **Chez Better.** Fieldstone walls and casement windows create a classy ambience for this branch of a popular European sausage house. Although the decor is upscale, the limited menu keeps prices down, to only $3.95 in the case of the "Better Special," a satisfying sandwich of a sausage on freshly baked bread. It's a convenient refueling stop if you're touring Vieux-Montréal. The Notre-Dame restaurant is more elegant. ✉ *160 rue Notre-Dame Est,* ☏ *514/861–2617;* ✉ *5400 chemin Côte-des-Neiges,* ☏ *514/344–3971. AE, MC, V.*

Delicatessens

$ ✕ **Bens.** This big, brassy deli serves up cheesecake smothered in chocolate sauce, drinks the color of electric cherry juice, and a "Big Ben Sandwich"—two slices of rye bread enclosing a pink pile of juicy smoked meat (Montréal's version of corned beef). The decor is strictly '50s, with yellow and green walls and institutional furniture. The waiters are often wisecracking characters but incredibly efficient. Beer, wine, and cocktails are served. ✉ *990 blvd. de Maisonneuve Ouest,* ☏ *514/844–1000. Reservations not accepted. MC, V.*

$ ✕ **Schwartz's Delicatessen.** Its proper name is the Montreal Hebrew Delicatessen, but everyone calls it Schwartz's. The sandwiches are huge; the steaks are tender and come with grilled liver appetizers. To drink you'll find nothing stronger than a Coke. The furniture looks like it was rescued from a Salvation Army depot, and the waiters are briskly efficient. Don't ask for a menu (there isn't one) and avoid the lunch hour unless you don't mind long lines. ✉ *3895 blvd. St-Laurent,* ☏ *514/842–4813. Reservations not accepted. No credit cards.*

$ ✕ **Wilensky's Light Lunch.** Since 1932 the Wilensky family has served up its special: salami and bologna on a "Jewish" (kaiser) roll, generously slathered with mustard. You can also get a chopped-egg sandwich, which comes with a pickle and a cherry or pineapple cola from the fountain (there's no liquor license). This neighborhood haunt was a setting for the film *The Apprenticeship of Duddy Kravitz,* from the

Allumette, **8**
Bazou, **11**
Beaver Club, **23**
Bens, **27**
Bleu Marin, **35**
Bocca d'Oro, **38**
Bonaparte, **17**
Bon Blé Riz, **12**
Le Café de Paris, **31**
Café Stash, **18**
Le Caveau, **29**
Champs-Elysées, **37**
Chez Better, **14**
Chez Clo, **10**
Chez Delmo, **16**
Entrecôte St-Jean, **33**
L'Express, **7**
Gibby's, **19**
Guy and Dodo Morali, **26**
Les Halles, **36**
Hélène de Champlain, **21**
Katsura, **32**
Magnan, **39**
Maison Kam Fung, **13**
Mediterraneo, **9**
Milos, **2**
Moishe's, **4**
Nuances, **22**
Le Passe-Partout, **40**
Piment Rouge, **24**
Pizzaiole, **1, 34**
Les Remparts, **15**
Salsa Thai, **25**
Schwartz's Delicatessen, **5**
Le Taj, **30**
Toqué, **6**
Les Trois Tilleuls, **20**
Wilensky's Light Lunch, **3**
Zen, **28**

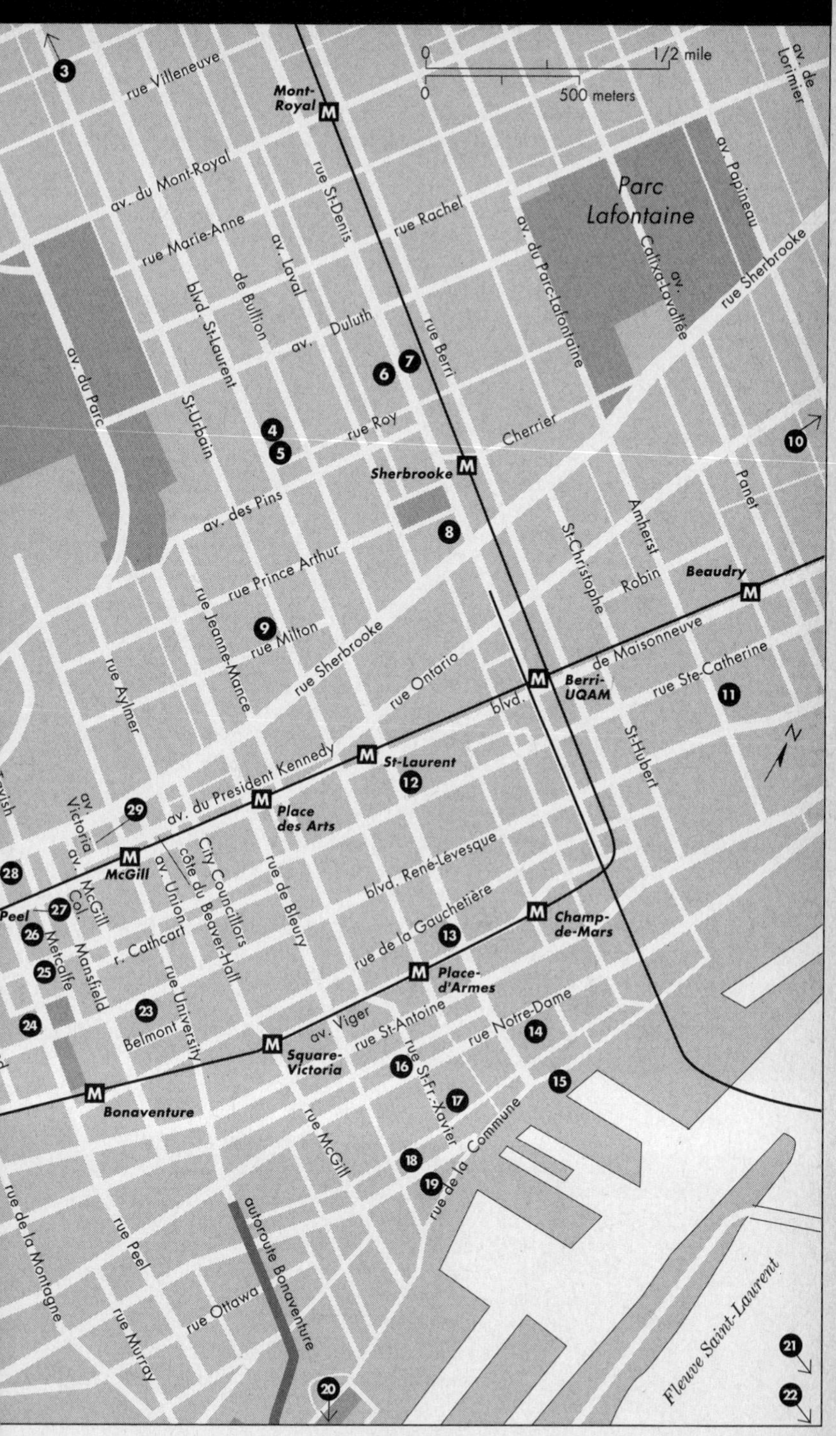

0
1/2 mile
0
500 meters
av. de Lorimier
Mont-Royal
rue Villeneuve
av. du Mont-Royal
rue St-Denis
Parc Lafontaine
av. Papineau
rue Rachel
av. du Parc-Lafontaine
av. Calixa-Lavallée
rue Marie-Anne
av. Laval
de Bullion
blvd. St-Laurent
av. du Parc
av. Duluth
rue Berri
rue Sherbrooke
St-Urbain
rue Roy
Cherrier
Sherbrooke
Panet
av. des Pins
rue Prince Arthur
Amherst
St-Christophe
Robin
Beaudry
rue Jeanne-Mance
rue Milton
de Maisonneuve
rue Sherbrooke
rue Aylmer
rue Ontario
blvd.
Berri-UQAM
rue Ste-Catherine
St-Hubert
St-Laurent
av. du President Kennedy
Place des Arts
av. Victoria
McGill
av. McGill Col.
av. Union
City Councillors
côte du Beaver-Hall
rue de Bleury
blvd. René-Lévesque
Peel
Metcalfe
Mansfield
r. Cathcart
rue University
rue de la Gauchetière
Champ-de-Mars
Place-d'Armes
Belmont
av. Viger
rue St-Antoine
rue Notre-Dame
Square-Victoria
Bonaventure
rue St-Fr.-Xavier
rue McGill
rue de la Commune
rue de la Montagne
rue Peel
autoroute Bonaventure
rue Ottawa
rue Murray
Fleuve Saint-Laurent
N

novel by Mordecai Richler. ✉ *34 rue Fairmount Ouest,* ☏ *514/271–0247. Reservations not accepted.* No credit cards. *Closed weekends.*

Eclectic

$$$–$$$$ ★ ✕ **Mediterraneo.** Sandstone floors, a space-age ceiling, and huge windows that wrap around two walls set off some of the trendiest food in Montréal. Dinner could start with tuna sashimi or spring rolls stuffed with chicken, spinach, and ricotta, and then move on to duck with sweet potatoes, dried cranberries, and a marmalade of pears and exotic fruits. ✉ *3500 blvd. St-Laurent,* ☏ *514/844–0027. Reservations essential. AE, MC, V.*

$$–$$$ ★ ✕ **Bazou.** The name means "jalopy," and a car theme appears in the decor and menu of this charming little eatery. To start, for example, you can have Crevettes Thais Suzuki (shrimp cooked with peanut butter, coriander, chili, and fried spinach), and one main dish is rabbit cooked in a "Mustang sauce" of cream, white wine, and mushrooms. This is one of the best of Montréal's many "bring-your-own-bottle" restaurants, so you can keep the bill low by buying your plonk at a grocery store or an outlet of the government-run Société des Alcools du Québec. ✉ *1271 rue Amherst,* ☏ *514/526–4940. AE, MC, V.*

French

$$$$ ★ ✕ **Toqué.** The name means "a bit crazy." Its young and innovative chef-owner, Normand Laprise, and partner Christin LaMarche are among the best and most eccentric chefs in the city. They whip market-fresh ingredients into dazzling combinations and colors. The menu often features salmon tournedos, smoked salmon, and warm foie gras, all flavored with fresh ingredients like red peppers, thinly shredded leeks, celery roots, and Québec goat cheese. The portions don't look big but are surprisingly filling. ✉ *3842 rue St-Denis,* ☏ *514/499–2084. Reservations essential. AE, DC, MC, V.*

$$$$ ✕ **Les Trois Tilleuls.** About an hour southeast of town, you can lunch or dine on delectable food next to the Rivière Richelieu. This small, romantic inn, one of the prestigious Relais et Châteaux chain, has a terrace and a large, airy dining room with beautiful sunset views. The chef specializes in cream of onion soup, sweetbreads, and game dishes. ✉ *290 rue Richelieu, St-Marc sur Richelieu,* ☏ *450/584–2231. Reservations essential. AE, DC, MC, V.*

$$$–$$$$ ★ ✕ **Allumette.** The chef focuses on ingredients from Québec—lamb from the salt marshes of Ile Verte grilled with crushed garlic flowers, or caribou cutlets from the tundra served with sweet-potato gnocchi. Good dessert choices are the chestnut soufflé and the crème brûlée with white chocolate. This small, elegant restaurant with red walls and plain white tables is just south of Carré St-Louis. ✉ *3434 rue St-Denis,* ☏ *514/284–4239. AE, D, DC, MC, V. No lunch weekends.*

$$$–$$$$ ✕ **Beaver Club.** This fine French restaurant was a social club for the city's elite in the 19th century, and it still has the atmosphere of an exclusive men's club, even if it's open to anyone with a reservation. The menu lists such classics as roast prime rib of beef au jus, but more adventurous offerings include appetizers like cold lobster carpaccio—paper-thin slices of raw lobster tail served with wasabi-based sauce—and main dishes like panfried salmon fillets sandwiching a layer of grilled eggplant and tomato. There's dancing on Saturday. Service is excellent, and the bar serves the best martini in the city. ✉ *Le Reine Elizabeth hotel, 900 blvd. René-Lévesque Ouest,* ☏ *514/861–3511. Jacket and tie. AE, D, DC, MC, V. Closed Sun. and July. No dinner Mon.*

$$$–$$$$ ★ ✕ **Bonaparte.** Piped-in Mozart serenades diners surrounded by exposed brick walls in a wonderful little restaurant in the heart of Vieux-Mont-

réal. The traditional French dishes here have a light touch. You could start with a wild mushroom ravioli seasoned with fresh sage and move on to a lobster stew flavored with vanilla and served with a spinach fondue, or a roast rack of lamb in a port wine sauce. Lunch is a good value. At press time the restaurant planned to open a little auberge upstairs. ✉ *443 rue St-François-Xavier,* ☎ *514/844–4368. AE, D, DC, MC, V. No lunch weekends.*

$$$–$$$$ ✕ **Le Café de Paris.** Patrons sit at large, well-spaced tables in a room ablaze with flowers and with light streaming through the French windows. The Ritz garden, with its picturesque duck pond, is open for summer dining alfresco. You can choose from such classics as *escalope de veau Viennoise* or steak tartare. At meal's end the waiter will trundle over the dessert cart; the *royale chocolat* and the *îles flottant* (puffs of soft meringue in custard) are favorites. ✉ *Ritz-Carlton Kempinski, 1228 rue Sherbrooke Ouest,* ☎ *514/842–4212. Reservations essential. Jacket required. AE, D, DC, MC, V.*

$$$–$$$$ ✕ **Champs Elysées.** Unobtrusive elegance lets the food do the talking in this dining room in the Golden Square Mile. You could start with snails with Parma ham or a simple goat-cheese salad before moving on to quail with grapes or sea bass with fennel. Peach crumble or a crème brûlée lightly flavored with jasmine completes the experience. ✉ *1800 rue Sherbrooke Ouest,* ☎ *514/499–2084. AE, DC, MC, V.*

$$$–$$$$ ✕ **Les Halles.** Main dishes like Grapefruit Marie-Louise with scallops and lobster or roasted duck with pears sit comfortably beside the chef's ventures into nouvelle cuisine, such as his lobster with herbs and butter. The desserts are classic—the Paris-Brest, a puff pastry with praline cream inside, is one of the best in town. Mirrors, murals, and light colors are part of the Paris-market decor. ✉ *1450 rue Crescent,* ☎ *514/844–2328. Reservations essential. AE, DC, MC, V. Closed Sun. No lunch Mon. or Sat.*

$$$–$$$$ ✕ **Hélène de Champlain.** The food here is good if unadventurous (rack of lamb, fillet of sole amandine, veal marsala, filet mignon with roasted peppers), but people come for the setting. The restaurant is in the middle of the park on Ile Ste-Hélène, with views over the river and the city. The large dining room with its two fireplaces and antique furnishings is delightful. ✉ *Ile Ste-Hélène near Métro station,* ☎ *514/395–2424. Reservations essential. AE, DC, MC, V.*

$$$–$$$$ ★ ✕ **Le Passe-Partout.** New York–born James MacGuire might make the best bread in Montréal—moist but airy with a tight, crispy crust. He and his wife, Suzanne Baron-Lafrenière, sell this delicacy, along with homemade pâtés and terrines, in a bakery next door to their restaurant. The handwritten menu is short and changes according to mood and availability. You might start with smoked salmon, a potage of curried sweet potatoes, or perhaps a venison terrine. Entrées include swordfish steak served with a puree of red cabbage or loin of veal with poached cucumbers and noodles. ✉ *3857 blvd. Décarie (5-min walk south from Villa Maria Métro),* ☎ *514/487–7750. Reservations essential. AE, DC, MC, V. No lunch Sat.–Mon., no dinner Sun.–Wed.*

$$$–$$$$ ✕ **Les Remparts.** A stone-walled cellar under the Auberge du Vieux-Port showcases innovative French cooking in an atmosphere redolent of Nouvelle France. Wild mushroom soup with walnut croutons and quail with squash and sage gnocchi are some of the enticing appetizers, fitting preparation for main courses such as venison steak with parsley, salsify root and juniper berries and Atlantic salmon cooked with endives, shallots, and red wine. ✉ *97 rue de la Commune Est,* ☎ *514/392–1649. AE, DC, MC, V.*

$$–$$$$ ✕ **L'Express.** This Paris-style bistro has mirrored walls, a smoky atmosphere, and noise levels that are close to painful on weekends. But the food's good, the service fast, and the prices reasonable. The steak

tartare with french fries, the salmon with sorrel, and the calves' liver with tarragon are marvelous. Jars of gherkins, fresh baguettes, and cheeses aged to perfection make the pleasure last longer. L'Express has one of the best and most original wine cellars in town. ✉ *3927 rue St-Denis,* ☎ *514/845–5333. Reservations essential. AE, DC, MC, V.*

$$–$$$$ ✕ **Guy and Dodo Morali.** Pale yellow walls and lots of art decorate this comfortable restaurant in the very exclusive Cours Mont-Royal shopping plaza. In summer, dining spills out onto a little terrace on rue Metcalfe. Guy's cooking is classic French with a splash of modern flair; his menu is 70% seafood. His daily table d'hôte menu is the best bet, with openers such as excellent lobster bisque followed by *agneau en croûte* (lamb in a pastry) with thyme sauce (a house specialty), or fillet of halibut with leeks. For dessert try the *tatan,* apples and caramel with crème anglaise. ✉ *Les Cours Mont-Royal, 1444 rue Metcalfe,* ☎ *514/842–3636. Reservations essential. AE, D, DC, MC, V.*

$$–$$$ ★ ✕ **Le Caveau.** Lost among the glass-and-steel towers of downtown is an eccentric Victorian house where buttery sauces, creamy desserts, and fairly reasonable prices have survived the onslaughts of inflation and nouvelle cuisine. Appetizers include sautéed brains with a caper mousseline and snails cooked in meat glaze, butter, and Danish blue cheese. A main course might be rabbit cooked with sweet wine, spices, and raisins, or rack of lamb crusted with bread crumbs, mustard, garlic, and herbs. A children's menu—rare in restaurants as fine as Le Caveau—is available. ✉ *2063 av. Victoria,* ☎ *514/844–1624. AE, DC, MC, V.*

Greek

$$$$ ✕ **Milos.** Nets, ropes, and floats hang from Milos's walls and ceilings. The real display, however, is in the refrigerated cases and on the beds of ice in the back by the kitchen—octopus, squid, shrimp, crabs, oysters, and sea urchins. The main dish at Milos is usually fish grilled over charcoal and seasoned with parsley, capers, and lemon juice. It's done to a turn and is achingly delicious. The fish are priced by the pound, and you can order one large fish to serve two or more. You'll also find lamb and veal chops, cheeses, and olives. Milos is a healthy walk from Métro Laurier. ✉ *5357 av. du Parc,* ☎ *514/272–3522. Reservations essential. AE, D, DC, MC, V. No lunch Sat.*

Indian

$$ ✕ **Le Taj.** The cuisine of the north of India, less spicy and more refined than that of the south, is showcased here. The tandoori ovens seal in the flavors of the grilled meat and fish. Vegetarian dishes include the *taj-thali,* made of lentils; basmati rice; and *saag panir*—spicy white cheese with spinach. A nine-course lunch buffet is under $10, and at night there's an "Indian feast" for $20. The desserts—pistachio ice cream or mangoes—are often decorated with pure silver leaves. ✉ *2077 rue Stanley,* ☎ *514/845–9015. AE, MC, V.*

Italian

$$$–$$$$ ✕ **Bocca d'Oro.** This restaurant next to Métro Guy has a huge menu. One pasta specialty is *tritico di pasta*: one helping each of spinach ravioli with salmon and caviar, shellfish marinara, and spaghetti primavera. Also recommended is the *pasta mistariosa*—no cream, no butter, no tomatoes, but delicious nonetheless. With dessert and coffee, the waiters bring out a bowl of walnuts for you to crack at your table. The two-floor dining area is inexplicably decorated with a huge display of golf pictures, and Italian pop songs play in the background. The staff is extremely friendly and professional; if you're in a hurry, they'll serve your meal in record time. ✉ *1448 rue St-Mathieu,* ☎ *514/933–8414. Reservations essential. AE, DC, MC, V. Closed Sun.*

$ ✕ **Pizzaiole.** Pizzaiole brought the first wood-fired pizza ovens to Montréal, and it's still the best in the field. Whether you choose a simple tomato-cheese or a ratatouille on a whole-wheat crust—there are about 30 possible combinations—all the pizzas are made to order and brought to your table piping hot. The calzone is worth the trip. ✉ *1446A rue Crescent,* ☎ *514/845–4158;* ✉ *5100 rue Hutchison,* ☎ *514/274–9349. AE, DC, MC, V.*

Japanese

$$–$$$ ✕ **Katsura.** The sushi chefs in this elegant Japanese restaurant create an assortment of raw seafood delicacies, as well as their own delicious invention, the cone-shaped Canada roll (smoked salmon and salmon caviar). Service is excellent, but if you sample all the sushi, the tab can be exorbitant. ✉ *2170 rue de la Montagne,* ☎ *514/849–1172. Reservations essential. AE, DC, MC, V. No lunch weekends.*

Polish

$–$$ ✕ **Café Stash.** On chilly nights many Montrealers turn to Café Stash in Vieux-Montréal for sustenance—for pork chops or duck, hot borscht, pierogi, or cabbage and sausage—in short, for all the hearty specialties of a Polish kitchen. Diners sit on pews from an old chapel at refectory tables from an old convent. ✉ *200 rue St-Paul Ouest,* ☎ *514/845–6611. AE, MC, V.*

Seafood

$$–$$$$ ✕ **Chez Delmo.** The long, shiny wooden bar at Chez Delmo is crammed at lunchtime with lawyers and businesspeople gobbling oysters and fish. In the back is a more relaxed and cheerful dining room. The poached salmon with hollandaise is a nice slab of perfectly cooked fish served with potatoes and broccoli. Also excellent are the arctic char and the Dover sole. ✉ *211–215 rue Notre-Dame Ouest,* ☎ *514/849–4061. Reservations essential. AE, DC, MC, V. Closed Sun., 3 wks in midsummer, and 3 wks at Christmas.*

$$–$$$ ✕ **Bleu Marin.** Fish here comes with an Italian touch. Antipasto Bleu Marin, for example, includes little plates of baby clams, mussels, and oysters with a light gratinée of crumbs and cheese. All fish are baked or steamed; a main course could be fillets of sea bass, baked in their own juices with olive oil, lemon juice, white wine, and capers. ✉ *1437A rue Crescent,* ☎ *514/847–1123. AE, D, DC, MC, V.*

Steak

$$$–$$$$ ★ ✕ **Gibby's.** While the extensive menu is rich in items like broiled lobster, Dover sole meunière, and Cajun-blackened grouper, it was Gibby's first-class steaks—some say the best in the city—that made this restaurant famous. Gibby's also boasts its own on-site bakery and makes its own ice cream. The thick gray stone walls here date to 1825, and the attention to service and detail also seems to belong to another age. ✉ *298 Pl. d'Youville,* ☎ *514/282–1837. AE, D, DC, MC, V.*

$$$–$$$$ ✕ **Moishe's.** The steaks here are big and marbled, and the Lighter brothers still age them in their own cold rooms for 21 days before charcoal grilling them, just the way their father did when he opened Moishe's more than 50 years ago. There are other things on the menu, such as lamb and grilled arctic char—but people come for the beef. The selection of single-malt Scotches is exquisite. ✉ *3961 blvd. St-Laurent,* ☎ *514/845–3509. AE, DC, MC, V. No lunch.*

$–$$ ✕ **Magnan.** The atmosphere in this tavern in working-class Pointe St-Charles is decidedly and defiantly masculine. The decor is upscale warehouse, and the half dozen television sets are noisily stuck on professional sports. You can't beat the roast beef, though, and the industrial-strength steaks that range from 6 to 22 ounces. Everyone eats here—from dock workers to corporate executives. In summer the tavern adds Québec lobster to its menu and turns its parking lot into an outdoor dining room. It also has excellent beer from several local microbreweries on tap. ✉ *2602 rue St-Patrick,* ☎ *514/935–9647. AE, DC, MC, V.*

$ ✕ **Entrecôte St-Jean.** The shortest menu in the city can be found in this restaurant in the heart of downtown. The choices are a walnut salad followed by french fries and a steak cooked in a special sauce, or the same meal bracketed by the soup du jour and chocolate profiteroles. Lots of brass and polished wood give the place the air of a Paris bistro. ✉ *2002 rue Peel,* ☎ *514/281–6492. AE, DC, MC, V.*

Thai

$ ✕ **Salsa Thai.** It began as a tiny hole in the wall in Chinatown, but Salsa Thai's popularity enabled the owners to move into plusher digs on Square Dorchester. Prices are still reasonable, though, and portions are generous. Some appealing choices are hot-and-sour seafood soup with coconut milk; squid salad with onion, hot chilies, and mint leaves; and deep-fried whole pomfret (butterfish) flavored with garlic and hot green peppers, onions, basil, and Thai seasonings. Frogs' legs are fried with pepper, garlic, and sesame seeds; beef with satay sauce comes on a sizzling hot plate. ✉ *1237 rue Metcalfe,* ☎ *514/874–9047. MC, V.*

LODGING

Keep in mind that during peak season (May–August) it may be difficult to find a bed without reserving, and most, but not all, hotels raise their prices. Rates often drop from mid-November to early April. Throughout the year a number of the better hotels have two-night, three-day double-occupancy packages that offer substantial discounts.

CATEGORY	COST*
$$$$	over $160
$$$	$120–$160
$$	$85–$120
$	under $85

**All prices are for a standard double room, excluding 14.5% tax, in Canadian dollars.*

$$$$ **Le Centre Sheraton.** This huge 37-story complex is well placed between the downtown business district and the restaurant-lined streets of Crescent and Bishop. It offers services to both the business and tourist crowds. Rooms have coffeemakers, irons, and ironing boards. The 10-story Club section is geared toward business travelers, and there are lots of meeting rooms for conventions. The bar in the busy lobby is in a pleasant forest of potted trees, some of them 30 ft tall. ✉ *1201 blvd. René-Lévesque Ouest, H3B 2L7,* ☎ *514/878–2000 or 800/325–3535,* FAX *514/878–3958. 784 rooms, 25 suites. Restaurant, 2 bars, indoor pool, beauty salon, health club, baby-sitting, business services. AE, D, DC, MC, V.*

$$$$ **Delta Montréal.** The Delta has the city's most complete exercise and pool facility and an extensive business center. The hotel's public areas spread over two stories and are decorated to look a bit like a French château, with a huge baronial chandelier and gold patterned carpets.

Rooms are big, with plush broadloom, pastel walls, mahogany-veneer furniture, and windows that overlook the mountain or downtown. The Cordial Music bar serves lunch on weekdays. ✉ *475 av. President-Kennedy, H3A 1J7,* ☎ *514/286–1986 or 800/268–1133,* FAX *514/284–4306. 453 rooms, 10 suites. 2 restaurants, bar, indoor and outdoor pools, hot tub, sauna, aerobics, health club, squash, recreation room, video games, baby-sitting, business services. AE, D, DC, MC, V.*

$$$$ **Hotel Inter-Continental Montréal.** On the edge of Vieux-Montréal, this luxury hotel is part of the Montréal World Trade Center, a block-long retail and office development. Rooms are in a modern 26-story brick tower with fanciful turrets and pointed roofs. They're large, with lush carpets, pastel walls, heavy drapes, and big windows overlooking downtown or Vieux-Montréal and the waterfront. The main lobby is home to Le Continent, which serves fine international cuisine. ✉ *360 rue St-Antoine Ouest, H2Y 3X4,* ☎ *514/987–9900 or 800/327–0200, 800/361–3600 in the U.S. and Canada,* FAX *514/847–8550. 335 rooms, 22 suites. 2 restaurants, room service, indoor pool, sauna, health club, concierge, meeting rooms. AE, D, DC, MC, V.*

$$$$ ★ **Loews Hôtel Vogue.** Tall windows and a facade of polished rose granite grace this chic hotel in the heart of downtown, right across the street from Ogilvy department store. The lobby's focal point, L'Opéra Bar, has an expansive bay window overlooking the trendy rue de la Montagne. Room furnishings are upholstered with striped silk, and the beds are draped with lacy duvets. The bathrooms have whirlpool baths, televisions, and phones. ✉ *1425 rue de la Montagne, H3G 1Z3,* ☎ *514/285–5555 or 800/465–6654,* FAX *514/849–8903. 126 rooms, 16 suites. Restaurant, bar, exercise room. AE, D, DC, MC, V.*

$$$$ ★ **Ritz-Carlton Kempinski.** This is the closest Montréal comes to a grand hotel. Power meals are the rule at Le Café de Paris (☞ Dining, *above*). Guest rooms are a successful blend of Edwardian style—some suites have working fireplaces—with such modern accessories as electronic safes. Careful and personal attention are hallmarks of the Ritz-Carlton's service: Your shoes get shined, there's fresh fruit in your room, and everyone calls you by name. It was good enough for Elizabeth Taylor and Richard Burton, who celebrated one of their weddings here. ✉ *1228 rue Sherbrooke Ouest, H3G 1H6,* ☎ *514/842–4212 or 800/223–6800,* FAX *514/842–3383. 201 rooms, 39 suites. Restaurant, bar, piano bar, room service, barbershop. AE, DC, MC, V.*

$$$$ ★ **Le Westin Mont-Royal.** Service and hospitality make the Westin stand out among Montréal's best hotels. Its concierge desk can organize anything. The clientele here is primarily corporate, and the large rooms are decorated to serve that market: floral chintzes, plush carpeting, and traditional English furnishings. One of the city's best Chinese restaurants is the Zen (☞ Dining, *above*), downstairs. The revamped ground floor holds Opus II, a contemporary French restaurant with a glassed-in atrium. ✉ *1050 rue Sherbrooke Ouest, H3A 2R6,* ☎ *514/284–1110 or 800/228–3000,* FAX *514/845–3025. 300 rooms, 28 suites. 2 restaurants, lobby lounge, minibars, room service, pool, hot tub, 2 saunas, health club. AE, D, DC, MC, V.*

$$$–$$$$ ★ **Bonaventure Hilton International.** The large Hilton occupies the top three floors of the Place Bonaventure exhibition center. From the outside the massive building is uninviting, but you step off the elevator into an attractive reception area flanked by an outdoor swimming pool (heated year-round) and 2½ acres of gardens—all refurbished with new lighting and a marble floor in the lobby. All rooms have sleek modern furniture, pastel walls, plug-ins for computers, and irons and ironing boards. The Bonaventure has excellent access to the Métro and the Underground City. ✉ *1 Pl. Bonaventure, H5A 1E4,* ☎ *514/878–2332 or*

Auberge de la Fontaine, **27**
Auberge du Vieux-Port, **23**
Auberge les Passants du Sans Soucy, **21**
Bonaventure Hilton International, **18**
Le Centre Sheraton, **7**
Château Versailles, **3**
Delta Montréal, **15**
Holiday Inn Select, **22**
Hostelling International, **5**
Hôtel l'Abri du Voyageur, **24**
Hôtel de la Montagne, **8**
Hôtel du Fort, **2**
Hôtel du Parc, **14**
Hôtel Inter-Continental Montréal, **20**
Hôtel Lord Berri, **25**
Hôtel Radisson des Gouverneurs de Montréal, **19**
Hôtel Thrift Lodge, **26**
Loews Hôtel Vogue, **9**
Le Marriott Château Champlain, **16**
McGill Student Apartments, **13**
Le Nouvel Hôtel, **4**
Le Reine Elizabeth, **17**
Ritz-Carlton Kempinski, **11**
Université de Montréal Residence, **1**
Le Westin Mont-Royal, **12**
YMCA, **10**
YWCA, **6**

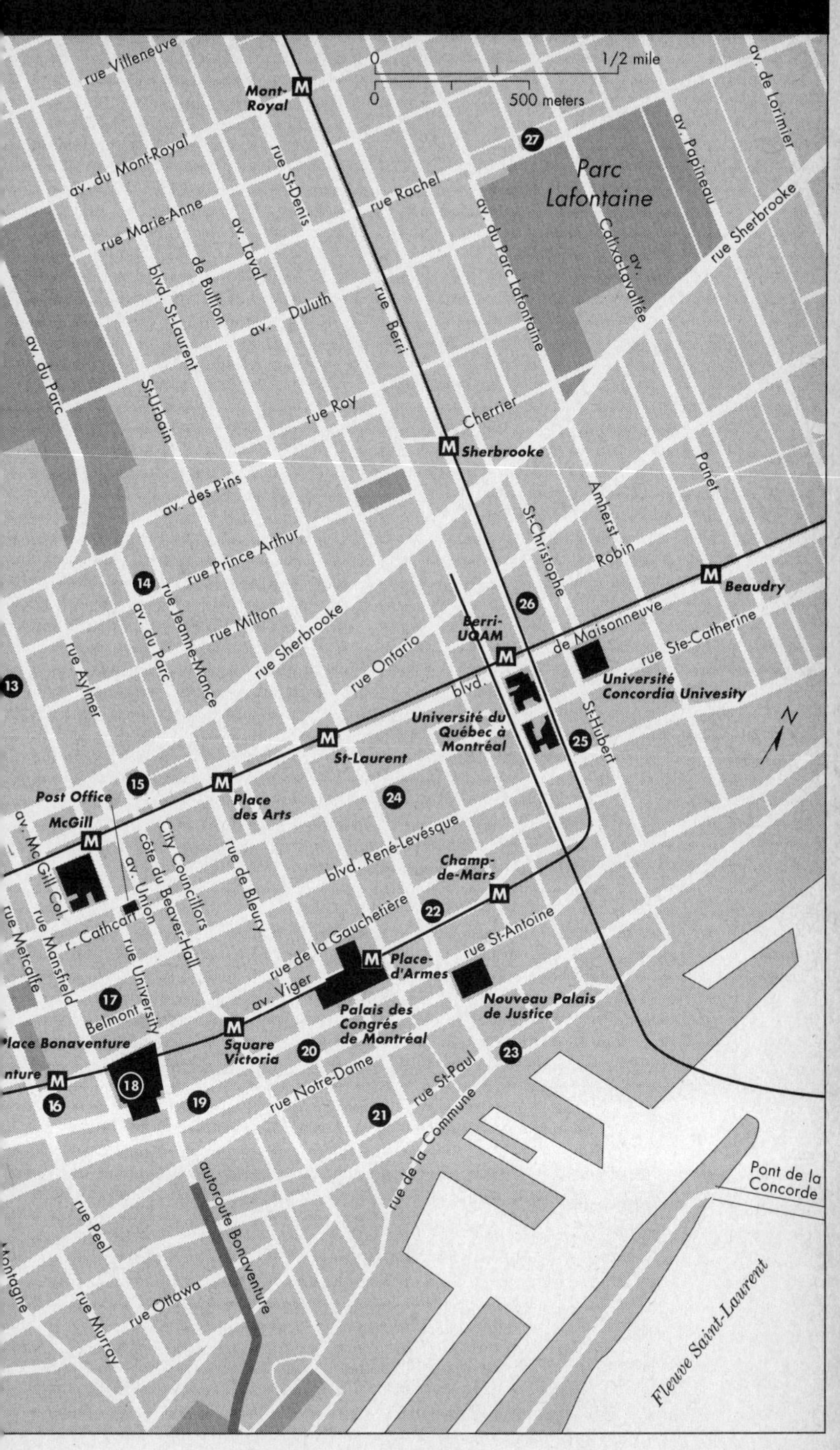

0
1/2 mile
0
500 meters
Mont-Royal
Parc Lafontaine
Sherbrooke
Beaudry
Berri-UQAM
Université Concordia Univesity
Université du Québec à Montréal
St-Laurent
Place des Arts
Post Office
McGill
Champ-de-Mars
Place-d'Armes
Palais des Congrés de Montréal
Nouveau Palais de Justice
Square Victoria
Place Bonaventure
Pont de la Concorde
Fleuve Saint-Laurent
rue Villeneuve
av. du Mont-Royal
rue Marie-Anne
rue Rachel
av. Duluth
rue Roy
Cherrier
av. des Pins
rue Prince Arthur
rue Milton
rue Sherbrooke
rue Ontario
blvd. de Maisonneuve
rue Ste-Catherine
blvd. René-Levésque
rue de la Gauchetière
av. Viger
rue St-Antoine
rue Notre-Dame
rue St-Paul
rue de la Commune
rue St-Denis
av. Laval
de Bullion
blvd. St-Laurent
St-Urbain
av. du Parc
rue Berri
av. du Parc Lafontaine
av. Calixa-Lavallée
av. Papineau
av. de Lorimier
St-Christophe
Amherst
Robin
Panet
St-Hubert
rue Jeanne-Mance
rue Aylmer
av. McGill Col.
City Councillors
côte du Beaver-Hall
av. Union
rue de Bleury
r. Cathcart
rue Metcalfe
rue Mansfield
rue University
Belmont
autoroute Bonaventure
rue Peel
rue Ottawa
rue Murray
13
14
15
16
17
18
19
20
21
22
23
24
25
26
27

800/267–2575, FAX 514/028–1442. 395 rooms. 3 restaurants, minibars, room service, pool, shops, business services. AE, D, DC, MC, V.

$$$–$$$$ ★ **Hôtel de la Montagne.** Upon entering the reception area you'll be greeted by a naked, butterfly-winged nymph who rises out of a fountain; an enormous crystal chandelier hangs from the ceiling. The decor resembles Versailles rebuilt with a dash of art nouveau, although management prefers to describe it as a mix of Early American and rococo. The rooms are tamer, large and comfortable. There's a piano bar and a rooftop terrace, and a tunnel connects the hotel to Thursdays/Les Beaux Jeudis, a popular singles bar, restaurant, and dance club. ✉ *1430 rue de la Montagne, H3G 1Z5,* ☎ *514/288–5656 or 800/361–6262,* FAX *514/288–9658. 135 rooms. 2 restaurants, bar, pool, concierge. AE, D, DC, MC, V.*

$$$–$$$$ **Le Reine Elizabeth.** In the center of the city, this Canadian Pacific hotel sits on top of the Gare Centrale train station. The lobby is a bit too much like a railroad station—hordes march this way and that—but upstairs the rooms are modern, spacious, and spotless, with lush pale carpets, striped Regency wallpapers, and chintz bedspreads. The Penthouse floors—20 and 21—have business services, and the Gold Floor is a hotel within a hotel with its own elevator, check-in, and concierge. The hotel is home to the Beaver Club (☞ Dining, *above*). Conventions are a specialty here. ✉ *900 blvd. René-Lévesque Ouest, H3B 4A5,* ☎ *514/861–3511 or 800/441–1414,* FAX *514/954–2256. 1,020 rooms. 2 restaurants, 3 bars, indoor pool, beauty salon, health club, baby-sitting. AE, D, DC, MC, V.*

$$–$$$$ ★ **Holiday Inn Select.** This Chinatown hotel is full of surprises, from the two pagodas on the roof to the Chinese garden in the lobby. Its restaurant, Chez Chine, is excellent. An executive floor has all the usual business facilities. The hotel has a pool and a small exercise room, but guests also have access to a plush private health and leisure club downstairs with a whirlpool, saunas, a billiard room, and a bar. The hotel is catercorner to the Palais des Congrès and a five-minute walk from the World Trade Center. ✉ *99 av. Viger Ouest, H2Z 1E9,* ☎ *514/878–9888 or 888/878–9888,* FAX *514/878–6341. 235 rooms. Restaurant, bar, pool, exercise room, business services. AE, D, DC, MC, V.*

$$–$$$$ **Hôtel du Fort.** All rooms here have good views of the city, the river, or the mountain. The hotel is in the west end of downtown in a residential neighborhood known as Shaughnessy Village, close to shopping at the Faubourg Ste-Catherine and Square Westmount, and just around the corner from the Canadian Center for Architecture. Rates include Continental breakfast served in the charming Louis XV Lounge, which doubles as a bar in the evening. ✉ *1390 rue du Fort, H3H 2R7,* ☎ *514/938–8333 or 800/565–6333,* FAX *514/938–2078. 127 rooms. Bar, exercise room. AE, DC, MC, V.*

$$$ **Hôtel Radisson des Gouverneurs de Montréal.** Abutting the stock exchange, the Radisson rises above a three-story atrium-reception area and is attractive to convention crowds. It's near Place Bonaventure, the western fringe of Vieux-Montréal, and the Square Victoria Métro (accessible via an underground passage). There's an exclusive floor for higher-paying guests and a shopping arcade on the underground level. The Tour de Ville on the top floor is the city's only revolving restaurant, and its bar has live music nightly. ✉ *777 rue University, H3C 3Z7,* ☎ *514/879–1370 or 800/333–3333,* FAX *514/879–1831. 550 rooms, 25 suites. 2 restaurants, bar, indoor pool, steam room, health club. AE, DC, MC, V.*

$$$ **Le Marriott Château Champlain.** At the southern end of Place du Canada is this 36-floor skyscraper with distinctive half-moon-shape windows that give the rooms a Moorish feel. The furniture is elegantly French and the bedspreads are brightly patterned. Underground

passageways connect the Champlain with the Bonaventure Métro station and Place Ville-Marie. ✉ *1050 rue de la Gauchetière Ouest, H3B 4C9,* ☎ *514/878–9000 or 800/200–5909,* FAX *514/878–6761. 611 rooms, 33 suites. Restaurant, bar, no-smoking rooms, indoor pool, sauna, health club. AE, DC, MC, V.*

$$–$$$ ★ **Auberge de la Fontaine.** The decor of this small hotel in the heart of the trendy Plateau Mont-Royal district sounds wild—contrasting purple and bare-brick walls, a red molding separating yellow walls from a green ceiling—but the hotel is delightful. Its 21 rooms are scattered over three floors in two turn-of-the-century residences. Some of them have whirlpool baths and a few have private balconies. Guests can use the little ground-floor kitchen and take whatever they like from its fridge full of snacks. The hotel is right on one of the city's bicycle paths and just across the street from Parc Lafontaine. ✉ *1301 rue Rachel Est, H2J 2K1,* ☎ *514/597–0166 or 800/597–0597,* FAX *514/597–0496. 21 rooms. Meeting room. AE, DC, MC, V.*

$$–$$$ ★ **Auberge du Vieux-Port.** A splendid little hotel—27 rooms over five floors—backs onto fashionable rue St-Paul and overlooks the Vieux-Port. The Vieux-Montréal building dates to the 1880s. Rooms have stone or brick walls, tall casement windows, brass beds, and massive exposed beams; many have whirlpool tubs. In summer guests can watch the fireworks competitions from a rooftop terrace. Rates include a full breakfast in Les Remparts, the hotel's French restaurant (☞ Dining, *above*). ✉ *97 rue de la Commune Est, H2Y 1J1,* ☎ *514/876–0081,* FAX *514/876–8923. 27 rooms. Restaurant, coffee shop. AE, DC, MC, V.*

$$–$$$ ★ **Auberge les Passants du Sans Soucy.** A little gem on rue St-Paul, the inn is a former fur warehouse dating to 1836—the foundations date to 1684. The lobby is also an art gallery that opens onto the street. Behind it are a living room and a breakfast room separated by a fireplace that crackles with burning hardwood in winter. This is one of the most romantic city hostelries you'll find anywhere, with brass beds, bare stone walls, exposed beams, soft lighting, whirlpool baths, and lots of fresh-cut flowers. A full breakfast is included in the rates. ✉ *171 rue St-Paul Ouest, H2Y 1Z5,* ☎ *514/842–2634,* FAX *514/842–2912. 8 rooms, 1 suite. Breakfast room. AE, DC, MC, V.*

$$–$$$ **Hôtel du Parc.** This L-shape brick tower overlooks Parc du Mont-Royal; the McGill University campus is a five-minute walk to the west. The hotel is a briskly efficient operation, the rooms are large, and the decor is modern with blond wood and pastel shades. A large, comfortable bar dominates the lobby. ✉ *3625 av. du Parc, H2X 3P8,* ☎ *514/288–6666 or 800/363–0735,* FAX *514/288–2469. 429 rooms, 20 suites. Restaurant, bar, café, no-smoking floors. AE, D, DC, MC, V.*

$$–$$$ **Le Nouvel Hôtel.** This hotel has brightly colored and functional studios and 2½-room apartments. It is near the restaurants and bars on rues Crescent, de la Montagne, and Bishop and is two blocks from the Guy-Concordia Métro station. It is also home to the Comedy Nest Cabaret (☞ Nightlife and the Arts, *below*). ✉ *1740 blvd. René-Lévesque Ouest, H3H 1R3,* ☎ *514/931–8841 or 800/363–6063,* FAX *514/931–3233. 126 rooms. Restaurant, bar, pool, comedy club. AE, DC, MC, V.*

$$ ★ **Château Versailles.** This charming hotel occupies a row of four converted mansions on rue Sherbrooke Ouest near Métro Guy-Concordia. The public areas are decorated with antique paintings and tapestries. Some guest rooms have ornate moldings and plaster decorations, and most are generously sized, with comfortable but functional furnishings. Half the rooms have king-size beds. Across the street, at 1808 rue Sherbrooke Ouest, is the 107-room Tour Versailles, a converted apartment hotel that serves as an annex to the original town houses. There is a fine French restaurant, the Champs-Elysées (☞ Dining, *above*), in La

Tour, and a breakfast room in the Château. The staff is extremely helpful and friendly. ✉ *1659 rue Sherbrooke Ouest, H3H 1E3,* ☎ *514/933–3611 or 800/361–3664, 800/361–7199 in Canada,* FAX *514/933–7102. 70 rooms in Château; 105 rooms, 2 suites in La Tour. Restaurant, breakfast room. AE, DC, MC, V.*

$–$$ 🏨 **Hôtel Lord Berri.** Rooms in this hotel near the restaurants and nightlife of rue St-Denis have brightly colored bedspreads, modern furniture, and in-room movies. The restaurant, Il Cavaliere, serves Italian food and is popular with locals. ✉ *1199 rue Berri, H2L 4C6,* ☎ *514/845–9236 or 888/363–0363,* FAX *514/849–9855. 154 rooms. Restaurant, no-smoking floors, meeting rooms. AE, DC, MC, V.*

$ 🏨 **Hostelling International.** This hostel in the heart of downtown has same-sex dorms that sleep 4, 6, or 10 people. Members pay $17.50 for a bed and nonmembers $22. Some rooms are available for couples and families. There are kitchen facilities and lockers for valuables. Reserve early during summer. ✉ *1030 rue Mackay, H3G 2H1,* ☎ *514/843–3317,* FAX *514/934–3251. 263 beds. Coin laundry. DC, MC, V.*

$ 🏨 **Hôtel l'Abri du Voyageur.** Price and location are this little hotel's main selling points, but it manages to squeeze in some unassuming charm as well, with high ceilings, bare brick walls, original pine and maple floors, and paintings by local artists (including a few by owner Guy Bisson). The hotel's three floors are over a restaurant in a pre–World War I commercial building. Bathrooms are shared, but each room has a TV and a sink. ✉ *9 rue Ste-Catherine Ouest, H2X 1Z7,* ☎ *514/849–2922,* FAX *514/499–0151. 30 rooms without bath. MC, V.*

$ 🏨 **Hôtel Thrift Lodge.** The Thrift Lodge is adjacent to the Terminus Voyageur bus station (buses park directly beneath one wing of the hotel), and some of the bus-station aura has rubbed off on the place: It's a little dingy. But if you're stumbling after a long bus ride and want somewhere to stay *now,* the rooms are large and clean, the service is friendly, and the price is right. It's also handy to the Berri-UQAM Métro station. ✉ *1600 rue St-Hubert, H2L 3Z3,* ☎ *514/849–3214,* FAX *514/849–9812. 147 rooms. Restaurant. AE, MC, V.*

$ 🏨 **McGill Student Apartments.** From mid-May to mid-August, when McGill is on summer recess, you can stay in its dorms on the grassy, quiet campus in the heart of the city. Nightly rates are $32 for students, $38 for nonstudents (single rooms only); some more expensive rooms include a kitchenette. As a visitor, you may use the campus swimming pool and gym facilities for a fee. The university cafeteria is also open during the week, serving breakfast and lunch. Be sure to book early. ✉ *3935 rue University, H3A 2B4,* ☎ *514/398–6367,* FAX *514/398–6770. 1,000 rooms without baths. MC, V.*

$ 🏨 **Université de Montréal Residence.** The university's student housing accepts visitors from early May to late August. It's on the other side of Mont-Royal from downtown and Vieux-Montréal but is right next to the Edouard-Monpetit Métro station. The rooms have phones for local calls; common lounges have microwaves and TVs. For a fee you may use the campus sports facilities. Rates are $23 per night or $141 per week. ✉ *2350 blvd. Edouard-Montpetit, H3T 1J4,* ☎ *514/343–6531,* FAX *514/343–2353. 750 rooms without baths. MC, V.*

$ 🏨 **YMCA.** This clean Y is downtown, next to Peel Métro station. Men should book at least two days in advance; women should book seven days ahead, because there are fewer rooms with showers for them. Anyone staying summer weekends must book at least a week ahead. There is a full gym facility and a typical Y cafeteria. ✉ *1450 rue Stanley, H3A 2W6,* ☎ *514/849–8393,* FAX *514/849–8017. 353 rooms, 3 with bath. Cafeteria, health club. AE, MC, V.*

$ 🏨 **YWCA.** Very close to dozens of restaurants, the Y is right downtown, one block from rue Ste-Catherine. Although men can eat at the café, the overnight facilities and health club are for women only. If you want a room with any amenities, you must book in advance; not all the rooms come with a sink and bath. There are single, double, and triple rooms. ✉ *1355 blvd. René-Lévesque, H3G 1P3,* ☎ *514/866–9941,* FAX *514/861–1603. 63 rooms. Café, pool, sauna, aerobics, exercise room, shops. MC, V.*

NIGHTLIFE AND THE ARTS

The Friday Preview section of the *Gazette,* the English-language daily paper, has an especially good list of all events at the city's concert halls, theaters, clubs, dance spaces, and movie houses. Other publications listing what's on include the *Mirror, Hour, Scope,* and *Voir* (in French), distributed free at restaurants and other public places. You can also phone **Info-Arts (Bell)** (☎ 514/790–2787) for events information.

For **tickets** to major pop and rock concerts, shows, festivals, and hockey and baseball games, go to the individual box offices or call Admission (☎ 514/790–1245 or 800/361–4595). Call **Ticketmaster** (☎ 514/790–1111) for tickets to Théâtre St-Denis. **Place des Arts** tickets may be purchased at its box office underneath the Salle Wilfrid-Pelletier, next to the Métro station.

The Arts

Dance

Traditional and contemporary dance companies thrive in Montréal, though many take to the road or are on hiatus in the summer. **Ballets Classiques de Montréal** (☎ 514/866–1771) performs mostly classical programs. **Les Ballets Jazz de Montréal** (☎ 514/982–6771) experiments with new musical forms. **Les Grands Ballets Canadiens** is the leading Québec company (☎ 514/849–8681 or 514/849–0269). **LaLaLa Human Steps** (☎ 514/277–9090) is an avant-garde, exciting powerhouse of a company. **Margie Gillis Fondation de Danse** (☎ 514/845–3115) gives young dancers and choreographers opportunities to develop their art. **Montréal Danse** (☎ 514/845–2031) is a postmodern dance repertory company. **Ouest Vertigo Danse** (☎ 514/251–9177) stages innovative, postmodern performances. **Tangente** (☎ 514/525–1860) is a nucleus for many of the more avant-garde dance troupes.

Montréal's dancers have a downtown performance and rehearsal space, the **Agora Dance Theatre** (✉ 840 rue Chérrier Est, ☎ 514/525–1500), affiliated with the Université de Montréal dance faculty. When not on tour, many dancers can be seen at Place des Arts or at any of the **Maisons de la Culture** (☎ 514/872–6211) performance spaces around town. Every other September (that is, in the odd-numbered years, such as 1999), the **Festival International de Nouvelle Danse** (☎ 514/287–1423 or 514/521–1212 for tickets) brings "new" dance to various venues around town. Tickets for this event always sell quickly.

Music

The city is home to one of the best chamber orchestras in Canada, **I Musici de Montréal** (☎ 514/982–6037). McGill University's Pollack Concert Hall (☎ 514/398–4547) is the site of concerts, notably by the **McGill Chamber Orchestra.** The **Orchestre Métropolitain de Montréal** (☎ 514/598–0870) stars at Place des Arts most weeks during the October–April season. The **Orchestre Symphonique de Montréal** (☎ 514/842–9951) has gained world renown under the baton of Charles Dutoit. When the group is not on tour, its regular venue is the Salle Wilfrid-Pelletier at the Place des Arts. The orchestra also gives Christmas and summer concerts in Notre-Dame Basilica and pop concerts at the

Arena Maurice Richard in Olympic Park. Also check the *Gazette* listings for its free summertime concerts in Montréal's city parks.

The **Spectrum** (✉ 318 rue Ste-Catherine Ouest, ☎ 514/861–5851) is an intimate concert hall. **Stade Olympique** (✉ Olympic Park, ☎ 514/252–8687) hosts rock and pop concerts. The 2,500-seat **Théâtre St-Denis** (✉ 1594 rue St-Denis, ☎ 514/849–4211) is the second-largest auditorium in Montréal (after Salle Wilfrid-Pelletier in Place des Arts).

Opera

L'Opéra de Montréal (☎ 514/985–2258) stages four productions a year at Place des Arts.

Theater

French-speaking theater lovers will find a wealth of dramatic productions. There are at least 10 major companies in town, some that have an international reputation. Anglophones have less to choose from. **Théâtre de Quat'Sous** (✉ 100 av. des Pins Est, ☎ 514/845–7277) performs modern, experimental, and cerebral plays. **Théâtre du Nouveau Monde** (✉ 84 rue Ste-Catherine Ouest, ☎ 514/866–8667) is the North American temple of French classics. **Théâtre du Rideau Vert** (✉ 4664 rue St-Denis, ☎ 514/844–1793) specializes in modern French repertoire.

The **Centaur Theatre** (✉ 453 rue St-François-Xavier, ☎ 514/288–3161), the best-known English theatrical company, stages Beaux Arts–style productions in the former stock exchange building in Vieux-Montréal. English-language plays can also be seen at the **Saidye Bronfman Centre** (✉ 5170 chemin de la Côte Ste-Catherine, ☎ 514/739–2301 or 514/739–7944), a multidisciplinary institution that is a focus of cultural activity for Montréal as a whole and for the Jewish community in particular. Many of its activities, such as gallery exhibits, lectures on public and Jewish affairs, performances, and concerts, are free. The center is home to the Yiddish Theatre Group, one of the few Yiddish companies performing today in North America. Touring companies of Broadway productions can often be seen at the **Théâtre St-Denis** (✉ 1594 rue St-Denis, ☎ 514/849–4211), as well as at Place des Arts (☎ 514/842–2112)—especially during summer.

Festivals

Montréal loves a party, and every summer festivals celebrate everything from beer to Yiddish theatre; here are some of the largest.

At the **Concours d'Art International Pyrotechnique** (International Fireworks Competition, ☎ 514/935–5161 or 800/678–5440, 800/361–4595 in Canada), held every Saturday and Sunday in June and July, teams from around the world compete to see who can best light up the sky. Their launch site is La Ronde on Ile Ste-Hélène, and you can buy a ticket, which includes an amusement park pass, to watch from a reserved seat. But thousands of Montrealers take their lawn chairs and blankets down to the Vieux-Port or across the river to the park along the South Shore and watch the show for nothing.

The **Festival International de Jazz de Montréal,** the world's biggest jazz festival, brings together more than 2,000 musicians for more than 400 concerts over a period of 11 days, from the end of June to the beginning of July. About 75% of concerts are presented free on outdoor stages. You can also hear blues, Latin rhythms, gospel, Cajun, and world music. Bell Info-Jazz (☎ 514/871–1881 or 888/515–0515) answers all queries about the festival and about travel packages. You can charge tickets over the phone (☎ 514/790–1245 or 800/678–5440, 800/361–4595 in Canada).

At the **Festival International des Films du Monde** (World Film Festival, ☎ 514/848–3883) at the end of August and the beginning of September, international stars and directors show off their best.

The **Festival Juste pour Rire** (Just for Laughs Comedy Festival, ☎ 514/790–4242) begins in early July; the comics show up for a 12-day festival that attracts about 650 performers and 350,000 spectators. Highlight acts have included Bobby Slayton and illusionists Penn and Teller.

Nightlife

Casino

The **Casino de Montréal** (✉ 1 av. du Casino, ☎ 514/392–2746 or 800/665–2274), on Ile Notre-Dame in the St. Lawrence River, is one of the world's 10 biggest, with 1,835 slot machines and 88 tables for baccarat, blackjack, and roulette. The government has tried to capture the elegance of Monte Carlo: The building glitters with glass and murals and offers stunning city views. There's a strict dress code, and croupiers are trained in politeness as well as math. The casino has five restaurants, including Nuances (☞ Dining, *above*), and a delightfully bilingual cabaret theater. There are some oddities for those used to Vegas—no drinking on the floor, no crap games (dice games are illegal in Canada), and no tipping the croupiers. The casino is a $10 cab ride from downtown, or you can take the Métro to the Ile Ste-Hélène station and transfer to Bus 167. Driving here is a hassle. It's open daily 9 AM–5 AM.

Comedy

The **Comedy Nest** (✉ 1740 blvd. René-Lévesque Ouest, ☎ 514/932–6378) has shows by name performers and up-and-comers.

Dance Clubs

Club 737 (✉ 1 Place Ville-Marie, ☎ 514/397–0737), on top of Place Ville-Marie, does the disco number every Thursday, Friday, and Saturday night. This has become very popular with the upscale, mid-20s to mid-30s crowd. The view is magnificent and there's an open-air rooftop bar. **Hard Rock Cafe** (✉ 1458 rue Crescent, ☎ 514/987–1420) is Montréal's version of this establishment. **Kokino** (✉ 3556 blvd. St-Laurent, ☎ 514/848–6398) is *the* place for the beautiful people, with jazz, Brazilian, and house music. **Thursdays/Les Beaux Jeudis** (✉ 1449 rue Crescent, ☎ 514/288–5656) is a popular dance club.

Folk Music

An enthusiastic crowd sings along with Québécois performers at the **Deux Pierrots Boîte aux Chansons** (✉ 104 rue St-Paul Est, ☎ 514/861–1270). **Hurley's Irish Pub** (✉ 1225 rue Crescent, ☎ 514/861–4111) attracts some of the city's best Celtic musicians and dancers.

Jazz

The best-known jazz club is Vieux-Montréal's **L'Air du Temps** (✉ 191 rue St-Paul Ouest, ☎ 514/842–2003). This small, smoky club presents 90% local talent and 10% international acts from 5 PM on into the night. Downtown, duck into **Biddle's** (✉ 2060 rue Aylmer, ☎ 514/842–8656), where bassist Charles Biddle holds forth most evenings. Biddle's serves pretty good ribs and chicken. You might try the **Quai des Brumes Dancing** (✉ 4481 rue St-Denis, ☎ 514/499–0467).

Rock

Rock clubs seem to spring up, flourish, then fizzle out overnight. **Club Soda** (✉ 5240 av. du Parc, ☎ 514/270–7848), the granddaddy of them all, sports a neon martini glass complete with neon effervescence outside. Inside it's a small hall with a stage, three bars, and room for about 400 people. International rock acts play here, as does local talent. It's also a venue for the comedy and jazz festivals. The club is open only for shows. Phone the box office to find out what's on. **Déjà Vu** (✉ 1224 rue Bishop, ☎ 514/866–0512), a rock club with a nostalgia theme, is popular with young English-speakers. **L'Ours Qui Fume** (✉ 2019 rue St-Denis, ☎ 514/845–6998), or the Smoking Bear, is loud, raucous, and very Francophone.

OUTDOOR ACTIVITIES AND SPORTS

Most Montrealers would probably claim they hate winter, but the city is rich in cold-weather activities—skating rinks, cross-country ski trails, toboggan runs, and even a downhill ski run. In summer there are tennis courts, miles of bicycle trails, golf courses, and two lakes for boating and swimming.

Participant Sports

Biking

The island of Montréal—except for Mont-Royal itself—is quite flat, and there are more than 20 cycling paths in the metropolitan area. Bikes are welcome on the first and last cars of Métro trains during non–rush hours. Ferries at the Vieux-Port will take you to Ile Ste-Hélène and the South Shore of the St. Lawrence River.You can rent bicycles at **Vélo Aventure** on the grounds of the Vieux-Port (☎ 514/847–0666).

One interesting path starts at the Vieux-Port and follows the **Lachine Canal** (1825) from Vieux-Montréal to the shores of Lac St-Louis in suburban Lachine. Along the way you can stop at the bustling Atwater Farmer's Market (✉ 110 av. Atwater) to buy the makings of a picnic or take a break at Magnan (☞ Dining, *above*) in summer for a steak or a cheap lobster. In Lachine you can visit the Fur Trade at Lachine Historic Site (✉ 1255 blvd. St-Joseph, Lachine, ☎ 514/637–7433). **Parks Canada** (☎ 514/283–6054 or 514/637–7433) conducts guided cycling tours along the Lachine Canal every summer weekend.

Boating

In Montréal you can get in a boat at a downtown wharf and be crashing through Class V white water minutes later. Jack Kowalski of **Lachine Rapids Tours Ltd.** (✉ 105 rue de la Commune, or Quai de l'Horloge, or Clock Tower Pier, ☎ 514/284–9607) takes thrill seekers on a 45-minute voyage through the rapids in big, sturdy aluminum jet boats. He supplies heavy-water gear. You can also choose a half-hour trip around the islands in 10-passenger boats that can go about 100 kph (60 mph). Reservations are required; trips are narrated in French and English. There are five trips daily through the rapids from May through September; cost is $48. Rafting trips are also available.

Golf

For a complete listing of the many golf courses in the Montréal area, call **Tourisme-Québec** (☎ 514/873–2015 or 800/363–7777).

Ice-Skating

The city has at least 195 outdoor and 21 indoor rinks. There are huge ones on Ile Ste-Hèléne and at the Vieux-Port. Call the **Parks and Recreation Department** (☎ 514/872–6211) for information.You can skate year-round in the **Amphithéatre Bell** (☎ 514/395–0555, ext. 237) in Le 1000 rue de la Gauchetière.

Jogging

There are paths in most city parks, but for running with a panoramic view, head to the dirt track in **Parc du Mont-Royal** (take rue Peel, then the steps up to the track).

Skiing

CROSS-COUNTRY

Trails crisscross most city parks, including Parc des Iles, Maisonneuve, and Mont-Royal, but the best are probably the 46 km (28 mi) in the 900-acre **Cap St-Jacques Regional Park** (✉ Off blvd. Gouin, ☎ 514/280–6871) in Pierrefonds on the west end of Montréal Island.

DOWNHILL

For the big slopes you'll have to go northwest to the Laurentians (☞ Chapter 4) or south to the Eastern Townships (☞ Chapter 4), an hour or two away by car. There is a small slope in Parc du Mont-Royal. A "Ski-Québec" brochure is available from **Tourisme-Québec** offices (☎ 514/873–2015 or 800/363–7777).

Squash

Court time should be reserved three days ahead at **Nautilus Centre St-Laurent Côte-de-Liesse Racquet Club** (✉ 8305 chemin Côte-de-Liesse, ☎ 514/739–3654).

Swimming

There is a large indoor pool at the Olympic Park's **Centre Aquatique** (✉ 4141 av. Pierre-de-Coubertin, ☎ 514/252–4622). **Centre Sportif et des Loisirs Claude-Robillard** (✉ 1000 av. Emile Journault, ☎ 514/872–6900) has a big indoor pool. The outdoor pool on **Ile Ste-Hélène** is a popular (and crowded) gathering place, open June–Labor Day. The city-run beach, **Plage de l'Ile Notre-Dame** (☎ 514/872–6211), on Ile Notre-Dame is the only natural swimming hole in Montréal.

Tennis

There are public courts in the Jeanne-Mance, Kent, Lafontaine, and Somerled parks. For details call the **Parks and Recreation department** (☎ 514/872–6211).

Windsurfing and Sailing

Sailboards and small sailboats can be rented at **L'Ecole de Voile de Lachine** (✉ 2105 blvd. St-Joseph, Lachine, ☎ 514/634–4326) and the **Société du Parc des Iles** (✉ 12 Pl. de la Concorde, ☎ 514/872–4537).

Spectator Sports

Baseball

The National League's **Montréal Expos** (☎ 514/253–3434 or 800/463–9767) play at Olympic Stadium April–September.

Football

The venerable **Montréal Alouettes** (☎ 514/254–2400 for information, 514/254–1818 for tickets) of the Canadian Football League play the Canadian version of the game—bigger field, just three downs, and a far more wide-open style—on real grass under open skies at McGill University's Molson Stadium June–October. It's one of the best sporting deals in town.

Grand Prix

The annual **Player's Grand Prix du Canada** (☎ 514/392–0000 or 514/350–4731), which draws top Formula 1 racers from around the world, takes place every June at Circuit Gilles Villeneuve on Ile Notre-Dame.

Hockey

The **Montréal Canadiens,** winners of 23 Stanley Cups, meet National Hockey League rivals at the Centre Molson (✉1250 rue de la Gauchetière Ouest, ☎ 514/932–2582) October–April. Buy tickets in advance.

SHOPPING

Montrealers *magasinent* (go shopping) with a vengeance, so it's no surprise that the city has 160 multifaceted retail areas encompassing some 7,000 stores. The law allows shops to stay open weekdays 9–9 and weekends 9–5. However, many merchants close Monday–Wednesday evenings and on Sunday. Many specialty service shops are closed on Monday, too. Just about all stores, with the exception of some bargain outlets and a few selective art and antiques galleries, accept major credit cards. Most purchases are subject to a federal goods and services tax (GST) of 7% as well as a provincial tax of 8%.

If you think you might be buying fur, it is wise to check with your country's customs officials before leaving to find out which animals are considered endangered and cannot be imported. Do the same if you think you might be buying Inuit carvings, many of which are made of whalebone and ivory and cannot be brought into the United States.

Montréal Specialties

Many visitors usually reserve at least one day to hunt for either exclusive fashions along rue Sherbrooke. But there are specific items that you should seek out in Montréal.

Antiques and Secondhand Books

The fashionable place for antiquing is a once run-down five-block strip of rue Notre-Dame Ouest between rue Guy and avenue Atwater (a five-minute walk south from the Lionel-Groulx Métro station). **Antiquités Landry** (✉ 1726 rue Notre-Dame Ouest, ☎ 514/937–7040) has solid pine furniture. **Deuxièmement** (✉ 1880 rue Notre-Dame Ouest, ☎ 514/933–8560) sells a fascinating jumble of objects from every age. **Héritage Antique Métropolitain** (✉ 1645 rue Notre-Dame Ouest, ☎ 514/931–5517) has elegant English and French furniture. A Sunday tour might begin with brunch at **Salon de Thé Ambiance** (✉ 1874 rue Notre-Dame Ouest, ☎ 514/939–2609), a charming restaurant that also sells antiques. **Viva Gallery** (✉ 1970 rue Notre-Dame Ouest, ☎ 514/932–3200) specializes in Asian antiques.

Antiques stores are beginning to pop up along **rue Amherst** between rues Ste-Catherine and Ontario (a five-minute walk west of the Beaudry Métro station). The area is shabbier than rue Notre-Dame but a lot cheaper. **L'Antiquaire Joyal** (✉ 1475 rue Amherst, ☎ 514/524–0057) includes rosaries, crucifixes, and religious art among its two floors of Victorian and earlier furniture. **Antiquités Curiosités** (✉ 1769 rue Amherst, ☎ 514/525–8772) has a wide selection of well-priced wooden toys and Victorian-era tables and tallboys. **Cité Déco** (✉ 1761 rue Amherst, ☎ 514/528–0659) specializes in the chrome and plastic furnishings of the '50s.

Biblomania (✉ 1841A rue Ste-Catherine Ouest, ☎ 514/933–8156) has some gems among its extensive shelves of secondhand books. **Ex Libris** (✉ 1628B rue Sherbrooke Ouest, ☎ 514/932–1689) houses a fine collection of secondhand books in an elegant graystone on rue Sherbrooke. One of the most fascinating bookstores in Montréal is **Russell Books** (✉ 275 rue St-Antoine Ouest, ☎ 514/866–0564), a huge, dusty place full of remainders, secondhand paperbacks, children's books, and shelves of old volumes on every subject from algebra to zoology. The back rooms are full of treasures that have never been catalogued. Lovers of old books can browse through the shelves at **S.W. Welch** (✉ 3878 blvd. St-Laurent, ☎ 514/848–9358).

Fur

Montréal is one of the fur capitals of the world. Close to 85% of Canada's fur manufacturers are based in the city, as are many of their retail outlets. Many of them are clustered along rue Mayor and boulevard de Maisonneuve between rue de Bleury and rue Aylmer. **Alexandor** (✉ 2055 rue Peel, ☎ 514/288–1119) is nine blocks west of the main fur trade area, and its storefront showroom caters to the downtown trade. **Birger Christensen at Holt Renfrew** (✉ 1300 rue Sherbrooke Ouest, ☎ 514/842–5111) is perhaps the most exclusive showroom of the lot, with prices to match. **Grosvenor** (✉ 400 blvd. de Maisonneuve Ouest, ☎ 514/288–1255) caters more to the wholesale trade but has several showrooms where customers can view its decidedly European styles. **McComber** (✉ 402 blvd. de Maisonneuve Ouest, ☎ 514/845–1167) has been in business for 100 years; its present owner has a flair for mink designs.

Downtown

Downtown is Montréal's largest retail district. It takes in rue Sherbrooke, boulevard de Maisonneuve, rue Ste-Catherine, and the side streets between them. Because of the proximity and variety of shops, it's the best shopping bet if you're in town overnight or over a weekend. The area bounded by rues Sherbrooke and Ste-Catherine, and rues de la Montagne and Crescent has antiques and art galleries in addition to designer salons. Rue Sherbrooke is lined with fashion boutiques and art and antiques galleries. Rue Crescent is a tempting blend of antiques, fashions, and jewelry displayed beneath colorful awnings.

Brisson et Brisson (✉ 1472 rue Sherbrooke Ouest, ☎ 514/937–7456) is perhaps the most exclusive men's store in the city. **Casa del Habano** (✉ 1434 rue Sherbrooke Ouest, ☎ 514/849–0037) stocks the finest cigars Cuba produces. (Warning: U.S. law forbids its citizens to buy Cuban products.) **Galerie Tansu** (✉ 1622 rue Sherbrooke Ouest, ☎ 514/864–1039) has Chinese and Japanese antiques. The craftspeople at **Kaufmann de Suisse** (✉ 2195 rue Crescent, ☎ 514/848–0595) make finely wrought jewelry.

Complexe Desjardins

Complexe Desjardins (✉ Blvd. René-Lévesque and rue Jeanne Mance) is filled with splashing fountains and exotic plants. To get here, take the Métro to the Place des Arts and follow the tunnels to Desjardins' multitiered atrium mall. The roughly 80 stores include budget outlets like Le Château for clothing as well as the exclusive Jonathan Roche Monsieur for men's fashions.

Les Cours Mont-Royal

Les Cours Mont-Royal (✉ 1550 rue Metcalfe) is *très élégant.* This mall is linked to both the Peel and McGill Métro stations and caters to expensive tastes, but even bargain hunters find it an intriguing spot for window shopping. Beware: The interior layout can be disorienting.

Department Stores

La Baie (✉ 585 rue Ste-Catherine Ouest, ☎ 514/281–4422)—the Bay in English—has been a department store since 1891. It's known for its duffel coats and Hudson Bay red-, green-, and white-striped blankets. La Baie also sells the typical department store fare.

Eaton (✉ 677 rue Ste-Catherine Ouest, ☎ 514/284–8411) is the city's leading department store and part of Canada's largest chain. Founded in Toronto by Timothy Eaton, the first Montréal outlet appeared in 1925. It now sells everything—from fashions and furniture to meals in the Art Deco top-floor restaurant and zucchini loaves in the basement bakery. Everything, that is, except tobacco. Timothy was a good Methodist, and his descendants honor his principles.

Exclusive **Holt Renfrew** (✉ 1300 rue Sherbrooke Ouest, ☎ 514/842–5111) is known for furs and fashions. It has supplied coats to four generations of British royalty, and when Queen Elizabeth II got married in 1947, Holt's gave her a priceless Labrador mink. Holt carries the pricey line of furs by Denmark's Birger Christensen, as well as the haute couture and prêt-à-porter collections of Yves Saint Laurent.

A kilted piper regales shoppers at **Ogilvy** (✉ 1307 rue Ste-Catherine Ouest, ☎ 514/842–7711) every day at noon. Founded in 1865, the department store still stocks traditional apparel by retailers like Aquascutum and Jaeger. The store has been divided into individual designer boutiques selling pricier lines than La Baie or Eaton. It used to be Ogilvy's (just as Eaton used to be Eaton's) before Québec's French-only sign laws made apostrophes illegal.

Faubourg Ste-Catherine

The Faubourg Ste-Catherine (✉ 1616 rue Ste-Catherine Ouest, at rue Guy) is a vast bazaar abutting the Gray Nuns' convent grounds. There are clothing and crafts boutiques, but the main product is food—fresh bagels, pastries, fruits and vegetables, and gourmet meats. A dozen or so very reasonably priced lunch counters sell ethnic foods.

Place Bonaventure

Place Bonaventure (✉ Rues de la Gauchetière and University) is one of Canada's largest commercial exhibition centers. It's directly above the Bonaventure Métro station and has a mall with some 120 stores, including the trendy Au Coton and Bikini Village and the practical Bata Shoes. There are also a number of fun shops: Ici-Bas for outrageous hose, Le Rouet for handicrafts, and Miniatures Plus for exquisite dolls' furniture and tiny gifts.

Place Montréal Trust

Place Montréal Trust (✉ 1600 rue McGill College, at rue Ste-Catherine Ouest) is the lively entrance to an imposing glass office tower. Shoppers, fooled by the aqua and pastel decor, may think they have stumbled into a California mall. Prices at the 110 outlets range from hundreds (for designs by Alfred Sung, haute couture at Gigi, or men's fashions at Rodier) to only a few dollars (for T-shirts or steak-and-kidney pies at the outpost of famed British department store Marks & Spencer). This shopping center is linked to the McGill Métro station.

Place Ville-Marie

Weatherproof shopping began in 1962 beneath the 42-story cruciform towers of Place Ville-Marie (✉ Blvd. René-Lévesque and rue University). Stylish men and women head to Place Ville-Marie's 100-plus retail outlets for the clothes—Tristan & Iseut, Cactus, and Aquascutum at the upper end and Dalmys and Reitmans for more affordable fashions. For shoes try Mayfair, Brown's, François Villon, and French.

Les Promenades de la Cathédrale

The Promenades de la Cathédrale (✉ 625 rue Ste-Catherine Ouest) are directly beneath Christ Church Cathedral, the seat of Montréal's Anglican (Episcopal) bishop. Les Promenades, which is connected to the McGill Métro station, has Canada's largest Linen Chest outlet, with hundreds of bedspreads and duvets draped over revolving racks plus aisles of china, crystal, linen, and silver. It's also home to the Anglican Church's Diocesan Book Room, which sells an unusually good and ecumenical selection of books as well as religious objects.

Rue Chabanel

In the north end of the city, rue Chabanel is the soul of Montréal's extensive garment industry. Every Saturday, from about 8:30 to 1, many of the manufacturers and importers in the area open their doors to the general public. At least they do if they feel like it. What results is part bazaar, part circus, and often all chaos—but friendly chaos. When Montrealers say "Chabanel," they mean the eight-block stretch just west of boulevard St-Laurent. The factories and shops there are tiny—dozens of them are crammed into each building. The goods seem to get more stylish and more expensive the farther west you go. For really cheap leather goods, sportswear, children's clothes, and linens, try the shops at 99 rue Chabanel. For more deluxe options drop into 555 rue Chabanel. The manufacturers and importers here have their work areas on the upper floors and have transformed the mezzanine into a glitzy mall with bargains in men's suits, winter coats, knitted goods, and stylish leather jackets. A few places on Chabanel accept credit cards, but bring cash anyway. It's easier to bargain if you can flash bills, and if you pay cash, the price will often "include the tax."

Square Westmount and Avenue Greene

Square Westmount (☒ Rue Ste-Catherine Ouest and av. Greene) has some of the city's finest shops, which is hardly surprising—it serves the mountainside suburb of Westmount, home to executives and former prime ministers. Humbler types can get there easily by taking the Métro to the Atwater station and following the tunnel to Square Westmount. **Collange** (☎ 514/933–4634) sells lacy lingerie. **Hugo Nicholson** (☎ 514/937–1937) carries exclusive fashions for men and women. **Ma Maison** (☎ 514/933–0045) stocks quality housewares. The very elegant **Marché de Westmount** has an array of gourmet boutiques that sell pastries, cheeses, pâtés, fruits, cakes, and chocolates. You can assemble your own picnic and eat it at one of the little tables scattered among the stalls. If shopping tires you out, you can stop in at the **Spa de Westmount** (☎ 514/933–9966) for a massage.

Square Westmount opens onto **avenue Greene,** two flower-lined blocks of restored redbrick row houses full of boutiques, restaurants, and shops. The **Coach House** (☒ 1325 av. Greene, ☎ 514/937–6191) is a source for antique silverware. **Double Hook** (☒ 1235A av. Greene, ☎ 514/932–5093) sells only Canadian books.

Upper Boulevard St-Laurent and Avenue Laurier Ouest

Upper boulevard St-Laurent—which runs roughly from avenue du Mont-Royal north to rue St-Viateur and climbs the mountain to rue Bernard—has blossomed into one of Montréal's most chic *quartiers.* It's not entirely surprising, given that much of this area lies within or adjacent to Outremont, an enclave of wealthy Francophone Montrealers, with restaurants, boutiques, nightclubs, and bistros catering to the upscale visitor. **J. Schrecter** (☒ 4350 blvd. St-Laurent, ☎ 514/845–4231) had been supplying work duds for blue-collar workers for decades when the grunge look suddenly made the store trendy. **Scandale** (☒ 3639 blvd. St-Laurent, ☎ 514/842–4707) has designs for the very hip as well as great lingerie and a secondhand-clothes store.

Shoppers flock to the two blocks of **avenue Mont-Royal** just east of boulevard St-Laurent for a series of shops that sell secondhand clothes and recycled clothes (things like housecoats chopped into sassy miniskirts). **Eva B** (☒ 2013 blvd. St-Laurent, ☎ 514/849–8246) sells new clothes as well as used. **Hatfield & McCoy** (☒ 156 av. Mont-Royal

Est, ☏ 514/982–0088) recycles elegant lounge clothes from the 1930s to the 1970s. **Scarlett O'Hara** (✉ 254 av. Mont-Royal Est, ☏ 514/844–9435) started the whole secondhand trend.

Avenue Laurier Ouest, from boulevard St-Laurent to chemin de la Côte-Ste-Catherine, is roughly an eight-block stretch; you'll crisscross it many times as you explore its fashionable and trendy shops, which carry everything from crafts and clothing to books and paintings. Asian and African crafts are sold at **Artefact** (✉ 102 av. Laurier Ouest, ☏ 514/278–6575). **Boutique Gabriel Filion** (✉ 1127 av. Laurier Ouest, ☏ 514/274–0697) sells interesting imported toys and marvelous dolls, dolls' clothes, stuffed animals, and music boxes. **Tilley Endurables** (✉ 1050 av. Laurier Ouest, ☏ 514/272–7791) sells the famous Canadian-designed Tilley hat and other easy-care travel wear.

Vieux-Montréal

Despite Vieux-Montréal's abundance of garish souvenir shops, a shopping spree there can be worthwhile. Both rues Notre-Dame and St-Jacques, from rue McGill to Place Jacques-Cartier, are lined with low to moderately priced fashion boutiques and shoe stores. **Desmarais et Robitaille** (✉ 60 rue Notre-Dame Ouest, ☏ 514/845–3194), a store that supplies churches with vestments and liturgical aids, has Québécois carvings and handicrafts as well as tasteful religious articles.

Rue St-Paul has some interesting shops and art galleries. At the **Cerf Volanterie** (✉ 224 rue St-Paul Ouest, ☏ 514/845–7613), Claude Thibaudeau makes sturdy, gloriously colored kites that he signs and guarantees for three years. **Drags** (✉ 367 rue St-Paul Est, ☏ 514/866–0631) is crammed with fragments of military uniforms and loads of clothes, shoes, hats, and accessories from the '30s and '40s. **L'Empreinte Coopérative** (✉ 272 rue St-Paul Est, ☏ 514/861–4427) has a fine collection of Québec handicrafts. The **Galerie Art & Culture** (✉ 227 rue St-Paul Ouest, ☏ 514/843–5980) specializes in Canadian landscapes. **Galerie des Arts Relais des Époques** (✉ 234 rue St-Paul Ouest, ☏ 514/844–2133) sells some fascinating work by contemporary Montréal painters. **La Guilde Graphique** (✉ 9 rue St-Paul Ouest, ☏ 514/844–3438) has an exceptional selection of original prints, engravings, and etchings. **Rita R. Giroux** (✉ 206 rue St-Paul Ouest, ☏ 514/844–4714) makes flamboyant creations with fresh, dried, and silk flowers.

MONTRÉAL A TO Z

Arriving and Departing

By Bus

For information about bus companies, contact the city's downtown bus terminal, **Terminus Voyageur** (✉ 505 blvd. de Maisonneuve Est, ☏ 514/842–2281), which connects with the Berri-UQAM Métro station. **Greyhound** (☏ 800/231–2222) has coast-to-coast service and serves Montréal with buses arriving from and departing for various cities in North America. **Vermont Transit** (☏ 800/231–2222), a Greyhound subsidiary, serves Montréal via Boston, New York, and other points in the Northeast. **Voyageur** and Voyageur-Colonial service destinations primarily within Québec and Ontario.

By Car

Montréal is accessible from the rest of Canada via the Trans-Canada Highway (Highway 1), which enters the city from the east and west via Routes 20 and 40. The New York State Thruway (I–87) becomes Route 15 at the Canadian border, and then it's 47 km (29 mi) to the outskirts of Montréal. U.S. I–89 becomes two-lane Route 133, which eventually joins Route 10, at the border. From I–91 from Massachusetts, you must take Routes 55 and 10 to reach Montréal. At the border you must clear Canadian Customs, so be prepared with proof of citizenship and your vehicle's ownership papers. On holidays and during the peak summer season, expect waits of a half hour or more at the major crossings.

Once you're in Québec, the road signs will be in French, but they're designed to be understandable to everyone. The speed limit is posted in kilometers; on highways the limit is 100 kph (about 62 mph). There are heavy penalties for driving while intoxicated, and drivers and front-seat passengers must wear over-the-shoulder seat belts. Gasoline is sold in liters (3¾ liters equal 1 U.S. gallon), and lead-free is called *sans plomb*. New York, Maine, and Ontario residents should drive with extra care in Québec: Traffic violations in the province are entered on their driving records back home (and vice versa).

By Plane

Flying time from New York is 1½ hours; from Chicago, two hours; from Los Angeles, 6½ hours (with a connection). **Dorval International** (✉ 975 blvd. René-Vachon, ☎ 514/633–3105), 22½ km (14 mi) west of the city, handles all scheduled flights foreign and domestic and some charter operations. **Mirabel International** (✉ 12600 rue Aérogare, ☎ 514/476–3010), 54½ km (34 mi) northwest of the city, serves most charter traffic. Major **airlines** serving Montréal are Air Canada, American Airlines, Canadian Airlines International, Delta, and US Airways (☞ Air Travel *in* the Gold Guide). A $10 airport tax (for capital improvements) is charged when you leave. You can pay cash or with a credit card.

A **taxi** from Dorval to downtown will cost $25; from Mirabel, about $56. All taxi companies in Montréal must charge the same rates by law. **Autobus Connaisseur** (☎ 514/934–1222) is a much cheaper alternative to taxis into town from Mirabel and Dorval. Shuttle service from Mirabel to the terminal next to the Gare Centrale (✉ 777 rue de la Gauchetière) is frequent and costs only $7.25. The shuttle from Dorval runs about every half hour and stops at Le Centre Sheraton, Le Château Champlain, Le Reine Elizabeth, and the Voyageur terminal. It costs $9. If you plan to use the bus to go back to either airport, you can save by buying a round-trip ticket.

By Train

The Gare Centrale, on rue de la Gauchetière between rues University and Mansfield (behind Le Reine Elizabeth), is the rail terminus for all trains from the United States and from other Canadian provinces. It is connected underground to the Bonaventure Métro station.

Amtrak's (☎ 800/872–7245) *Adirondack* leaves New York's Penn Station every morning for the 10½-hour trip through scenic upstate New York to Montréal. Amtrak also has bus connections with the *Vermonter* in St. Albans, Vermont.

VIA Rail (☎514/989–2626 or 800/561–3949, 800/361–5390 in Québec Province) connects Montréal with all the major cities of Canada, including Québec City, Halifax, Ottawa, Toronto, Winnipeg, Edmonton, and Vancouver.

Getting Around

By Bus and Métro

Public transportation is easily the best and cheapest way to get around. The **Métro** (subway) is clean, quiet (it runs on rubber wheels), and safe, and it's heated in winter and cooled in summer. Métro hours on the Orange, Green, and Yellow lines are weekdays 5:30 AM–12:58 AM, Saturday 5:30 AM–1:28 AM, and Sunday 5:30 AM–1:58 AM. The Blue Line runs daily from 5:30 AM to 11 PM. Trains run as often as every three minutes on the most crowded lines—Orange and Green at rush hours. The Métro is also connected to the 29 km (18 mi) of the Underground City. Each of the 65 Métro stops has been individually designed and decorated; Berri-UQAM has stained glass, and at Place d'Armes a small collection of archaeological artifacts is exhibited. The stations between Snowdon and Jean-Talon on the Blue Line are worth a visit, particularly Outremont, with its glass-block design. Each station connects with one or more bus routes, which cover the rest of the island. The STCUM (Société de Transport de la Communauté Urbaine de Montréal) administers both the Métro and the buses, so the same tickets and transfers (free) are valid on either service. You should be able to get within a few blocks of anywhere in the city on one fare. At press time rates were: single ticket $1.85, six tickets $7.75, monthly pass $44.50. Visitors can buy a day pass for $5 or a three-day pass for $12. They're available at some major hotels, at Berri-UQAM and some other downtown stations, and at Info-Touriste (☞ Visitor Information *in* Contacts and Resources, *below*) at place Jacques-Cartier.

Free maps may be obtained at Métro ticket booths. Try to get the *Carte Réseau* (system map); it's the most complete. Transfers from Métro to buses are available from the dispenser just beyond the ticket booth inside the station. Bus-to-bus and bus-to-Métro transfers may be obtained from the bus driver. For more information on reaching your destination call the **Société de Transport de la Communauté de Montréal** (☏ 514/288–6287).

By Car

Finding your way around Montréal by car is not difficult. The streets are laid out in a fairly straightforward grid, and one-way streets are clearly marked. But parking is difficult and the narrow cobbled streets of Vieux-Montréal can be a trial. It's much easier to park near a Métro station and walk and use public transit.

Montréal police have a diligent tow-away and fine system for cars double-parked or stopped in no-stopping zones in downtown Montréal during rush hours and business hours. A parking ticket will cost between $35 and $40. All Montréal parking signs are in French, so brush up on your *gauche* (left), *droit* (right), *ouest* (west), and *est* (east). If your car is towed away while illegally parked, it will cost an additional $35 to retrieve it. Be especially alert in winter: Montréal's snow-clearing crews are the best in the world and a joy to watch in action after a blizzard—but they're ruthless in dealing with any parked cars in their way. If they don't tow them, they'll bury them.

In winter, remember that your car may not start on extra cold mornings unless it has been kept in a heated garage. And if you drive in the city, remember two things: Québec law forbids you to turn right on a red light, and Montrealers are notorious jaywalkers.

By Taxi

Taxis in Montréal all run on the same rate: $2.25 minimum and $1 per kilometer (½ mi). They're usually reliable, although they may be hard to find on rainy nights after the Métro has closed. Each carries on its roof a white or orange plastic sign that is lit when available and off when occupied.

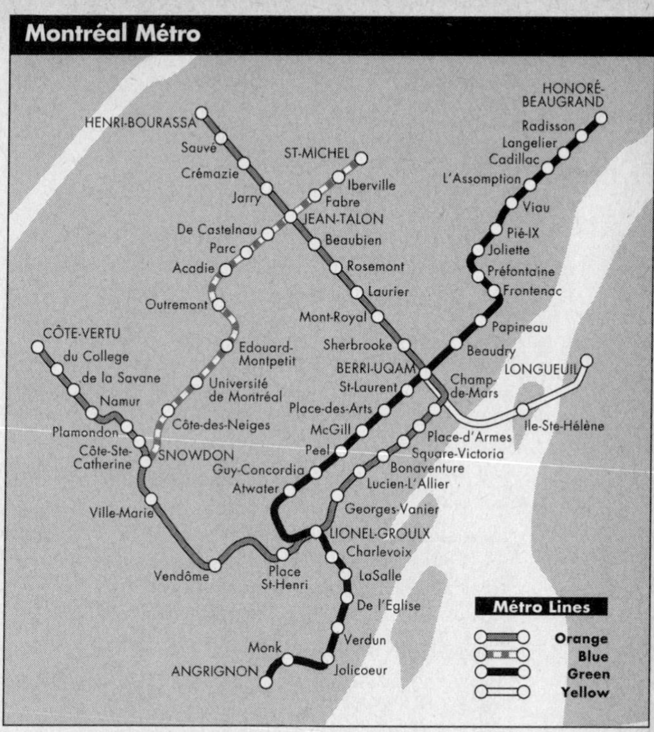

Contacts and Resources

Car Rentals

Avis (☏ 514/866–7906 or 800/879–2847). **Budget** (☏ 514/938–1000 or 800/268–8900). **Discount** (☏ 514/286–1554 or 800/357–0123). **Enterprise** (☏ 514/931–3722 or 800/736–8222). **Hertz** (☏ 514/842–8537 or 800/263–0600). **National/Tilden** (☏ 514/878–2771 or 800/387–4747). **Via Route** (☏ 514/521–5221).

Consulates

United States (✉ 1155 rue St-Alexandre, ☏ 514/398–9695) is open weekdays 8:30–4:30. **United Kingdom** (✉ 1000 rue de la Gauchetière Ouest, ☏ 514/866–5863) is open weekdays 9–5.

Doctors and Dentists

The **U.S. Consulate** cannot recommend specific doctors and dentists but does provide a list of various specialists in the Montréal area. Call in advance (☏ 514/398–9695) to make sure the consulate is open.

Dental clinic (☏ 514/342–4444) is open 24 hours; Sunday appointments are for emergencies only. **Montréal General Hospital** (☏ 514/937–6011). **Québec Poison Control Centre** (☏ 800/463–5060). **Touring Club de Montréal–AAA, CAA, RAC** (☏ 514/861–7111).

Emergencies

Ambulance, fire, police (☏ 911).

English-Language Bookstores

Chapters (✉1171 rue Ste-Catherine Ouest, ☏ 514/849–8825), a branch of the Canadian chain, has books, magazines, and a coffee shop. **Double Hook** (✉1235A av. Greene, ☏ 514/932–5093) sells only Canadian books. **Paragraphe** (✉ 2065 rue Mansfield, ☏ 514/845–5811) has a café.

Guided Tours

BOAT

From May through October, **Amphi Tour** (☎ 514/849–5181 or ☎ 514/386–1298 for cell phone in season only) offers a unique one-hour tour of Vieux-Montréal and the Vieux-Port on both land and water in an amphibious bus. **Bateau-Mouche** (☎ 514/849–9952) runs four harbor excursions and an evening supper cruise every day from May through October. The boats are reminiscent of the ones that cruise the canals of the Netherlands—wide-beamed and low-slung, with a glassed-in passenger deck. Boats leave from the Jacques Cartier Pier at the foot of Place Jacques-Cartier in the Vieux-Port (Métro Champs-de-Mars).

CALÈCHE RIDES

Open **horse-drawn carriages**—fleece-lined in winter—leave from Place Jacques-Cartier, Square Dorchester, Place d'Armes, and rue de la Commune. An hour-long ride costs about $50 (☎ 514/653–0751).

ORIENTATION

Gray Line (☎ 514/934–1222) has nine different tours of Montréal in the summer and one tour during the winter. It has pickup service at the major hotels or at Info-Touriste (✉ 1001 Sq. Dorchester). **Murray Hill Trolley Buses** (☎ 514/871–4733) follow a 14-stop circuit of the city. Passengers can get off and on as often as they like and stay at each stop as long as they like. There's pickup service at major hotels.

Late-Night Pharmacies

Many pharmacies are open until midnight. **Jean Coutu** (✉ 501 Mont-Royal Est, ☎ 514/521–3481; ✉ 5510 Côte-des-Neiges, ☎ 514/344–8338) is open until midnight. **Pharmaprix** (✉ 1500 rue Ste-Catherine Ouest, ☎ 514/933–4744; ✉ 5157 rue Sherbrooke Ouest, ☎ 514/484–3531) stays open until midnight. **Pharmaprix** (✉ Promenades du Musée; ✉ 5122 Côte-des-Neiges, ☎ 514/738–8464; ✉ 901 rue Ste-Catherine Est, ☎ 514/842–4915) is open 24 hours.

Lodging Reservations

Bed and Breakfast à Montréal (✉ Marian Kahn, Box 575, Snowdon Station, H3X 3T8, ☎ 514/738–9410 or 800/738–4338, FAX 514/735–7493) represents more than 50 homes in downtown and in the elegant neighborhoods of Westmount and Outremont. Singles run $45–$55, doubles $60–$95.

Downtown B&B Network (✉ Bob Finkelstein, 3458 av. Laval, H2X 3C8, ☎ 514/289–9749 or 800/267–5180) represents 75 homes and apartments, mostly around the downtown core and along rue Sherbrooke, that have one or more rooms available for visitors. Singles are $30–$40, doubles $40–$65.

There is a room reservation service at **Info-Touriste** (☎ 800/665–1528), which can find you a room in one of 80 hotels, motels, and bed-and-breakfasts.

Museum Pass

The Montréal **museum pass** allows access to 19 major museums. A day pass costs $15, a three-day pass $28; family passes are $30 for one day and $60 for three days. They are available at museums or Centre Info-Touriste (✉ 1001 Sq. Dorchester).

Travel Agencies

American Express (✉ 1141 blvd. de Maisonneuve Ouest, ☎ 514/284–3300). **Canadian Automobile Club** (✉ 1180 rue Drummond, ☎ 514/861–5111). **Vacances Tourbec** (✉ 595 blvd. de Maisonneuve Ouest, ☎ 514/842–1400). **Voyages Campus** (✉ McGill University, 3480 rue McTavish, ☎ 514/398–0647).

Visitor Information

Centre Info-Touriste (✉ 1001 Sq. Dorchester, ☎ 514/873–2015 or 800/363–7777) on Square Dorchester is open June 10–Labor Day, daily 8:30–7:30, and Labor Day–June 9, daily 9–6. A second branch (✉ 174 rue Notre-Dame Est, at Pl. Jacques-Cartier, ☎ 514/873–2015) is open Labor Day–mid-May, daily 9–1 and 2–5, and mid-May–Labor Day, daily 9–7.

3 Québec City

Whether you're strolling along the Plains of Abraham or exploring the Vieux-Port, Québec City will give you a feeling for centuries of history and French civilization. The city, which has one of the most spectacular settings in North America, is perched on a cliff above a narrow point in the St. Lawrence River. It is the capital of, as well as the oldest municipality in, Québec province.

Updated by Elizabeth Thompson

NO EXCURSION TO FRENCH-SPEAKING Canada is complete without a visit to exuberant, romantic Québec City, which can claim one of the most beautiful natural settings in North America. The well-preserved Vieux-Québec (Old Québec) is small and dense, steeped in four centuries of history and French tradition. Here are 17th- and 18th-century buildings, the ramparts that once protected the city, and numerous parks and monuments. The Québec government has completely restored many of the centuries-old buildings of Place Royale, one of the oldest districts on the continent. Because of its immaculate preservation as the only fortified city remaining in North America, UNESCO has designated Vieux-Québec a World Heritage Site.

Perched on a cliff above a narrow point in the St. Lawrence River, Québec City is the oldest municipality in Québec province. In the 17th century the first French explorers, fur trappers, and missionaries came here to establish the colony of New France. Today it still resembles a French provincial town in many ways; its family-oriented residents have strong ties to their past. An estimated 96% of the Québec City region's population of more than 650,000 are French-speaking.

In 1535 French explorer Jacques Cartier first came upon what the Algonquin people called "Kebec," meaning "where the river narrows." New France, however, was not actually founded in the vicinity of what is now Québec City until 1608, when another French explorer, Samuel de Champlain, recognized the military advantages of the location and set up a fort. On the banks of the St. Lawrence, on the spot now called Place Royale, this fort developed into an economic center for fur trade and shipbuilding. Twelve years later, Champlain realized the French colony's vulnerability to attacks from above and expanded its boundaries to the top of the cliff, where he built the fort Château St-Louis on the site of the present-day Château Frontenac.

During the early days of New France, the French and British fought for control of the region. In 1690, when an expedition led by Admiral Sir William Phipps arrived from England, Comte de Frontenac, New France's most illustrious governor, defied him with the statement, "Tell your lord that I will reply with the mouth of my cannons."

The French, preoccupied with scandals at the courts of Louis XV and Louis XVI, gave only grudging help to their possessions in the New World. The French colonists built walls and other military structures and had the strong defensive position on top of the cliff, but they still had to contend with Britain's naval supremacy. On September 13, 1759, the British army, led by General James Wolfe, scaled the colony's cliff and took the French troops led by General Louis-Joseph Montcalm by surprise. The British defeated the French in a 20-minute battle on the Plains of Abraham, and New France came under British rule.

The British brought their mastery of trade to the region. During the 18th century, Québec City's economy prospered because of the success of the fishing, fur-trading, shipbuilding, and timber industries. Wary of new invasions, the British continued to expand upon the fortifications left by the French. They built a wall encircling the city and a star-shape citadel, both of which mark the city's urban landscape today. The constitution of 1791 established Québec City as the capital of Lower Canada until the 1840 Act of Union united Upper and Lower Canada and made Montréal the capital. The city remained under British rule until 1867, when the Act of Confederation united several Canadian

Metropolitan Québec City

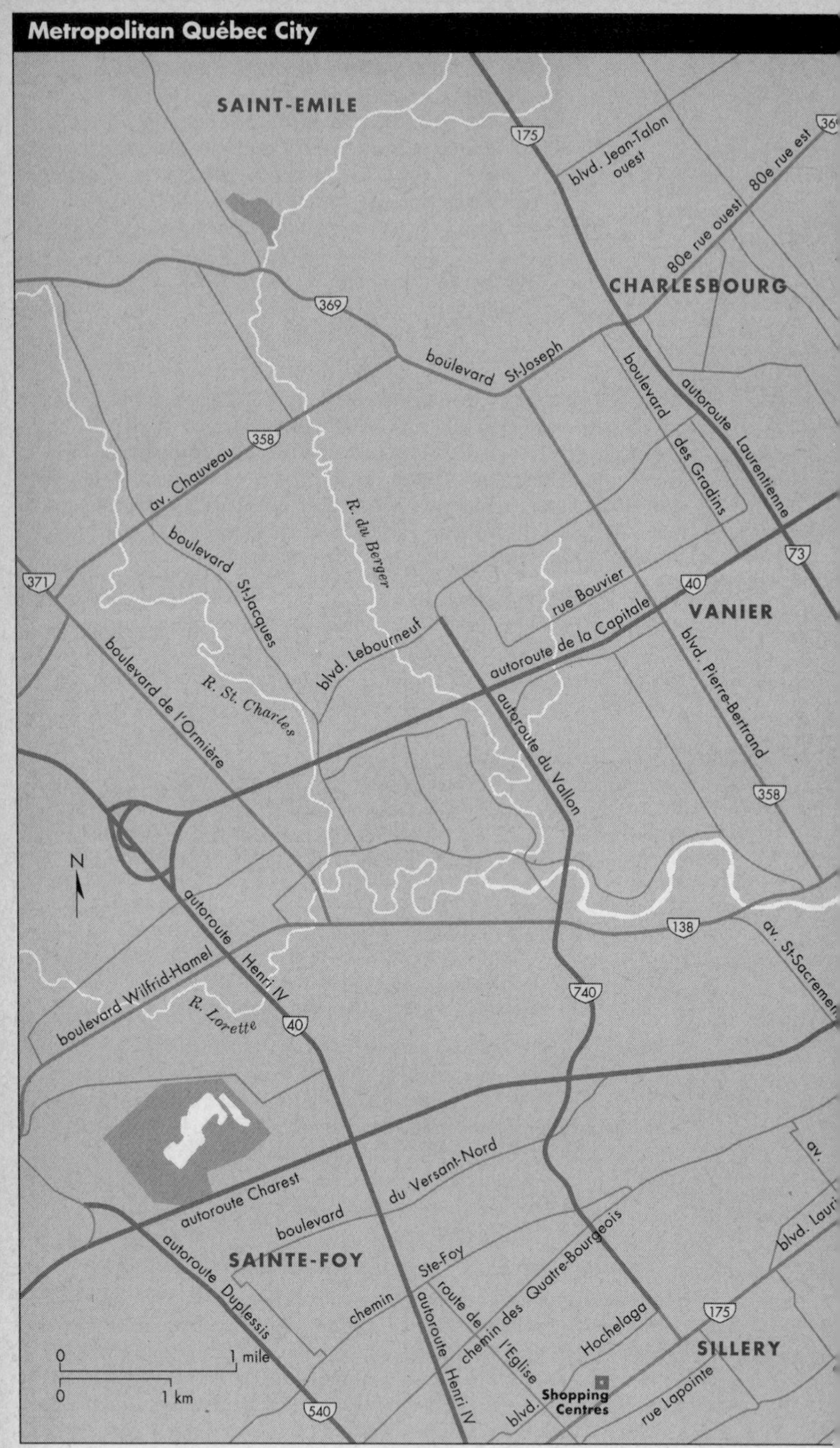
SAINT-EMILE
CHARLESBOURG
VANIER
SAINTE-FOY
SILLERY
blvd. Jean-Talon ouest
80e rue est
80e rue ouest
boulevard St-Joseph
boulevard des Gradins
autoroute Laurentienne
av. Chauveau
R. du Berger
boulevard St-Jacques
rue Bouvier
blvd. Lebourneuf
autoroute de la Capitale
blvd. Pierre-Bertrand
boulevard de l'Ormière
R. St. Charles
autoroute du Vallon
autoroute Henri IV
boulevard Wilfrid-Hamel
R. Lorette
av. St-Sacrement
autoroute Charest
boulevard du Versant-Nord
chemin Ste-Foy
route de l'Eglise
chemin des Quatre-Bourgeois
Hochelaga
autoroute Duplessis
blvd. Lauri
rue Lapointe
blvd.
Shopping Centres
175
369
358
371
40
73
138
740
540
0
1 mile
1 km
N

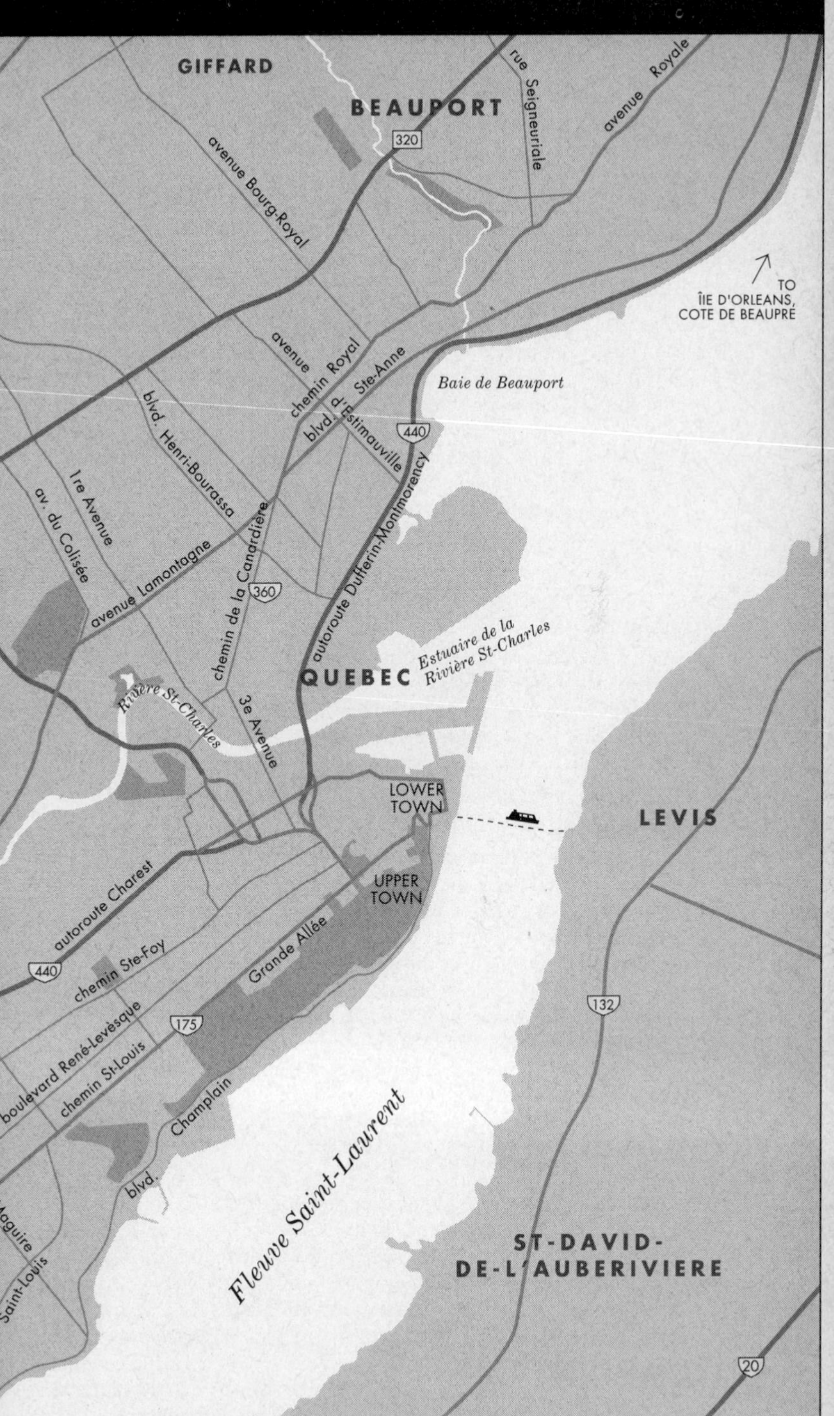

GIFFARD
BEAUPORT
320
rue Seigneuriale
avenue Royale
avenue Bourg-Royal
TO
ÎIE D'ORLEANS,
COTE DE BEAUPRÉ
avenue
chemin Royal
blvd. d'Estimauville
Ste-Anne
Baie de Beauport
440
blvd. Henri-Bourassa
1re Avenue
av. du Colisée
autoroute Dufferin-Montmorency
avenue Lamontagne
chemin de la Canardière
360
Estuaire de la
Rivière St-Charles
QUEBEC
Rivière St-Charles
3e Avenue
LOWER
TOWN
LEVIS
UPPER
TOWN
autoroute Charest
440
chemin Ste-Foy
Grande Allée
132
boulevard René-Levèsque
175
chemin St-Louis
Champlain
blvd.
Fleuve Saint-Laurent
Maguire
Saint-Louis
ST-DAVID-
DE-L'AUBERIVIERE
20

provinces (Québec, Ontario, New Brunswick, and Nova Scotia) and established Québec City as capital of the province of Québec.

In the mid-19th century, the economic center of eastern Canada shifted west from Québec City to Montréal and Toronto. Today, government is Québec City's main business: About 27,000 full- or part-time civil-service employees work and live in the area. Office complexes continue to spring up outside the older part of town; modern malls, convention centers, and imposing hotels now cater to a business clientele.

Pleasures and Pastimes

Dining

Gone are the days when Québec City dining consisted mostly of classic French and hearty Québécois cuisine, served in restaurants in the downtown core. Nowadays the city's finest eateries, found both inside and outside the city's walls, offer lighter contemporary fare, often with Asian or Italian as well as French and Québécois influences. You will still find fine French restaurants, though, and be able to sample French-Canadian cuisine, composed of robust, uncomplicated dishes that make use of the region's bounty of foods, including fowl and wild game (quail, caribou, venison), maple syrup, and various berries and nuts. Other specialties include *cretons* (pâtés), *tourtière* (meat pie), and *tarte au sucre* (maple-syrup pie).

Lodging

With more than 35 hotels within its walls and an abundance of family-run bed-and-breakfasts, Québec City has a range of lodging options. Landmark hotels stand as prominent as the city's most historic sites; modern high-rises outside the ramparts have spectacular views of the old city. Another choice is to immerse yourself in the city's historic charm by staying in an old-fashioned inn where no two rooms are alike.

Walking

Québec City is a wonderful place to wander on foot. From Parc Montmorency, you can see the Laurentian Mountains jutting majestically above the St. Lawrence River. Even more impressive vistas are revealed on a walk along the city walls or a climb to the city's highest point, Cap Diamant, near the Citadelle. It's possible to spend days investigating the narrow cobblestone streets of Vieux-Québec, visiting historic sites, or browsing for local arts and crafts in the boutiques of quartier Petit-Champlain. A stroll on the Promenade des Gouverneurs and the Plains of Abraham provides a view of the river as well as the Laurentian foothills and the Appalachian Mountains.

EXPLORING QUÉBEC CITY

Québec City's split-level landscape divides Upper Town on the cape from Lower Town, along the shores of the St. Lawrence. If you look out from the Terrasse Dufferin boardwalk in Upper Town, you will see the rooftops of Lower Town buildings directly below. Separating these two sections of the city is steep and precipitous rock, against which were built more than 25 *escaliers* (staircases). A *funiculaire* (funicular) climbs and descends the cliff between Terrasse Dufferin and the Maison Jolliet in Lower Town. There's plenty to see in the oldest sections of town, as well as in the modern city beyond the walls.

Numbers in the text correspond to numbers in the margin and on the Upper and Lower Towns (Haute-Ville, Basse-Ville), Outside the Walls, and Ile d'Orléans and Côte de Beaupré maps.

Great Itineraries

Whether you take a weekend or almost a week, there's enough history, scenery, and entertainment for even the most seasoned traveler. On a weekend or four-day trip, you can take in the historic sites of Vieux-Québec, walking along ancient streets and the boardwalk by the river before dining at some of the city's fine restaurants. A longer stay allows you to wander beyond the city proper.

IF YOU HAVE 2 DAYS

With only a couple of days, you should devote one day to Lower Town, where you will find the earliest site of French civilization in North America, and the second day to Upper Town, where more of the later British influence can be seen. On Day 1, stroll through the narrow streets of the Petit-Champlain, visiting the Maison Chevalier and browsing through the many handicraft boutiques. Moving on to Place Royale, you'll find the Église Notre-Dame-des-Victoires; in summer there's a wide variety of entertainment in the square. On Day 2, take the time to view the St. Lawrence River from Terrasse Dufferin and visit the impressive buildings of Upper Town, where 17th- and 18th-century religious and educational institutions predominate.

IF YOU HAVE 4 DAYS

A four-day trip allows you to wander farther afield, outside the walls of the Old Town. On Day 3, watch the pomp and ceremony of the changing of the guard at the Citadelle; roam the Plains of Abraham, site of the battle that decided the fate of New France; and tour the National Assembly, where the battles for power are still being waged. On Day 4, you can take a more in-depth look at the Musée du Québec or the Musé de la Civilisation. See the city from a different vantage point—aboard a horse-drawn calèche or from a walk atop the ramparts. In summer, do what the locals do—grab a seat on an outdoor *terrasse,* sip a cool drink, and watch the world go by.

IF YOU HAVE 6 DAYS

A trip this length gives you time to experience some of Quebec's scenic countryside. Follow the itinerary above for a four-day trip. On Day 5, you could spend more time exploring the Old Town. Or you could take historic avenue Royale (Route 360) east to the Basilica of Ste-Anne-de-Beaupré and Montmorency Falls, higher than Niagara. Afterward, you can cross the bridge to explore the farms and woodlands of Ile d'Orléans. On Day 6, do something you've never done before. In summer, you can take a boat cruise along the St. Lawrence or raft down the Jacques Cartier River. In winter, strap on skis and head to Mont Ste-Anne. Try ice canoeing on the St. Lawrence, dogsledding, or even ice climbing at the Montmorency Falls.

Upper Town

The most prominent buildings of Québec City's earliest European inhabitants, who set up political, educational, and religious institutions, stand here. Haute-Ville, or Upper Town, became the political capital of the colony of New France and, later, of British North America. Historic buildings with thick stone walls, large wood doors, glimmering copper roofs, and majestic steeples fill the heart of the city.

A Good Walk

Begin your walk where rue St-Louis meets rue du Fort at **Place d'Armes** ①, a large plaza bordered by government buildings. To your right is the colony's former treasury building, **Maison Maillou,** interesting for its 18th-century architecture. A little farther along, at 25 rue St-Louis, is Maison Kent, where the terms of the surrender of Québec to the British were signed in 1759. South of Place d'Armes stands Québec City's most celebrated landmark, **Château Frontenac** ②, an impressive green-turreted hotel on the site of what was once the administrative and military headquarters of New France. As you head to the boardwalk behind the Frontenac, notice the glorious bronze statue of Samuel de Champlain, standing where he built his residence.

Walk south along the boardwalk called the **Terrasse Dufferin** ③ for a panoramic view of the city and its surroundings. As you pass to the southern side of the Frontenac, you will come to a small park called **Jardin des Gouverneurs** ④. From the north side of the park, follow rue Haldimand and turn left on rue St-Louis; then make a right and follow rue du Parloir until it intersects with tiny rue Donnacona. Here you'll find the **Couvent des Ursulines** ⑤, a private school that houses a museum and has a lovely chapel next door.

On the nearby rue des Jardins, you'll see the **Holy Trinity Anglican Cathedral** ⑥, a dignified church with precious objects on display. Next come two buildings interesting for their Art Deco details: the **Hôtel Clarendon** ⑦, just east of the cathedral, on the corner of rue des Jardins and rue Ste-Anne, and, next door, the **Edifice Price** ⑧. Continue along rue Ste-Anne up to rue St-Stanislas and **Morrin College** ⑨, a building that started out as a prison and now houses the Literary and Historical Society library. Walk along rue St-Stanislas and turn left up rue Dauphine to the **Chapelle des Jésuites** ⑩ at the corner of rues Dauphine and d'Auteuil. Turn right on rue d'Auteuil and head down the hill to rue St-Jean and the entrance to the **Parc de l'Artillerie** ⑪, a complex of 20 military, industrial, and civilian buildings.

On your way out of Artillery Park, turn left, away from the walls, and walk along rue St-Jean, one of Québec City's most colorful thoroughfares; turn left on rue Collins. The cluster of stone buildings at the end of the street is the **Monastère des Augustines de l'Hôtel-Dieu de Québec** ⑫, which can be toured. Turn right along rue Charlevoix, then left on rue Hamel to rue des Remparts. To the right, on rue des Remparts between rues Hamel and St-Flavien, is the **Maison Montcalm** ⑬, the former home of General Montcalm.

Continue along rue des Remparts and then turn right on rue Ste-Famille. When you reach côte de la Fabrique, you will find the iron entrance gates of the **Séminaire du Québec** ⑭. Head north across the courtyard to the **Musée de l'Amérique Française** ⑮. Next, you can visit the seminary's Chapelle Extérieure, at the seminary's west entrance.

Nearby, at the corner of rue Ste-Famille and rue Buade you'll see the historic **Basilique Notre-Dame-de-Québec** ⑯, which has an ornate interior. Turn left on rue Buade; then cross the street halfway down the block and wander through the outdoor art gallery of **rue du Trésor** ⑰. At the end of the alley, turn left on rue Ste-Anne and wind up your walk (and rest your feet) with a 30-minute recap of the six sieges of Québec City at the **Musée du Fort** ⑱.

TIMING

Plan on spending at least a day visiting the sites and museums in Upper Town. Lunchtime should find you around Parc de l'Artillerie and rue St-Jean, where there is a good selection of restaurants. Those who prefer a leisurely pace could take two days, stopping to watch street performers and enjoy long lunches. May through October are the best months for walking, July and August being the busiest.

Sights to See

16 **Basilique Notre-Dame-de-Québec.** This basilica has the oldest parish in North America, dating from 1647. It's been rebuilt three times: in the early 1700s, when François de Montmorency Laval was the first bishop; in 1759, after cannons at Lévis fired upon it during the siege of Québec; and in 1922, after a fire. The basilica's somberly ornate interior includes a canopy dais over the episcopal throne, a ceiling of clouds decorated with gold leaf, richly colored stained-glass windows, and a chancel lamp that was a gift of Louis XIV. The large and famous crypt was Québec City's first cemetery; more than 900 people are interred here, including 20 bishops and four governors of New France. Samuel de Champlain is believed to be buried near the basilica: Archaeologists have searched for his tomb since 1950. In summer the indoor Act of Faith sound-and-light show uses the basilica as a backdrop to tell the history of the city and the basilica. ✉ *16 rue Buade,* ☎ *418/692–2533.* 🎫 *Basilica free, sound-and-light show $7.* ⏲ *Oct.–May, daily 7:30–4:30; June–Sept., daily 7:30–3, followed by sound-and-light show.*

Centre Marie-de-l'Incarnation. Next to the ☞ **Musée des Ursulines** is this bookstore with an exhibit on the life of the Ursulines' first superior, who came from France and cofounded the convent. ✉ *10 rue Donnacona,* ☎ *418/ 694–0413.* 🎫 *Free.* ⏲ *Feb.–Nov., Tues.–Sat. 10–11:30 and 1:30–4:30, Sun. 1:30–4:30.*

10 **Chapelle des Jésuites** (Jesuits' Chapel). Built in 1820 from plans by architect François Baillairgé, the chapel and its sculptures and paintings are considered one of the monuments of Québec art of the period. Sculptor Pierre-Noël Levasseur contributed the delicately carved high altar and wooden statues of the Blessed Virgin and St. Joseph. ✉ *20 rue Dauphine,* ☎ *418/694–9616.* 🎫 *Free.* ⏲ *Weekdays 11–1:30.*

Chapelle des Ursulines (Ursuline Chapel). On the grounds of the ☞ **Couvent des Ursulines** stands a little chapel where French general Louis-Joseph Montcalm was buried after he died in the 1759 battle. The exterior was rebuilt in 1902, but the interior contains the original chapel, which took sculptor Pierre-Noël Levasseur from 1726 to 1736 to complete. The votive lamp was lit in 1717 and has never been extinguished. ✉ *12 rue Donnacona.* 🎫 *Free.* ⏲ *May–Oct., Tues.–Sat. 10–11:30 and 1:30–4:30, Sun. 1:30–4:30.*

★ 2 **Château Frontenac.** Québec City's most celebrated landmark, this imposing green-turreted castle with its copper roof stands on the site of what was the administrative and military headquarters of New France. It owes its name to the Comte de Frontenac, governor of the French colony between 1672 and 1698. Looking at the magnificence of the château's location, you can see why Frontenac said, "For me, there is no site more beautiful nor more grandiose than that of Québec City." Samuel de Champlain, who founded Québec City in 1608, was responsible for Château St-Louis, the first structure to appear on the site of the Frontenac; it was built between 1620 and 1624 as a residence for colonial governors. In 1784, Château Haldimand was constructed here, but it was demolished in 1892 to make way for Château Frontenac (☞ Lodging, *below*). The latter was built as a hotel in 1893, and it was considered to be remarkably luxurious at that time: Guest rooms contained fireplaces, bathrooms, and marble fixtures, and a special commissioner purchased antiques for the establishment. The hotel was designed by New York architect Bruce Price, who also worked on Québec City's Gare du Palais (rail station) and other Canadian landmarks, such as Montréal's Windsor Station. The Frontenac was completed in 1925 with the addition of a 20-story central tower. Owned by Canadian Pacific Hotels, it has accumulated a star-studded guest roster, including

Antiques district, **28**
Basilique Notre-Dame-de-Québec, **16**
Chapelle des Jésuites, **10**
Château Frontenac, **2**
Couvent des Ursulines, **5**
Edifice Price, **8**
Eglise Notre-Dame-des-Victoires, **24**
Holy Trinity Anglican Cathedral, **6**
Hôtel Clarendon, **7**
L'Ilot des Palais, **29**
Jardin des Gouverneurs, **4**
Maison Chevalier, **22**
Maison Louis-Jolliet, **19**
Maison Montcalm, **13**
Monastère des Augustines de l'Hôtel-Dieu de Québec, **12**
Morrin College, **9**
Musée de la Civilisation, **26**
Musée de l'Amérique Française, **15**
Musée du Fort, **18**
Parc de l'Artillerie, **11**
Place d'Armes, **1**
Place de Paris, **25**
Place Royale, **23**
Rue du Petit-Champlain, **21**
Rue du Trésor, **17**
Séminaire du Québec, **14**
Terrasse Dufferin, **3**
Verrerie La Mailloche, **20**
Vieux-Port de Québec, **27**

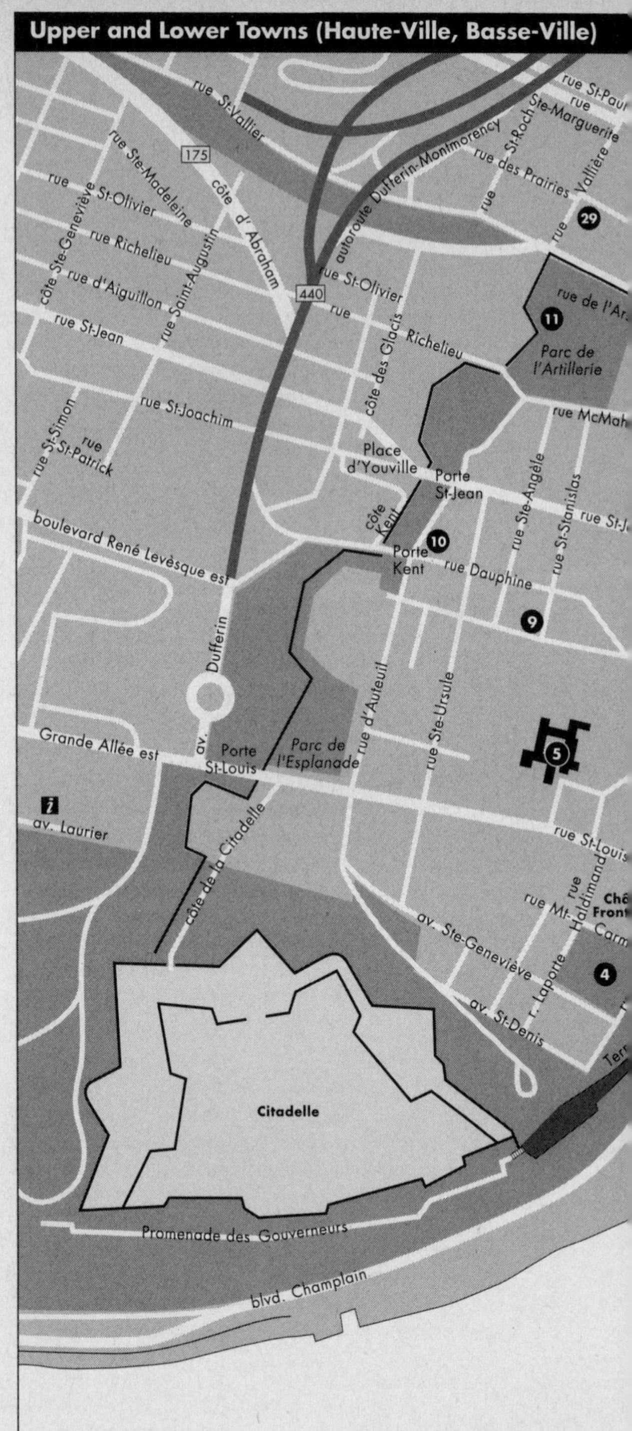

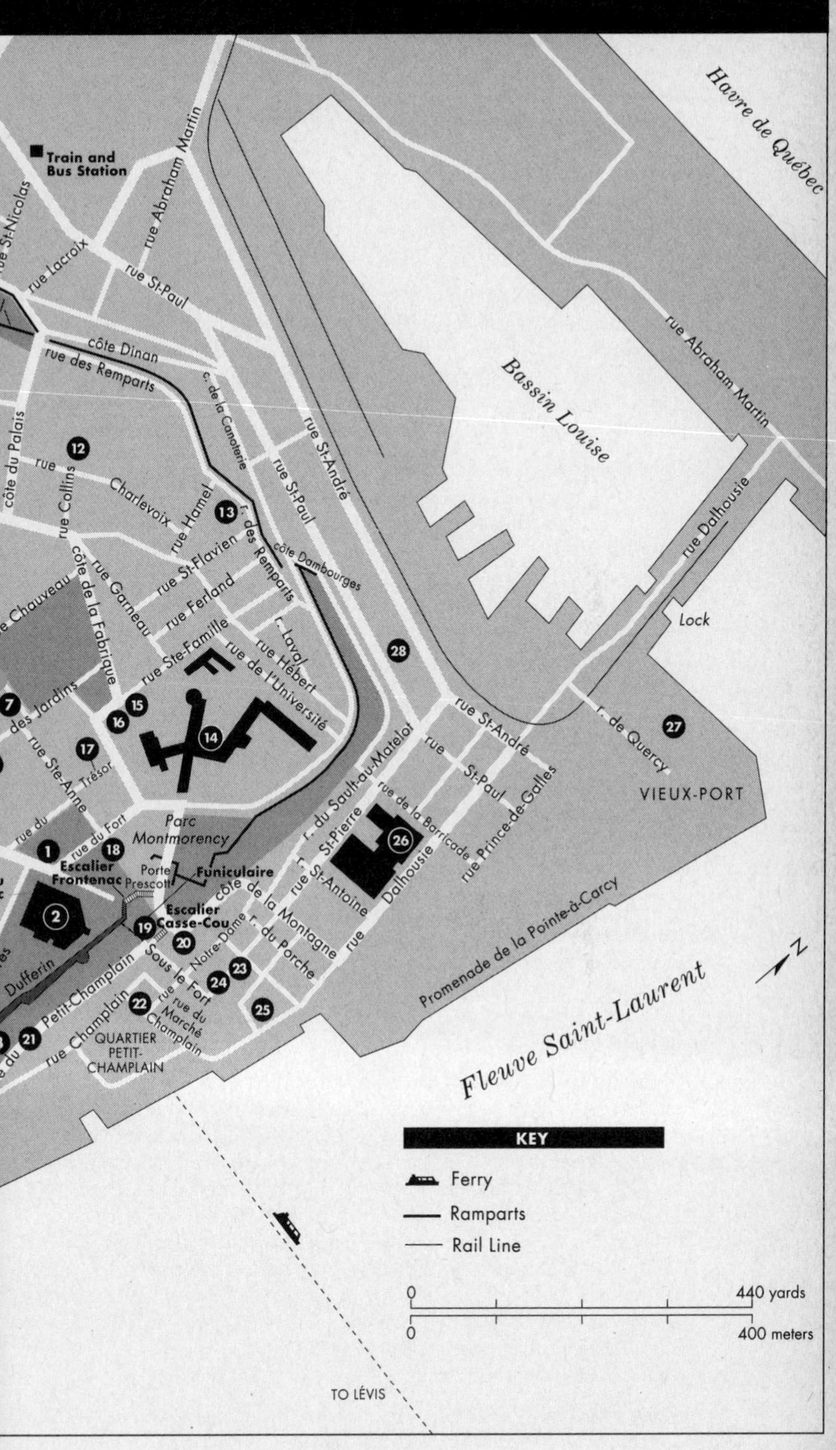

Havre de Québec
Train and Bus Station
rue Abraham Martin
rue St-Nicolas
rue Lacroix
rue St-Paul
côte Dinan
rue des Remparts
c. de la Canoterie
rue St-André
rue St-Paul
Bassin Louise
rue Abraham Martin
rue Dalhousie
Lock
côte du Palais
rue Charlevoix
rue Collins
rue Hamel
r. des Remparts
côte Dambourges
rue St-Flavien
rue Ferland
rue Chauveau
côte de la Fabrique
rue Garneau
rue Ste-Famille
r. Laval
rue Hébert
rue de l'Université
des Jardins
rue Ste-Anne
Trésor
rue St-André
r. de Quercy
VIEUX-PORT
rue St-Paul
rue Prince-de-Galles
r. du Sault-au-Matelot
rue de la Barricade
rue St-Pierre
rue Dalhousie
rue St-Antoine
Parc Montmorency
rue du Fort
Escalier Frontenac
Porte Prescott
Funiculaire
côte de la Montagne
Escalier Casse-Cou
r. du Porche
Notre-Dame
Sous le Fort
Dufferin
rue du Petit-Champlain
rue Champlain
rue du Marché Champlain
QUARTIER PETIT-CHAMPLAIN
Promenade de la Pointe-à-Carcy
Fleuve Saint-Laurent
N
KEY
Ferry
Ramparts
Rail Line
0
440 yards
0
400 meters
TO LÉVIS

Queen Elizabeth and Ronald Reagan as well as Franklin Roosevelt and Winston Churchill, who convened here in 1943 and 1944 for two wartime conferences. ✉ *1 rue des Carrières,* ☎ *418/692–3861.*

★ ❺ **Couvent des Ursulines** (Ursuline Convent). The site of North America's oldest teaching institution for girls, still a private school, was founded in 1639 by two French nuns. The convent has many of its original walls still intact. On its property are the ☞ **Musée des Ursulines** and the ☞ **Chapelle des Ursulines,** which you may visit. Next door is an interesting bookstore, the ☞ **Centre Marie-de-l'Incarnation.** ✉*18 rue Donnacona.*

★ ❽ **Edifice Price** (Price Building). The city's first skyscraper, a 15-story Art Deco structure, was built in 1929 and served as headquarters of the Price Brothers Company, the lumber firm founded in Canada by Sir William Price. Don't miss the interior: Exquisite copper plaques depict scenes of the company's early pulp and paper activities, while the two maple-wood elevators are '30s classics. ✉ *65 rue Ste-Anne.*

❻ **Holy Trinity Anglican Cathedral.** This stone church dates from 1804 and was one of the first Anglican cathedrals built outside the British Isles. Its simple, dignified facade is reminiscent of London's St. Martin-in-the-Fields. The cathedral's land was originally given to the Recollet fathers (Franciscan monks from France) in 1681 by the king of France for a church and monastery. When Québec came under British rule, the Recollets made the church available to the Anglicans for services. Later, King George III of England ordered construction of the present cathedral, with an area set aside for members of the royal family. A portion of the north balcony still remains exclusively for the use of the reigning sovereign or her representative. The church houses precious objects donated by George III; wood for the oak benches was imported from the Royal Forest at Windsor. The cathedral's impressive rear organ has more than 2,500 pipes. ✉ *31 rue des Jardins,* ☎ *418/692–2193.* 🎫 *Free.* ⏲ *May–June, daily 9–5; July–Aug., daily 9–9; Sept.–Oct., weekdays 10–4; Nov.–Apr., services only; Sun. services in English 8:30 and 11* AM, *and in French 9:30* AM.

❼ **Hôtel Clarendon.** One of Québec City's finest Art Deco structures is the Clarendon, Québec's oldest hotel (☞ Lodging, *below*). Although the Clarendon dates from 1866, it was reconstructed in its current style—with geometric patterns of stone and wrought iron decorating its interior—in 1930. ✉ *57 rue Ste-Anne, at rue des Jardins,* ☎ *418/692–2480.*

❹ **Jardin des Gouverneurs** (Governors' Park). This small park on the southern side of the Château Frontenac is home to the **Wolfe-Montcalm Monument,** a 50-ft obelisk that is unique because it pays tribute to both a winning (English) and a losing (French) general. The monument recalls the 1759 battle on the Plains of Abraham, which ended French rule of New France. British general James Wolfe lived only long enough to hear of his victory; French general Louis-Joseph Montcalm died shortly after Wolfe with the knowledge that the city was lost. During the French regime, the public area served as a garden for the governors who resided in Château St-Louis. On the south side of the park is **avenue Ste-Geneviève,** lined with well-preserved Victorian houses dating from 1850 to 1900 that have been converted to old-fashioned inns.

Maison Maillou. The colony's former treasury building typifies the architecture of New France with its sharply slanted roof, dormer windows, concrete chimneys, shutters with iron hinges, and limestone walls. Built between 1736 and 1753, it stands at the end of ☞ **rue du Trésor.** Maison Maillou now houses the Québec City Chamber of Commerce and is not open for tours. ✉ *17 rue St-Louis.*

13 **Maison Montcalm.** This was the home of French general Louis-Joseph Montcalm from 1758 until the capitulation of New France. A plaque dedicated to the general is on the right side of the house. ⊠ *Rue des Remparts between rues Hamel and St-Flavien. Closed to public.*

12 **Monastère des Augustines de l'Hôtel-Dieu de Québec** (Augustine Monastery). Augustine nuns arrived from Dieppe, France, in 1639 with a mission to care for the sick in the new colony; they established the first hospital north of Mexico, the **Hôtel-Dieu,** the large building west of the monastery. The **Musée des Augustines** (Augustine Museum) is in hospital-like quarters with large sterile corridors leading into a ward that has a small exhibit of antique medical instruments, such as a pill-making device from the 17th century. Upon request the Augustines also offer guided tours of the **chapel** (1800) and the cellars used by the nuns as a shelter, beginning in 1659, during bombardments by the British. ⊠ *32 rue Charlevoix,* ☎ *418/692–2492.* 🎟 *Guided tour $2.* ⏲ *Tues.–Sat. 9:30–noon and 1:30–5, Sun. 1:30–5.*

★ 9 **Morrin College.** This stately graystone building was once Québec City's first prison (the cells can still be seen in the basement), where wrong-doers were hanged outside the front door. In 1868, it was turned into one of the city's early private schools, Morrin College. The **Literary and Historical Society library** has been on the site since then. Its superb collection includes some of the earliest books printed in North America, and the librarian's desk once belonged to Sir Georges-Étienne Cartier, one of Canada's fathers of Confederation. A statue of General Wolfe, on the second-floor balcony that wraps around the interior of the library, dates from 1779. The society, founded in 1824, is the oldest of its kind in North America and a forerunner to Canada's National Archives. ⊠ *44 rue St-Stanislas,* ☎ *418/694–9147.* 🎟 *Free.* ⏲ *Weekdays 9:30–4:30, Sat. 10–4.*

15 **Musée de l'Amérique Française.** Housed in a former student residence of the Québec Seminary–Laval University (☞ **Séminaire du Québec**), this museum focuses on the history of the French presence in North America. There are more than 400 landscape and still-life paintings dating to the 15th century, rare Canadian money from colonial times, and scientific instruments acquired for the purposes of research and teaching. The museum uses historical documents and movies to tell the story as well. A former chapel has been renovated and is used for exhibits, conferences, and cultural activities. ⊠ *9 rue de l'Université,* ☎ *418/692–2843.* 🎟 *$4; free Tues. Sept.–June 23.* ⏲ *Tues., Thurs., Fri. 9:30–4:30, Wed. 9:30–6:30, weekends 10–4.*

Musée des Ursulines (Ursuline Museum). Within the walls of the ☞ **Couvent des Ursulines** is the former residence of one of the convent's founders, Madame de la Peltrie. The museum provides an informative perspective on 120 years of the Ursulines' life under the French regime, from 1639 to 1759. It took an Ursuline nun nine years of training to attain the level of a professional embroiderer; the museum contains magnificent pieces of ornate embroidery, such as altar frontals with gold and silver threads intertwined with precious jewels. ⊠ *12 rue Donnacona,* ☎ *418/694–0694.* 🎟 *$3.* ⏲ *May–Oct., Tues.–Sat. 10–noon and 1–5, Sun. 12:30–5.*

NEED A BREAK? The brick-wall **Bistro Taste-Vin** (⊠ 32 rue St-Louis, ☎ 418/692–4191), on the corner of rue des Jardins and rue St-Louis, is a good place to sample delicious salads, pastries, and desserts.

18 **Musée du Fort** (Fort Museum). This museum's sole exhibit is a sound-and-light show that reenacts the area's important battles, including the

Battle of the Plains of Abraham and the 1775 attack by American generals Arnold and Montgomery. ⊠ *10 rue Ste-Anne,* ☎ *418/692–1759.* 🎫 *$6.25.* ⏲ *June–Aug., daily 10–6; Apr.–May and Sept., daily 10–5; Oct.–Jan., by reservation; Feb.–Mar., Thurs.–Sun. noon–4.*

★ 11 **Parc de l'Artillerie** (Artillery Park). This national historic park is a complex of 20 military, industrial, and civilian buildings that were situated to guard the St. Charles River and the Old Port. Its earliest buildings served as headquarters for the French garrison and were taken over in 1759 by the British Royal Artillery soldiers. The defense complex was used as a fortress, barracks, and cartridge factory during the American siege of Québec in 1775 and 1776. The area served as an industrial complex providing ammunition for the Canadian army from 1879 until 1964. One of the three buildings open is a former **powder magazine,** which in 1903 became a shell foundry. The building houses a detailed model of Québec City in 1808, rendered by two surveyors in the office of the Royal Engineers Corps. Sent to Britain in 1813, it was intended to show officials the strategic importance of Québec so that more money would be provided to expand the city's fortifications. The model details the city's buildings, streets, and military structures. From April through October, the powder magazine is open daily 10–5; admission is $3. The **Dauphin Redoubt,** named in honor of the son of Louis XIV (the heir apparent), was constructed from 1712 to 1748. It served as a barracks for the French garrison until 1760, when it became an officers' mess for the Royal Artillery Regiment. It's open late June–early September, daily 10–5. The **Officers' Quarters,** a dwelling for Royal Artillery officers until 1871 when the British army departed, houses an exhibit on military life during the British regime. The Officers' Quarters are open late June–early September, daily 10–5. ⊠ *2 rue d'Auteuil,* ☎ *418/648–4205.*

1 **Place d'Armes.** For centuries, this square atop a cliff has been a gathering place for parades and military events. Upper Town's most central location, the plaza is bordered by government buildings; at its west side is the majestic **Ancien Palais de Justice** (Old Courthouse), a Renaissance-style building from 1887. The plaza is on land that was occupied by a church and convent of the Recollet missionaries (Franciscan monks), who in 1615 were the first order of priests to arrive in New France. The Gothic-style **fountain** at the center of Place d'Armes pays tribute to their arrival. ⊠ *Rue St-Louis and rue du Fort.*

17 **Rue du Trésor.** The road that colonists took on their way to pay rent to the king's officials is now a narrow alley where colorful prints, paintings, and other artworks are on display. You won't necessarily find masterpieces, but this walkway is a good stop for a souvenir sketch or two. In summer, activity on this street and nearby rue Ste-Anne, lined with eateries and boutiques, starts early in the morning and continues until late at night. Stores stay open, artists paint, and street musicians perform as long as there is an audience, even if it's one o'clock in the morning. At 8 rue du Trésor is the **Québec Experience** (☎ 418/694–4000), a multimedia sound-and-light show that traces Québec's history from the first explorers until modern days; cost is $6.75.

14 **Séminaire du Québec.** Behind these gates lies a tranquil courtyard surrounded by austere stone buildings with rising steeples; these structures have housed classrooms and student residences since 1663. Québec Seminary was founded by François de Montmorency Laval, the first bishop of New France, to train priests in the new colony. In 1852 the seminary became Université Laval, the first Catholic university in North America. In 1946 the university moved to a larger campus in suburban Ste-Foy. Today priests live on the premises, and Laval's architec-

ture school occupies part of the building. The **Musée du Séminaire** has tours of the seminary in summer. The small Roman-style chapel, **Chapelle Extérieure** (Outer Chapel), at the west entrance of Québec Seminary, was built in 1888 after fire destroyed the first chapel, which dated from 1750. ✉ *1 côte de la Fabrique,* ☎ *418/692–3981.*

❸ **Terrasse Dufferin.** This wide boardwalk with an intricate wrought-iron guardrail has a panoramic view of the St. Lawrence River, the town of Lévis on the opposite shore, Ile d'Orléans, and the Laurentian Mountains. It was named for Lord Dufferin, governor of Canada between 1872 and 1878, who had this walkway constructed in 1878. At its western end begins the **Promenade des Gouverneurs**, which skirts the cliff and leads up to Québec's highest point, Cap Diamant, and also to the Citadelle (☞ Outside the Walls, *below*).

Lower Town

New France first began to flourish in the streets of the Basse-Ville, or Lower Town, along the banks of the St. Lawrence River. These streets became the colony's economic crossroads, where furs were traded, ships came in, and merchants established their residences. Despite the status of Lower Town as the oldest neighborhood in North America, its narrow and time-worn thoroughfares have a new and polished look. In the 1960s, after a century of decay as the commercial boom moved west and left the area abandoned, the Québec government committed millions of dollars to restore the district to the way it had been during the days of New France. Today modern boutiques, restaurants, galleries, and shops catering to visitors occupy the former warehouses and residences.

A Good Walk

Begin this walk on the northern tip of rue du Petit-Champlain at **Maison Louis-Jolliet** ⑲ at the foot of the **Escalier Casse-Cou.** Across the street is the **Verrerie La Mailloche** ⑳, where master glassblowers turn molten glass into contemporary works of art. Heading south on **rue du Petit-Champlain** ㉑, the city's oldest street, you'll notice the cliff on the right that borders this narrow thoroughfare, with Upper Town on the heights above. At the point where rue du Petit-Champlain intersects with boulevard Champlain, make a U-turn to head back north on rue Champlain. One block farther, at the corner of rue du Marché-Champlain, you'll find **Maison Chevalier** ㉒, a stone house in the style of urban New France. Walk east to rue Notre-Dame, which leads directly to **Place Royale** ㉓, formerly the heart of New France. The small stone church at the south side of Place Royale is the **Église Notre-Dame-des-Victoires** ㉔, the oldest church in Québec.

On the east side of Place Royale, take rue de la Place, which leads to an open square, **Place de Paris** ㉕. You may want to stop at **Explore,** a sound-and-light show on rue Dalhousie. Continue north on rue Dalhousie until you come to the **Musée de la Civilisation** ㉖, devoted to Québécois culture and civilization. Head east toward the river to the **Vieux-Port de Québec** ㉗, at one time the busiest on the continent. The breezes from the St. Lawrence provide a cool reprieve on a hot summer's day, and you can browse through a farmer's market here. You are now in the ideal spot to explore Québec City's **antiques district** ㉘.

In summer, walk west along rue St-Paul, past the train station built in 1915 in the style of the castles in France's Loire Valley, and turn left on rue Vallière to **L'Îlot des Palais** ㉙, an archaeological museum that has the remnants of the first two palaces of the French colonial intendants (administrators) and a unique dig.

TIMING

This is a good day of sightseeing. A morning stroll will take you to two of the city's most famous squares, Place Royale and Place de Paris. You can see the city from the Lévis ferry or pause for lunch before touring the Musée de la Civilisation and the antiques district. After browsing along rue St-Paul, explore L'Îlot des Palais.

Sights to See

28 **Antiques district.** Antiques shops cluster along rue St-Pierre and rue St-Paul. Rue St-Paul was once part of a business district where warehouses, stores, and businesses abounded. After World War I, shipping and commercial activities plummeted; low rents attracted antiques dealers. Today numerous cafés, restaurants, and art galleries have turned this area into one of the town's more fashionable sections.

24 **Église Notre-Dame-des-Victoires** (Our Lady of Victory Church). The oldest church in Québec was built on the site of Samuel de Champlain's first residence, which also served as a fort and trading post. The church was built in 1688 and was restored twice. Its name comes from two French victories against the British: one in 1690 against Admiral William Phipps and another in 1711 against Sir Hovendon Walker. The interior contains copies of paintings by such European masters as Van Dyck, Rubens, and Boyermans; its altar resembles the shape of a fort. A scale model suspended from the ceiling represents *Le Brezé,* the boat that transported French soldiers to New France in 1664. The side chapel is dedicated to Ste-Geneviève, the patron saint of Paris. ✉ *Pl. Royale,* ☎ *418/692–1650.* 🎫 *Free.* ⏲ *Mid-May–mid-Oct., Sun.–Fri. 9–4:30, Sat. 9–4, except during Mass (Sun. at 9, 10, and noon; Sat. at 7* PM*), marriages, and funerals; mid-Oct.–mid-May, daily 9–4:30, except during Mass, marriages, and funerals.*

Escalier Casse-Cou. The steepness of the city's first iron stairway, an ambitious 1893 design by city architect and engineer Charles Baillairgé, is ample evidence of how it got its name: Breakneck Steps. The steps were built on the site of the original 17th-century stairway that linked the Upper Town and Lower Town during the French regime. Today shops, quaint boutiques, and restaurants are at various levels.

Explore. This 30-minute sound-and-light show uses high-tech visual art to re-create the story of the founding of the city. You can sail up the St. Lawrence River with Jacques Cartier and Samuel de Champlain to Québec and witness their first encounter with the area's native people. ✉ *63 rue Dalhousie,* ☎ *418/692–2063 or 418/692–1759.* 🎫 *$5.50.* ⏲ *June–Aug., daily 11–5; Sept.–May, by reservation only.*

29 **L'Ilot des Palais.** More than 300 years of history have been laid bare at this archaeological museum on the site of the first two palaces of New France's colonial intendants. The first palace, erected as a brewery by Jean Talon in 1669, was turned into the intendant's residence in 1685 and destroyed by fire in 1713. In 1716, a second palace was built facing the first. It was later turned into a modern brewery, but the basement vaults remain. On the site of the first palace, the dig that lasted 10 years has been conserved and turned into a unique archaeological display. ✉ *8 rue Vallière,* ☎ *418/691–6092.* 🎫 *Free.* ⏲ *May–June 23 and Labor Day–Oct., Tues.–Sun. 10–5; June 24–Labor Day, daily 10–5.*

OFF THE BEATEN PATH

LÉVIS–QUÉBEC FERRY –En route to the opposite shore of the St. Lawrence River, you get a striking view of Québec City's skyline, with the Château Frontenac and the Québec Seminary high atop the cliff. The view is even more impressive at night. *E Rue Dalhousie, 1 block south of Place* *de Paris,* ☎ *418/644-3704.* ⊠ *$1.25.* ⊙ *See Getting Around in Québec City A to Z, below, for hrs.*

22 **Maison Chevalier.** This old stone house was built in 1752 for shipowner Jean-Baptiste Chevalier; the house's style, of classic French inspiration, clearly reflects the urban architecture of New France. The fire walls, chimneys, vaulted cellars, and original wood beams and stone fireplaces are noteworthy. ⊠ *60 rue du Marché-Champlain,* ☎ *418/643–2158.* ⊠ *Free.* ⊙ *May 6–June 22 and Sept. 8–Oct., Tues.–Sun. 10–6; June 23–Sept. 7, daily 10–6; Nov.–May 5, weekends 10–5.*

19 **Maison Louis-Jolliet.** Built in 1683, this house is the lower station of the funicular and was used by the first settlers of New France as a base for further westward explorations. A monument commemorating Louis Jolliet's discovery of the Mississippi River in 1672 stands in the park next to the house. At the north side of the house is the ☞ Escalier Casse-Cou. ⊠ *16 rue du Petit-Champlain.*

26 **Musée de la Civilisation** (Museum of Civilization). Wedged into the foot of the cliff, this spacious museum with a striking limestone-and-glass facade has been artfully designed by architect Moshe Safdie to blend into the landscape. Its campanile echoes the shape of church steeples throughout the city. The museum has innovative exhibits devoted to aspects of Québec's culture. It tells the story of how the first settlers lived, and how they survived such harsh winters. It illustrates to what extent the Roman Catholic Church dominated the people and explains the evolution of Québec nationalism. Several of the shows, with their imaginative use of artwork, video screens, computers, and sound, will appeal to both adults and children. The museum's thematic, interactive approach also extends to exhibits of an international nature. ⊠ *85 rue Dalhousie,* ☎ *418/643–2158.* ⊠ *$7; free Tues. in winter.* ⊙ *June 24–Aug., daily 10–7; Sept.–June 23, Tues.–Sun. 10–5.*

25 **Place de Paris.** This square, a newcomer (1987) to these historic quarters, is dominated by a black-and-white geometric sculpture, *Dialogue avec l'Histoire* (*Dialogue with History*), a gift from France positioned on the site where the first French settlers landed. ⊠ *Rue Dalhousie.*

NEED A BREAK?

Café du Monde (⊠ 57 rue Dalhousie, ☎ 418/692–4455), with an impressive view of the St. Lawrence River, specializes in brunch on Saturday and Sunday. Omelets, sausages, waffles with maple syrup, and *moules et frites* (mussels with french fries) are popular.

23 **Place Royale.** The cobblestone square is encircled by the former homes of wealthy merchants, which have steep Normandy-style roofs, dormer windows, and several chimneys. Until 1686 the area was called Place du Marché, but its name was changed when a bust of Louis XIV was erected at its center. During the late 1600s and early 1700s, when Place Royale was continually under threat of attacks from the British, the colonists progressively moved to higher and safer quarters atop the cliff in Upper Town. Yet after the French colony fell to British rule in 1759, Place Royale flourished again with shipbuilding, logging, fishing, and fur trading. An **information center** (⊠ 215 Marche Finlay, ☎ 418/646–3167) about the square is open June 3–September 29.

21 **Rue du Petit-Champlain.** The oldest street in the city was the main street of a former harbor village, with trading posts and the homes of rich merchants. Today it has pleasant boutiques and cafés. Natural-fiber weaving, Inuit carvings, hand-painted silks, and enameled copper crafts are some of the local specialties that are good buys here.

⑳ **Verrerie La Mailloche.** The glassblowing techniques used in this combination workshop, boutique, and museum are as old as Ancient Egypt, but the results are contemporary. In the workshop, master glassblower Jean Vallières turns 1092°C (2000°F) molten glass into works of art and answers questions. Examples of his work have been presented by the Canadian government to visiting dignitaries such as Queen Elizabeth and former president Ronald Reagan. ✉ *58 rue Sous-le-Fort,* ☎ *418/694–0445.* *Free.* *Workshop June–Oct., Wed.–Sun. 10–4:30; Nov.–June, weekdays 10–4:30. Boutique regular store hrs in winter, daily 9* AM*–10* PM *in summer.*

㉗ **Vieux-Port de Québec** (Old Port of Québec). Today this historic 72-acre area encompasses several parks. The old harbor dates from the 17th century, when ships first arrived from Europe bringing supplies and settlers to the new colony. At one time this port was among the busiest on the continent: Between 1797 and 1897, Québec shipyards turned out more than 2,500 ships, many of which passed the 1,000-ton mark. The port saw a rapid decline after steel replaced wood and the channel to Montréal was deepened to allow larger boats to reach a good port upstream. You can stroll along the riverside promenade, where merchant and cruise ships are docked. At the port's northern end, where the St. Charles meets the St. Lawrence, a lock protects the marina in the Louise Basin from the generous Atlantic tides that reach even this far up the St. Lawrence. In the northwest section of the port, an exhibition center, **Port de Québec in the 19th Century** (✉ 100 rue St-André, ☎ 418/648–3300), presents the history of the port in relation to the lumber trade and shipbuilding. Admission to the center is $2.75; it is open May–Labor Day, daily 10–5; Labor Day–Thanksgiving, noon–4; Thanksgiving–April, by reservation only. At the port's northwestern tip is the **Marché du Vieux-Port** (Old Port Market), where farmers sell their fresh produce. The market is open May–October, daily 8–8.

Outside the Walls

In the 20th century, Québec City grew into a modern metropolis outside the confines of the city walls. Beyond the walls lies a great deal of the city's military history, in the form of its fortifications and battlements, as well as a number of museums and other attractions.

A Good Walk

Start close to Porte St-Louis (St-Louis Gate) at the **Parc de l'Esplanade** ㉚, the site of a former military parade ground. From the powder magazine in the park, head south on côte de la Citadelle, which leads directly to **La Citadelle** ㉛, a historic fortified base. Retrace your steps down côte de la Citadelle to Grande Allée. Continue west until you come to the **Parliament Buildings** ㉜, which mark Parliament Hill, headquarters of the provincial government. Across the street, in the modern concrete building, are the offices of Quebec's premier. Farther along Grande Allée is the Manège Militaire, a turreted armory built in 1888 that is still a drill hall for the 22nd Regiment.

Continue along **Grande Allée** ㉝, Québec City's version of the Champs-Elysées, with its cafés, clubs, and restaurants. If you turn left on Place Montcalm, you'll be facing the **Montcalm Monument** ㉞. Continue south on Place Montcalm to the historic and scenic **Parc des Champs-de-Bataille** ㉟. Within the park are the **Plains of Abraham** ㊱, site of the famous 1759 battle that decided the fate of New France.

Take avenue Laurier, which runs parallel to the park, a block west until you come to a neatly tended garden called **Parc Jeanne d'Arc** ㊲. If you

Outside the Walls

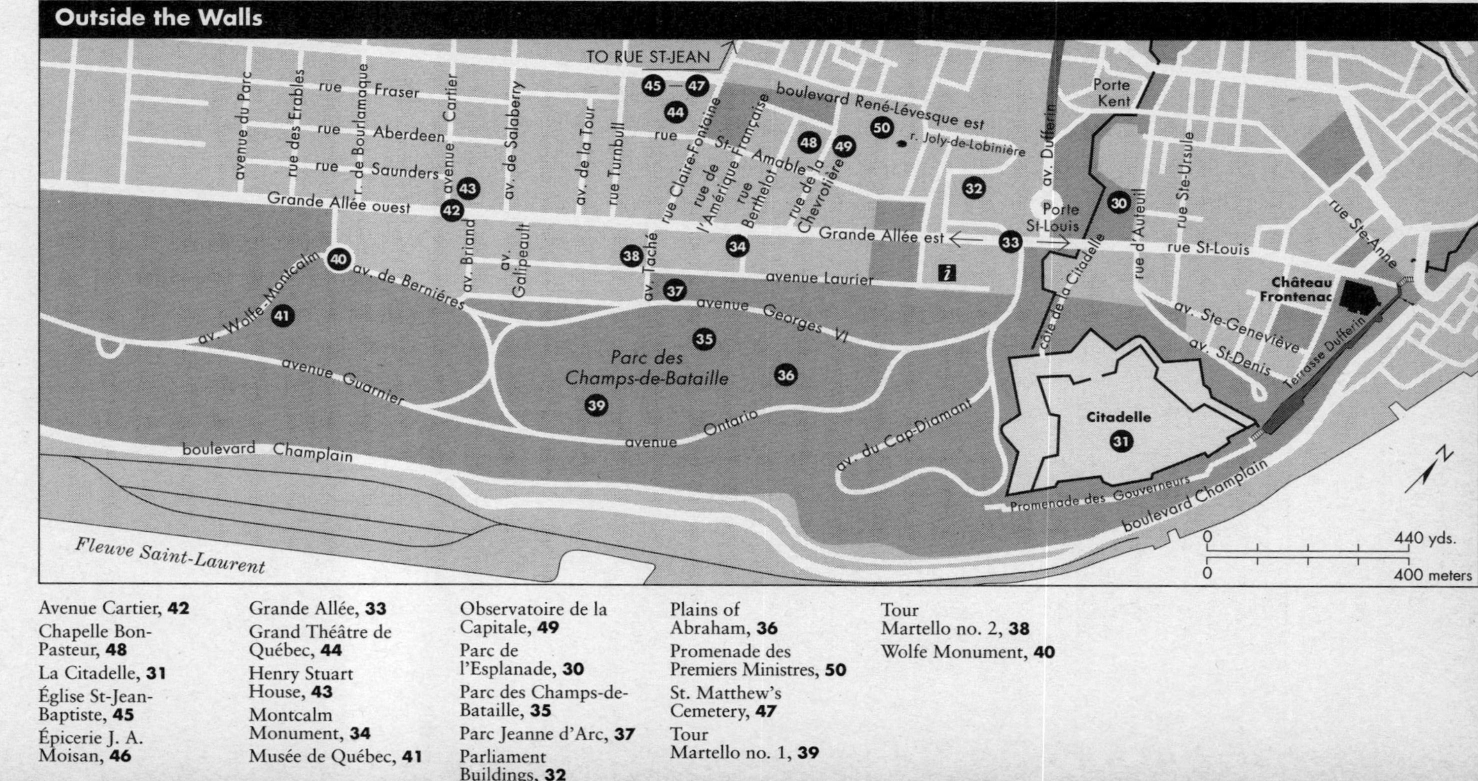

Avenue Cartier, **42**
Chapelle Bon-Pasteur, **48**
La Citadelle, **31**
Église St-Jean-Baptiste, **45**
Épicerie J. A. Moisan, **46**
Grande Allée, **33**
Grand Théâtre de Québec, **44**
Henry Stuart House, **43**
Montcalm Monument, **34**
Musée de Québec, **41**
Observatoire de la Capitale, **49**
Parc de l'Esplanade, **30**
Parc des Champs-de-Bataille, **35**
Parc Jeanne d'Arc, **37**
Parliament Buildings, **32**
Plains of Abraham, **36**
Promenade des Premiers Ministres, **50**
St. Matthew's Cemetery, **47**
Tour Martello no. 1, **39**
Tour Martello no. 2, **38**
Wolfe Monument, **40**

continue west on avenue Laurier, you'll see a stone oval defense tower, **Tour Martello no. 2** ㊳; on the left, toward the south end of the park, stands **Tour Martello no. 1** ㊴. Continue a block west on rue de Bernières and then follow avenue George-VI along the outskirts of the Parc des Champs-de-Bataille until it intersects with avenue Wolfe-Montcalm. You'll come to the tall **Wolfe Monument** ㊵, which marks the place where the British general died. Turn left on avenue Wolfe-Montcalm to visit the **Musée de Québec** ㊶.

From the museum head north on avenue Wolfe-Montcalm, turning right on Grande Allée and walking a block to **avenue Cartier** ㊷. At the corner of avenue Cartier is the **Henry Stuart House** ㊸, which once marked the city's outskirts. If you continue north along avenue Cartier, the first major intersection is boulevard René-Lévesque Est. Turn right and walk two blocks to the concrete modern building of the **Grand Théâtre de Québec** ㊹, a performing arts center. The high-waving flags east of the Grand Théâtre are in the Parc de l'Amérique-Française, dedicated to places in North America with a French-speaking population.

Turn left on rue Claire-Fontaine and walk down the hill to rue St-Jean, where the **Église St-Jean-Baptiste** ㊺ dominates the neighborhood. Turn right and stroll down rue St-Jean past trendy shops in century-old buildings to **Épicerie J. A. Moisan** ㊻, which claims the title of the oldest grocery store in North America. Farther down the street you will come to **St. Matthew's Cemetery** ㊼, the oldest remaining cemetery in Québec City. Cut through the cemetery to rue St-Simon, walk up the hill, cross the street, and turn right on boulevard René-Lévesque to rue de la Chevrotière. On the west side of the street is the **Chapelle Bon-Pasteur** ㊽, a church surrounded by modern office buildings. Across the street is the entrance to Edifice Marie-Guyart, whose observation tower, **Observatoire de la Capitale** ㊾, provides a spectacular view. In summer, you can end your walk by turning right after you leave the building and strolling along the **Promenade des Premiers Ministres** ㊿, which tells the stories of Quebec's premiers. This will take you past the National Assembly and within sight of the St-Louis Gate. A number of other sites are in nearby suburbs, including an aquarium, a zoo, and several gardens.

TIMING

This walk will take a full day. In summer, you should try to catch the colorful 10 AM changing of the guard at the Citadelle. For lunch, try one of the many restaurants around avenue Cartier or bring a picnic and eat on the Plains of Abraham. In the afternoon, you can head down to the area around Église St-Jean-Baptiste and then see the city from the observatory. Other afternoon choices are the aquarium, the zoo, and gardens outside the city.

Sights to See

Aquarium du Québec. The aquarium, about 10 km (6 mi) from the city center, contains more than 340 species of marine life, including reptiles, exotic fish, and seals from the lower St. Lawrence River. A wooded picnic ground makes this spot ideal for a family outing. The Québec City transit system, Société de Transport de la Communauté Urbaine de Québec, or STCUQ (☎ 418/627–2511), runs Buses 13 and 25 here. ✉ *1675 av. des Hôtels, Ste-Foy,* ☎ *418/659–5264 or 418/659–5266 (reservations required for groups of 15 or more).* *$9.50.* *Daily 9–5; seals fed and put on a show at 10:15 and 3:15.*

㊷ **Avenue Cartier.** Here you can indulge in the pleasures offered by the many good restaurants, clubs, and cafés lining the street.

48 **Chapelle Bon-Pasteur.** Charles Baillargé designed this slender church with a steep sloping roof in 1868. Its ornate Baroque-style interior has carved-wood designs painted elaborately in gold leaf. The chapel houses 32 religious paintings done by the nuns of the community from 1868 to 1910. Classical concerts are performed here year-round. ⊠ *1080 rue de la Chevrotière,* ☎ *418/641–1069 or 418/648–9710.* 🎟 *Free.* ⊙ *July–Aug., Tues.– Sat. 1:30–4, Sun. 9–1; Sept.–June by reservation; musical artists' Mass Sun. 10:45.*

31 **La Citadelle** (Citadel). Built at the city's highest point, on Cap Diamant, the Citadel is the largest fortified base in North America still occupied by troops. The 25-building fortress was intended to protect the port, prevent the enemy from taking up a position on the Plains of Abraham, and provide a refuge in case of an attack. Having inherited incomplete fortifications, the British sought to complete the Citadel to protect themselves against retaliations from the French. By the time the Citadel was completed in 1832, the attacks against Québec City had ended. Since 1920 the Citadel has served as a base for the Royal 22nd Regiment. Firearms, uniforms, and decorations from the 17th century are displayed in the **Royal 22nd Regiment Museum,** in the former powder magazine, built in 1750. If weather permits, you can watch the Changing of the Guard, a ceremony in which the troops parade before the Citadel in red coats and black fur hats. Admission is by guided tour only. ⊠ *1 côte de la Citadelle,* ☎ *418/694–2815.* 🎟 *$5.* ⊙ *Apr.–mid-May, daily 10–4; mid-May–June 23, daily 9–5; June 24–Aug., daily 9–6; Sept., daily 9–4; Oct., daily 10–3, Nov.–Mar., groups only (reservations required). Changing of the guard, mid-June–Labor Day, daily 10 AM. Retreat ceremony, July–Aug., daily 6 PM.*

★ 45 **Église St-Jean-Baptiste.** Architect Joseph Ferdinand Peachy's crowning glory, this church was inspired by the facade of the Église de la Trinité in Paris and rivals the Basilique Notre-Dame-de-Québec in beauty and size. The first church on the site, built in 1847, burned in the 1881 fire that destroyed much of the neighborhood. Seven varieties of Italian marble were used in the soaring columns, statues, and pulpit of the present church, which dates to 1884. Its 36 stained-glass windows consist of 30 sections each, and the organ, like the church, is classified as a historical monument. ⊠ *410 rue St-Jean,* ☎ *418/525–7188.* ⊙ *May–Sept., weekdays 3–5:30, Sat. afternoon, and all day Sun. In other months or outside regular opening hrs, knock at the presbytery (⊠ 490 rue St-Jean) to see the church.*

46 **Épicerie J. A. Moisan.** Founded in 1871 by Jean-Alfred Moisan, this store claims the title of the oldest grocery store in North America. The original display cases, woodwork, tin ceilings, and antiques preserve that old-time feel. The store stocks a wide variety of products, including difficult-to-find delicacies from other regions of Québec. ⊠ *699 rue St-Jean,* ☎ *418/522–8268.*

33 **Grande Allée.** One of the city's oldest streets, Grande Allée was the route people took from outlying areas to sell their furs in town. Now trendy cafés, clubs, and restaurants line the road. The street actually has four names: inside the city walls, it is rue St-Louis; outside the walls, Grande Allée; farther west, chemin St-Louis; and farther still, boulevard Laurier.

44 **Grande Théâtre de Québec.** Opened in 1971, the theater incorporates two main halls, named for 19th-century Canadian poets. Louis-Frechette was the first Québec poet and writer to be honored by the French Academy; Octave-Crémazie stirred the rise of Québec nationalism in the mid-19th century. A three-wall mural by Québec sculptor

Jordi Bonet depicts death, life, and liberty. Bonet wrote "La Liberté" on one wall to symbolize the Québécois' struggle for freedom and cultural distinction. ✉ *269 blvd. René-Lévesque Est,* ☎ *418/646–0609.*

OFF THE BEATEN PATH

GROSSE ILE NATIONAL PARK – For thousands of immigrants from Europe in the 1800s, the first glimpse of North America was the hastily erected quarantine station at Grosse Ile—Canada's equivalent of Ellis Island. For far too many passengers on the plague-racked ships, particulary the Irish fleeing the potato famine, Grosse Ile became a final resting place. Several buildings have been restored to tell the story of that tragic period. From Québec City, head south on the Pierre Laporte Bridge and follow the signs for Autoroute 20 East for about an hour to Berthier-sur-Mer or Montmagny. In either town, follow the signs to the marina and you will find ferries to take you across to the island. ☎ *418–248–8888 or 800/463–6769.* *$26–$48, including ferry.* *May–June and Sept.–Oct., 8:30–6:30; late June–Aug., 8:30–8:30.*

43 **Henry Stuart House.** Built in 1849, this Regency-style cottage was home to the Stuart family from 1918 to 1987, when it was designated a historic monument by the Ministry of Culture. Its decor has remained unchanged since 1930. Most of the furniture was imported from England in the second half of the 19th century. ✉ *82 Grande Allée Ouest,* ☎ *418/647–4347.* *$5.* *June–Aug., Wed.–Mon. 11–5; Sept.–May, Thurs. and Sun. 11–5 or by reservation.*

NEED A BREAK?

Halles Petit-Cartier (✉ 1191 av. Cartier, ☎ 418/688–1630), a food mall near the Henry Stuart House, has restaurants and shops that sell French delicacies—cheeses, pastries, breads, vegetables, and candies.

Jardin Roger Van den Hende. A water garden, more than 2,000 plant species from North and South America, Europe, and Asia, and a collection of trees, small shrubs, and remarkable rhododendrons are highlights of this botanical garden. The Metrobus and Buses 11 and 801 run to the gardens. ✉ *Pavillon de l'Environtron, 2480 blvd. Hochelaga, Ste-Foy,* ☎ *418/656–3410.* *Free.* *May–Oct., daily 9–8.*

Jardin Zoologique du Québec. This zoo is especially scenic because of the DuBerger River, which traverses the grounds. About 200 animal species live here, including bears, wildcats, primates, and birds of prey, as well as farm animals. You can cross-country ski on the grounds in winter. The zoo is 11 km (7 mi) west of Québec City on Route 73 and is served by city bus 801 (☎ 418/627–2511). ✉ *9300 rue de la Faune, Charlesbourg,* ☎ *418/622–0313.* *June–Aug. $9.50, Sept.–May $6.* *Daily 9–5.*

34 **Montcalm Monument.** France and Canada joined together to erect this monument honoring Louis-Joseph Montcalm, the general who claimed his fame by winning four major battles in North America. His most famous battle, however, was the one he lost, when the British conquered New France on September 13, 1759. Montcalm was north of Québec City at Beauport when he learned that the British attack was imminent. He quickly assembled his troops to meet the enemy and was wounded in battle in the leg and stomach. Montcalm was carried into the walled city, where he died the next morning. ✉ *Pl. Montcalm.*

★ 41 **Musée de Québec** (Québec Museum). A neoclassical Beaux Arts showcase, the museum has more than 20,000 traditional and contemporary pieces of Québec art. The portraits by artists well known in the area, such as Ozias Leduc (1864–1955) and Horatio Walker (1858–1938), are particularly notable. The museum's very formal and dignified building in Parc des Champs-de-Bataille was designed by Wilfrid Lacroix and erected in 1933 to commemorate the tricentennial of the founding of Québec. The museum has renovated the original building, incorporating the space of an abandoned prison dating from 1867. A hallway of cells, with the iron bars and courtyard still intact, has been preserved as part of a permanent exhibition of the prison's history. ✉ *1 av. Wolfe-Montcalm,* ☎ *418/643–2150.* 🎫 *$5.75; Sept.–mid-May, free Wed.* ⏲ *Sept.–mid-May, Tues. and Thurs.–Sun., 11–5:45, Wed. 11–8:45; mid-May–Aug., Thurs.–Tues. 10–6, Wed. 10–9:30.*

49 **Observatoire de la Capitale.** This observation gallery is on top of Edifice Marie-Guyart, Québec City's tallest office building. The gray, modern concrete tower, 31 stories high, has by far the best view of the city and the environs. There's an express elevator. ✉*1037 rue de la Chevrotière,* ☎ *418/644–9841.* 🎫 *$4.* ⏲ *June–Sept., daily 10–7; Oct.–May, daily 10–5.*

30 **Parc de l'Esplanade** (Esplanade Park). In the early 19th century, this was a clear space surrounded by a picket fence and poplar trees. Today you'll find the **Poudrière de l'Esplanade** (✉ 100 rue St-Louis, ☎ 418/648–7016), the powder magazine that the British constructed in 1820; it houses a model depicting the evolution of the wall surrounding Vieux-Québec. There's a $2.75 charge to enter the magazine, which is open April–October, daily 10–5. The French began building ramparts along the city's natural cliff as early as 1690 to protect themselves from British invaders. The colonists had trouble convincing the French government back home, though, to take the threat of invasion seriously, and by 1759, when the British invaded for control of New France, the walls were still incomplete. The British, despite attacks by the Americans during the War of Independence and the War of 1812, took a century to finish them. The park is also the starting point for walking the city's 4½ km (3 mi) of walls; in summer, guided tours begin here.

35 **Parc des Champs-de-Bataille** (Battlefields Park). One of North America's largest and most scenic parks, this 250-acre area of gently rolling slopes has unparalleled views of the St. Lawrence River. Within the park and just west of the Citadel are the ☞ **Plains of Abraham,** the site of the famous 1759 battle that decided the fate of New France.

37 **Parc Jeanne d'Arc.** An equestrian statue of Joan of Arc is the focus of this park, which is bright with colorful flowers in summer. A symbol of courage, the statue stands in tribute to the heroes of 1759 near the place where New France was lost to the British. The park also commemorates the Canadian national anthem, "O Canada"; it was played here for the first time on June 24, 1880. ✉ *Avs. Laurier and Taché.*

32 **Parliament Buildings.** These buildings, erected between 1877 and 1884, are the seat of L'Assemblée Nationale (the National Assembly) of 125 provincial representatives. Québec architect Eugène-Étienne Taché designed the stately buildings in the late-17th-century Renaissance style of Louis XIV, with four wings set in a square around an interior court. In front of the Parliament, statues pay tribute to important figures of Québec history: Cartier, Champlain, Frontenac, Wolfe, and Montcalm. There's a 30-minute tour (in English or French) of the President's Gallery, the Legislative Council Chamber, and the National Assembly Chamber, which is blue, white, and gold. ✉ *Av. Honoré-Mercier and Grande Allée Est, Door 3,* ☎ *418/643–7239.* 🎫 *Free.* ⏲ *Guided tours (reservations required for groups) weekdays 9–4:30; late June–Labor Day, also open weekends 10–4:30.*

★ 36 **Plains of Abraham.** This park, named after the river pilot Abraham Martin, is the site of the famous 1759 battle that decided the fate of New France. People cross-country ski here in winter and use their in-line skates in summer. Sleigh rides are available in winter. The interpretation center is open year-round; in summer a bus serves as shuttle and guided tour, with commentary in French and English, around the Plains of Abraham, making seven stops. Call Pavillon Baillargé in the Québec Museum (☎ 418/648–4071) for departure times. 🎟 *Tour $1.* ⏲ *Tours June–Sept., daily 10:30–6.*

50 **Promenade des Premiers Ministres.** Inaugurated in 1997, the promenade has a series of panels that tell the story of the premiers who have led the province and their contributions to its development. The panels are in French, but at press time there were plans to print booklets with English and Spanish translations. *Closed in winter.*

47 **St. Matthew's Cemetery.** The burial place of many of the earliest English settlers in Canada was opened in 1771 and is the oldest cemetery remaining in Québec City. Closed in 1860, it has been turned into a park. Next door, St. Matthew's Anglican Church is now a public library; it has a book listing most of the original tombstone inscriptions, including those that disappeared to make way for the city's modern convention center. ✉ *755 rue St-Jean.*

39 **Tour Martello no. 1.** Of the 16 Martello towers in Canada, 4 were built in Québec City because the British government feared an invasion after the American Revolution. Tour Martello no. 1, which exhibits the history of the four structures, was built between 1802 and 1810. (For Tour Martello no. 2, ☞ *below.*) Tour no. 3 guarded westward entry to the city, but it was demolished in 1904. Tour no. 4 is on rue Lavigueur overlooking the St. Charles River but is not open to the public. ✉ *South end of Parc Jeanne d'Arc.* 🎟 *$2.* ⏲ *May–Sept., daily 10–5:30.*

38 **Tour Martello no. 2.** This Martello tower, which has an astronomy display, was built in the early 19th century to slow an enemy approach (☞ Tour Martello no. 1, *above*). ✉ *Avs. Taché and Laurier.* 🎟 *$2.* ⏲ *May–Sept., daily 10–5:30.*

Villa Bagatelle. A romantic 19th-century villa is now home to an exhibition on the villas and garden estates of Sillery. Its English garden, where groups can have tea, has more than 300 varieties of indigenous and exotic plants. ✉ *1563 chemin St-Louis, Sillery,* ☎ *418/688–8074.* 🎟 *$2.* ⏲ *Mar.–Dec., Wed.–Sun. 1–5.*

40 **Wolfe Monument.** This tall monument marks the place where the British general James Wolfe died in 1759. Wolfe landed his troops about 3 km (2 mi) from the city's walls; the 4,500 English soldiers scaled the cliff and opened fire on the Plains of Abraham. Wolfe was mortally wounded in battle and was carried behind the lines to this spot. ✉ *Rue de Bernières and av. Wolfe-Montcalm.*

DINING

Most dining establishments have a selection of dishes à la carte, but more creative specialties are often found on the table d'hôte, a two- to four-course meal chosen daily by the chef. At dinner many restaurants will offer a *menu dégustation,* a five- to seven-course dinner of the chef's finest creations. Note that lunch generally costs about 30% less than dinner, and many of the same dishes are available. Lunch is usually served 11:30 to 2:30; dinner, 6:30 until about 11. You should tip about 15% of the bill.

CATEGORY	COST*
$$$$	over $35
$$$	$25–$35
$$	$15–$25
$	under $15

per person, in Canadian dollars, excluding drinks, service, 7% GST, and 7.5% provincial sales tax

Upper Town

$$$$ ★ ✕ **Le Saint-Amour.** Here are all the makings of a true haute-cuisine establishment without the pretentious atmosphere. A light and airy atrium, with a retractable roof for outdoor dining in summer, creates a relaxed dining ambience. Chef Jean-Luc Boulay returns regularly to France for inspiration; his studies pay off in such creations as stuffed quail in port sauce and salmon with chive mousse. Sauces are light, with no flour or butter. The *menu découvert* has nine courses, and the *menu dégustation* has seven. If you plan to order one of these menus, mention it when you make your reservation. The chef's true expertise shines in his desserts—try the crème brûlée sweetened with maple syrup. ✉ *48 rue Ste-Ursule,* ☎ *418/694–0667. Reservations essential on weekends. AE, DC, MC, V.*

$$$–$$$$ ✕ **Aux Anciens Canadiens.** This establishment is named for a book by Philippe-Aubert de Gaspé, who once resided here. The house, dating from 1675, has five dining rooms with different themes. The *vaisselier* (dish room) is bright and cheerful, with colorful antique dishes and a fireplace. People come for the authentic French-Canadian cooking; hearty specialties include duck in maple glaze, caribou with blueberry wine sauce, and a blueberry cake with warm maple syrup sauce. The restaurant also serves the best caribou drink (a local beverage known for its kick) in town, using its own special mix of sherry and vodka. ✉ *34 rue St-Louis,* ☎ *418/692–1627. AE, DC, MC, V.*

$$$–$$$$ ✕ **Le Continental.** If Québec City had a dining hall of fame, Le Continental would be there among the best. Since 1956, the Sgobba family has been serving award-winning Continental cuisine. Deep blue walls, mahogany paneling, and crisp white tablecloths create a stately ambience, and house specialties like orange duckling and filet mignon Continental are flambéed at your table. Other favorites are rack of lamb Victoria, partridge Périgourdine, and fish and seafood dishes. ✉ *26 rue St-Louis,* ☎ *418/694–9995. AE, DC, MC, V.*

$$$–$$$$ ★ ✕ **La Maison Serge Bruyère.** This restaurant, serving classic French cuisine presented with plenty of crystal, silver, and fresh flowers, put Québec City on the map of great gastronomic cities. It was opened in 1980 by the late Serge Bruyère, a native of Lyon, France. The highlight at La Grande Table is the *menu découvert,* a seven-course meal for about $58. Among chef Jean-Claude Crouzet's dishes are *aiguillettes* (thin strips) of duck with green pepper honey and raspberry vinegar and *noisettes* (small pieces) of stag with apples and cider jelly. Downstairs, Chez Livernois is less formal and less expensive, with such dishes as chicken breasts with sesame seeds and lime. ✉ *1200 rue St-Jean,* ☎ *418/694–0618. Reservations essential. AE, DC, MC, V.*

$$–$$$ ✕ **Portofino Bistro Italiano.** By joining two 18th-century houses, owner James Monti has created a cozy Italian restaurant with a bistro flavor. The room is distinctive: burnt sienna walls, a wood pizza oven set behind a semicircular bar, deep-blue tablecloths and chairs. Not to be missed are the thin-crust pizza and its accompaniment of oils flavored with pepper and oregano, and *pennini al'arrabiata*—tubular pasta with a spicy tomato sauce. Don't miss the homemade tiramisu—ladyfingers dipped in espresso with a whipped cream and mascarpone-cheese fill-

Dining
Apsara, **14**
Aux Anciens Canadiens, **29**
Casse-Crêpe Breton, **21**
Chez Temporel, **25**
Chez Victor, **2**
Le Cochon Dingue, **35**
Le Commensal, **17**
Le Continental, **28**
L'Echaudé, **39**
La Fenouillère, **1**
Le Graffiti, **7**
Laurie Raphaël, **40**
La Maison Serge Bruyère, **23**
Le Marie Clarisse, **37**
Mistral Gagnant, **41**
Montego Resto Club, **5**
Paparazzi, **4**
Le Paris Brest, **9**
Le Parlementaire, **13**
La Point des Amériques, **18**
Portofino Bistro Italiano, **24**
Le Saint-Amour, **15**

Lodging
L'Auberge du Quartier, **6**
Auberge St-Antoine, **38**
L'Auberge St-Louis, **30**
Château de la Terrasse Dufferin, **34**
Le Château de Pierre, **31**
Château Frontenac, **36**
Germain de Près, **3**
Hilton International Québec, **12**
Hôtel Château Bellevue, **32**
Hôtel Clarendon, **27**
L'Hôtel du Capitole, **19**
L'Hôtel du Vieux Québec, **22**
Hôtel Loews Le Concorde, **8**
Hôtel Manoir Victoria, **20**
Hôtel Marie Rollet, **26**
Hôtel Radisson Gouverneurs Québec, **11**
Manoir d'Auteuil, **16**
Manoir Lafayette, **10**
Manoir Ste-Geneviève, **33**

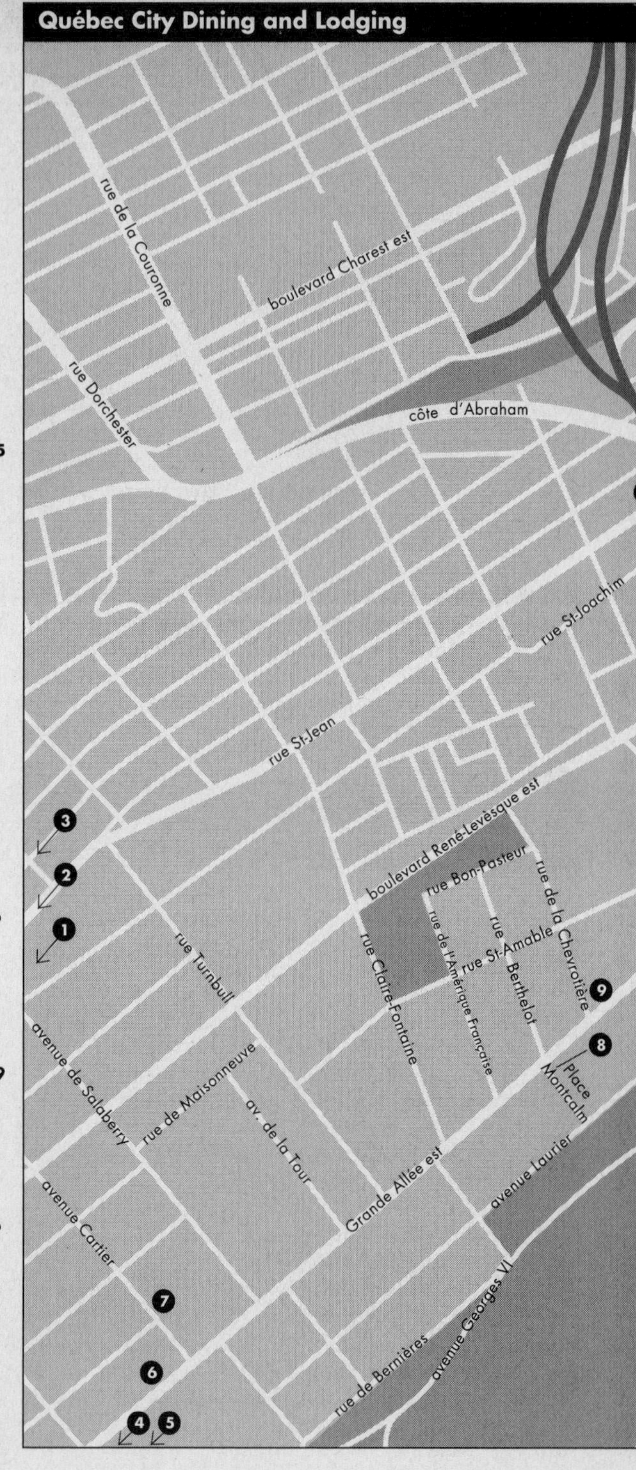

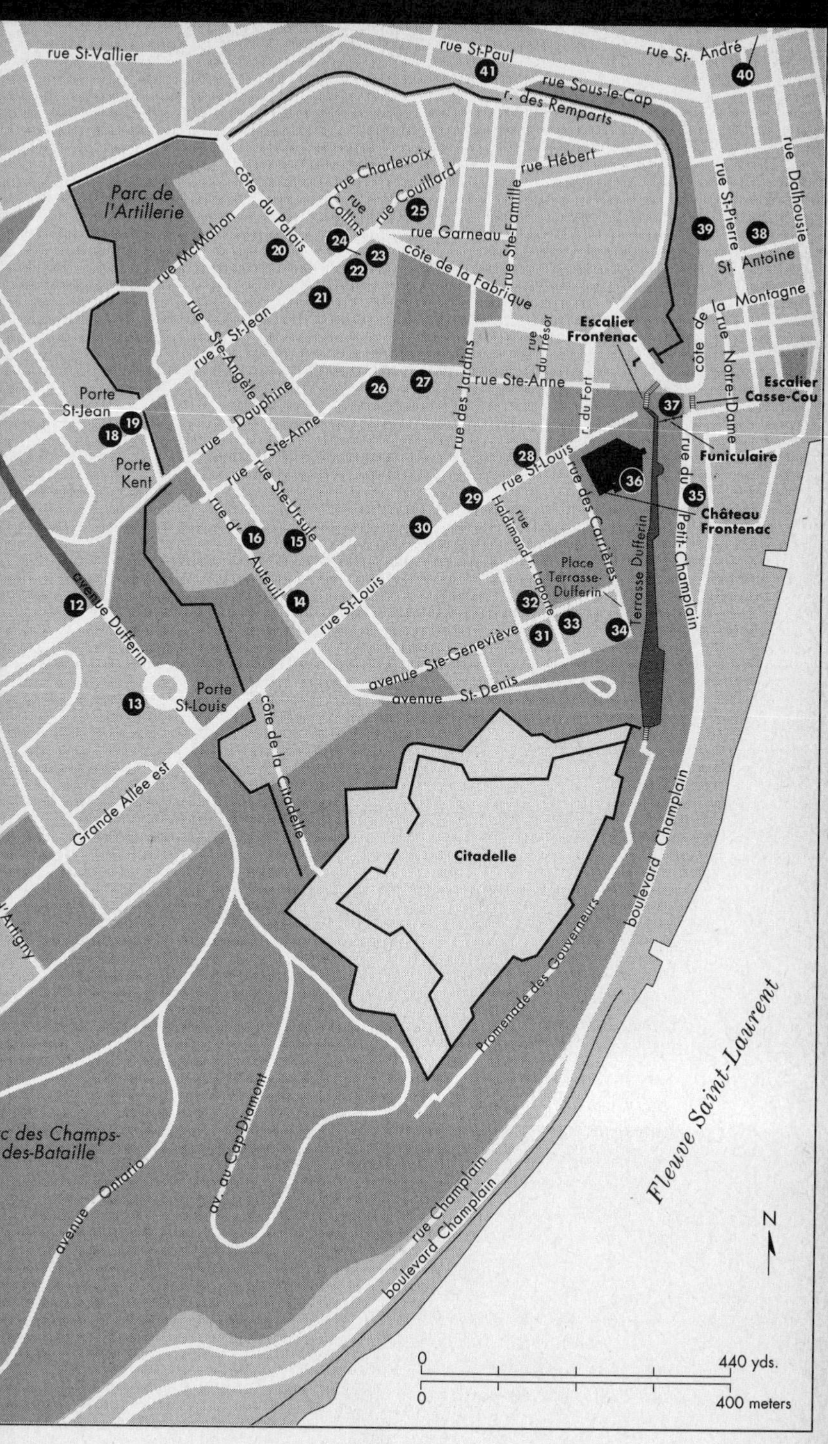
rue St-Vallier
rue St-Paul
rue St- André
r. des Remparts
rue Sous-le-Cap
Parc de l'Artillerie
rue Charlevoix
rue Couillard
rue Collins
rue Hébert
côte du Palais
rue McMahon
rue Garneau
côte de la Fabrique
rue Ste-Famille
rue St-Pierre
rue Dalhousie
St. Antoine
côte de la Montagne
rue St-Jean
rue Ste-Angèle
rue du Trésor
Escalier Frontenac
rue Ste-Anne
rue des Jardins
r. du Fort
rue Notre-Dame
Escalier Casse-Cou
Porte St-Jean
Porte Kent
rue Dauphine
rue Ste-Ursule
rue St-Louis
Funiculaire
Château Frontenac
rue des Carrières
rue du Petit-Champlain
rue Haldimand
r. Laporte
Place Terrasse-Dufferin
Terrasse Dufferin
rue d'Auteuil
avenue Dufferin
avenue Ste-Geneviève
avenue St-Denis
Porte St-Louis
côte de la Citadelle
Grande Allée est
Citadelle
boulevard Champlain
Promenade des Gouverneurs
Fleuve Saint-Laurent
rc des Champs-des-Bataille
avenue Ontario
av. au Cap-Diamant
rue Champlain
N
0
440 yds.
0
400 meters

ing. There's a prix-fixe meal of the day, and from 3 to 7 the restaurant serves a beer and pizza meal for about $10. ✉ *54 rue Couillard,* ☎ *418/692–8888. Reservations essential. AE, DC, MC, V.*

$–$$ ✕ **Apsara.** The Cambodian family that owns this restaurant near the St-Louis Gate excels at using both subtle and tangy spices to create unique flavors. Decor combines Western and Eastern motifs, with flowered wallpaper, Asian art, and small fountains. Innovative dishes from Vietnam, Thailand, and Cambodia include such starters as *fleur de pailin* (a rice-paste roll filled with fresh vegetables, meat, and shrimp) and *mou sati* (pork kebabs with peanut sauce and coconut milk). The assorted miniature Cambodian pastries are delicious with tea. ✉ *71 rue d'Auteuil,* ☎ *418/694–0232. AE, DC, MC, V.*

$ ★ ✕ **Casse-Crêpe Breton.** Crepes in generous proportions are served in this café-style restaurant on rue St-Jean. From a menu of more than 20 fillings, pick your own chocolate or fruit combinations; design a larger meal with cheese, ham, and vegetables; or sip a bowl of Viennese coffee topped with whipped cream. Many tables surround three round hot plates at which you watch your creations being made. Crepes made with two to five fillings cost under $6. ✉ *1136 rue St-Jean,* ☎ *418/692–0438. No credit cards.*

$ ✕ **Chez Temporel.** Tucked behind rue St-Jean and côte de la Fabrique, this homey café filled with the aroma of fresh coffee is an experience *très français.* The rustic decor incorporates wooden tables, chairs, and benches, and a tiny staircase winds to an upper level. Croissants are made in-house; the staff will fill them with Gruyère and ham or anything else. Equally delicious are the *croques monsieur* (grilled ham and cheese sandwiches) and quiche Lorraine. ✉ *25 rue Couillard,* ☎ *418/694–1813. V.*

Lower Town

$$$$ ★ ✕ **Laurie Raphaël.** At this hot spot in town, the setting is classic yet unpretentious, with high ceilings, white linen tablecloths, and sheer white drapery. Award-winning chef Daniel Vezina, a rising star of Québec cuisine, is known for innovative recipes that mix classic French cuisine with international flavors. Among his creations are goat cheese fondue, wrapped in nuts and served with caramelized pears, and an Australian rack of lamb that comes with a shallot sauce, blue potatoes from nearby Charlevoix, and goat cheese. The wine list ranges from $23 to $700 per bottle; some wines are sold by the glass. ✉ *117 rue Dalhousie,* ☎ *418/692–4555. Reservations essential. AE, D, MC, V.*

$$$–$$$$ ✕ **Le Marie Clarisse.** This restaurant in an ancient building at the bottom of Escalier Casse-Cou near Place Royale is known for unique seafood dishes, such as halibut with nuts and honey and scallops with port and paprika. The menu usually lists a good game dish, such as caribou with curry. The *menu du jour* has about seven entrées; dinner includes soup, salad, dessert, and coffee. Wood-beam ceilings, stone walls, sea-blue decor, and a fireplace make this one of the coziest spots in town. ✉ *12 rue du Petit-Champlain,* ☎ *418/692–0857. Reservations essential. AE, DC, MC, V. No lunch weekends Oct.–Apr.*

$$–$$$$ ★ ✕ **L'Echaudé.** A chic black-and-white bistro, L'Echaudé attracts a mix of business and tourist clientele because of its location between the financial and antiques districts. Lunch offerings include *cuisse de canard confit* (duck confit) with french fries and fresh salad. Highlights of the three-course brunch for Sunday antiques shoppers are giant croissants, eggs Benedict, and tantalizing desserts. The modern decor consists of a stark dining area with a mirrored wall and a stainless-steel bar where you dine atop high stools. ✉ *73 Sault-au-Matelot,* ☎ *418/692–1299. AE, DC, MC, V. No dinner Sun. Sept.–May.*

$$$ ✕ **Mistral Gagnant.** Don't be surprised if the pottery bowl on your table or the antique armoire you are sitting beside is sold midway through your meal: Much of what you see in this sunny tearoom comes from Provence and is for sale. Though limited, the menu à la carte is delicious and includes a gourmet salad that changes with the season, daily quiches, and a few desserts. An ever-changing table d'hôte offers more hearty meat, seafood, and pasta dishes; the restaurant is famous for its lemon meringue pie. ✉ *160 rue St-Paul,* ☎ *418/692–4260. AE, MC, V. Closed some evenings in winter; call ahead.*

$–$$$ ✕ **Le Cochon Dingue.** Across the street from the ferry in Lower Town is the boulevard Champlain location of this chain, a cheerful café whose name translates to "The Crazy Pig." Sidewalk tables and indoor dining rooms artfully blend the chic and the antique; black-and-white checkerboard floors contrast with ancient stone walls. Café fare includes delicious mussels, homemade quiches, thick soups, and such desserts as maple-sugar pie. ✉ *46 blvd. Champlain,* ☎ *418/692–2013;* ✉ *46 blvd. René-Lévesque Ouest,* ☎ *418/523–2013;* ✉ *1326 av. Maguire, Sillery,* ☎ *418/684–2013. AE, DC, MC, V.*

Outside the Walls

$$$–$$$$ ✕ **La Fenouillère.** Although this restaurant is connected to a standard chain hotel, inside you will find an elegant, spacious dining room, with a view of the Pierre Laporte bridge. Chef Yvon Godbout has served a constantly rotating table d'hôte since 1986, going out of his way to offer seasonal products. The house specialty is salmon, but lamb is done to a turn and is very popular among the restaurant's regular customers. ✉ *Hotel Best Western Aristocrate, 3100 chemin St-Louis, Ste-Foy,* ☎ *418/653–3886. AE, DC, MC, V.*

$$$–$$$$ ★ ✕ **Le Paris Brest.** This busy restaurant on Grande Allée serves a gregarious crowd attracted to its tastefully prepared French dishes. Traditional fare, such as *escargots au Pernod* (snails with Pernod) and steak tartare, is presented artistically. Some popular choices are lamb with *herbes de Provence* and beef Wellington. A generous side platter of vegetables accompanies à la carte and main-course dishes; wine prices range from $22 to $400. Angular halogen lighting and soft yellow walls add a fresh, modern touch to the historic building. ✉ *590 Grande Allée Est,* ☎ *418/529–2243. AE, DC, MC, V.*

$$–$$$ ✕ **Le Graffiti.** A good alternative to Vieux-Québec dining, this restaurant housed in a modern gourmet food mall serves French cuisine. The romantic setting has dark mahogany-paneled walls and large bay windows that look out onto the passersby along avenue Cartier. On the distinctive seasonal menu are such dishes as *escalope de veau* (thin slices of veal) with a white wine, cream, and tomato sauce; and angel-hair pasta with pesto, pine nuts, black olives, and dried tomatoes. The table d'hôte is reasonably priced. ✉ *1191 av. Cartier,* ☎ *418/529–4949. AE, DC, MC, V.*

$$–$$$ ✕ **Montego Resto Club.** The sun shines year-round at this trendy bistro where Californian, Italian, French, and Szechuan cuisine share the bill. The red-and-yellow Sante Fe decor pays close attention to detail; each rainbow-colored light is a work of art, and every table setting has a unique twist. The inventive menu lists rib steak served with avocado, peppers, and fresh and sun-dried tomatoes, and linguine al Montego, with prosciutto, sun-dried tomatoes, cantaloupe, and peppers. Montego Resto Club is a 15-minute drive west of the old city. ✉ *1460 av. Maguire, Sillery,* ☎ *418/688–7991. AE, D, MC, V.*

$$–$$$ ✕ **Paparazzi.** The food at this Italian restaurant competes with that of many of the finer dining establishments in town, but without the high prices. Paparazzi has a sleek bistro ambience—bare wood tables, halogen lighting, and wrought-iron accents. Pizza Paparazzi comes with wild mushrooms, fresh tomatoes, and a mix of cheeses; desserts are interesting. The restaurant is a 15-minute drive west of Vieux-Québec. ✉ *1365 av. Maguire, Sillery,* ☏ *418/683–8111. AE, DC, MC, V.*

$–$$$ ✕ **La Pointe des Amériques.** Adventurous pizza lovers should explore the fare at this bistro, where the original brick walls of the century-old building just outside the St-Jean Gate contrast boldly with modern mirrors and arty wrought-iron lighting. Some pizza combos (marinated alligator, smoked Gouda, Cajun sauce, and hot peppers) are strange. But don't worry—there are more than 25 different pizzas as well as meat and pasta dishes, soups, and salads. Connected to the restaurant is the Biloxi Bar, which has live jazz and the same menu. ✉ *964 rue St-Jean,* ☏ *418/694–1199. AE, DC, MC, V.*

$–$$ ✕ **Le Parlementaire.** With its magnificent Beaux Arts interior and some of the most reasonable prices in town, the National Assembly's restaurant is nevertheless one of the best-kept secrets in Québec City. Chef Rél Therrien prepares contemporary cuisine that employs products from Québec's various regions. While the restaurant is usually open Tuesday–Friday for breakfast and lunch, opening hours follow the National Assembly's schedule and can vary; it is wise to call ahead. ✉ *Av. Honoré-Mercier and Grande Allée Est, Door 3,* ☏ *418/643–6640. AE, MC, V. Closed Sat.–Mon. No dinner.*

$ ★ ✕ **Chez Victor.** It's no ordinary burger joint: This cozy café with brick walls attracts an artsy crowd to rue St-Jean where trendy turns dreary. Lettuce, tomatoes, onions, mushrooms, pickles, hot mustard, mayonnaise, and a choice of cheeses (mozzarella, Swiss, blue, goat, and cream) top hearty gourmet burgers. French fries are served with a dollop of mayo and poppy seeds. You will find salads, sandwiches, and a daily dessert as well. ✉ *145 rue St-Jean,* ☏ *418/529–7702. MC, V.*

$ ✕ **Le Commensal.** At a kind of upscale cafeteria, diners serve themselves from an outstanding informal vegetarian buffet and then grab a table in the vast dining room, where brick walls and green plants add a touch of class. Plates are weighed to determine the price. Hot and cold dishes run the gamut of health-conscious cooking and include stir-fry tofu and ratatouille (vegetables in mild sauce with couscous). ✉ *860 rue St-Jean,* ☏ *418/647–3733. AE, DC, MC, V.*

LODGING

Be sure to make a reservation if you visit during peak season (May–September) or during the Winter Carnival, in February. During busy times, hotel rates usually rise 30%. From November through April, many lodgings offer weekend discounts and other promotions.

CATEGORY	COST*
$$$$	over $160
$$$	$120–$160
$$	$85–$120
$	under $85

**All prices are for a standard double room, excluding 7% GST, 7.5% provincial sales tax, and an optional service charge, in Canadian dollars.*

Upper Town

$$$$ ★ **Château Frontenac.** Towering above the St. Lawrence River, the Château Frontenac (☞ Upper Town *in* Exploring, *above*) is Québec City's most renowned landmark. Its public rooms—from the intimate piano bar to the 700-seat ballroom reminiscent of the Hall of Mirrors at Versailles—have the opulence of years gone by. Reserve well in ad-

vance, especially from late June–mid-October. At Le Champlain, classic French cuisine is served by waiters in traditional French costumes. Because the hotel is a tourist attraction, the lobby can be busy. ✉ *1 rue des Carrières, G1R 4P5,* ☎ *418/692–3861 or 800/441–1414,* FAX *418/692–1751. 589 rooms, 24 suites. 2 restaurants, piano bar, snack bar, indoor pool, beauty salon, health club. AE, DC, MC, V.*

$$–$$$$ **Hôtel Clarendon.** Built in 1866 and considered the oldest hotel in Québec, the Clarendon (☞ Upper Town *in* Exploring, *above*) has been entirely refurbished in its original Art Deco and Art Nouveau styles. Most rooms have excellent views of Old Québec. ✉ *57 rue Ste-Anne, G1R 3X4,* ☎ *418/692–2480 or 800/463–5250,* FAX *418/692–4652. 147 rooms, 3 suites. Restaurant, café, meeting rooms. AE, D, DC, MC, V.*

$$–$$$$ **Hôtel Manoir Victoria.** This European-style hotel with a good fitness center is well situated near the train station. Its discreet, old-fashioned entrance gives way to a large, wood-paneled foyer. A substantial buffet breakfast is included in some packages. ✉ *44 côte du Palais, G1R 4H8,* ☎ *418/692–1030,* FAX *418/692–3822. 142 rooms, 3 suites. 2 restaurants, indoor pool, beauty salon, sauna, health club, meeting rooms. AE, D, DC, MC, V.*

$$–$$$ **L'Hôtel du Capitole.** In 1992 this abandoned, turn-of-the-century theater just outside the St-Jean Gate was transformed into an exclusive lodging, an Italian bistro, and an elaborate 1920s cabaret-style dinner theater, Théâtre Capitole (☞ Nightlife and the Arts, *below*). A glitzy showbiz theme prevails throughout the hotel, with stars on carpets, doors, and keys. Rooms are small and simple, highlighted with a few rich details. Painted ceilings have a blue-and-white sky motif; white down-filled comforters dress the beds. ✉ *972 rue St-Jean, G1R 1R5,* ☎ *418/694–4040 or 800/363–4040,* FAX *418/694–1916. 36 rooms, 3 suites. Restaurant, bar, theater. AE, DC, MC, V.*

$$–$$$ **L'Hôtel du Vieux Québec.** In the heart of the Latin Quarter on rue St-Jean, this brick hotel is surrounded by striking historic structures. Once an apartment building, it still has the long-term visitor in mind. The interior design is simple, with sparsely furnished but comfortable rooms decorated in pastel colors. Many rooms have kitchens (dishes and cooking utensils can be rented for $10); some have air-conditioning. ✉ *1190 rue St-Jean, G1R 1S6,* ☎ *418/692–1850,* FAX *418/692–5637. 41 rooms. AE, MC, V.*

$$–$$$ **Hôtel Marie Rollet.** An intimate little inn in the heart of Vieux-Québec, built in 1876 by the Ursuline Order, is an oasis of warm woodwork and antique charm. Two rooms have working fireplaces. A rooftop terrace has a garden view. ✉ *81 rue Ste-Anne, G1R 3X4,* ☎ *418/694–9271. 10 rooms. MC, V.*

$$–$$$ **Manoir d'Auteuil.** Originally a private home, this lodging is one of the more lavish manors in town. A major renovation reinstated many of its Art Deco and Art Nouveau details. An ornate sculpted iron banister wraps around four floors, and guest rooms blend modern design with the Art Deco structure. Each room is different; one was formerly a chapel, and another has a tiny staircase leading to its bathroom. The room with a blue bathroom has a shower with seven showerheads. Some rooms look out onto the wall between the St-Louis and St-Jean gates. Note that rooms on the fourth floor are cheaper. ✉ *49 rue d'Auteuil, G1R 4C2,* ☎ *418/694–1173,* FAX *418/694–0081. 16 rooms. Breakfast room. AE, D, DC, MC, V.*

$–$$$ **Château de la Terrasse Dufferin.** This four-story inn has something that many others lack: a view of the St. Lawrence River from rooms in the front. The interior, with its high ceilings and stained glass in the large bay windows, hints at having once possessed a refined and elegant decor. These days rooms are furnished in a mix of styles but are tastefully put together. ✉ *6 Pl. Terrasse Dufferin, G1R 4N5,* ☎ *418/694–9472,* FAX *418/694–0055. 26 rooms. AE, DC, MC, V.*

$$ **Le Château de Pierre.** Built in 1853, this tidy Victorian manor on a picturesque street has kept its English origins alive. The high-ceilinged halls have ornate chandeliers, and Victorian rooms are imaginatively decorated with floral themes; some have either a balcony or vanity room. Several rooms in the front have bay windows with a view of Governors' Park. ✉ *17 av. Ste-Geneviève, G1R 4A8,* ☎ *418/694–0429,* FAX *418/694–0153. 15 rooms. AE, MC, V.*

$$ **Manoir Ste-Geneviève.** Quaint and elaborately decorated, this hotel dating from 1880 stands near the Château Frontenac, on the southwest corner of Governors' Park. A plush Victorian ambience is created with fanciful wallpaper and stately English manor furnishings, such as marble lamps, large wooden bedposts, and velvet upholstery; you'll feel as if you are staying in a secluded country inn. Service is personal and genteel. Some rooms have air-conditioning. ✉ *13 av. Ste-Geneviève, G1R 4A7,* ☎ FAX *418/694–1666. 9 rooms. No credit cards.*

$–$$ **Hôtel Château Bellevue.** Just behind the Château Frontenac, this hotel offers comfortable accommodations at reasonable prices in a good location. Guest rooms are modern, with standard hotel furnishings; many have a view of the St. Lawrence River. The rooms vary considerably in size, and package deals are available in winter. ✉ *16 rue de la Porte, G1R 4M9,* ☎ *418/692–2573 or 800/463–2617,* FAX *418/692–4876. 57 rooms. Meeting room. AE, DC, MC, V.*

$ **L'Auberge St-Louis.** For convenience, this inn's central location on the main street of the city can't be beat. A lobby resembling one in a European pension and tall staircases lead to small guest rooms with comfortable but bare-bones furniture. Six budget rooms are on the fourth floor. The service here is friendly. ✉ *48 rue St-Louis, G1R 3Z3,* ☎ *418/692–2424,* FAX *418/692–3797. 27 rooms, 14 with bath. MC, V.*

Lower Town

$$$–$$$$ **Auberge Saint-Antoine.** This charming little find is within comfortable walking distance of all the Old Town's attractions. The hotel seems much older than it is because of its location in an old maritime warehouse and the generally rustic atmosphere. Each room is styled differently, but all have a combination of antiques and contemporary pieces. Some rooms have river views; others have terraces. ✉ *10 rue St-Antoine, G1K 4C9,* ☎ *418/692–2211 or 800/267–0525,* FAX *418/692–1177. 24 rooms, 7 suites. AE, DC, MC, V.*

Outside the Walls

$$$$ **Hilton International Québec.** Just outside St-Jean Gate, the spacious Hilton rises from the shadow of Parliament Hill. The lobby, which can be chaotic at times, has a bar and an open-air restaurant. The hotel is next to the Parliament Buildings and connected to the convention center and a mall, Place Québec, which has 45 shops and restaurants. Standard yet ultramodern rooms have tall windows; those on upper floors have fine views of Vieux-Québec. Guests on executive floors are offered a free breakfast and an open bar from 5 to 10 PM. ✉ *1100 blvd. René-Lévesque Est, G1K 7M9,* ☎ *418/647–2411 or 800/447–2411,* FAX *418/647–6488. 487 rooms, 36 suites. Restaurant, piano bar, pool, sauna, health club. AE, D, DC, MC, V.*

$$$$ **Hôtel Radisson Gouverneurs Québec.** This large, full-service establishment opposite the Parliament Buildings is part of a Québec chain. Its light and spacious rooms have luminous pastel decor, wood furniture, and marble bathrooms. VIP floors were designed to lure the business traveler. The hotel occupies the first 12 floors of a tall office complex; views of Vieux-Québec are limited to the higher floors. ✉ *690 blvd. René-Lévesque Est, G1R 5A8,* ☎ *418/647–1717 or 888/910–1111,* FAX *418/647–2146. 371 rooms, 6 suites. Restaurant, pool, sauna, health club. AE, D, DC, MC, V.*

$$$–$$$$ ★ **Hôtel Loews Le Concorde.** When Le Concorde was built in 1974, the shockingly tall concrete structure aroused controversy because it supplanted 19th-century Victorian homes. Still, visitors love its location on Grande Allée, where cafés, restaurants, and bars dot the street. Rooms have good views of Battlefields Park and the St. Lawrence River, and nearly all have been redone in modern decor combined with traditional furnishings. Amenities for business travelers have expanded. ✉ *1225 Pl. Montcalm, G1R 4W6,* ☎ *418/647–2222 or 800/463–5256,* FAX *418/647–4710. 424 rooms. 2 restaurants, bar, pool, sauna, health club, business services. AE, D, DC, MC, V.*

$$$ **Germain des Près.** One popular hotel for the business crowd is in Ste-Foy, close to Place Laurier and with easy access to Québec City and the airports. Its ultramodern rooms—in black and white or black and tan—have white comforters on the beds. ✉ *1200 av. Germain-des-Près, Ste-Foy, G1V 3M7,* ☎ *418/658–1224 or 800/463–5263,* FAX *418/658–8846. 126 rooms with shower or bath. Restaurant, business services, meeting rooms. AE, DC, MC, V.*

$$–$$$ **Manoir Lafayette.** In 1882 this graystone building was a lavish, private home; today it is a simple hotel. Considering the location on Grande Allée—a street crowded with restaurants and trendy bars—the clean, comfortable accommodations are reasonably priced. The lobby is open and welcoming, with leather sofas surrounding a decorative fireplace and television. Rooms in the newer wing—although fresher—resemble those in the old part: All are quite small, with high ceilings, wooden furniture, and floral bedspreads and drapes. Rooms facing Grande Allée may be noisy. ✉ *661 Grande Allée Est, G1R 2K4,* ☎ *418/522–2652 or 800/363–8203,* FAX *418/522–4400. 67 rooms. Restaurant, baby-sitting. AE, DC, MC, V.*

$ **L'Auberge du Quartier.** A small, amiable inn in a house dating from 1852 benefits from a personal touch. The cheerful rooms are modestly furnished but well maintained. A suite of rooms on the third floor can accommodate a family at a reasonable cost. A 15-minute walk west from the old city, L'Auberge du Quartier is convenient to avenue Cartier and Grande Allée nightlife; joggers can use Battlefields Park across the street. ✉ *170 Grande Allée Ouest, G1R 2G9,* ☎ *418/525–9726. 11 rooms, 1 suite. Breakfast room. AE, DC, MC, V.*

NIGHTLIFE AND THE ARTS

Considering its size, Québec City has a wide variety of cultural institutions, from the renowned Québec Symphony Orchestra to several small theater companies. The arts scene changes significantly depending on the season. From September through May, a steady repertory of concerts, plays, and performances is presented in theaters and halls. In summer, indoor theaters close to make room for outdoor stages. For arts and entertainment listings in English, consult the *Québec Chronicle-Telegraph,* published on Wednesday. The French-language daily newspaper *Le Soleil* has listings on a page called "Où Aller à Québec" ("Where to Go in Québec"). Also, *Voir,* a weekly devoted to arts listings and reviews, appears on the street every Thursday.

Tickets for most shows can be purchased through **Billetech,** with outlets at the Bibliothèque Gabrielle-Roy (✉ 350 rue St-Joseph Est, ☎ 418/691–7400), Colisée de Québec (✉ 2205 av. du Colisée, Parc de l'Exposition, ☎ 418/691–7211), Grand Théâtre de Québec (✉ 269 blvd. René-Lévesque Est, ☎ 418/643–8131), La Baie department store (✉ Pl. Laurier, 2e, ☎ 418/627–5959), Palais Montcalm (✉ 995 Pl. d'Youville, ☎ 418/670–9011), Salle Albert-Rousseau (✉ 2410 chemin Ste-Foy, Ste-Foy, ☎ 418/659–6710), and Théâtre Périscope (✉ 2 rue Crémazie Est, ☎ 418/529–2183). Hours vary, and in some cases tickets must be bought at the outlet.

The Arts

Dance

Dancers appear at Bibliothèque Gabrielle-Roy (☞ Music, *below*), Salle Albert-Rousseau, and the Palais Montcalm (☞ Theater, *below*). **Grand Théâtre de Québec** (✉ 269 blvd. René-Lévesque Est, ☎ 418/643–8131) presents a dance series with Canadian and international companies.

Film

Most theaters present French films and American films dubbed into French. Three popular theaters are **Cinéma Cinéplex Odéon** (✉ 5700 blvd. des Gradins, ☎ 418/622–1077), **Cinéma de Paris** (✉ 966 rue St-Jean, ☎ 418/694–0891), and **Cinéma Place Charest** (✉ 500 rue du Pont, ☎ 418/529–9745). **Cinéma des Galeries** (✉ 5401 blvd. des Galeries, ☎ 418/628–2455) almost always shows some films in English. **Le Clap** (✉ 2360 chemin Ste-Foy, Ste-Foy, ☎ 418/650–2527) has a repertoire of foreign, offbeat, and art films. **IMAX Theatre** (✉ Galeries de la Capitale, 5401 blvd. des Galeries, ☎ 418/627–4629, 418/627–4688, or 800/643–4629) has extra-large-screen movies and translation headsets.

Music

L'Orchestre Symphonique de Québec (Québec Symphony Orchestra) is Canada's oldest. It performs at Louis-Frechette Hall in the Grand Théâtre de Québec (✉ 269 blvd. René-Lévesque Est, ☎ 418/643–8131).

Tickets for children's concerts at the **Joseph Lavergne auditorium** must be purchased in advance at the Bibliothèque Gabrielle-Roy (✉ 350 rue St-Joseph Est, ☎ 418/691–7400). For classical concerts at the **Salle de l'Institut Canadien** (✉ 42 rue St-Stanislas), buy tickets in advance at the Bibliothèque Gabrielle-Roy (☞ *above*).

Popular music concerts are often booked at the **Colisée de Québec** (✉ Parc de l'Exposition, 2205 av. du Colisée, Parc de l'Exposition, ☎ 418/691–7211).

An annual highlight is the July **Festival d'Eté International de Québec** (☎ 418/692–4540), an 11-day music festival with more than 400 shows and concerts (many of them free) from classical music to Francophone song. Events are held in more than 10 locations, including outdoor stages and public squares. Dates for 1999 are July 8–18.

Theater

Most theater productions are in French. The following theaters schedule shows September–April: **Grand Théâtre de Québec** (✉ 269 blvd. René-Lévesque Est, ☎ 418/643–8131) offers classic and contemporary plays staged by the leading local company, le Théâtre du Trident (☎ 418/643–5873). **Palais Montcalm** (✉ 995 Pl. d'Youville, ☎ 418/670–9011), a municipal theater outside St-Jean Gate, presents a broad range of productions. A diverse repertoire, from classical to comedy, is staged at **Salle Albert-Rousseau** (✉ 2410 chemin Ste-Foy, Ste-Foy, ☎ 418/659–6710). **Théâtre Capitole** (✉ 972 rue St-Jean, ☎ 418/694–4444), a restored turn-of-the-century cabaret-style theater, schedules pop music and musical comedy shows. **Théâtre Périscope** (✉ 2 rue Crémazie Est, ☎ 418/529–2183), a multipurpose theater, stages about 200 shows a year, including performances for children.

SUMMER THEATER

In summer, open-air concerts are presented at Place d'Youville (just outside St-Jean Gate) and on the Plains of Abraham.

Nightlife

Québec City nightlife is centered on the clubs and cafés of rue St-Jean, avenue Cartier, and Grande Allée. In winter, evening activity is livelier toward the end of the week, beginning on Wednesday. As warmer temperatures set in, the café-terrace crowd emerges, and bars are active seven days a week. Most bars and clubs stay open until 3 AM.

Bars and Lounges

Cosmos Café (✉ 575 Grande Allée, ☎ 418/640–0606) is a lively club and restaurant. Upstairs, Chez Maurice has dancing. **Le Pub Saint-Alexandre** (✉ 1087 rue St-Jean, ☎ 418/694–0015), a popular English-style pub, was formerly a men-only tavern. It serves 200 kinds of beer, 20 on tap. You'll find mainly yuppies at **Vogue** (✉ Upstairs at 1170 rue d'Artigny, ☎ 418/529–9973), which has dancing.

Dance Clubs

There's a little bit of everything—live rock bands to loud disco—at **Chez Dagobert** (✉ 600 Grande Allée Est, ☎ 418/522–0393), a large and popular club. **Merlin** (✉ 1179 av. Cartier, ☎ 418/529–9567), a second-story dance club with an English pub below, is packed nightly.

Folk, Jazz, and Blues

French-Canadian folk songs fill **Chez Son Père** (✉ 24 rue St-Stanislas, ☎ 418/692–5308), a smoky pub on the second floor of an old building in the Latin Quarter. Singers perform nightly. **Le d'Auteuil** (✉ 35 rue d'Auteuil, ☎ 418/692–2263), a converted church across from Kent Gate, is a place to hear rhythm and blues, jazz, and blues.The first jazz bar in Québec City, **L'Emprise at Hôtel Clarendon** (✉ 57 rue Ste-Anne, ☎ 418/692–2480), is the preferred spot for enthusiasts. The Art Deco decor sets the mood for Jazz Age rhythms. **Maison de la Chanson** (✉ Théâtre Petit Champlain, 68 rue du Petit-Champlain, ☎ 418/692–4744) is a fine spot for contemporary Québec music.

OUTDOOR ACTIVITIES AND SPORTS

Two parks are central to Québec City: the 250-acre Battlefields Park, with its panoramic views of the St. Lawrence River, and Cartier-Brébeuf Park, which runs along the St. Charles River. Both are favorites for jogging, biking, and cross-country skiing. Scenic rivers and mountains close by (no more than 30 minutes by car) make this city ideal for the sporting life. For information about sports and fitness, contact **Québec City Tourist Information Office** (✉ 835 av. Laurier, G1R 2L3, ☎ 418/ 649–2608) or **Québec City Bureau of Parks and Recreation** (✉ 65 rue Ste-Anne, 5ᵉ, G1R 3S9, ☎ 418/691–6284).

Participant Sports and Outdoor Activities

Biking

Bike paths along rolling hills traverse Battlefields Park, at the south side of the city. For a longer ride over flat terrain, take the path north of the city skirting the St. Charles River; this route can be reached from rue St-Roch, rue Prince-Edouard, and Pont Dorchester (Dorchester Bridge). Paths along the côte de Beaupré, beginning at the confluence of the St. Charles and St. Lawrence rivers, are especially scenic. They begin northeast of the city at rue de la Verandrye and boulevard Montmorency or rue Abraham-Martin and Pont Samson (Samson Bridge) and continue 10 km (6 mi) along the coast to Montmorency Falls.

You can rent bicycles for $25 a day or $15 a half-day at **Auberge de la Paix** (✉ 31 rue Couillard, ☎ 418/694–0735).

Boating

Lakes in the Québec City area have facilities for boating. **Lac Beauport** (✉ 78 chemin du Brûlé, ☎ 418/849–2821) is one of the best nearby resorts. Take Route 73 north of the city to St-Dunstan de Lac Beauport; then take Exit 157, boulevard du Lac. Just west of Québec City, on the St. Lawrence River, boats can be rented at **Parc Nautique du Cap-Rouge** (✉ 4155 chemin de la Plage Jacques Cartier, Cap-Rouge, ☎ 418/650–7770).

Dogsledding

Adventure Nord-Bec (✉ 665 rue St-Aimé, St-Lambert de Lévis, GOS 2WO, ☎ 418/889–8001), 20 minutes from the city, teaches people how to mush in the forest. Overnight camping trips are available.

Fishing

Permits are needed for fishing in Québec. Most sporting goods stores and all Canadian Tire stores sell permits; try **Canadian Tire** (✉ 1170 rte. de l'Église, Ste-Foy, ☎ 418/659–4882). The **Ministry of Wildlife and the Environment** (✉ 675 blvd. René-Lévesque Est, ☎ 418/643–3127) publishes a pamphlet on fishing regulations that is available at tourist information offices.

Réserve Faunique des Laurentides (☎ 418/686–1717), a wildlife reserve with good lakes for fishing, is approximately 48 km (30 mi) north of Québec City via Route 73.

Golf

The Québec City region has 18 golf courses, and several are open to the public. Reservations are essential in summer. **Club de Golf de Beauport** (✉ 3533 rue Clemenceau, Beauport, ☎ 418/663–1578), a 9-hole course, is 20 minutes from the city by car via Route 73 North. The 18-hole, par-70 course at **Club de Golf de Cap-Rouge** (✉ 4600 rue St-Felix, ☎ 418/653–9381) in Cap-Rouge is one of the closest to Québec City. **Parc du Mont Ste-Anne** (✉ Rte. 360, Beaupré, ☎ 418/827–3778), a half-hour drive north of Québec, has one of the best 18-hole courses in the region.

Health and Fitness Clubs

One of the city's most popular health clubs is **Club Entrain** (✉ Pl. de la Cité, 2600 blvd. Laurier, ☎ 418/658–7771). Facilities include a weight room with Nautilus, a sauna, a whirlpool, aerobics classes, and squash courts. **Hilton International Québec** (✉ 1100 blvd. René-Lévesque Est, ☎ 418/647–2411) has a health club with weights, a sauna, and a year-round heated outdoor pool available to nonguests for a $10 fee. Nonguests at **Hôtel Radisson des Gouverneurs** (✉ 690 blvd. René-Lévesque Est, ☎ 418/647–1717) can use the health club facilities, which include weights, a sauna, a whirlpool, and an outdoor heated pool (in summer), for a $5 fee. Nonmembers can use the pool at the **YMCA du Vieux-Québec** (✉ 650 av. Wilfred Laurier, ☎ 418/522–0800) for a $2.30 fee. Pool facilities cost $2.35 at the **YWCA** (✉ 855 av. Holland, ☎ 418/683–2155).

Hiking and Jogging

The Parc Cartier-Brébeuf, north of Vieux-Québec along the banks of the St. Charles River, has about 13 km (8 mi) of hiking trails. For more mountainous terrain, head 19 km (12 mi) north on Route 73 to Lac

Beauport. For jogging, Battlefields Park, Parc Cartier-Brébeuf, and Bois-de-Coulonge park in Sillery are the most popular places.

Horseback Riding

Jacques Cartier Excursions (✉ 978 av. Jacques-Cartier Nord, Tewkesbury, ☏ 418/848–7238), also known for rafting, offers summer and winter horseback riding. A summer excursion includes an hour of instruction and three hours of riding; the cost is $32–$50.

Ice Canoeing

This sport entails propelling the vessel (a cross between a canoe and a rowboat) over the uneven ice of the St. Lawrence to open water, at which time you jump in the boat and row. To propel the boat on the ice, you straddle it, one knee inside, the other leg pushing like a skateboard. This sport is best restricted to those in good shape. The guides at **Le Mythe des Glaces** (✉ 735 blvd. du Lac, Charlesbourg, G1H 7B1, ☏ 418/849–6131) will suit you up from head to toe. A half day costs $60, a full day with dinner is $120, and a two-day excursion is $265.

Ice-Skating

The ice-skating season runs December–March.There is a 1-km (½-mi) stretch for skating along the **St. Charles River,** between the Dorchester and Drouin bridges; season is January–March, depending on the ice. Rentals and changing rooms are nearby. For information contact Marina St-Roch (☏ 418/691–7188).

From December through March, try the **Patinoire de la Terrasse** adjacent to the Château Frontenac (☏ 418/692–2955), open from 11 to 11; skates can be rented for $4 daily. **Place d'Youville,** just outside St-Jean Gate, has an outdoor rink open November–April. Nighttime skating is an option at **Village des Sports** (✉ 1860 blvd. Valcartier, St-Gabriel-de-Valcartier, ☏ 418/844–3725).

Rafting

The Jacques Cartier River, about 48 km (30 mi) northwest of Québec City, provides good rafting. **Jacques Cartier Excursions** (✉ 978 av. Jacques-Cartier Nord, Tewkesbury, ☏ 418/848–7238) runs rafting trips May–October on the Jacques Cartier River. Tours originate from Tewkesbury, a half-hour drive from Québec City. A half-day tour costs about $45, a full day $65; wet suits are $16. In winter, snow-rafting excursions include all-day mountain sliding in river rafts for $44.

Village des Sports (✉ 1860 blvd. Valcartier, St-Gabriel-de-Valcartier, ☏ 418/844–2200) has excursions on the Jacques Cartier River from mid-May through October. A three-hour excursion costs $49. It also offers boogie boarding—running the rapids on surfboards.

Skiing

Brochures about ski centers in Québec are available at the Québec Tourism and Convention Bureaus or by calling 800/363–7777. The **Hiver Express** (☏ 418/525–5191) winter shuttle is a taxi service between major hotels in Vieux-Québec, Ste-Foy, ski centers, and the Village des Sports (☞ Snow Slides, *below*). It leaves hotels at 8:30 and returns at 4:30. The cost is $18; reserve in advance at hotels. For people staying in ski areas who want to visit the city, the bus leaves at 9:30 and returns at 3:30.

CROSS-COUNTRY

You can ski cross-country on many trails; **Battlefields Park,** which you can reach from Place Montcalm, has scenic marked trails. Thirty-two ski centers in the Québec area offer 2,000 km (1,240 mi) of groomed trails and heated shelters; for information, call **Regroupement des Stations de Ski de Fond** (☏ 418/653–5875). **Le Centre de Randonnée à**

Skis de Duchesnay (✉ 143 rue de Duchesnay, St-Catherine-de-Jacques-Cartier, ☎ 418/875–2147), just north of Québec City, has 11 marked trails totaling 125 km (77 mi). **Parc du Mont Ste-Anne** (✉ Rte. 360, Beaupré, ☎ 418/827–4561), 40 km (25 mi) northeast of Québec City, has 21 trails over 223 km (138 mi). Lac Beauport, 19 km (12 mi) north of the city, has more than 20 marked trails (150 km, or 93 mi); contact **Les Sentiers du Moulin** (✉ 99 chemin du Moulin, Lac Beauport, ☎ 418/849–9652).

DOWNHILL

Three alpine ski resorts, all with night skiing, are within a 30-minute drive of Québec City. There are 25 trails and a vertical drop of 734 ft at the relatively small **Le Relais** (✉ 1084 blvd. du Lac, Lac Beauport, G0A 2C0, ☎ 418/849–1851). **Station Mont Ste-Anne** (✉ Rte. 360, C.P. 400, Beaupré, G0A 1E0, ☎ 418/827–4561, 800/463–1568 for lodging) is the largest resort in eastern Canada, with a vertical drop of 2,050 ft, 54 downhill trails, 12 lifts, and a gondola. **Station Touristique Stoneham** (✉ 1420 av. du Hibou, Stoneham, G0A 4P0, ☎ 418/848–2411), with a vertical drop of 1,377 ft, is known for its long, easy slopes, with 25 downhill runs and 10 lifts.

Snow Slides

At **Glissades de la Terrasse** (☎ 418/692–2955), adjacent to the Château Frontenac (☞ Lodging, *above*), a wooden toboggan takes you down a 700-ft snow slide. Cost is $1 per ride per person.

Visitors to **Village des Sports** can use inner tubes or carpets on the two 300-ft snow slides, or join 6–12 others for a snow raft ride down one of seven groomed trails. ✉ *1860 blvd. Valcartier, St-Gabriel-de-Valcartier,* ☎ *418/844–3725.* 🎫 *Rafting and sliding $18.50 per day; $20 with skating.* ⏲ *Sun.–Thurs. 10–10, Fri.–Sat. 10 AM–10:30 PM.*

Tennis and Racquet Sports

At **Montcalm Tennis Club** (✉ 901 blvd. Champlain, Sillery, ☎ 418/687–1250), south of Québec City, four indoor and seven outdoor courts are open daily from 8 AM to midnight. **Tennisport** (✉ 6280 blvd. Hamel, Ancienne Lorette, ☎ 418/872–0111) has 10 indoor tennis courts, two squash courts, two racquetball courts, and eight badminton courts.

Winter Carnival

One winter highlight is the **Québec Winter Carnival** (✉ 290 rue Joly, GIL 1N8, ☎ 418/626–3716), famous for its joie de vivre. The whirl of activities over three weekends in January and/or February includes night parades, a snow-sculpture competition, and a canoe race across the St. Lawrence River. You can participate in or watch every activity imaginable in the snow from dogsledding to ice climbing. Dates for 1999 are January 29 to February 14.

Spectator Sports

Tickets for sporting events can be purchased at **Colisée de Québec** (✉ 2205 av. du Colisée, ☎ 418/691–7211). You can order tickets through **Billetech** (☞ Nightlife and the Arts, *above*).

Harness Racing

There's horse racing at **Hippodrome de Québec** (✉ Parc de l'Exposition, 250 blvd. Wilfrid-Hamel, ☎ 418/524–5283).

Hockey

An International Hockey League team, the **Québec Rafales,** plays at the Colisée de Québec (✉ 2205 av. du Colisée, ☎ 418/522–5225 or 418/691–7211).

SHOPPING

Shopping is European-style on the fashionable streets of Québec City. The boutiques and specialty shops clustered along narrow streets such as rue du Petit-Champlain, and rue Buade and rue St-Jean in the Latin Quarter, have one of the most striking historic settings on the continent. Prices in Québec City tend to be on a par with those in Montréal and other North American cities. When sales occur, they are usually listed in the French daily newspaper *Le Soleil.*

Stores are generally open Monday–Wednesday 9:30–5:30, Thursday and Friday until 9, Saturday until 5, and Sunday noon–5. In summer, shops may be open seven days a week, and most have later evening hours.

Department Stores

Large department stores can be found in the malls of the suburb of Ste-Foy, but some have outlets inside Québec City's walls. **La Baie** (⊠ Pl. Laurier, Ste-Foy, ☎ 418/627–5959) is Québec's version of the Canadian Hudson's Bay Company conglomerate, founded in 1670 by Montréal trappers Pierre Radisson and Médard Chouart des Groseilliers. Today La Baie carries clothing for the entire family and household wares. **Holt Renfrew & Co., Ltd.** (⊠ Pl. Ste-Foy, Ste-Foy, ☎ 418/656–6783), one of the country's more exclusive stores, carries furs, perfume, and tailored designer collections for men and women. **Simons** (⊠ 20 côte de la Fabrique, ☎ 418/692–3630), one of Québec City's oldest family stores, used to be its only source for fine British woolens and tweeds; now the store also has a large selection of designer clothing, linens, and other household items.

Shopping Malls

A 20-minute drive from the old city, the **Galeries de la Capitale** (⊠ 5401 blvd. des Galeries, ☎ 418/627–5800) has 250 stores and an indoor amusement park with a roller coaster. **Place Québec** (⊠ 880 autoroute Dufferin-Montmorency, ☎ 418/529–0551), the mall closest to the old city, is a multilevel shopping complex and convention center with 45 stores and restaurants; it is connected to the Hilton International Hotel.

The following shopping centers are approximately a 15-minute drive west along Grande Allée. **Place Ste-Foy** (⊠ 2450 blvd. Laurier, Ste-Foy, ☎ 418/653–4184) has 125 stores. **Place de la Cité** (⊠ 2600 blvd. Laurier, Ste-Foy, ☎ 418/657–6920) has 125 boutiques. The massive **Place Laurier** (⊠ 2700 blvd. Laurier, Ste-Foy, ☎ 418/653–9318) has more than 350 stores.

Quartier Petit-Champlain (☎ 418/692–2613) in Lower Town is a pedestrian mall with some 40 boutiques, local businesses, and restaurants. This popular district is the best area for native Québec arts and crafts, such as wood sculptures, weaving, ceramics, and jewelry. **Pot-en-Ciel** (⊠ 27 rue du Petit-Champlain, ☎ 418/692–1743) carries ceramics. **Pauline Pelletier** (⊠ 38 rue du Petit-Champlain, ☎ 418/692–4871) has porcelain.

Specialty Stores

Antiques

Québec City's antiques district is on rue St-Paul and rue St-Pierre, across from the Old Port. French Canadian, Victorian, and Art Deco furniture along with clocks, silverware, and porcelain are some of the rare collectibles found here. Authentic Québec pine furniture, characterized by simple forms and lines, is becoming increasingly rare and costly.

Antiquités Zaor (✉ 112 rue St-Paul, ☎ 418/692–0581), the oldest store on rue St-Paul, is still the best place in the neighborhood to find excellent English, French, and Canadian antiques. **L'Héritage Antiquité** (✉ 109 rue St-Paul, ☎ 418/692–1681) specializes in 18th- and 19th-century Québécois pine furniture, clocks, oil lamps, and porcelain.

Art

Aux Multiples Collections (✉ 43 rue Buade, ☎ 418/692–4298) has Inuit art and antique wood collectibles. **Galerie Brousseau et Brousseau** (✉ 35 rue St-Louis, ☎ 418/694–1828) has Inuit art. **Galerie Madeleine Lacerte** (✉ 1 côte Dinan, ☎ 418/692–1566), in Lower Town, sells contemporary art and sculpture. A source for less expensive artwork or work by young artists who may become famous in the future is **Rue du Trésor,** where local artists display their sketches, paintings, and etchings. Fine portraits of Québec City and the region are plentiful.

Books

English-language books are difficult to find in Québec. **Librairie du Nouveau-Monde** (✉ 103 rue St-Pierre, ☎ 418/694–9475) stocks titles in French and English. **Librairie Smith** (✉ 2700 blvd. Laurier, Place Laurier, ☎ 418/653–8683) has both English and French books. **La Maison Anglaise** (✉ 2600 blvd. Laurier, Place de la Cité, Ste-Foy, ☎ 418/654–9523) has English-language titles only, specializing in fiction.

Clothing

François Côté Collections (✉ 35 rue Buade, ☎ 418/692–6016) is a chic boutique with fashions for men and women. **Louis Laflamme** (✉ 1192 rue St-Jean, ☎ 418/692–3774) has a large selection of stylish men's clothes. **La Maison Darlington** (✉ 7 rue Buade, ☎ 418/692–2268) carries well-made woolens, dresses, and suits for men, women, and children by fine names in couture.

Crafts

Les Trois Colombes Inc. (✉ 46 rue St-Louis, ☎ 418/694–1114) sells handmade items, including clothing made from handwoven fabric, native and Inuit carvings, jewelry and pottery.

Food

Chocolate becomes a work of art at **Chocolaterie Érico** (✉ 634 rue St-Jean, ☎ 418/524–2122), where *chocolatier* Éric Normand will handcraft whatever you like out of chocolate within a few days. At **Marché du Vieux-Port,** farmers from the Québec countryside sell fresh produce in the Old Port near rue St-André, May–October, 8–8.

Fur

The fur trade has been an important industry here for centuries. Québec City is a good place to purchase high-quality furs at fairly reasonable prices. The department store **J. B. Laliberté** (✉ 595 rue St-Joseph Est, ☎ 418/525–4841) carries furs. Since 1894, one of the best furriers in town has been **Richard Robitaille Fourrures** (✉ 1500 rue des Taneurs, ☎ 418/681–7297).

Gifts

Collection Lazuli (✉ 774 rue St-Jean, ☎ 418/525–6528; ✉ 2600 blvd. Laurier, Pl. de la Cité, Ste-Foy, ☎ 418/652–3732) offers a good choice of unusual art objects and international jewelry.

Jewelry

Joaillier Louis Perrier (✉ 48 rue du Petit-Champlain, ☎ 418/692–4633) has Québec-made gold and silver jewelry. Exclusive jewelry can be found at **Zimmermann** (✉ 46 côte de la Fabrique, ☎ 418/692–2672).

SIDE TRIPS FROM QUÉBEC CITY

Several easy excursions will show you another side of the province and provide more insight into its past. The spectacular Montmorency Falls and the Basilique Ste-Anne-de-Beaupré can be seen in a day trip. A drive around the Ile d'Orléans, just east of the city, is an easy way to experience rural Québec. The farms, markets, and churches here evoke the island's long history. The island can be toured in an energetic day, though rural inns make it tempting to extend a visit.

Côte de Beaupré and Montmorency Falls

As legend tells it, when explorer Jacques Cartier first caught sight of the north shore of the St. Lawrence River in 1535, he exclaimed, "*Quel beau pré!*" ("What a lovely meadow!"), because the area was the first inviting piece of land he had spotted since leaving France. Today this fertile meadow, first settled by French farmers, is known as Côte de Beaupré (Beaupré Coast), stretching 40 km (25 mi) east from Québec City to the famous pilgrimage site of Ste-Anne-de-Beaupré. Historic Route 360, or avenue Royal, winds its way from Beauport to St-Joachim, east of St-Anne-de-Beaupré. The impressive Montmorency Falls are midway between Québec City and Ste-Anne-de-Beaupré.

Montmorency Falls

51 *10 km (6 mi) east of Québec City.*

As it cascades over a cliff into the St. Lawrence River, the Montmorency River (named for Charles de Montmorency, who was a governor of New France) is one of the most beautiful sights in the province. The falls, at 274 ft, are 50% higher than Niagara Falls. A cable car runs to the top of the falls in **Parc de la Chute-Montmorency** (Montmorency Falls Park) from late April–early November. During very cold weather, the falls' heavy spray freezes and forms a giant loaf-shape ice cone (hill) known to Québécois as the Pain du Sucre (Sugarloaf); this phenomenon attracts sledders and sliders from Québec City. Ice climbers come to scale the falls; a school trains novices for only a few days to make the ascent. In the warmer months, you can visit an observation tower in the river's gorge that is continuously sprayed by a fine drizzle from water pounding onto the cliff rocks. The top of the falls can be observed from avenue Royale.

The park is also historic. The British general Wolfe, on his way to conquer New France, set up camp here in 1759. In 1780, Sir Frederick Haldimand, then the governor of Canada, built a summer home—now a good restaurant called Manoir Montmorency—on top of the cliff. Prince Edward, Queen Victoria's father, rented this villa from 1791 to 1794. Unfortunately, the structure burned down several years ago; what stands is a re-creation. ⊠ *2490 av. Royale, Beauport,* ☎ *418/663–2877.* 🎫 *Cable car $7 round-trip; car parking $7.* ⏲ *Cable car Apr. 25–June 19 and Sept. 2–Oct. 25, daily 9–7; June 20–Aug. 2, daily 9 AM–11 PM; Aug. 3–Sept. 1, daily 9–9; Oct. 26–Nov. 1, daily 9–4. It functions on winter weekends for the Sugarloaf slide.*

Ste-Anne-de-Beaupré

40 km (25 mi) east of Québec City.

The small town of Ste-Anne-de-Beaupré is famous for an impressive shrine
★ 52 with the same name.The monumental and inspiring **Basilique Ste-Anne-de-Beaupré** is surrounded by aged, modest homes and tacky souvenir shops that emphasize its grandeur. The basilica has become a popular attraction as well as an important Catholic shrine: More than a half-million people visit the site each year.

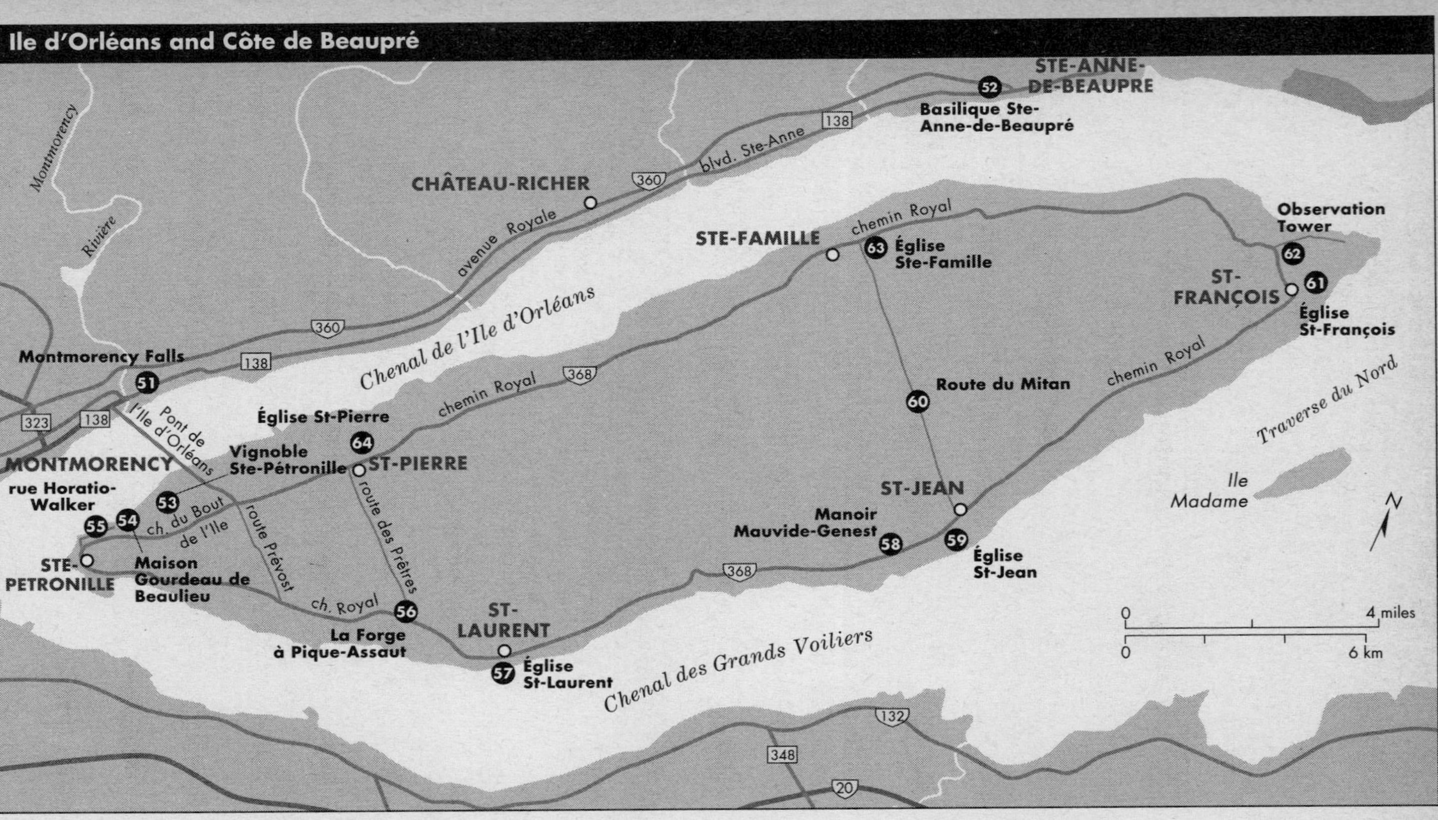
Ile d'Orléans and Côte de Beaupré
STE-ANNE-DE-BEAUPRE
Basilique Ste-Anne-de-Beaupré
Montmorency Rivière
CHÂTEAU-RICHER
avenue Royale
blvd. Ste-Anne
138
360
STE-FAMILLE
chemin Royal
Église Ste-Famille
Observation Tower
ST-FRANÇOIS
Église St-François
Chenal de l'Ile d'Orléans
Montmorency Falls
323
368
Route du Mitan
Traverse du Nord
Pont de l'Ile d'Orléans
Église St-Pierre
Vignoble Ste-Pétronille
ST-PIERRE
MONTMORENCY
rue Horatio-Walker
ch. du Bout de l'Ile
route Prévost
route des Prêtres
ST-JEAN
Manoir Mauvide-Genest
Ile Madame
Église St-Jean
STE-PETRONILLE
Maison Gourdeau de Beaulieu
ch. Royal
La Forge à Pique-Assaut
ST-LAURENT
Église St-Laurent
Chenal des Grands Voiliers
0
4 miles
6 km
N
132
348
20
51
52
53
54
55
56
57
58
59
60
61
62
63
64

The French brought their devotion to St. Anne (the patron saint of those in shipwrecks) with them when they sailed across the Atlantic to New France. In 1650, Breton sailors caught in a storm vowed to erect a chapel in honor of this patron saint at the exact spot where they landed. The present-day neo-Roman basilica constructed in 1923 was the fifth to be built on the site where the sailors first touched ground.

According to local legend, St. Anne was responsible over the years for saving voyagers from shipwrecks in the harsh waters of the St. Lawrence. Tributes to her miraculous powers can be seen in the shrine's various mosaics, murals, altars, and ceilings. A bas-relief at the entrance depicts St. Anne welcoming her pilgrims, and ceiling mosaics represent her life. Numerous crutches and braces posted on the back pillars have been left by those who have felt the saint's healing powers.

The basilica, in the shape of a Latin cross, has two granite steeples jutting from its gigantic structure. Its interior has 22 chapels and 18 altars, as well as round arches and numerous ornaments in the Romanesque style. The 214 stained-glass windows by Frenchmen Auguste Labouret and Pierre Chaudière, finished in 1949, tell a story of salvation through personages who were believed to be instruments of God over the centuries. Other features of the shrine are intricately carved wood pews decorated with various animals and several smaller altars (behind the main altar) dedicated to different saints.

The original, 17th-century wood chapel in the village of Ste-Anne-de-Beaupré was built too close to the St. Lawrence and was swept away by river flooding. In 1676 the chapel was replaced by a stone church that was visited by pilgrims for more than a century, but this structure was also demolished in 1872. The first basilica, which replaced the stone church, was destroyed by a fire in 1922. The following year architects Maxime Rosin from Paris and Louis N. Audet from Québec province designed the basilica that now stands. ✉ *10018 av. Royale,* ☎ *418/827–3781.* 🎫 *Free.* 🕑 *Reception booth mid-May–mid-Oct., daily 8:30–7:30. Guided tours daily at 1 in summer; Sept.–mid-May, call in advance to arrange a tour.*

The **Commemorative Chapel,** across from the basilica on avenue Royale, was designed by Claude Bailiff and built in 1878. The memorial chapel was constructed on the location of the transept of a stone church built in 1676 and contains the old building's foundations. Among the remnants housed here are the old church's bell, dating from 1696; an early 18th-century altar designed by Vezina; a crucifix sculpted by François-Noël Levasseur in 1775; and a pulpit designed by François Baillargé in 1807.

Côte de Beaupré and Montmorency Falls A to Z

ARRIVING AND DEPARTING

To reach Montmorency Falls, take Route 440 (Autoroute Dufferin-Montmorency) east from Québec City approximately 9½ km (6 mi) to the exit for Montmorency Falls. To drive directly to Ste-Anne-de Beaupré, continue east on Route 440 for approximately 29 km (18 mi) and exit at Ste-Anne-de-Beaupré.

An alternative way to reach Ste-Anne-de-Beaupré is to take Route 360, or avenue Royale. Take Route 440 from Québec City, turn left at d'Estimauville, and right on boulevard Ste-Anne until it intersects with Route 360. Also called *le chemin du Roi* (the King's Road), this panoramic route is one of the oldest in North America, winding 30 km (19 mi) along the steep ridge of the Côte de Beaupré. The road borders 17th- and 18th-century farmhouses, historic churches, and Normandy-style homes with half-buried root cellars.

GUIDED TOURS

Gray Line (☎ 418/653–9722, FAX 418/653–9834) and **Maple Leaf Sight-seeing Tours** (☎ 418/649–9226) lead day excursions along the Côte de Beaupré, with stops at Montmorency Falls and the Ste-Anne-de-Beaupré Basilica. Cost is about $32 per tour.

VISITOR INFORMATION

The **Beaupré Coast Interpretation Center,** in the old mill Petit-Pré, built in 1695, has displays on the history of the region. ✉ *7007 av. Royale, Château-Richer,* ☎ *418/824–3677.* *$2.* ⊙ *Mid-May–mid-Oct., daily 10–5.* **Quebec City Tourist Information** has a bureau in Beauport (✉ 4300 blvd. Ste-Anne, Rte. 138) in Montmorency Falls Park. It's open mid-June–October 12, daily 9–5:45.

Ile d'Orléans

The Algonquins called it Minigo, the "Bewitched Place," and over the years the island's tranquil rural beauty has inspired poets and painters. The Ile d'Orléans is only 15 minutes from downtown Québec City, but a visit here is one of the best ways to get a feel for traditional life in rural Québec. The road that rings the island is dotted with centuries-old homes and some of the oldest churches in the region. Ile d'Orléans is at its best in summer when the boughs of trees in lush orchards bend under the weight of apples, plums, or pears, and the fields are bursting with strawberries and raspberries. Roadside stands sell woven articles, maple syrup, baked goods, jams, fruits, and vegetables. Visitors can also pick their own produce at about two dozen farms. The island, immortalized by one of its most famous residents, the late poet and songwriter Félix Leclerc, is still fertile ground for artists and artisans.

The island was discovered at about the same time as Québec City, in 1535. Explorer Jacques Cartier noticed an abundance of vines and called it the Island of Bacchus, after the Greek god of wine. (Today, native Québec vines are being crossbred with European varieties at Ste-Pétronille's fledgling vineyard.) In 1536 Cartier renamed the island in honor of the duke of Orléans, son of the French king François I. Its fertile soil and abundant fishing made it so attractive to settlers that its population once exceeded Québec City's.

Ile d'Orléans, about 8 km (5 mi) wide and 34 km (21 mi) long, is composed of six small villages that have sought over the years to retain their identities. The island's bridge to the mainland was built in 1935, and in 1970 the island was declared a historic area to protect it from urban development.

Ste-Pétronille

17 km (10½ mi) from Québec City.

The lovely village of Ste-Pétronille, the first to be settled on Ile d'Orléans, lies to the west of the bridge to the island. Founded in 1648, the community was chosen in 1759 by British general James Wolfe for his headquarters. With 40,000 soldiers and a hundred ships, the English bombarded French-occupied Québec City and Côte de Beaupré.

During the late 19th century, the English population of Québec developed Ste-Pétronille into a resort village. This area is considered to be the island's most beautiful, not only because of its spectacular views of Montmorency Falls and Québec City but also for the Regency-style English villas and exquisitely tended gardens.

53 At the **Vignoble de Ste-Pétronille,** hardy native Québec vines have been crossbred with three types of European grapes to produce a surprisingly good dry white wine. A guided tour of the vineyard includes

a taste testing. ⊠ *1A chemin Royal,* ☎ *418/828–9554.* 🎫 *$2.50.* ⊙ *Mid-June–mid-Oct., daily 10–6.*

At the **Plante family farm** (⊠ 20 chemin Royal, ☎ 418/828–9603) you can stop to pick apples (in season) or buy fresh fruits and vegetables.

54 The island's first home, the **Maison Gourdeau de Beaulieu** (⊠ 137 chemin Royal) was built in 1648 for Jacques Gourdeau de Beaulieu, who was the first seigneur (a landholder who distributed lots to tenant farmers) of Ste-Pétronille. Remodeled over the years, this white house with blue shutters now incorporates both French and Québécois styles. Its thick walls and dormer windows are characteristic of Breton architecture, but its sloping bell-shape roof, designed to protect buildings from large amounts of snow, is typically Québécois. The house is not open to the public.

55 The tiny street called **rue Horatio-Walker,** off chemin Royal, was named after the turn-of-the-century painter known for his landscapes of the island. Walker lived on this street from 1904 until his death in 1938. At 11 and 13 rue Horatio-Walker are his home and workshop, but they are not open to the public.

DINING AND LODGING

$$$–$$$$ ✕🏨 **La Goéliche.** This English-style country manor, rebuilt in 1996–97 following a fire, stands just steps away from the St. Lawrence River. Antiques decorate the cozy, elegant rooms, all with river views. Sinks are in the rooms instead of the baths to maximize space. Classic French cuisine includes fillet of trout rolled with spinach and cheese from Charlevoix, and breast of duck in an orange sauce perfumed with Grand Marnier. The romantic dining room overlooks the river; an outdoor terrace is used in summer. ⊠ *22 chemin du Quai,* ☎ *418/828–2248,* FAX *418/828–2745. 18 rooms. Restaurant. AE, MC, V.*

SHOPPING

Chocolaterie de lle d'Orléans (⊠ 196 chemin Royal, ☎ 418/828–2252) combines Belgian chocolate with local ingredients to create handmade treats. Some choices are chocolates filled with maple butter or the *framboisette* made from raspberries. In summer there are homemade ice creams and sherbets.

St-Laurent

9 km (5½ mi) from Ste-Pétronille.

Founded in 1679, St-Laurent is one of the island's maritime villages. Until as late as 1935, residents here used boats as their main means of
56 transportation. The **La Forge à Pique-Assaut** (⊠ 2200 chemin Royal, ☎ 418/828–9300) belongs to the talented and well-known local artisan Guy Bel, who has done ironwork restoration for Québec City. He was born in Lyon, France, and studied there at the Ecole des Beaux Arts. In summer he can be seen hard at work daily; his stylish candlesticks, chandeliers, fireplace tools, and other ironworks are for sale. In winter his workshop is closed on weekends.

The **Parc Maritime de St-Laurent,** at a former boatyard, is where craftspeople specializing in boatbuilding practiced their trade. Now you can picnic here, rent a rowboat, and visit the Chalouperie Godbout (Godbout Longboat), which houses a complete collection of tools used during the golden era of boatbuilding. You can try your hand at some boatbuilding skills and practice tying sailors' knots. ⊠ *120 chemin de la Chalouperie,* ☎ *418/828–9672.* 🎫 *Park $2, parking $3.* ⊙ *Mid-June–Aug., daily 10–5; Sept.–early Oct., weekends 10–5 or by reservation; mid-May–mid-June by reservation.*

57 The tall, inspiring **Église St-Laurent,** which stands next to the village marina on chemin Royal, was built in 1860 on the site of an 18th-century church that had to be torn down. One of the church's procession chapels is a miniature stone replica of the original. ✉ *1532 chemin Royal.* 🎫 *Free.* ⏱ *Summer, daily.*

DINING AND LODGING

$$–$$$$ ✕ **Moulin de St. Laurent.** This is an early 18th-century stone mill in which you can dine in the herb-and-flower garden out back in season. Scrumptious snacks, such as quiches, bagels, and salads, are available at the café-terrace. Evening dishes include local game such as stuffed rabbit. ✉ *754 chemin Royal,* ☎ *418/829–3888. AE, DC, MC, V.*

$–$$ ✕🏨 **Le Canard Huppé.** He's barely 30, but award-winning chef Philip Rae's inventive use of fresh island ingredients and his often spectacular presentations have already won rave reviews at this restaurant ($$$–$$$$). As the inn's name suggests, the contemporary cuisine usually showcases at least one dish with duck, whether it's duck with pineapple chutney and cedar sauce or red (from beet juice) ravioli stuffed with conserve of duck and smoked snails. Upstairs, each of the inn's rooms has its own personality. Rooms are decorated with original paintings by Québec City area artists and unusual antiques—some from as far away as Polynesia. ✉ *2198 chemin Royal,* ☎ *418/828–2292,* FAX *418/828–0966. 8 rooms. Restaurant. DC, MC, V.*

St-Jean

12 km (7 mi) from St-Laurent.

The southernmost point of the island, St-Jean is a village whose inhabitants were once river pilots and navigators. Most of its small, homogeneous row homes were built between 1840 and 1860. Being at sea most of the time, the sailors did not need large homes and plots of land, as did the farmers.

58 St-Jean's beautiful Normandy-style manor, **Manoir Mauvide-Genest,** was built in 1734 for Jean Mauvide—surgeon to Louis XV—and his wife, Marie-Anne Genest. Most notable about this house, which still has its original thick walls, ceiling beams, and fireplaces, is the degree to which it has held up over the years, in spite of being targeted by English guns during the 1759 siege of Québec City. The indentations left by cannonballs can still be seen on the facade. The home is a pleasure to explore; all rooms are furnished with antiques from the 18th and 19th centuries. There's also an exhibit on French architecture. ✉ *1451 chemin Royal,* ☎ *418/829–2630.* 🎫 *$4.* ⏱ *June–Aug., daily 10:30–5:30; Sept.–mid-Oct., weekends by reservation.*

59 At the eastern end of the village is **Église St-Jean,** a massive granite structure with large red doors and a towering steeple built in 1749. The church resembles a ship; it is big and round and appears to be sitting right on the river. Paintings of the patron saints of seamen line the interior walls. The church's cemetery is also intriguing, especially if you can read French. Back in the 18th century, piloting the St. Lawrence was a dangerous profession. The cemetery tombstones recall the tragedies of lives lost in these harsh waters. ✉ *2001 chemin Royal,* ☎ *418/829–3182.* 🎫 *Free.* ⏱ *Summer, daily 9–5.*

60 Outside St-Jean, chemin Royal crosses **route du Mitan,** the most beautiful on the island. In old French, *mitan* means "halfway." This road, dividing the island in half, has views of acres of tended farmland, apple orchards, and maple groves. If you need to end your circuit of the island here, take route du Mitan, which brings you to Ste-Famille; head west on chemin Royal to return to the bridge to the mainland.

St-François

12 km (7 mi) from St-Jean.

Sprawling open fields separate 17th-century farmhouses in St-François, the island's least-toured and most rustic village. This community at the eastern tip of the island was originally settled mainly by farmers. St-François is also the perfect place to visit one of the island's *cabanes à sucre* (maple-sugaring shacks), found along chemin Royal. Stop at a hut for a tasting tour; sap is gathered from the maple groves and boiled until it turns to syrup. When it is poured on ice, it tastes like a delicious toffee. The maple syrup season is late March–April.

61 **Église St-François** (✉ 106 chemin Royal, ☎ 418/829–3440), built in 1734, is one of eight provincial churches dating from the French regime. At the time the English seized Québec City in 1759, General Wolfe knew St-François to be a strategic point along the St. Lawrence. Consequently, he stationed British troops here and used the church as a military hospital. In 1988, a car crash set the church on fire and most of the interior treasures were lost. A separate children's cemetery stands as a silent witness to the difficult life of early residents.

62 A picnic area with a wood **observation tower** is perfectly situated for viewing the majestic St. Lawrence. In spring and fall, wild Canada geese can be seen here. The area is about 2 km (1 mi) north on chemin Royal from St-François Church.

Ste-Famille

14 km (9 mi) from St-François.

The village of Ste-Famille, founded in 1661, has exquisite scenery, including abundant apple orchards and strawberry fields with views of Côte de Beaupré and Mont Ste-Anne in the distance. But it also has plenty of historic charm, claiming the area's highest concentration of stone houses dating from the French regime.

63 The impressive **Église Ste-Famille,** constructed in 1749, is the only church in the province to have three bell towers at the front. Its ceiling was redone in the mid-19th century with elaborate designs in wood and gold. The church also holds a famous painting, *L'Enfant Jésus Voyant la Croix (Baby Jesus Looking at the Cross),* done in 1670 by Frère Luc (Father Luc), who was sent from France to decorate churches in the area. ✉ *3915 chemin Royal.* *Free.* *Summer, daily.*

DINING

$$$–$$$$ ✕ **L'Atre.** After you park your car, you'll be driven in a 1954 Chrysler to the 17th-century Normandy-style house furnished with Québécois pine antiques. True to the establishment's name, which means "hearth," all the dishes are cooked and served from a fireplace. The menu emphasizes hearty fare, such as beef bourguignonne and tourtière, with maple-sugar pie for dessert. Halfway through the meal, diners visit the attic for a nip of maple-syrup liqueur. ✉ *4403 chemin Royal,* ☎ *418/829–2474. Reservations essential. AE, MC, V. Closed Nov.–Apr.*

St-Pierre

14 km (9 mi) from St-Famille.

St-Pierre, on the northwest side of the island, was established in 1679. Set on a plateau that has the island's most fertile land, the town has long been the center of traditional farming industries. The best products grown here are potatoes, asparagus, and corn, and the many dairy farms have given the village a reputation for butter and other dairy products. If you continue west on chemin Royal, just up ahead is the bridge back to the mainland and Route 440.

64 **Église St-Pierre,** the oldest on the island, dates from 1717. It is no longer open for worship, but it was restored during the 1960s and is open to visitors. Many of the original components are still intact, such as benches with compartments below, where hot bricks and stones were placed to keep people warm during winter services. Félix Leclerc (1914–88), the first Québécois singer to make his mark in Europe, is buried in the cemetery nearby. ✉ *1243 chemin Royal.* 🎫 *Free.* ⏲ *Summer, daily.*

La Ferme Monna has won international awards for its crème de cassis de l'Ile d'Orléans, a liqueur made from black currants. The farm has free samples of the strong, sweet cassis or one of Monna's black currant wines, and a tour explains how they are made. ✉ *723 chemin Royal,* ☎ *418/828–1057.* 🎫 *Free; guided tours $4.* ⏲ *June–Sept., daily 10–6; Mar. and Oct.–Dec., weekends 10–5.*

Ile d'Orléans A to Z

ARRIVING AND DEPARTING

From Québec City, take Route 440 (Autoroute Dufferin-Montmorency) northeast. After a drive of about 10 km (6 mi) take the bridge Pont de l'Ile d'Orléans to the island. Ile d'Orléans has no public transportation; cars are the only way to get around, unless you take a guided tour (☞ Guided Tours, *below*). Parking can sometimes be a problem, but you can leave your car in the church parking lot and explore each village on foot. Cycling is also a popular option, although there are no separate bicycle lanes. The main road, chemin Royal (Route 368), extends 67 km (42 mi) through the island's six villages; street numbers along chemin Royal begin at No. 1 for each municipality.

B&B RESERVATION SERVICE

Reservations are necessary at the island's 50 B&Bs, which cost about $50–$100 per night for a double-occupancy room. The **Chamber of Commerce** (☎ 418/828–9411) has a referral service for B&Bs.

EMERGENCIES

Centre Médical Prévost (✉ 1015 Rte. Prévost, St-Pierre, ☎ 418/828–2213) is the principal medical clinic on the island.

GUIDED TOURS

Québec City tour companies, including **Maple Leaf Sight-seeing Tours** (☎ 418/649–9226) and **Gray Line** (☎ 418/653–9722), have bus tours of the western tip of the island, combined with sightseeing along the Côte de Beaupré. The island's **Chamber of Commerce** rents a cassette tape for $8 with an interesting 90-minute tour of the island by car; it's available at the tourist kiosk (☞ Visitor Information, *below*).

Any of the offices of the **Québec City Region Tourism and Convention Bureau** (☞ Visitor Information *in* Québec City A to Z, *below*) can provide information on tours and accommodations on the island.

VISITOR INFORMATION

The island's **Chamber of Commerce** operates a tourist information kiosk at the west corner of côte du Pont and chemin Royal in St-Pierre. ✉ *490 côte du Pont, St-Pierre,* ☎ *418/828–9411.* ⏲ *June–Sept., daily 8:30–7; Oct.–May, weekdays 9–5.*

QUÉBEC CITY A TO Z

Arriving and Departing

By Bus

Orléans Express Inc. provides service from Montréal to Québec City daily, departing hourly 6 AM–10 PM, with an additional bus at midnight. The three-hour ride costs $35.90 one-way, and a round-trip is double that; but a round-trip costs $53.27 if you return within 10 days and do not travel on Friday or certain days during holiday periods. You can purchase tickets only at one of the terminals (☞ *below*).

TERMINALS

Montréal: Terminus Voyageur (✉ 505 blvd. de Maisonneuve Est, ☎ 514/842–2281). **Québec City:** Downtown Terminal (✉ 320 rue Abraham-Martin, ☎ 418/525–3000); Ste-Foy Terminal (✉ 925 av. de Rochebelle, ☎ 418/525–3000).

By Car

Montréal and Québec City are linked by Autoroute 20 on the south shore of the St. Lawrence River and by Autoroute 40 on the north shore. On both highways, the ride between the two cities is about 240 km (149 mi) and takes about three hours. U.S. I–87 in New York, U.S. I–89 in Vermont, and U.S. I–91 in New Hampshire connect with Autoroute 20. Highway 401 from Toronto links up with Autoroute 20.

Driving northeast from Montréal on Autoroute 20, follow signs for Pont Pierre-Laporte (Pierre Laporte Bridge) as you approach Québec City. After you've crossed the bridge, turn right onto boulevard Laurier (Route 175), which becomes the Grande Allée leading into Québec City. Also *see* Getting Around by Car, *below.*

By Plane

Jean Lesage International Airport (✉ 500 rue Principale, Ste-Foy, ☎ 418/640–2600) is about 19 km (12 mi) from downtown. Few U.S. **airlines** fly directly to Québec City. You usually have to stop in Montréal, Toronto, or Ottawa and take a regional or commuter airline, such as Air Canada's Air Alliance or Canadian Airlines International's Inter-Canadien. Air Alliance and Delta offer some direct flights (☞ Air Travel *in* the Gold Guide).

BETWEEN THE AIRPORT AND QUÉBEC CITY

The ride from the airport into town should be no longer than 30 minutes. Most hotels do not have an airport shuttle, but they will make a reservation for you with a bus company. If you're not in a rush, a shuttle bus offered by Autobus La Québécoise Inc. (☞ *below*) is convenient and half the price of a taxi.

By Bus. Autobus La Québécoise Inc. (✉ 5480 rue Rideau, ☎ 418/570–5379) has a shuttle bus from the airport to hotels; cost is less than $10 one-way. Reservations are necessary for the trip to the airport.

By Car. If you're driving from the airport, take Route 540 (Autoroute Duplessis) to Route 175 (blvd. Laurier), which becomes Grande Allée and leads right to Vieux-Québec. The ride is about 30 minutes and may be only slightly longer (45 minutes or so) during rush hours (7:30–8:30 AM into town and 4–5:30 PM leaving town).

By Limousine. Private limo service is expensive, starting at $50 for the ride from the airport into Québec City. Try **Groupe Limousine A-1** (✉ 361 rue des Commissaires Est, ☎ 418/523–5059).

By Taxi. Taxis are available immediately outside the airport exit near the baggage claim area. A ride into the city costs about $25.Two local taxi firms are **Taxi Québec** (✉ 975 8e av., ☎ 418/522–2001) and **Taxi Coop de Québec** (✉ 496 2e av., ☎ 418/525–5191), the largest company in the city.

By Train

VIA Rail (☎ 418/692–3940, 800/361–5390 in Québec), Canada's passenger rail service, runs trains from Montréal to Québec City four times daily Tuesday–Friday, and three times daily on Saturday, Sunday, and Monday. The trip takes less than three hours, with a stop in Ste-Foy. Tickets must be purchased in advance at any VIA Rail office or travel agent. The basic one-way rate, including taxes, is about $54, but a limited quantity of seats are reduced to $32 if tickets are bought at least five days in advance. First-class service costs about $95 each way and includes early boarding, seat selection, and a three-course meal with wine.

The train arrives in Québec City at the 19th-century **Gare du Palais** (✉ 450 rue de la Gare du Palais, ☎ 418/524–6452), in the heart of the old city.

Getting Around

By Bus

The city's transit system, **Société de Transport de la Communauté Urbaine de Québec (STCUQ)** (☎ 418/627–2511) runs buses approximately every 15 to 30 minutes that stop at major points around town. The cost is $2; you'll need exact change. Bus tickets are available for $1.60 ($4.35 for day pass) at major convenience stores. All buses stop in Lower Town at Place Jacques-Cartier and outside St-Jean Gate at Place d'Youville in Upper Town. Transportation maps are available at visitor information offices.

By Car

It is necessary to have a car only if you plan to visit outlying areas. The narrow streets of the old city leave few two-hour metered parking spaces available. However, several parking garages at central locations charge about $10 a day. Main garages are at City Hall, Place d'Youville, Edifice Marie-Guyart, Complex G, Place Québec, Château Frontenac, Québec Seminary, rue St-Paul, and the Old Port.

By Ferry

The **Québec–Lévis ferry** (☎ 418/644–3704) crosses the St. Lawrence River to the town of Lévis. Although the crossing takes 15 minutes, waiting time can increase that to an hour. The cost is $1.50 in winter and $1.75 in summer. From December through April, the first ferry from Québec City leaves daily at 6:30 AM from the pier at rue Dalhousie, across from Place Royale. Crossings run every half hour from 7:30 AM until 6:30 PM, then hourly until 2:15 AM. From May through November, the ferry adds extra service every 20 minutes during rush hours: 7:20–9 AM and 4–6 PM.

By Foot

Walking is the best way to explore the city. Vieux-Québec measures 11 square km (about 6 square mi), and most historic sites, hotels, and restaurants are within the walls or a short distance outside. City maps are available at visitor information offices.

By Horse-Drawn Carriage

Hire a calèche on rue d'Auteuil between the St-Louis and Kent gates from **André Beaurivage** (☎ 418/687–9797), **Balades en Calèche et Diligence** (☎ 418/624–3062), or **Les Calèches du Vieux-Québec** (☎ 418/683–9222). The cost is about $50 without tax or tip for a 45-minute tour of Vieux-Québec. Some drivers talk about Québec's history and others don't; if you want a storyteller, ask in advance.

By Limousine

Groupe Limousine A-1 (✉ 361 rue des Commissaires Est, ☎ 418/523–5059) has 24-hour service.

By Taxi

Taxis are stationed in front of major hotels and the Hôtel de Ville (City Hall), along rue des Jardins, and at Place d'Youville outside St-Jean Gate. Passengers are charged an initial $2.25, plus $1 for each kilometer (½ mi). For radio-dispatched cars, try **Taxi Coop de Québec** (☎ 418/525–5191) or **Taxi Québec** (☎ 418/522–2001).

Contacts and Resources

B&B Reservation Agencies

Québec City has many accommodations in hostels and B&Bs, which are becoming known as Couette & Cafés. To guarantee a room in peak season, reserve in advance. **Québec City Tourist Information** (✉ 835 av. Laurier, G1R 2L3, ☎ 418/649–2608) has B&B listings.

Car Rentals

Hertz Canada (Airport, ☎ 418/871–1571; Vieux-Québec, ✉ 44 Côte du Palais, ☎ 418/694–1224, 800/263–0600 in English, 800/263–0678 in French). **Tilden** (Airport, ☎ 418/871–1224; ✉ 295 St. Paul St., ☎ 418/694–1727). **Via Route** (✉ 2605 Hamel Blvd., ☎ 418/682–2660).

Consulate

The **U.S. Consulate** (✉ 2 Pl. Terrasse Dufferin, ☎ 418/692–2096) faces the Governors' Park near the Château Frontenac.

Dentists and Doctors

Clinique Dentaire Darveau, Dablois and Tardif (✉ 1175 rue Lavigerie, Edifice Iberville 2, Room 100, Ste-Foy, ☎ 418/653–5412) is open Monday–Tuesday 8–8, Wednesday 8–5, Thursday 8–6, and Friday 8–4.

Pavillon Centre Hospitalier de l'Université Laval (CHUL) (✉ 2705 blvd. Laurier, ☎ 418/656–4141) is in Ste-Foy. **Pavillon Hôtel-Dieu** (✉ 11 côte du Palais, ☎ 418/691–5151, 418/691–5042 for emergencies) is the main hospital inside Vieux-Québec.

Emergencies

Distress Center (☎ 418/686–2433). **Fire, police** (☎ 911 or 418/691–7882 outside the 911 area). **Poison Center** (☎ 418/656–8090). **Provincial police** (☎ 418/623–6262).

English-Language Bookstore

La Maison Anglaise (✉ 2600 blvd. Laurier, Place de la Cité, Ste-Foy, ☎ 418/654–9523).

Guided Tours

BOAT

Croisières AML Inc. (✉ Pier Chouinard, 10 rue Dalhousie, beside the Québec-Lévis ferry terminal, ☎ 418/692–1159) runs cruises on the St. Lawrence River aboard the MV *Louis-Jolliet.* The 1½- to 3-hour cruises from May through mid-October start at $20.

ORIENTATION

Tours cover such sights as Québec City, Montmorency Falls, and Ste-Anne-de-Beaupré; combination city and harbor-cruise tours are also available. Québec City tours operate year-round; excursions to outlying areas may operate only in summer. Tickets for **Gray Line** bus tours (☎ 418/653–9722) can be purchased at most major hotels or at the kiosk at Terrasse Dufferin at Place d'Armes. Tours run year-round and cost $20–$80; departure is from Château Frontenac terrace. **Maple Leaf Sight-seeing Tours** (✉ 240 3[e] rue, ☎ 418/649–9226) offers guided tours in a minibus or trolley. Call for a reservation, and the company will pick you up at your hotel. Prices are $21–$89.

WALKING

Adlard Tours (✉ 13 rue Ste-Famille, ☎ 418/692–2358) leads walking tours of the old city amid the narrow streets that buses cannot enter. The $14 cost includes a refreshment break; unilingual tours are available in many languages. Tours leave from 12 rue Ste-Anne.

Late-Night Pharmacy

Pharmacie Brunet (✉ Les Galeries Charlesbourg, 4250 1re av., north of Québec City in Charlesbourg, ☎ 418/623–1571), is open daily, 24 hours a day.

Opening and Closing Times

Most banks are open Monday–Wednesday 10–3 and close later on Thursday and Friday. **Bank of Montréal** (✉ Pl. Laurier, 2700 blvd. Laurier, Ste-Foy, ☎ 418/525–3786) is open Saturday 11–2. For currency exchange, **Echange de Devises Montréal** (✉ 12 rue Ste-Anne, ☎ 418/694–1014) is open September–mid-June, daily 9–5, and mid-June–Labor Day, daily 8:30–7:30.

Museum hours are typically 10–5, with longer evening hours during summer months. Most are closed on Monday. For store hours, *see* Shopping, *above*. In winter many attractions and shops change their hours; visitors are advised to call ahead.

Road Conditions

Seasonal information is available November–April (☎ 418/643–6830).

Travel Agencies

American Express (✉ 2700 blvd. Laurier, Place Laurier, ☎ 418/ 658–8820). **Inter-Voyage** (✉ 1095 rue de l'Amérique Française, ☎ 418/524–1414).

Visitor Information

Québec City Region Tourism and Convention Bureau has two visitor information centers that are open year-round and a mobile information service that operates between mid-June and September 7 (look for the mopeds with a big question mark).

The **Québec City** (✉ 835 av. Laurier, G1R 2L3, ☎ 418/649–2608) center is open June–September 7, daily 8:30–7:45; September 8–October 12, daily 8:30–5:15; October 13–May, daily 9–4:45. **Québec Government Tourism Department** (✉ 12 rue Ste-Anne, Pl. d'Armes, ☎ 800/363–7777) has a center that is open fall–winter, daily 9–5, and summer, daily 8:30–7:30. The **Ste-Foy** (✉ 3300 av. des Hôtels, G1W 5A8: look for the big question mark) center, a drop-in office (no telephone), is open June–September 7, daily 8:30–7:45; September 8–October 12, daily 8:30–5:45; October 13–May, daily 9–4:45.

4 Province of Québec

The Laurentians, the Eastern Townships, Charlevoix, the Gaspé Peninsula

Québec has a distinct personality forged by its French heritage and culture. The land, too, is memorable: Within its boundaries lie thousands of lakes and rivers—the highways for intrepid explorers, fur traders, and pioneers. Echoes of the past remain in the charming rural communities of Charlevoix and the Eastern Townships. The Laurentians with their ski resorts and the forested coastline of the Gulf of St. Lawrence also lend a unique flavor to La Belle Province.

By Dorothy Guinan

Updated by Helga Loverseed

AMONG THE PROVINCES OF CANADA, Québec is set apart by its strong French heritage, a matter not only of language but of customs, religion, and political structure. Québec covers a vast area—almost one-sixth of Canada's total—although the upper three-quarters is only sparsely inhabited. Most of the population lives in the southern cities, especially Montréal (☞ Chapter 2) and Québec City (☞ Chapter 3). Outside the cities, however, you'll find serenity and natural beauty in the province's innumerable lakes, streams, and rivers; in its farmlands and villages; in its great mountains and deep forests; and in its rugged coastline along the Gulf of St. Lawrence. Though the winters are long, there are plenty of winter sports to while away the cold months, especially in the Laurentians, with their many ski resorts.

The first European to arrive in Québec was French explorer Jacques Cartier, in 1534; another Frenchman, Samuel de Champlain, arrived in 1603 to build French settlements in the region, and Jesuit missionaries followed in due course. Louis XIV of France proclaimed Canada a crown colony in 1663, and the land was allotted to French aristocrats in large grants called seigneuries. As tenants, known as habitants, settled upon farms in Québec, the Roman Catholic Church took on an importance that went beyond religion. Priests and nuns also acted as doctors, educators, and overseers of business arrangements between the habitants and between French-speaking fur traders and English-speaking merchants. An important doctrine of the church in Québec, one that took on more emphasis after the British conquest of 1759, was *survivance,* the survival of the French people and their culture. Couples were encouraged to have large families, and they did—until the 1950s families with 10 or 12 children were common.

Québec's recent threats to secede from the Canadian union are part of a long-standing tradition of independence. Although the British won control of Canada in the French and Indian War, which ended in 1763, Parliament passed the Québec Act in 1774, which ensured the continuation of French civil law in Québec and left provincial authority in the hands of the Roman Catholic Church. In general the law preserved the traditional French-Canadian way of life. Tensions between French- and English-speaking Canada have continued throughout the 20th century, however, and in 1974 the province proclaimed French its sole official language, much the same way the provinces of Manitoba and Alberta had taken steps earlier in the century to make English their sole official language. In 1990 the Canadian government failed to add Québec's signature to changes it had brought about in the Canadian Constitution and in 1992 failed to have its proposed constitutional changes accepted by the Canadian population in a referendum. Today Québec is part of the Canadian union and a signatory to its constitution, but it has not accepted the changes made in that document during the 1980s.

Being able to speak French can make a visit to the province more pleasant—many locals, at least outside Montréal, do not speak English. If you don't speak French, arm yourself with a phrase book or at least a knowledge of some basic phrases. It's also worth your while to sample the hearty traditional Québécois cuisine, for this is a province where food is taken seriously.

Pleasures and Pastimes

Dining

Whether you choose a croissant and espresso at a sidewalk café or order *poutine* (a heaped plate of *frites*—french fries—smothered with gravy and melted cheese curds) from a fast-food emporium, you won't soon forget your meals here. There is no such thing as simply "eating out" in the province; restaurants are an integral slice of Québec life. Outside Montréal and Québec City, restaurants offer both good value and classic cuisine. Cooking in the province tends to be hearty, with such fare as cassoulet, *tourtières* (meat pies), onion soup, and apple pie heading up menus. In the Laurentians, chefs at some of the finer inns have attracted international followings.

The Eastern Townships are one of Québec's foremost regions for fine cuisine and for traditional Québéçois dishes. Specialties include such mixed-game meat pies as *cipaille* and sweet, salty dishes like ham and maple syrup. Actually, maple syrup—much of it produced locally—is a mainstay of Québécois dishes. In addition, cloves, nutmeg, cinnamon, and pepper—spices used by the first settlers—have never gone out of style here, and local restaurants make good use of them.

Early reservations are essential. Monday or Tuesday is not too soon to book weekend tables at the best provincial restaurants.

CATEGORY	COST*
$$$$	over $35
$$$	$25–$35
$$	$15–$25
$	under $15

**per person, in Canadian dollars, excluding drinks, service, 7% GST, and 7.5% provincial tax*

Lodging

The full spectrum of accommodation options in Québec ranges from large resort hotels in the Laurentians and elegant Relais & Châteaux properties in the Eastern Townships to simple accommodations near the heart of the Gaspé. Year-round or in high season (winter in the Laurentians and other ski areas, summer elsewhere), many inns operate on the Modified American Plan (MAP) and include two meals, usually breakfast and dinner, in the cost of a night's stay. Be sure to ask what's included, and expect prices to be lower off-season. In addition, some inns require a minimum two-night stay; always ask.

CATEGORY	COST*
$$$$	over $160
$$$	$120–$160
$$	$85–$120
$	under $85

**All prices are for a standard double room, excluding 10% service charge, 7% GST, and 7.5% provincial tax, in Canadian dollars.*

Outdoor Activities and Sports

FISHING

There are more than 60 outfitters (some of whom are also innkeepers) in the northern Laurentians area, where provincial parks and game sanctuaries abound. Pike, walleye, and lake and speckled trout are plentiful just a three-hour drive north of Montréal. Open year-round in most cases, their lodging facilities range from the most luxurious first-class resorts to log cabins. As well as supplying trained guides, all offer services and equipment to allow neophytes or experts the best

Lower Québec

NEWFOUNDLAND
Labrador City
Gagnon
Havre-St-Pierre
Rivière-aux-Graines
Sept-Iles
Baie-Ste-Clair
Port-Cartier
Anticosti Island
Pipmuacan Reservoir
Godbout
Anse-Pleureuse
Rivière-au-Renard
Baie-Comeau
River
Gaspésie Prov. Park
Gaspé
Forillon Nat. Park
St. Lawrence
Matane
Cascapedia R.
Bonaventure R.
Forestville
Mont-Joli
Percé
Amqui
Chandler
Les Escoumins
Rimouski
New Richmond
Gulf of St. Lawrence
Chicoutimi
Saguenay R.
Trois-Pistoles
Dalhousie
Baie des Chaleurs
Campbellton
Saint-Siméon
Rivière-du-Loup
Cabano
Edmundston
Chatham
Grand Falls
NEW BRUNSWICK
Montmagny
Île d'Orleans
Saint John R.
Prince Edward Island
Northumberland Strait
Cape Tormentine
Thetford Mines
Houlton
St. John R.
Fredericton
Fundy Nat. Park
Moosehead Lake
Lac Mégantic
Westfield
Saint John
St. George
Bay of Fundy
Halifax
MAINE
Calais
Campobello Island
NOVA SCOTIA
Kennebec R.
Grand Manan
Bar Harbour
Rossignol
Yarmouth
N
ATLANTIC OCEAN
0
50 miles
0
75 km
KEY
Rail Lines
Ferry
Trans-Canada Hwy.

possible fishing in addition to boating, swimming, river rafting, windsurfing, ice fishing, cross-country skiing, or hiking.

RAFTING

The Rivière Rouge in the Laurentians rates among the best in North America, so it's not surprising that this river has spawned a miniboom in the sport. Just an hour's drive north of Montréal, the Rouge cuts across the rugged Laurentians through canyons and alongside beaches. From April through October, you can experience what traversing the region must have meant in the days of the voyageurs, though today's trip is much safer and more comfortable. (For outfitter information, ☞ Contacts and Resources *in* Québec A to Z, *below.*)

SKIING

The Laurentians are well known internationally as a downhill destination, from St-Sauveur to majestic Mont-Tremblant. Night skiing is available at many slopes. Cross-country skiing is popular throughout the area from December to the end of March, especially at Val David, Val Morin, and Ville l'Estérel. Each has a cross-country ski center and at least a dozen groomed trails.

The Eastern Townships have more than 900 km (558 mi) of cross-country trails. Three inns here offer a weeklong package of cross-country treks from one inn to another. The area is also popular as a downhill ski center, with ski hills on four mountains that dwarf anything the Laurentians have to offer, with the exception of Mont-Tremblant.

Charlevoix has three main ski areas with excellent facilities for both the downhill and cross-country skier.

Sugar Shacks

Every March the combination of sunny days and cold nights causes the sap to run in the maple trees. *Cabanes à sucre* (sugar shacks) go into operation, boiling the sap collected from the trees in buckets (now, at some places, complicated tubing and vats do the job). The many commercial enterprises scattered over the area host "sugaring offs" and tours of the process, including the tapping of maple trees, the boiling of the sap in vats, and *tire sur la neige,* when hot syrup is poured over cold snow to give it a taffy consistency just right for "pulling" and eating. A number of cabanes serve hearty meals of ham, baked beans, and pancakes, all drowned in maple syrup.

Exploring Québec

Two major recreational areas beyond Montréal attract stressed-out urbanites and anyone else who wants to relax: the Laurentians and the Eastern Townships. The Laurentians are a resort area with thousands of miles of wilderness and world-famous ski resorts. The mountains begin only 60 km (37 mi) north of Montréal. Rolling hills and farmland make the Eastern Townships, in the southwest corner of the province, popular year-round, with outdoor activities on ski slopes and lakes and in provincial parks. Cultural attractions are other pleasures here. The Townships start just 80 km (50 mi) east of Montréal.

Charlevoix is often called the Switzerland of Québec because of its landscape, which includes mountains, valleys, streams, and waterfalls. Charming villages stretch along the north shore of the St. Lawrence River for about 200 km (124 mi), from Ste-Anne-de-Beaupré east of Québec City to the Saguenay River. The knobby Gaspé Peninsula is where the St. Lawrence River meets the Gulf of St. Lawrence. This isolated peninsula, which begins about 200 km (124 mi) east of Québec

City, has a wild beauty all its own; mountains and cliffs tower above its beaches. The drive around the Gaspé is 848 km (526 mi).

Numbers in the text correspond to numbers in the margin and on the Laurentians (les Laurentides), Eastern Townships (les Cantons de l'Est) and Montérégie, Charlevoix, and Gaspé Peninsula (Gaspésie) maps.

Great Itineraries

IF YOU HAVE 2 DAYS

If you have only a few days for a visit, you'll need to concentrate on one area, and the Laurentians, outside Montréal, are a good choice. This resort area has recreational options (depending on the season) that include golf, hiking, and great skiing. Pick a resort town to stay in, whether it's **St-Sauveur-des-Monts** ④, **Ste-Adèle** ⑥, or **Mont-Tremblant,** near the vast **Parc du Mont-Tremblant** ⑪, and use that as a base to visit some of the surrounding towns. There's good eating and shopping here—and even a reconstructed historic village in Ste-Adèle.

If your starting point is Québec City, you could take two days to explore the towns of Charlevoix (☞ If You Have 10–12 Days, *below*) east of the city, with an overnight in the elegant resort town of **La Malbaie** ㉖.

IF YOU HAVE 5 DAYS

You can combine a taste of the Eastern Townships with a two-day visit to the Laurentians. Get a feeling for the Laurentians by staying overnight in **St-Sauveur-des-Monts** ④ or **Ste-Adèle** ⑥ and exploring such surrounding towns as **St-Jérôme** ③ and **Morin Heights** ⑤. Then head back south of Montréal to the Townships, which extend to the east along the border with New England. Overnight in **Granby** ⑫ or **Bromont** ⑬; Granby has a zoo and Bromont is known for its factory outlets. The next day, you can shop in pretty **Knowlton** ⑮ and explore regional history in such towns as **Valcourt** ⑰, where a museum is dedicated to the inventor of the snowmobile. Spend a night or two in the appealing resort town of **Magog** ⑯, along Lac Memphrémagog, or the quieter **North Hatley** ⑳, on Lac Massawippi. You'll have good dining in either. Save a day for some outdoor activity, whether it's golfing, skiing, biking on former railroad lines, or hiking.

IF YOU HAVE 10–12 DAYS

A longer visit can show you a number of regions in Québec, but you must do some driving between them. You can spend a few days in either the Laurentians or the Eastern Townships before heading east to Québec City and historic Charlevoix, the heart of what was New France, along the St. Lawrence River. The drive from Montréal or Sherbrooke to Québec City is more than 240 km (149 mi); Charlevoix begins 33 km (20 mi) to the east, at **Ste-Anne-de-Beaupré** ㉓, with its famous basilica. Colonial-era homes and farmhouses dot several villages; some are still homes, and others are theaters, museums, or restaurants. Spend time in **Baie St-Paul** ㉔ and **La Malbaie** ㉖, or just drive lovely roads such as Route 362. There's whale-watching in **Tadoussac** ㉗. To go on to the Gaspé Peninsula, you have to cross the St. Lawrence River. An hour-long ferry ride from St-Siméon, between La Malbaie and Tadoussac, takes you to Rivière-du-Loup. From there it's a day to get to **Carleton** ㉘ on the Gaspé's southern shore. With mountains on one side and the ocean on the other, the peninsula offers one of the most scenic drives in North America; you can stop in **Percé** ㉙ and spend a day visiting **Bonaventure Island** ㉚ with its fascinating bird colony. The drive around the entire peninsula is more than 800 km (500 mi).

When to Tour Québec

The Laurentians are mainly a winter ski destination, but you can drive up from Montréal to enjoy the fall foliage, to hike, bike, or play golf, or to engage in spring skiing—and still get home before dark. The only slow periods are early November, when there is not much to do, and June, when there is plenty to do but the area is plagued by blackflies, admittedly less of a problem now than formerly, thanks to effective biological control programs.

The Eastern Townships are best in fall, when the foliage is at its peak. The region borders Vermont and has the same dramatic colors. It's possible to visit wineries at this time, although you should call ahead to see if visitors are welcome during the harvest, which can be busy. Charlevoix is lovely in fall, but winter is particularly magical. Although the roads aren't great in winter, the whole region, with its cozy villages and New France architecture, is charming. In summer there is a special silvery light, born of the mountains and the proximity of the sea: This is why the area attracts so many painters. Summer is really the only time to tour the Gaspé. Some attractions have already closed by Labor Day, and few hotels are open during winter. The weather can be harsh, too, and driving the coast road can be difficult.

THE LAURENTIANS

The Laurentians (les Laurentides) are divided into two major regions—the Lower Laurentians (les Basses Laurentides) and the Upper Laurentians (les Hautes Laurentides). But don't be fooled by the designations; they don't signify great driving distances. Avid skiers might call Montréal a bedroom community for the Laurentians; just 60 km (37 mi) to the north, they are home to some of North America's best-known ski resorts. The Laurentian range is ancient, dating to the Precambrian era (more than 600 million years ago). These rocky hills are relatively low, worn down by glacial activity, but they include eminently skiable hills, with a few peaks above 2,500 ft. World-famous Mont-Tremblant, at 3,150 ft, is the tallest.

The P'tit Train du Nord—the former railroad line that is now a 200-km (124-mi) linear park used by cyclists, hikers, skiers, and snowmobilers—made it possible to transport settlers and cargo easily to the Upper Laurentians. It also opened them up to skiing by the turn of the century. Before long, trainloads of skiers replaced settlers and cargo as the railway's major trade. The Upper Laurentians became known worldwide as the number one ski center in eastern North America—a position they still hold today. Initially a winter weekend getaway for Montrealers who stayed at boardinghouses and fledgling resorts while skiing its hills, the Upper Laurentians soon began attracting an international clientele.

Ski lodges, originally private family retreats for wealthy city dwellers, were accessible only by train until the 1930s, when Route 117 was built. Once the road opened up, cottages became year-round family retreats. Today there is an uneasy alliance between the longtime cottagers and resort-driven entrepreneurs. Both recognize the other's historic role in developing the Upper Laurentians, but neither espouses the other's cause. At the moment, commercial development seems to be winning out. A number of large hotels have added indoor pools and spa facilities, and efficient highways have brought the country closer to the city—45 minutes to St-Sauveur, 1½–2 hours to Mont-Tremblant.

The Lower Laurentians start almost immediately outside Montréal and are rich in historic and architectural landmarks. Beginning in the mid-

17th century, the governors of New France, as Québec was then called, gave large concessions of land to its administrators, priests, and top-ranking military, who became known as seigneurs. In the Lower Laurentians, towns like St-Eustache and Oka are home to the manors, mills, churches, and public buildings these seigneurs had built for themselves and their habitants—the inhabitants of these quasi-feudal villages.

The resort vacation area truly begins at St-Sauveur-des-Monts (Exit 60 on Autoroute 15) and extends as far north as Mont-Tremblant, where it turns into a wilderness of lakes and forests best visited with an outfitter. Laurentian guides planning fishing trips are concentrated around Parc Mont-Tremblant. To the first-time visitor, the hills and resorts around St-Sauveur, Ste-Adèle, Morin Heights, Val Morin, and Val David, up to Ste-Agathe, form a pleasant hodgepodge of villages, hotels, and inns that seem to blend one into another.

Oka

❶ *40 km (25 mi) west of Montréal.*

The town of Oka is known for a monastery that produces cheeses, a calvary, and its provincial park. To promote piety among the native people, the Sulpicians erected the **Oka Calvary** (✉ Rte. 344, across from Oka Provincial Park), representing the Stations of the Cross, between 1740 and 1742. Three of the seven chapels are still maintained, and every September 14 since 1870, Québécois pilgrims have congregated here from across the province to participate in the half-hour ceremony that proceeds on foot to the calvary's summit. A sense of the divine is inspired as much by the magnificent view of Lac des Deux-Montagnes as by religious fervor.

The **Abbaye Cistercienne d'Oka** is one of the oldest in North America. In 1887 the Sulpicians gave about 865 acres of their property near the Oka Calvary to the Trappist monks, who had arrived in New France in 1880 from Bellefontaine Abbey in France. Within 10 years they had built their monastery and transformed this land into one of the most beautiful domains in Québec. Famous for creating Oka cheese, the Trappists established the Oka School of Agriculture, which operated until 1960. Today, the monastery is a noted prayer retreat. The gardens and chapel are open to visitors. ✉ *1600 chemin d'Oka,* ☎ *514/479–8361.* 🎫 *Free.* ⏲ *Chapel daily 8–12:15 and 1–8; gardens and boutique weekdays 9:30–11:30 and 1–4:30, Sat. 9–4.*

Kanesatake, a Mohawk reserve near Oka, made headlines in 1990 when a 78-day armed standoff between Mohawk Warriors (the reserve's self-proclaimed paramilitary force) and Canadian and provincial authorities took place. The Mohawks of Kanesatake said they opposed the expansion of the Oka golf course, claiming the land was stolen from them 273 years before. When the standoff ended peacefully, the golf course was not expanded.

Lodging

$$$ 🏨 **Hotel du Lac Carling.** This modern hotel near Lachute (about 40 km, or 25 mi, northwest of Oka) caters to an upmarket clientele. Besides a large sports center and 20 km (12 mi) of cross-country ski trails, there's an excellent par-72 golf course. The hotel is owned by a real estate magnate with 23 castles and manor houses in his native Germany, and the rooms have oil paintings and priceless antiques shipped over from his various properties. ✉ *Rte. 327, Pinehill, J0V 1A0,* ☎ *514/533–9211 or 800/661–9211,* FAX *514/533–9197. 100 rooms. Restaurant, bar, pool, sauna, 18-hole golf course, exercise room, racquetball, squash, cross-country skiing. MAP. AE, DC, MC, V.*

The Laurentians (les Laurentides)

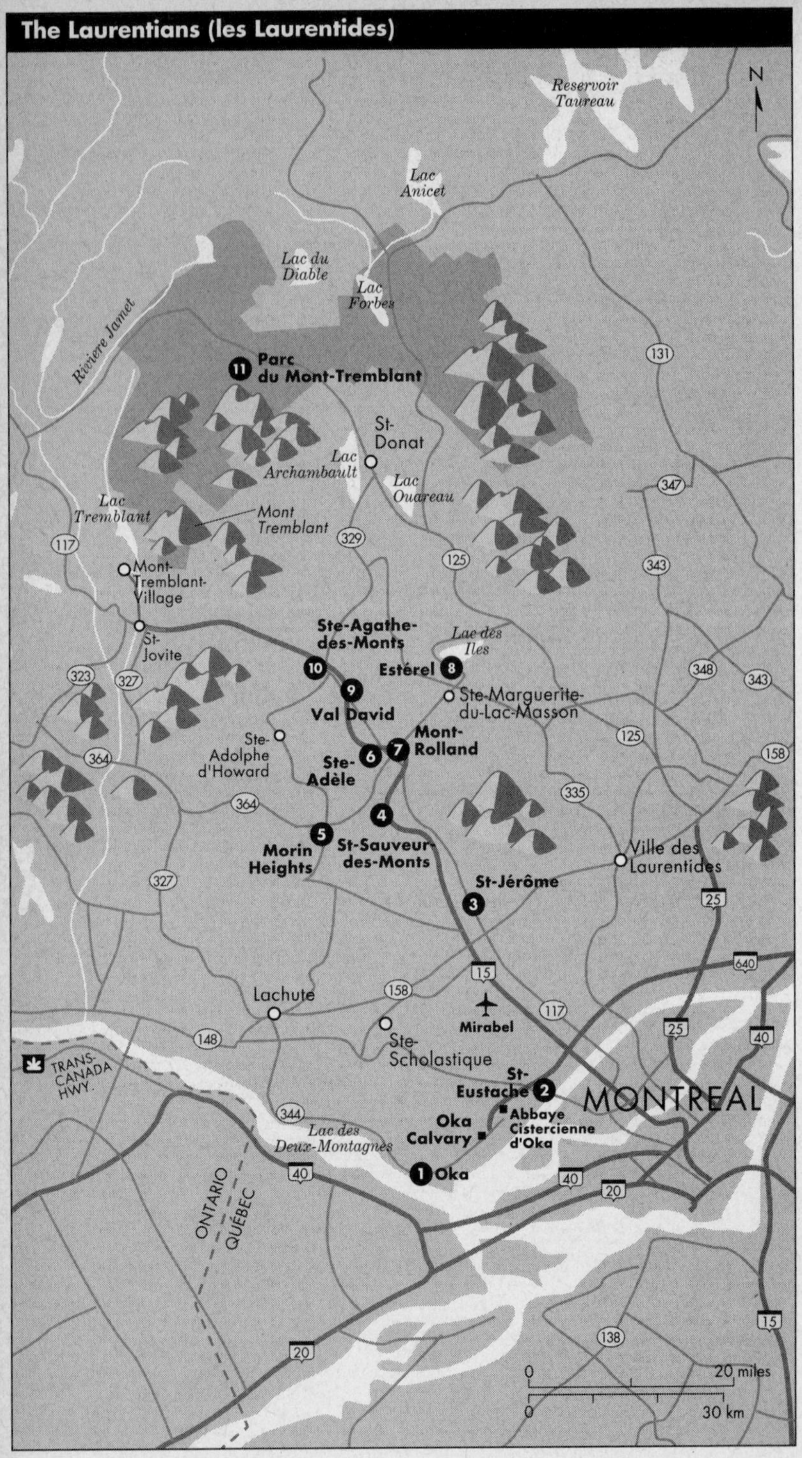

Reservoir Taureau
Lac Anicet
Lac du Diable
Lac Forbes
Rivière Jamet
11 Parc du Mont-Tremblant
St-Donat
Lac Archambault
Lac Ouareau
Lac Tremblant
Mont Tremblant
Mont-Tremblant-Village
St-Jovite
Ste-Agathe-des-Monts
Lac des Iles
10
Estérel 8
9
Val David
Ste-Marguerite-du-Lac-Masson
Ste-Adolphe d'Howard
Ste-Adèle 6
7 Mont-Rolland
4
5
Morin Heights
St-Sauveur-des-Monts
St-Jérôme
3
Ville des Laurentides
Lachute
Mirabel
Ste-Scholastique
TRANS-CANADA HWY.
St-Eustache 2
MONTREAL
Abbaye Cistercienne d'Oka
Oka Calvary
Lac des Deux-Montagnes
1 Oka
ONTARIO
QUÉBEC
131
347
343
117
329
125
348
323
327
364
125
158
335
25
640
15
158
117
148
25
40
344
40
40
20
138
15
20
0
20 miles
0
30 km
N

St-Eustache

❷ *25 km (16 mi) northeast of Oka.*

St-Eustache is a must for history buffs. One of the most important and tragic battles in Canadian history took place here during the 1837 Rebellion. Since the British conquest of 1759, French Canadians had been confined to preexisting territories while the new townships were allotted exclusively to the English. Adding to this insult was the government's decision to tax all imported products from England, which made them prohibitively expensive. The result? In 1834 the French Canadian Patriot party defeated the British party locally. Lower Canada, as it was then known, became a hotbed of tension between the French and English, with French resistance to the British government reaching an all-time high.

Rumors of rebellion were rife, and in December 1837, some 2,000 English soldiers led by General Colborne were sent in to put down the "army" of North Shore patriots by surrounding the village of St-Eustache. Jean-Olivier Chénier and his 200 patriots took refuge in the local church, which Colborne's cannons bombed and set afire. Chénier and 80 of his comrades were killed during the battle, and more than 100 of the town's houses and buildings erected during the seignorial regime were looted and burned down by Colborne's soldiers. Traces of the bullets fired by the English army cannons are visible on the facade of St-Eustache's church at 123 rue St-Louis.

Most of the town's period buildings are open to the public. The **Manoir Globensky** (✉ 235 rue St-Eustache, ☎ 514/974–5055) offers a guided tour or a free brochure that serves as a good walking-tour guide. There are tours from late June until early September at 1 and 3.

St-Jérôme

❸ *25 km (16 mi) north of St-Eustache.*

Rivaling St-Eustache in Québec's historic folklore is St-Jérôme, in the Upper Laurentians on Route 117. Founded in 1834, it is today a thriving economic center and cultural hub. It first gained prominence in 1868 when Curé Antoine Labelle became pastor of this parish on the shores of the Rivière du Nord. Curé Labelle devoted himself to opening up northern Québec to French Canadians. Between 1868 and 1890, he founded 20 parish towns—an impressive achievement given the harsh conditions of this vast wilderness. But his most important legacy was the famous P'tit Train du Nord railroad line, which he persuaded the government to build in order to open St-Jérôme to travel and trade. Today the railroad is a 200-km (124-mi) **linear park** for recreational use that begins in St-Jérôme.

St-Jérôme's **promenade,** a 4-km-long (2½-mi-long) boardwalk, follows the Rivière du Nord from rue de Martigny bridge to rue St-Joseph bridge, providing a walk through the town's history. Descriptive plaques en route highlight episodes of the Battle of 1837, a French Canadian uprising.The **Centre d'Exposition du Vieux-Palais,** housed in St-Jérôme's old courthouse, has changing exhibits of contemporary art, featuring mostly Québec artists. ✉ *185 rue du Palais,* ☎ *514/432–7171.* *Free.* *Wed.–Sun. noon–5, Tues. noon–8.*

Parc Régional de la Rivière-du-Nord was created as a nature retreat. Trails through the park lead to the spectacular **Wilson Falls.** The **Pavillon Marie-Victorin** has summer weekend displays and workshops devoted to nature, culture, and history. You can hike, bike, cross-country ski, snowshoe, or snow slide. ✉ *1051 blvd. International,* ☎

514/431–1676. 🎫 $3 per vehicle. ⏲ Fall–spring, daily 9–5; summer, daily 9–7.

Outdoor Activities and Sports

Para Vision (✉ C.P. 95, J7Z 5T7, ☎ 514/438–0855), a parachute school with a flying center in nearby Bellefeuille, caters to novices and seasoned flyers alike (courses are limited to ages 16 and up). Would-be parachutists are trained on the ground as well as in the air, and even first-timers get the chance to jump earthward from 3,500 ft.

St-Sauveur-des-Monts

❹ *25 km (16 mi) north of St-Jérôme.*

A focal point for area resorts, over the past 20 years St-Sauveur-des-Monts has changed from a sleepy Laurentian village of 4,000 residents to a thriving year-round town attracting some 30,000 cottagers and visitors on weekends. Its main street, rue Principale, once dotted with quaint French restaurants, now has dozens of eateries at all price levels; they serve everything from lamb brochettes to spicy Thai cuisine (a current craze among locals). The narrow strip is so choked in summertime with cars and tourists that it has earned the sobriquet Crescent Street of the North, borrowing its name from the action-filled street in Montréal. Despite all this development, St-Sauveur has maintained some of its charming, rural character.

For those who like their vacations—winter or summer—activity-filled, St-Sauveur is where the action rolls nonstop. In winter, skiing is the main thing. (Mont-St-Sauveur, Mont-Avila, Mont-Gabriel, and Mont-Olympia all offer special season passes and programs, and some ski-center passes can be used at more than one center in the region.)

Just outside St-Sauveur, the Mont-St-Sauveur **Water Park** and tourist center will keep children occupied with slides, a giant wave pool, a shallow wading pool, snack bars, and more. The rafting river attracts the older, braver crowd; the nine-minute ride follows the natural contours of steep hills and requires about 12,000 gallons of water to be pumped per minute. The latest attraction is tandem slides where plumes of water flow through figure-eight tubes. ✉ *350 rue St-Denis,* ☎ *514/871–0101 or 800/363–2426.* 🎫 *Full day $22, half-day $17, evening (after 5) $9; includes access to all activities.* ⏲ *June 8–Sept. 7, daily 10–7.*

Outdoor Activities and Sports

Blue signs on Route 117 and Autoroute 15 indicate where the area's ski hills are. **Station Touristique Mont-St-Saveur** (✉ 350 rue St-Denis, ☎ 800/363–2426), with a total of 28 downhill runs, is the collective name for the peaks around the village of St-Saveur-des-Monts. There are nine lifts; vertical drop is 762 ft. The runs are linked to Mont-Avila. **Ski Mont-Gabriel** (✉ Montée Mont-Gabriel, ☎ 514/227–1100) has a vertical drop of 660 ft, 16 runs, and 10 lifts. With a vertical drop of 660 ft, **Station de Ski Mont-Habitant** (✉ 12 blvd. des Skieurs, ☎ 514/393–1821) has nine runs and three lifts.

Shopping

Rue Principale has shops, fashion boutiques, and café terraces with bright awnings and flowers. Housed in a former bank, **Solo Mode** (✉ 239B rue Principale, ☎ 514/227–1234) carries such international labels as Byblos. **Les Factoreries St-Sauveur** (✉ 100 rue Guindon, Exit 60 from Autoroute 15, ☎ 514/227–1074) is a factory outlet mall with 12 boutiques. Canadian, American, and European manufacturers sell goods at reduced prices, from designer clothing to household items.

Morin Heights

❺ *10 km (6 mi) west of St-Sauveur-des-Monts.*

The town's architecture and population reflect its English settlers' origins, and most residents are English-speaking. Morin Heights has escaped the overdevelopment of St-Sauveur but still provides a good range of restaurants, bookstores, boutiques, and crafts shops to explore. During the summer months, windsurfing, swimming, and canoeing on the area's two lakes are popular pastimes.

In the summer, vacationers also head for the region's golf courses (including the 18-hole links at Mont-Gabriel), campgrounds at Val David, Lacs Claude and Lafontaine, and beaches; in the fall and winter, they come for the foliage as well as alpine and Nordic skiing.

Dining and Lodging

$$$ ✕ **Auberge le Clos Joli.** This farmhouse turned country inn, only two minutes from the ski slopes, is considered one of the top hostelries in the Laurentians. Intimate and cozy, the inn is decorated with original artwork by Québécois painters; the dining room has a fireplace. The menu highlights French cuisine but with some local touches, such as roast venison cooked with bilberries and ravioli stuffed with wild mushrooms. A specialty is *ris de veau* (veal sweetbreads) flavored with lemon and thyme. ✉ *19 chemin du Clos Joli, J0R 1H0,* ☎ *514/226–5401. 9 rooms. Restaurant, cross-country skiing, downhill skiing. MAP. AE, MC, V.*

Outdoor Activities and Sports

At **Ski Morin Heights** (✉ Autoroute 15 N, Exit 60, ☎ 514/227–2020 or 800/661–3535), snowboarding is the latest craze. The vertical drop at this downhill skiing center is 660 ft, and there are six lifts. Although it doesn't have overnight accommodations, Ski Morin Heights has a 44,000-square-ft chalet with hospitality services and sports-related facilities, eateries, après-ski activities, a pub, and a day-care center. Children ages two and up can join special ski-lesson programs.

Ste-Adèle

❻ *12 km (7 mi) north of Morin Heights.*

The busy town of Ste-Adèle is full of gift and Québec-crafts shops, boutiques, and restaurants. It also has an active nightlife, including a few dance clubs.

The reconstructed **Village de Seraphin**'s 20 small homes, grand country house, general store, and church recall the settlers who came to Ste-Adèle in the 1840s. This award-winning historic town also has a train tour through the woods. ✉ *Rte. 117,* ☎ *514/229–4777.* *$9.* *Late May–late June and Sept., weekends 10–6; late June–Aug., daily 10–6.*

Dining and Lodging

$$$$ ✕ **La Clef des Champs.** This family-owned restaurant, known for its gourmet French cuisine and cozy, romantic atmosphere, is tucked away among trees and faces a mountain. Game dishes are a specialty, including farm-raised rabbit flavored with mustard and medallions of roasted ostrich in pepper sauce. A good dessert choice is the *gâteau aux deux chocolats* (two-chocolate cake). ✉ *875 chemin Ste-Marguerite,* ☎ *514/229–2857. AE, DC, MC, V. Closed Mon. Oct.–May.*

$$$$ ★ ✕ **L'Eau à la Bouche.** Superb service, stunning rooms awash with color, and a terrace with a flower garden are highlights of this elegant inn. The auberge faces Le Chantecler's ski slopes, so skiing is literally at the door. Tennis, sailing, horseback riding, and a golf course are nearby.

The highly recommended restaurant superbly marries nouvelle cuisine and traditional Québec dishes. The care and inventiveness of chef-proprietor Anne Desjardins are extraordinary. Her menus change with the seasons, but some representative dishes are marinated Atlantic salmon and smoked scallops on a bed of julienned cucumber with a blend of mustards, and roast veal in a cognac and Roquefort sauce. ✉ *3003 blvd. Ste-Adèle, J0R 1L0,* ☎ *514/229–2991,* FAX *514/229–7573. 25 rooms. Restaurant, pool. EP, MAP. AE, DC, MC, V.*

$$$ **Le Chantecler.** This Montrealer favorite on Lac Ste-Adèle is nestled at the base of a mountain with 22 downhill ski runs. Skiing is the obvious draw—trails begin almost at the hotel entrance. The condominium units, hotel rooms, and chalets, furnished with Canadian pine, all have a rustic appeal. ✉ *1474 chemin Chantecler, C.P. 1048, J0R 1L0,* ☎ *514/229–3555, 800/363–2420 in Québec;* FAX *514/229–5593. 300 rooms, 20 suites. Restaurant, indoor pool, spa, 18-hole golf course, tennis court, beach, boating, downhill skiing. EP, MAP. AE, D, DC, MC, V.*

$ **Auberge aux Croissants.** At the foot of the Laurentians, the inn is only a five-minute drive from Mont-St-Sauveur. Although most rooms have no TV or telephone, such conveniences are found in one of the two lounges, and an impressive buffet-breakfast is included in the price. One room has a whirlpool bath. ✉ *750 chemin Ste-Marguerite, J0R 1L0,* ☎ *514/229–3838. 13 rooms, 1 suite. Pool. MC, V.*

Outdoor Activities and Sports

GOLF

The par-72 **Club de Golf Chantecler** (✉ Off Autoroute 15, Exit 67, 2520 chemin du Golf, ☎ 514/229–3742) has 18 holes.

SKIING

Ski Chantecler (☎ 514/229–3555) has a vertical drop of 663 ft, 8 lifts, and 22 runs (☞ Dining and Lodging, *above*). There are 50 km (31 mi) of cross-country trails, too. **Station de Ski Côtes** (☎ 514/229–2700) has six runs and a vertical drop of 392 ft.

Mont-Rolland

❼ *3 km (2 mi) east of Ste-Adèle.*

Mont-Rolland is the jumping-off point for the Mont-Gabriel ski area, about 16 km (10 mi) to the northeast.

Dining and Lodging

$$$$ ✕ **Auberge Mont-Gabriel.** At this deluxe resort spread out on a 1,200-acre estate, you can relax in a cozy, modern room with a view of the valley or be close to nature in a log cabin with a fireplace. The dining is superb here. Tennis, golf, and ski-week and -weekend packages are available. ✉ *Autoroute 15 (Exit 64), J0R 1G0,* ☎ *514/229–3547 or 800/668–5253,* FAX *514/229–7034. 126 rooms, 10 suites. Restaurant, indoor and outdoor pools, 18-hole golf course, 6 tennis courts. EP, MAP. AE, DC, MC, V.*

Nightlife and the Arts

The place for live music is **Bourbon Street** (✉ 2045 Rte. 117, ☎ 514/229–2905).

Outdoor Activities and Sports

Ski Mont-Gabriel (✉ Monté Mont-Gabriel, ☎ 514/227–1100 or 800/363–2426) has 10 lifts and 16 superb downhill trails primarily for intermediate and advanced skiers. The vertical drop is 660 ft. The most popular runs are the Tamarack and the O'Connell trails for advanced skiers and Obergurgl for intermediates.

Estérel

8 *12 km (7 mi) north of Mont-Rolland.*

The permanent population of the town of Estérel is a mere 95 souls, but visitors to Hôtel l'Estérel (☞ Dining and Lodging, *below*), a resort off Route 370, at Exit 69 near Ste-Marguerite Station, swell that number into the thousands. Founded in 1959 on the shores of Lac Dupuis, this 5,000-acre domain was bought by Fridolin Simard from Baron Louis Empain. Named Estérel by the baron because it evoked memories of his native village in Provence, Hotel l'Estérel soon became a household word for vacationers in search of a first-class resort area.

Dining and Lodging

$$$–$$$$ ✕ **Bistro à Champlain.** An astonishing selection of wines—26,000 bottles at last count—have made the bistro famous. Diners can tour the cellars, where some 2,000 brands are represented, with prices from $28 to $25,000. The restaurant is in a former general store built in 1864; next to the 150-seat dining room is a comfy lounge for cigar smokers. The paintings of Jean-Paul Riopelle adorn the walls. The *menu de dégustation* gives you a different wine with several courses for $62; typical dishes are marinated Atlantic smoked salmon and roast duckling with rosemary. ✉ *75 chemin Masson, Ste-Marguerite du Lac Masson,* ☎ *514/228–4988 or 514/225–4949. AE, DC, MC, V.*

$$$$ 🏨 **Hôtel l'Estérel.** If this all-inclusive resort were in the Caribbean, it would probably be run by Club Med, given the nonstop activities. Dogsledding and an ice-skating disco are two of the more unusual options, and there are buses to nearby downhill resorts. Comfortable rooms offer a view of either the lake or the beautiful flower gardens. ✉ *39 blvd. Fridolin Simard, J0T 1E0,* ☎ *514/228–2571 or 800/363–3623,* FAX *514/228–4977. 135 rooms. Restaurant, indoor pool, 18-hole golf course, tennis courts, exercise room, beach, dock, cross-country skiing, snowmobiling. EP, MAP. AE, DC, MC, V.*

Val David

9 *18 km (11 mi) west of Estérel.*

Val David is a rendezvous for mountain climbers, hikers, and summer or winter campers, besides a center for arts and crafts. Children know Val David for its **Santa Claus Village.** This is Santa Claus's summer residence, where children can sit on Santa's knee and speak to him in French or English. On the grounds is a petting zoo, with goats, sheep, horses, and colorful birds. Bumper boats and games are run here as well. ✉ *987 rue Morin,* ☎ *819/322–2146.* 🎫 *$8.* ⏲ *Late May–early June, weekends 10–6; early June–late Aug., daily 10–6.*

Dining and Lodging

$$$$ ✕🏨 **Hôtel La Sapinière.** Comfortable, freshly redecorated accommodations are offered in this homey, dark-brown frame hotel. The rooms, with country-style furnishings and pastel floral accents, come with such luxurious extras as thick terry-cloth bathrobes and hair dryers. Guests can relax in front of a blazing fire in one of several lounges. The property is best known for the French nouvelle cuisine in its fine dining room and its wine cellar. The minimum stay is two nights. ✉ *1244 chemin de la Sapinière, J0T 2N0,* ☎ *819/322–2020 or 800/567–6635,* FAX *819/322–6510. 70 rooms. Restaurant. MAP. AE, DC, MC, V.*

Outdoor Activities and Sports

Mont-Alta (✉ Rte. 117, ☎ 819/322–3206) has 22 runs and 2 lifts; the vertical drop is 587 ft. **Station de Ski Vallée-Bleue** (✉ 1418 chemin Vallée-Bleue, ☎ 819/322–3427) has 16 runs.

Shopping

Val David is a haven for artists, many of whose studios are open to the public. The **Atelier Bernard Chaudron, Inc.** (✉ 2449 chemin de l'Ile, ☎ 819/322–3944) sells hand-shaped lead-free pewter objets d'art.

Ste-Agathe-des-Monts

10 *5 km (3 mi) north of Val David, 96 km (60 mi) northwest of Montréal.*

Overlooking Lac des Sables is Ste-Agathe-des-Monts, the largest commercial center for ski communities farther north. It has many shops and a variety of restaurants and bars.

Dining, Lodging, and Camping

$$$–$$$$ ✕ **Chatel Vienna.** Run by Eberhards Rado and his wife, who is also the chef, this Austrian restaurant serves traditional, hearty Viennese and other Continental dishes in a lakeside setting. You may want to try the home-smoked trout, served with an herb-and-spice butter and garden-fresh vegetables. Other options are a variety of schnitzels, a sauerkraut plate, and venison. Hot spiced wine, Czech pilsner beer, and dry Austrian and other international white wines are some of the beverage choices. A Sunday buffet brunch has approximately 35 dishes. ✉ *6 rue Ste-Lucie,* ☎ *819/326–1485. Reservations essential. MC, V.*

$$ **Auberge du Lac des Sables.** A favorite with couples, this inn offers a quiet, relaxed atmosphere in a country setting with a magnificent view of Lac des Sables. All rooms have contemporary decor and a balcony. ✉ *230 St-Venant, J8C 2Z7,* ☎ *819/326–3994,* FAX *819/326–9159. 19 rooms. CP. MC, V.*

$ ⛺ **Au Parc des Campeurs.** This spacious campground is near a lively resort area. Canoes and kayaks can be rented here. ✉ *Tour du Lac and Rte. 329, J8C 1M9,* ☎ *819/324–0482. 556 sites. Miniature golf, tennis court, volleyball, bicycles, coin laundry.*

Outdoor Activities and Sports

Sailing is the favorite summer sport, especially during the "*24 Heures de la Voile,*" a weekend sailing competition (☎ 819/326–0457) that takes place each year in June. The ***Alouette*** touring launch (✉ Municipal dock, rue Principale, ☎ 819/326–3656) has guided tours of Lac des Sables.

Mont-Tremblant

25 km (16 mi) north of Ste-Agathe-des-Monts.

Mont-Tremblant, more than 3,000 ft high, is the highest peak in the Laurentians and a major center for skiing. The resort village at the foot of the mountain has accommodations and many restaurants, bars, and shops. An exciting ongoing development here has been the redevelopment of the Tremblant resort (☞ *below*).

The mountain and the hundreds of square miles of wilderness beyond
11 it constitute **Parc du Mont-Tremblant** (☎ 819/688–2281). Created in 1894, the park was once the home of the Algonquin people, who called this area Manitonga Soutana, meaning "mountain of the spirits." Today it is a vast wildlife sanctuary of more than 400 lakes and rivers protecting about 230 species of birds and animals, including moose, deer, bear, and beaver. In winter its trails are used by cross-country skiers, snowshoers, and snowmobile enthusiasts. Moose hunting is allowed in season, and camping and canoeing are the main summer activities. Entrance to the park is free, and the main entrance is through St-Donat.

Dining and Lodging

$$$$ ✕🏨 **Club Tremblant.** Built as a private retreat in the 1930s by a wealthy American, this hotel is across the lake from Station Mont-Tremblant. The original large, log-cabin lodge is furnished in colonial style, with wooden staircases and huge stone fireplaces. The rustic but comfortable main lodge has excellent facilities and an outstanding dining room serving ($$–$$$$) Continental cuisine. Both the main lodge and the deluxe condominium complex (with fireplaces, private balconies, kitchenettes, and split-level design), built just up the hill from the lodge, offer magnificent views of Mont-Tremblant and its ski hills. There is a golf course nearby. ✉ *Av. Cuttle, J0T 1Z0,* ☎ *819/425–2731,* FAX *819/425–9903. 113 rooms. Restaurant, indoor pool, tennis court, exercise room, boating, fishing. EP, MAP. AE, MC, V.*

$–$$ ✕🏨 **Auberge du Cog de Montagne.** Owners Nino and Kay Faragalli have earned a favorable reputation for their auberge on Lac Moore. The cozy, family-run inn is touted for its friendly service, great hospitality, and modern accommodations. Kudos have also been garnered for the great Italian cuisine served up nightly, which also draws a local crowd; reservations are essential. Year-round facilities and activities, on-site or nearby, include canoeing, kayaking, sailboarding, fishing, badminton, tennis, horseback riding, skating, and skiing. ✉ *2151 chemin Principal, C.P. 208, J0T 1Z0,* ☎ *819/425–3380 or 800/895–3380,* FAX *819/425–7846. 13 rooms. Restaurant, sauna, exercise room, beach. MAP in winter; EP, MAP in summer. AE, MC, V.*

$$$$ ★ 🏨 **Château Mont-Tremblant.** A new property built by Canadian Pacific Hotels is the attractive centerpiece of Tremblant's (☞ *below*) pedestrian village. Similar in style to the company's historic railway "castles" scattered throughout Canada—Banff Springs Hotel and Château Frontenac are two examples—the hotel has been decorated with wood paneling, copper, stained glass, stone fireplaces, and wrought-iron lamps with parchment shades. The ambience is elegant but sporty. Skiers can zoom off the mountain right into the ground-level deli or opt for a more formal meal in the dining room. On the menu are Brie wrapped in phyllo pastry, Laurentian rainbow trout, and pork chops grilled with local maple syrup. ✉ *3045 chemin Principal, Box 100, J0T 1Z0,* ☎ *819/681–7000. 360 rooms. Indoor pool, sauna, exercise room. AE, DC, MC, V.*

$$–$$$$ 🏨 **Tremblant.** This world-class resort, spread around the 14-km-long (9-mi-long) Lac Tremblant, has undergone a radical transformation. Intrawest Corporation has injected a much-needed $500 million (with more investment planned) into the mountain since the early '90s. It has quickly become the most fashionable vacation venue in Québec among sporty types and lovers of the great outdoors. The resort's hub is a pedestrian-only village that looks a bit like a displaced Québec City. The buildings—constructed in the style of New France with dormer windows and steep roofs—hold pubs, restaurants, boutiques, sports shops, a cinema, and accommodations ranging from rooms in hotels to self-catering condominiums. A new indoor water recreation complex includes pools, waterslides, and whirlpool baths. ✉ *3005 chemin Principal, J0T 1Z0,* ☎ *819/425–8711, 800/461–8711, or 800/567–6760 (hotel reservations),* FAX *819/425–9604. 1,050 rooms. Indoor lap pool, indoor-outdoor pool, wading pool, 2 18-hole golf courses, tennis courts, hiking, horseback riding, beach, windsurfing, boating, mountain bikes. AE, MC, V.*

Outdoor Activities and Sports

With a 2,131-ft vertical drop, **Mont-Tremblant** (☎ 819/425–8711 or 819/681–2000) offers 74 downhill trails, 10 lifts, and 90 km (56 mi) of cross-country trails. Downhill beginners favor the 6-km (4-mi)

Nansen trail; intermediate skiers head for the Beauchemin run. Experts choose the challenging Flying Mile on the south side and Duncan and Expo runs on the mountain's north side. The speedy Duncan Express is a quadruple chairlift.

THE EASTERN TOWNSHIPS

The Eastern Townships (also known as les Cantons de l'Est, and formerly as l'Estrie) refers to the area in the southwest corner of the province of Québec, bordering Vermont, New Hampshire, and Maine. Its northern Appalachian hills, rolling down to placid lakeshores, were first home to the Abenaki natives, long before "summer people" built their cottages and horse paddocks here. The Abenaki are gone, but the names they gave to the region's recreational lakes remain—Memphrémagog, Massawippi, Mégantic.

The Eastern Townships (or the Townships, as locals call them) were populated by United Empire Loyalists fleeing the Revolutionary War and, later, the newly created United States of America, to continue living under the English king in British North America. It's not surprising that the Townships, with their covered bridges, village greens, white church steeples, and country inns, are reminiscent of New England. The Loyalists were followed, around 1820, by the first wave of Irish immigrants—ironically, Catholics fleeing their country's union with Protestant England. Some 20 years later the potato famine sent more Irish pioneers to the Townships.

The area became more Gallic after 1850 as French Canadians moved in to work on the railroad and in the lumber industry. Around the turn of the century, English families from Montréal and Americans from the border states discovered the region and began summering at cottages along the lakes. During the Prohibition era, the area attracted even more cottagers from the United States. Lac Massawippi became a favorite summer resort of wealthy families, and those homes have since been converted into gracious inns and upscale bed-and-breakfasts.

Today the summer communities fill up with equal parts French and English visitors, though the year-round residents are primarily French. Nevertheless, the locals are proud of both their Loyalist heritage and their Québec roots. They boast of "Loyalist tours" and Victorian gingerbread homes and in the next breath direct visitors to the snowmobile museum in Valcourt, where, in 1937, native son Joseph-Armand Bombardier built the first *moto-neige* (snowmobile) in his garage. (Bombardier's other inventions were the basis of one of Canada's biggest industries, supplying New York City and Mexico City with subway cars and other rolling stock.)

Over the past two decades, the Townships have developed from a series of quiet farm communities and wood-frame summer homes to a thriving all-season resort area. In winter, skiers flock to seven downhill centers and some 900 km (558 mi) of cross-country trails. Three inns—Manoir Hovey, Auberge Hatley, and the Ripplecove Inn—offer the Skiwippi, a weeklong package of cross-country treks from one inn to another. The network covers some 32 km (20 mi). Still less crowded and commercialized than the Laurentians, the area has ski hills on four mountains that dwarf anything the Laurentians have to offer, with the exception of Mont-Tremblant. And, compared to those in Vermont, ski-pass rates are still a bargain. Owl's Head, Mont-Orford, Mont-Sutton, and Bromont have interchangeable lift tickets. The Townships' southerly location also makes this the balmiest corner of Québec, notable for its spring skiing.

By early spring, the sugar shacks are busy with the new maple syrup. In summer, boating, swimming, sailing, golfing, rollerblading, hiking, and bicycling take over. And every fall the inns are booked solid with leaf peepers eager to take in the brilliant foliage.

Granby

12 *80 km (50 mi) east of Montréal.*

Granby is the gateway to the Eastern Townships and home to a notable zoo. It also hosts a number of annual festivals—the **Festival of Mascots and Cartoon Characters** (July), a great favorite with youngsters and families; and the **Granby International,** an antique car competition held at the Granby Autodrome (also in July). The **Festival International de la Chanson,** a songfest of budding composers and performers that has launched several of Québec's current megastars, is a nine-day event in mid-September.

★ This town is best known for its zoo, the **Jardin Zoologique de Granby.** It houses some 1,000 animals from 230 species. Two rare snow leopards are on loan from Chicago's Lincoln Park Zoo and New York's Bronx Zoo. The complex includes amusement park rides and souvenir shops as well as a playground and picnic area. ✉ *347 rue Bourget,* ☎ *514/372–9113.* *$16.* *Mid-May–early Sept., daily 10–5; Sept., weekends 10–5.*

Outdoor Activities and Sports

Cyclists will find outdoor bliss on the paved l'Estriade path, which links Granby to Waterloo, and the Montérégiade between Granby and Farnham, both 21 km (13 mi) long. Mountain biking is big in the Townships: The season kicks off in early June with the **Tour de la Montagne,** a 25-km (15-mi) mountain bike rally. Competitions for serious mountain bikers are held throughout the summer (☎ 514/534–2453 for information).

Bromont

13 *8 km (5 mi) south of Granby.*

The town of Bromont is as lively at night as during the day. It has the only night skiing in the Eastern Townships and a slope-side disco, Le Bromontais, where the après-ski action continues into the night. Bromont and Orford (☞ *below*) are *stations touristiques* (tourist centers), meaning they offer a wide range of activities in all seasons—boating, camping, golf, horseback riding, swimming, tennis, biking, canoeing, fishing, hiking, cross-country and downhill skiing, and snowshoeing. Bromont has more than 100 km (62 mi) of maintained trails for mountain bikers. A former Olympic equestrian site, Bromont is horse country, and every year in late June it holds a **riding festival** (☎ 514/534–3255). **Bromont Aquatic Park** (✉ Autoroute 10, Exit 78, ☎ 514/534–2200) is a water-slide park.

Lodging

$$$ **Le Château Bromont Hotel Spa.** Massages, electropuncture, algae wraps, facials, and aromatherapy are just a few of the pampering services at this European-style resort spa. Rooms are large and comfortable, with contemporary furniture, but those facing the Atrium are a little somber. L'Equestre Bar, named for Bromont's equestrian interests, has a cocktail hour and live entertainment. ✉ *90 rue Stanstead, J0E 1L0,* ☎ *514/534–3433 or 800/304–3433,* FAX *514/534–0514. 147 rooms. Restaurant, bar, indoor pool, hot tubs, sauna, spa, badminton, racquetball, squash. EP, MAP. AE, D, DC, MC, V.*

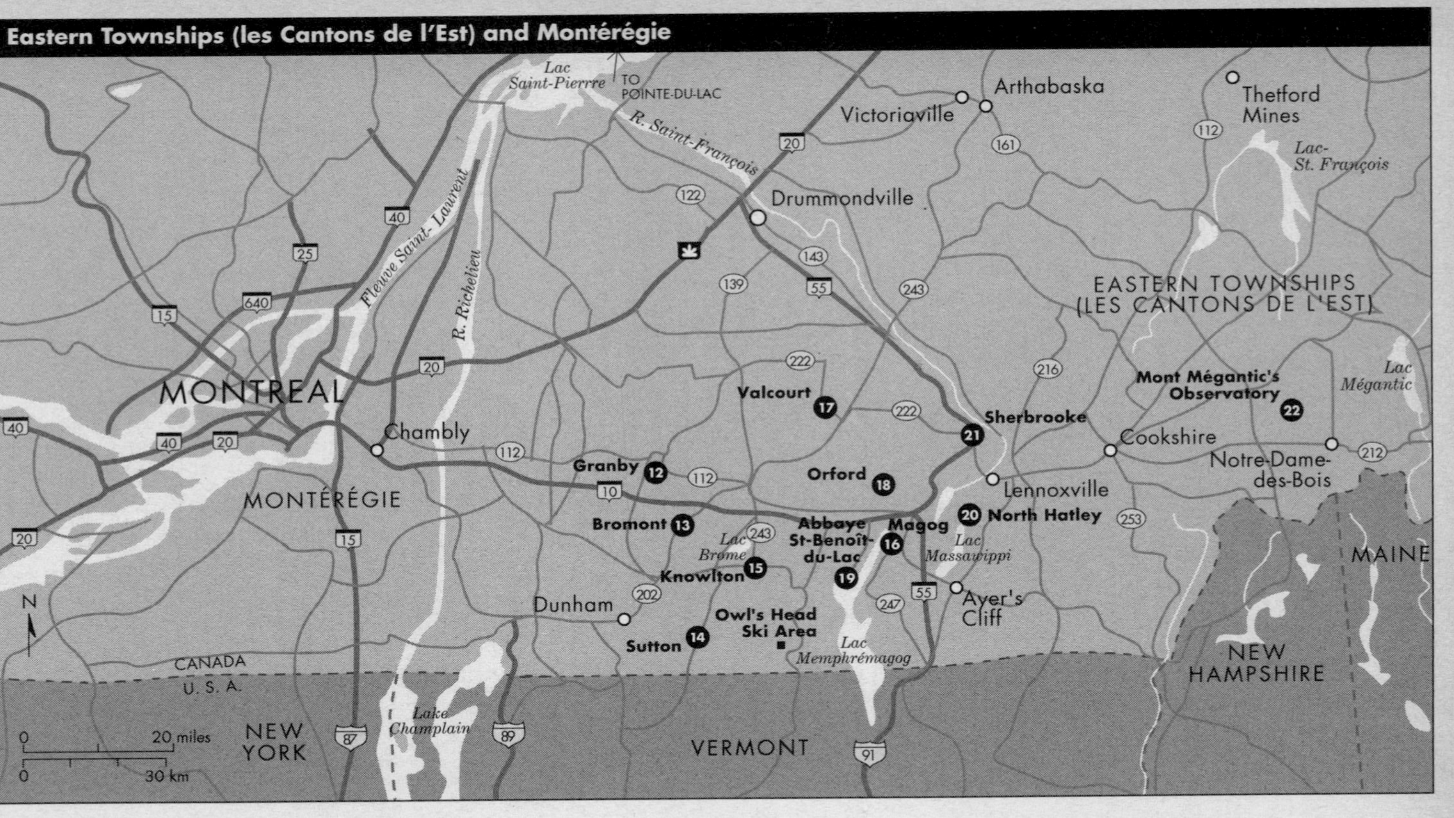

Eastern Townships (les Cantons de l'Est) and Montérégie
Lac Saint-Pierre
TO POINTE-DU-LAC
Arthabaska
Victoriaville
Thetford Mines
Lac-St. François
R. Saint-François
Drummondville
Fleuve Saint-Laurent
R. Richelieu
EASTERN TOWNSHIPS (LES CANTONS DE L'EST)
MONTREAL
Chambly
Valcourt 17
Mont Mégantic's Observatory 22
Lac Mégantic
Sherbrooke 21
Cookshire
Notre-Dame-des-Bois
Granby 12
Orford 18
Lennoxville
MONTÉRÉGIE
Bromont 13
Abbaye St-Benoît-du-Lac 19
Magog 16
20 North Hatley
Lac Brome
Lac Massawippi
Knowlton 15
Ayer's Cliff
Dunham
Owl's Head Ski Area
Sutton 14
Lac Memphrémagog
MAINE
N
CANADA
U. S. A.
NEW HAMPSHIRE
Lake Champlain
NEW YORK
VERMONT
0 20 miles
0 30 km
20
40
25
640
15
112
161
122
143
139
55
243
222
216
212
10
253
243
202
247
87
89
91

OFF THE BEATEN PATH

SAFARI TOUR LOOWAK – The brainchild of butterfly collector Serge Poirier, this oddball attraction 10 km (6 mi) from Bromont is a kind of Indiana Jones theme park where participants head off into the bush on treasure hunts and to look for downed planes. To make the game as authentic as possible, Poirier acquired a couple of wrecked aircraft that he has artfully hidden around his land. Needless to say, the place is a great hit with small fry, but parents quickly get caught up in the fantasy, too. Reservations are recommended. ✉ *475 Horizon Blvd., Waterloo, Exit 88 from Autoroute 10,* ☎ *514/539–0501.* *Trips begin at $10 per person (minimum 4 people).*

Outdoor Activities and Sports

Station de Ski Bromont (✉ 150 rue Champlain, ☎ 514/534–2200), with 22 trails for downhill skiing, was the site of the 1986 World Cup Slalom. The vertical drop is 1,336 ft, and there are six lifts.

Shopping

Factory outlet shopping is gaining popularity in the Townships—especially in Bromont, where shoppers can save between 30% and 70% on items carrying such national and international labels as Liz Claiborne, Vuarnet, and Oneida. Versants de Bromont and Promenades de Ma Maison are two centers off Exit 78 of Autoroute 10.

Sutton

14 *28 km (17mi) south of Bromont.*

Sutton is a well-established community with crafts shops, cozy eateries, and bars (La Paimpolaise is a favorite among skiers). **Arts Sutton** (✉ 7 rue Academy, ☎ 514/538–2563) is a long-established mecca for the visual arts.

Lodging

$$$ **Auberge la Paimpolaise.** This auberge is on Mont-Sutton, 50 ft from the ski trails. Nothing fancy is offered, but the location is hard to beat. Rooms are simple, comfortable, and clean, with a woodsy appeal. All-inclusive weekend ski packages are available. A complimentary breakfast is served. ✉ *615 rue Maple, J0E 2K0,* ☎ *514/538–3213 or 800/263–3213,* FAX *514/538–3970. 28 rooms. EP, MAP. AE, MC, V.*

Outdoor Activities and Sports

GOLF

Reservations must be made in advance at **Les Rochers Bleus** (✉ 550 Rte. 139, ☎ 514/538–2324), a par-72, 18-hole course.

SKIING

Mont-Sutton (✉ Rte. 139 South, Exit 106 from Autoroute 10, ☎ 514/538–2339), where skiers pay by the hour, has 53 downhill trails, a vertical drop of 1,518 ft, and nine lifts. This ski area attracts a die-hard crowd of mostly Anglophone skiers from Québec. It's also one of the area's largest resorts, with trails that plunge and wander through pine, maple, and birch trees slope-side.

Knowlton

15 *15 km (9 mi) northeast of Sutton.*

Along the shore of Lac Brome is the picturesque village of Knowlton, a great place to shop for antiques, clothes, and gifts. The village, which has a pond flanked by a brick church where ducks line up to be fed, is a treasure trove of Victoriana. Renovated clapboard buildings painted every shade of the rainbow have been turned into trendy stores, art galleries, and interesting little eateries. The distinctive Lake Brome ducks—white and plump—are found on local menus and celebrated, with exhibits, activities, and food, during the **Brome Lake Duck Festival** in mid-October.

Nightlife and the Arts

Théâtre Lac Brome (✉ 267 rue Knowlton, ☎ 514/242–2270 or 514/242–1395) stages plays, musicals, and productions of classic Broadway and West End hits. The company specializes in English productions but also has tried some bilingual productions and some new Canadian works. The 175-seat, air-conditioned theater is behind Knowlton's popular pub of the same name.

Outdoor Activities and Sports

Many Montrealers come for the downhill skiing at **Mont-Glen** (✉ Off Rte. 243, ☎ 514/243–6142).

Magog

⓰ *40 km (25) east of Knowlton.*

At the northern tip of Lac Memphrémagog, a large body of water reaching into northern Vermont, lies the bustling resort town of Magog, a four-season destination with bed-and-breakfasts, hotels, and restaurants. It has sandy beaches as well as activities that include boating, riding a ferry, bird-watching, sailboarding, horseback riding, dogsledding, rollerblading, and snowmobiling.

People can stroll or picnic (or skate and cross-country ski in winter) along the scenic linear park that skirts the lake, then turns into an off-road recreational trail leading to **Mont-Orford Provincial Park,** 13½ km (8 mi) from the center of town. The trail, which is for cyclists, walkers, and cross-country skiers, hugs the lake, then parallels Route 112 before winding through a forested area into the park.

The streets downtown are lined with century-old homes that have been converted into boutiques, stores, and dozens of eating places—from fast-food outlets to bistros serving Italian and French fare.

Dining and Lodging

$–$$$ ✕ **Auberge l'Étoile Sur-le-Lac.** This popular restaurant (which also has rooms) serves three meals a day in attractive surroundings. Large windows overlooking mountain-ringed Lac Memphrémagog make the dining room bright and airy. In summer you can sit outside and take in the smells and sounds, as well as the beautiful view. House specialties include wild game and Swiss fondue. ✉ *1150 rue Principale Ouest,* ☎ *819/843–6521 or 800/567–2727. AE, DC, MC, V.*

$$$$ ✕🏨 **Ripplecove Inn.** The Ripplecove vies with the Hatley and Hovey inns (☞ North Hatley, *below*) for best in the region. Its accommodations, service, and dining room are consistently excellent. The English pub–style room combines classical and French cuisine in such dishes as *petite timbale de sole et saumon fumé à l'algue nori* (timbale of sole and smoked salmon with seaweed) and the *gâteau de foie de volaille à la crème de porto* (gâteau of chicken livers in a port-flavored sauce). ✉ *700 chemin Ripplecove, C.P. 246, Ayer's Cliff (11 km, or 7 mi, south of Magog) J0B 1C0,* ☎ *819/838–4296 or 800/668–4296,* FAX *819/838–5541. 25 rooms. Restaurant, pool, 2 beaches, windsurfing, boating, cross-country skiing, meeting rooms. MAP. AE, MC, V.*

$$$$ ★ 🏨 **Centre de Santé d'Eastman.** The oldest spa in Québec has evolved from a simple health center into a bucolic haven for anyone seeking rest and therapeutic treatments. Owner Jocelyna Dubuc has resisted the temptation to turn the 350-acre property into a glitzy resort. In-

stead, she has created a relaxing world where people can, at reasonable prices, rejuvenate their bodies and minds through walking programs, massages, algae wraps, oxygen baths, and other energy-boosting programs. The brightly lit dining room (for guests only), with its wall of windows, serves flavorful vegetarian cuisine as well as innovative seafood and chicken dishes. Some spa goers, intent on shedding unwanted pounds, walk to nearby Eastman, an attractive hamlet with antiques and gift shops. ✉ *895 chemin Diligence, Eastman (15 km, or 9 mi, west of Magog) J0E 1P0,* ☎ *514/297–3009 or 800/665–5272. 19 rooms. Dining room, spa, cross-country skiing. AP. AE, MC, V.*

Nightlife and the Arts

THE ARTS

A theater-turned-church **Le Vieux Clocher** (✉ 64 rue Merry Nord, ☎ 819/847–0470) headlines well-known comedians and singers. Most performances are in French, but big names, like Jim Corcoran, Edith Butler, and Michel Rivard, perform here regularly.

NIGHTLIFE

Magog is lively after dark, with a variety of bars, cafés, bistros, and restaurants to suit every taste and pocketbook. **Auberge Orford** (✉ 20 rue Merry Sud, ☎ 819/843–9361) often has live entertainment. **La Grosse Pomme** (✉ 270 rue Principale Ouest, ☎ 819/843–9365) is a multilevel complex with huge video screens, dance floors, and restaurant service. **Resto-club Au Chat Noir** (✉ 266 rue Principale Ouest, ☎ 819/843–4337) is a gathering place for local jazz aficionados and musicians, who drop by for impromptu jam sessions that augment the regular performances.

Outdoor Activities and Sports

Owl's Head Ski Area (✉ Rte. 243 South, Exit 106 from Autoroute 10, ☎ 514/292–3342), 25 km (16 mi) south of Magog, is a mecca for skiers looking for fewer crowds. It has seven lifts, a 1,782-ft vertical drop, and 27 trails, including a 4-km (2½-mi) intermediate run, the longest in the Eastern Townships. From the trails you can see nearby Vermont and Lac Memphrémagog. (You might even see the lake's legendary sea dragon, said to have been sighted around 90 times since 1816.)

Valcourt

17 *50 km (31 mi) northwest of Magog.*

Valcourt is the birthplace of the inventor of the snowmobile, and the Eastern Townships are a world center for the sport, with more than 2,000 km (1,240 mi) of paths cutting through the woods and meadows. In February the town hosts the **Valcourt Snowmobiling Grand Prix** (☎ 514/532–3443), a five-day event with competitions and festivities. The **Musée Joseph-Armand Bombardier** displays innovator Bombardier's many inventions, including the snowmobile. ✉ *1001 av. Joseph-Armand Bombardier,* ☎ *514/532–5300.* 🎫 *$5.* ⏲ *Late June–Aug., daily 10–5:30; Sept.–late June, Tues.–Sun. 10–5.*

Orford

18 *40 km (25 mi) southeast of Valcourt.*

Orford is near a regional park, the Parc de Récréation du Mont-Orford, that's in use year-round, whether for skiing, camping, or hiking. Orford also has an annual arts festival, Festival Orford, highlighting classical music and chamber orchestra concerts. Since 1951, thousands of students have come to the **Orford Arts Centre** (☎ 819/843–3981, 800/567–6155 in Canada May–August) to study and perform classical music in the summer. Canada's internationally celebrated Orford String Quartet originated here.

Lodging

$$ **Auberge Estrimont.** An exclusive complex built of cedar, combining hotel rooms, condos, and larger chalets, Auberge Estrimont is close to ski hills, riding stables, and golf courses. Every room, whether in the hotel or in an adjoining condo unit, has a fireplace and a private balcony. ✉ *44 av. de l'Auberge, C.P. 98, Orford-Magog J1X 3W7,* ☎ *819/843–1616 or 800/567–7320,* FAX *819/843–4909. 76 rooms, 7 suites. Restaurant, bar, indoor and outdoor pools, hot tub, sauna, tennis, exercise room, racquetball, squash. AE, DC, MC, V.*

Outdoor Activities and Sports

Mont-Orford Ski Area (✉ Rte. 141, ☎ 819/843–6548), at the center of the provincial park here, has plenty of challenges for alpine and cross-country skiers, from novices to veterans. It has 41 runs, a vertical drop of 1,782 ft, and 8 lifts, as well as 56 km (35 mi) of cross-country trails.

Abbaye St-Benoît-du-Lac

★ 19 *17 km (11 mi) southwest of Magog.*

This abbey's slender bell tower juts up above the trees like a fairy-tale castle. Built by the Benedictines in 1912 on a wooded peninsula on Lac Memphrémagog, the abbey is home to some 60 monks, who sell apples and sparkling apple wine from their orchards as well as distinctive cheeses: Ermite, St-Benoît, and ricotta. Gregorian masses are sung daily and some are open to the public. To get to the abbey from Magog, take Route 112 and then follow the signs for the side road (R.R. 2, or rue des Pères) to the abbey. ✉ *R.R. 2,* ☎ *819/843–4080 for information about times of masses.* ⊙ *Store open between services; best time is 2–4.*

North Hatley

20 *36 km (22 mi) northeast of Abbaye St-Benoît-du-Lac.*

North Hatley, the small resort town on the tip of lovely Lac Massawippi, has a theater and a number of excellent inns and restaurants. The town, set among hills and farms, was discovered by well-to-do vacationers early in the century and has been drawing people ever since. A number of special events during the year are additional attractions.

Dining and Lodging

$$ ✕ **The Pilsen.** Québec's earliest microbrewery no longer brews beer on-site, but there's still Massawippi pale ale on tap at this lively spot. Good pub food—pasta, homemade soups, burgers, and the like—is served in the upstairs restaurant and the tavern, both of which overlook the water. ✉ *55 Main St.,* ☎ *819/842–2971. AE, MC, V.*

$$$$ ★ ✕ **Auberge Hatley.** Chef Alain Labrie specializes in regional dishes at this restaurant-inn, which has three times been voted the best in Québec. The menu changes seasonally, but the rich foie gras and Barbary duck are recommended if available. The yellow dining room has a panoramic view of Lake Massawippi; you can linger over your coffee or sip your selection from the wine cellar, which has more than 5,000 bottles. Guest rooms in this 1903 country manor are charmingly decorated; some have a whirlpool and a fireplace. ✉ *325 chemin Virgin, C.P. 330, J0B 2C0,* ☎ *819/842–2451,* FAX *819/842–2907. 25 rooms. Restaurant. MAP. AE, DC, MC, V. Closed last 2 wks in Nov.*

$$$$ ★ ✕ **Manoir Hovey.** Overlooking Lac Massawippi, this retreat maintains the ambience of a private estate and provides the activities of a

resort. Built in 1900, it resembles George Washington's home at Mount Vernon. Each wallpapered room has a mix of antiques and newer wood furniture, richly printed fabrics, and lace trimmings; many have fireplaces and private balconies. The dining room serves exquisite Continental and French cuisine; if it's in season, try warm roulades of Swiss chard with spring lamb, preserved apricots, and roasted hazelnuts or grilled tenderloin of beef marinated with juniper berries and a sauce of tarragon and horseradish. Dinner, breakfast, and most sports facilities are included in room rates. ✉ *575 chemin Hovey, C.P. 60, J0B 2C0,* ☎ *819/842–2421 or 800/661–2421,* FAX *819/842–2248. 40 rooms, 1 suite, 1 4-bedroom cottage. 2 bars, dining room, pool, tennis court, 2 beaches, ice fishing, mountain bikes, cross-country skiing, library, meeting rooms. MAP. AE, DC, MC, V.*

Nightlife and the Arts

The **Piggery** (✉ Rte. 108, ☎ 819/842–2432 or 819/842–2431), a theater that was once a pig barn, reigns supreme in the Townships' cultural life. The venue is renowned for its risk taking, often presenting new plays by Canadian playwrights and even experimenting with bilingual productions. The season runs June–August.

L'Association du Festival du Lac Massawippi (☎ 819/563–4141) presents an annual antiques and folk-arts show in July. The association also sponsors classical music concerts at the Église Ste-Elizabeth in North Hatley, on Sundays starting in late April and continuing through June. The biennial **Naive Arts Contest** (✉ Galerie Jeannine-Blais, 100 rue Main, ☎ 819/842–2784) shows the work of over 100 painters of naive art from 15 countries; the next show is in 2000.

Sherbrooke

㉑ *16 km (10 mi) north of North Hatley.*

The region's unofficial capital and largest city is Sherbrooke, named in 1818 for Canadian governor general Sir John Coape Sherbrooke. It was founded by Loyalists in the 1790s along the St-François River. Sherbrooke has a number of art galleries and museums, including the **Musée des Beaux-Arts de Sherbrooke.** This fine-arts museum has mostly oil paintings; there are occasional exhibits by regional artists and other changing shows. ✉ *241 rue Dufferin, J1H 4M3,* ☎ *819/821–2115.* 🎫 *$2.50.* ⏲ *Tues. and Thurs.–Sun. 1–5, Wed. 1–9.*

The **Sherbrooke Tourist Information Center** (✉ 48 rue Dépôt, ☎ 819/821–1919) conducts city tours late June–early September. Call for reservations.

Two **sugar shacks** near Sherbrooke give tours of their maple-syrup producing operations in the spring: It's best to call before visiting. Erablière Patoine (✉ 1105 chemin Beauvoir, ☎ 819/563–7455) is in Fleurimont. Bolduc (✉ 525 chemin Lower, ☎ 819/875–3022) is in Cookshire.

Dining and Lodging

$$–$$$$ ✕ **La Falaise St-Michel.** Chef and part-owner Patrick Laigniel serves up superb French cuisine in a warm redbrick and wood room that takes off any chill even before you sit down. A large selection of wines complements the table d'hôte. ✉ *Rues Webster and Wellington North, behind Banque Nationale,* ☎ *819/346–6339. AE, DC, MC, V.*

$$–$$$ ✕ **Restaurant au P'tit Sabot.** Specialties include dishes with wild boar, quail, and bison. The cozy room is a pleasant refuge from the bustle of Sherbrooke's main drag. A piano in the corner, pink decor, and room for only 35 patrons help set a romantic atmosphere. ✉ *1410 rue King Ouest,* ☎ *819/563–0262. AE, DC, MC, V.*

$ **Bishop's University.** If you are on a budget, the students' residences here are a great place to stay in summer. The prices can't be beat, and the location near Sherbrooke is good for touring. The university's grounds are lovely, with much of the architecture reminiscent of stately New England campuses. The Gothic-style chapel, paneled with richly carved ash, was built in 1857 and is a fine example of local craftsmanship. Reservations for summer guests are accepted as early as September, so book in advance. ✉ *Rue College, Lennoxville (5 km, or 3 mi, south of Sherbrooke), J1M 1Z7,* ☎ *819/822–9651,* FAX *819/822–9615. 564 beds in single or double rooms. Indoor pool, 18-hole golf course, tennis court, exercise room. MC, V. Closed Sept.–mid-May.*

Nightlife and the Arts

The **Centennial Theatre** (☎ 819/822–9692) at Bishop's University in Lennoxville, 5 km (3 mi) south of Sherbrooke, presents a roster of international, Canadian, and Québécois jazz, classical, and rock concerts, as well as dance, mime, and children's theater.

Mont-Mégantic's Observatory

22 *74 km (46 mi) east of Sherbrooke.*

Both amateur stargazers and serious astronomers are drawn to this site, in a beautifully wild and mountainous part of the Eastern Townships. The observatory (known as the Astrolab du Mont-Mégantic in French) is at the summit of the Townships' second-highest mountain (3,601 ft), whose northern face records annual snowfalls rivaling any other in North America. A joint venture by the University of Montréal and Laval University, the observatory has a powerful telescope that allows resident scientists to observe celestial bodies 10 million times smaller than the human eye can detect. At the Astrolab (a welcome center on the mountain's base), you can view an exhibition and a multimedia show and learn about the night sky. ✉ *189 Rte. du Parc, Notre-Dame-des-Bois,* ☎ *819/888–2822. Astrolab $10, night tour to summit $10. Astrolab late June–Labor Day, daily 10–6; night tour to summit late June–Labor Day, daily 8 PM.*

Dining and Lodging

$$ ✕ **Aux Berges de l'Aurore.** Although this tiny bed-and-breakfast has attractive furnishings and spectacular views (it sits at the foot of Mont-Mégantic), the draw here is the inn's cuisine. The restaurant ($$$) serves a five-course meal with ingredients supplied from the inn's huge fruit, vegetable, and herb garden, as well as wild game from the surrounding area: boar, fish, hare, and quail. ✉ *51 chemin de l'Observatoire, Notre-Dame-des-Bois,* ☎ *819/888–2715. 4 rooms. Restaurant. MC, V. Closed Jan.–May.*

CHARLEVOIX

Stretching along the St. Lawrence River's north shore, east of Québec City from Ste-Anne-de-Beaupré to the Saguenay River, Charlevoix embraces mountains rising from the sea and a succession of valleys, plateaus, and cliffs cut by waterfalls, brooks, and streams. The roads wind into villages of picturesque houses and huge tin-roof churches. The area has long been popular both as a summer retreat and as a haven for artists and craftspeople. In winter there are opportunities for both downhill and cross-country skiing.

New France's first historian, the Jesuit priest François-Xavier de Charlevoix, gave his name to the region. Charlevoix (pronounced sharle-*vwah*) was first explored by Jacques Cartier, who landed in

1535, although the first colonists didn't arrive until well into the 17th century. They developed a thriving shipbuilding industry, specializing in the sturdy schooner they called a *goelette,* which they used to haul everything from logs to lobsters up and down the coast in the days before rail and paved roads. Shipbuilding has been a vital part of the provincial economy until recent times; today wrecked and forgotten goelettes lie along beaches in the region.

Ste-Anne-de-Beaupré

23 *33 km (20 mi) east of Québec City.*

Charlevoix begins in the tiny town of Ste-Anne-de-Beaupré (named for Québec's patron saint). Each year more than a million pilgrims visit ★ the region's most famous religious site, the **Basilique Ste-Anne-de-Beaupré** (☞ Side Trips from Québec City *in* Chapter 3), which is dedicated to the mother of the Virgin Mary.

At the **Cap Tourmente Wildlife Reserve,** about 8 km (5 mi) northeast of Ste-Anne-de-Beaupré, more than 100,000 greater snow geese gather every October and May. This enclave on the north shore of the St. Lawrence River has 14 hiking trails; the park harbors hundreds of kinds of birds and mammals and more than 700 plant species. Naturalists give guided tours. ✉ *St-Joachim,* ☎ *418/827–4591 Apr.–Oct., 418/827–3776 Nov.–Mar.*

Outdoor Activities and Sports

Le Massif (✉ 1350 rue Principale, Petite Rivière St-François, ☎ 418/632–5876) is a three-peak ski resort that has the province's highest vertical drop—2,500 ft. The 18 trails are divided into runs for different levels (including one for extremely advanced skiers). Equipment can be rented on site. **Station Mont-Ste-Anne** (☞ Outdoor Activities and Sports *in* Chapter 3), outside Québec City, is on the World Cup downhill ski circuit.

Baie-St-Paul

24 *60 km (37 mi) northeast of Ste-Anne-de-Beaupré.*

Baie-St-Paul, Charlevoix's earliest settlement after Beaupré, is popular with craftspeople and artists. Here the high hills circle a wide plain, holding the village beside the sea. Many of Québec's greatest landscapists portray the area, and the work of some of them is for sale at the **Centre d'Art Baie-St-Paul** (✉ 4 rue Ambroise-Fafard, ☎ 418/435–3681). The **Centre d'Exposition de Baie-St-Paul** (✉ 23 rue Ambroise-Fafard, ☎ 418/435–3681) displays the work of various artists, some of them from the region.

Dining and Lodging

$$$$ ★ ✕▣ **Auberge la Maison Otis.** This inn offers calm and romantic accommodations in three buildings, including an old stone house, in the center of the village. Some of the country-style rooms have whirlpools, fireplaces, and antique furnishings. Summer lunches are served on an outdoor terrace. Skiing and ice-skating are available nearby. The restaurant serves creative Québec-oriented French cuisine like *ballotine de faisan* (pheasant) stuffed with quail and served in a venison sauce, followed by a delicious assortment of cheeses. It's in a 150-year-old Norman-style house, elegantly decorated in pastel pink, with a huge fireplace. ✉ *23 rue St-Jean-Baptiste, G0A 1B0,* ☎ *418/435–2255,* FAX *418/435–2464. 30 rooms, 4 suites. Restaurant, lounge, piano bar, indoor pool, sauna, health club. MAP. AE, MC, V.*

Charlevoix

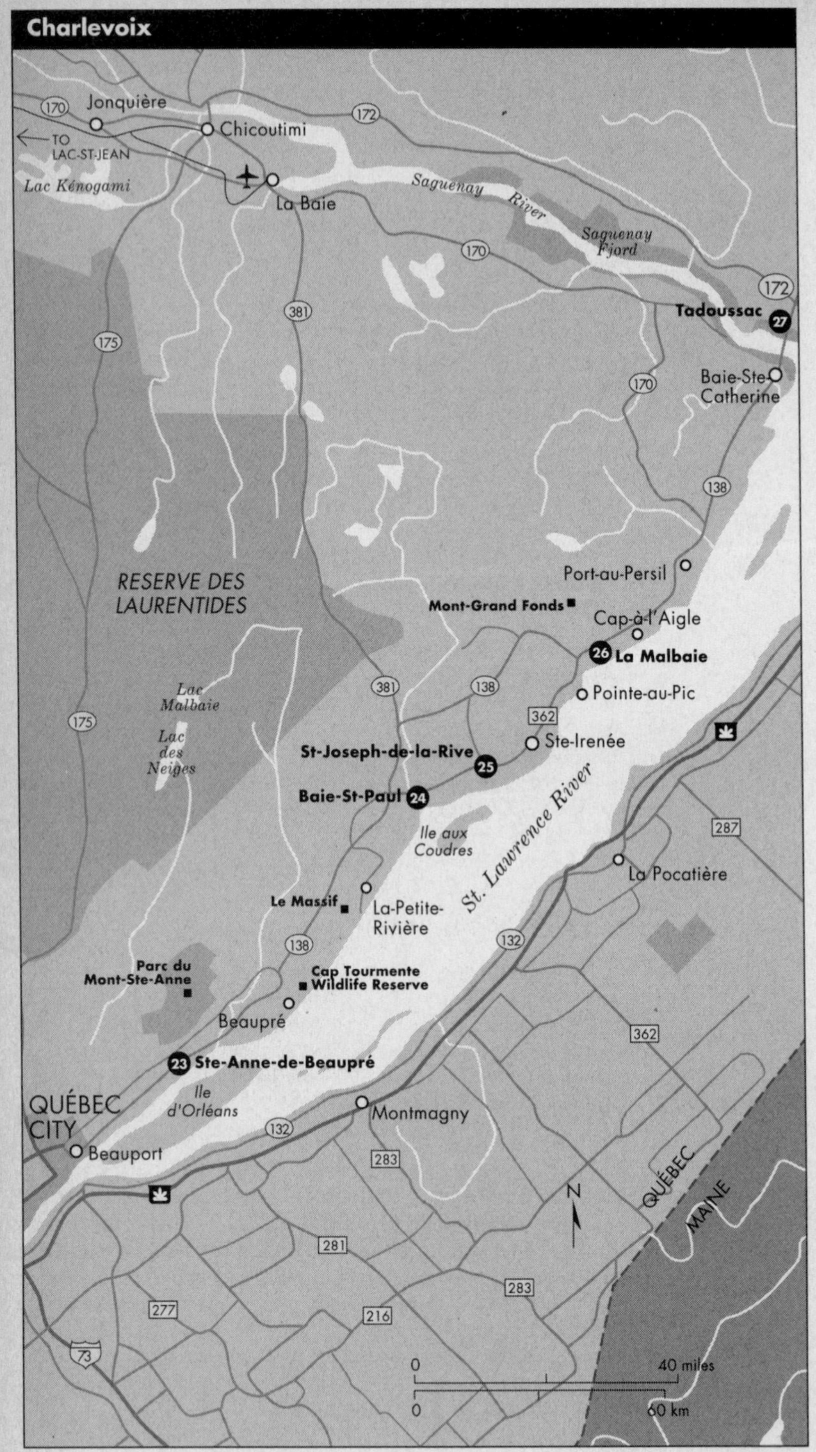

170
Jonquière
Chicoutimi
172
TO LAC-ST-JEAN
Lac Kénogami
La Baie
Saguenay River
Saguenay Fjord
170
172
Tadoussac
27
381
175
170
Baie-Ste-Catherine
138
Port-au-Persil
RESERVE DES LAURENTIDES
Mont-Grand Fonds
Cap-à-l'Aigle
26
La Malbaie
381
138
Pointe-au-Pic
Lac Malbaie
175
362
Lac des Neiges
Ste-Irenée
St-Joseph-de-la-Rive
25
Baie-St-Paul
24
St. Lawrence River
287
Ile aux Coudres
La Pocatière
Le Massif
La-Petite-Rivière
138
132
Parc du Mont-Ste-Anne
Cap Tourmente Wildlife Reserve
Beaupré
362
23
Ste-Anne-de-Beaupré
QUÉBEC CITY
Ile d'Orléans
Montmagny
132
Beauport
283
N
QUÉBEC
MAINE
281
283
277
216
73
0
40 miles
0
60 km

En Route From Baie-St-Paul, drivers have a choice of the open, scenic coastal drive on **Route 362** or the faster Route 138 to Pointe-au-Pic, La Malbaie, and Cap-à-l'Aigle. This section of Route 362 has memorable views of rolling hills—green, white, or ablaze with fiery hues, depending on the season—meeting the broad expanse of the "sea," as the locals like to call the St. Lawrence estuary.

St-Joseph-de-la-Rive

25 *15 km (9 mi) northeast of Baie-St-Paul.*

A secondary road leads sharply down into St-Joseph-de-la-Rive, with its line of old houses hugging the mountain base on the narrow shore road. The town has a number of peaceful inns and inviting restaurants. The small **Exposition Maritime** (Maritime Museum, ☎ 418/635–1131) commemorates the days of the St. Lawrence goelettes.

OFF THE BEATEN PATH **ILE AUX COUDRES** – From St-Joseph-de-la-Rive, a ferry (☎ 418/438–2743) travels to Ile aux Coudres, an island where Jacques Cartier's men gathered *coudres* (hazelnuts) in 1535. Since then, the island has produced many a goelette, and former captains now run several small inns. Larger inns have folk-dance evenings. You can bike around the island and see windmills, inns, water mills, and old schooners, or stop at boutiques selling paintings and local handicrafts, such as household linens.

Lodging

$$ ★ **Hôtel Cap-aux-Pierres.** This hotel provides top-notch accommodations in a traditionally Canadian main building and a motel section open in the summer only. About a third of the rooms have river views. The restaurant serves a mix of Québec standards and nouvelle cuisine, and entertainment includes folk dancing on summer Saturday evenings. ✉ *246 rue Principale, La Baleine, Ile aux Coudres G0A 2A0,* ☎ *418/438–2711 or 800/463–5250,* FAX *418/438–2127. 98 rooms. Restaurant, bar, indoor-outdoor pool. MAP. AE, DC, MC, V.*

Shopping

The **Papeterie St-Gilles** (✉ 304 rue F. A. Savard, ☎ 418/635–2430) produces unusual handcrafted stationery, using a 17th-century process.

La Malbaie

26 *35 km (22 mi) northeast of St-Joseph.*

La Malbaie is one of the most elegant and historically interesting resort towns in the province. It was known as Murray Bay in an earlier era when wealthy Anglophones summered here and in the neighboring villages of Pointe-au-Pic and Cap-à-l'Aigle. Once called the "summer White House," this area became popular with both American and Canadian politicians in the late 1800s when Ottawa Liberals and Washington Republicans partied decorously through the summer with members of the Québec judiciary. William Howard Taft built the first of three summer residences in Pointe-au-Pic in 1894, when he was the American civil governor of the Philippines. He became the 27th president of the United States in 1908.

Now many Taft-era homes serve as handsome inns, guaranteeing an old-fashioned coddling, with such extras as breakfast in bed, gourmet meals, whirlpools, and free shuttles to the ski areas in winter. Many serve lunch and dinner to nonresidents, so you can tour the area going from one gourmet's delight to the next. The cuisine, as elsewhere in Québec, is genuine French or regional fare.

Musée de Charlevoix traces the region's history as a vacation spot in a series of exhibits and is developing an excellent collection of local paintings and folk art. ✉ *1 chemin du Havre, Pointe-au-Pic (3 km, or 2 mi, south of La Malbaie),* ☎ *418/665–4411.*

The **Casino de Charlevoix,** styled after European casinos, welcomes visitors year-round. The minimum age is 18. ✉ *Hôtel Manoir Richelieu, 183 av. Richelieu, Pointe-au-Pic,* ☎ *418/665–5353 or 800/665–2274.* ⏲ *Sun.–Thurs. 10 AM–1 AM, Fri.– Sat. 10 AM–3 AM.*

Dining and Lodging

$$$$ ✕ **Auberge des 3 Canards.** The inn has made a name for itself in the region, not only for its accommodations but also for its award-winning restaurant. The menu may include *gratin d'escargots aux bluets* (snails with a blueberry and grapefruit sauce baked au gratin) as an appetizer, and stuffed pheasant—the breasts smothered in mustard sauce and the legs seasoned with spicy maple sauce—as a main course. Homemade desserts include *pomme de l'Ile aux Coudres*—cheese-topped apples with a touch of honey. Meals are elegantly presented in a rustic setting with natural wood and pale and deep blue touches throughout. ✉ *49 côte Bellevue, Pointe-au-Pic (3 km, or 2 mi, south of La Malbaie),* ☎ *418/665–3761. AE, MC, V.*

$$$$ ✕ **Auberge sur la Côte.** Simple white tablecloths, natural wood, and stone walls create a casual setting for fine French cuisine. A house specialty is *agneau de Charlevoix,* lamb seasoned with lemon and thyme, served with fresh vegetables. Lunch is served in summer only, but the dining room is open in the evening year-round. ✉ *205 chemin des Falaises,* ☎ *418/665–3972. AE, MC, V.*

$$$$ ★ ✕🏨 **Auberge la Pinsonnière.** An atmosphere of country luxury prevails at this inn, a Relais & Châteaux property. Each room is decorated differently; some have fireplaces, whirlpools, and king-size four-poster beds. The rooms overlook Murray Bay on the St. Lawrence River. The food here is excellent, and the auberge has one of the largest wine cellars in North America. ✉ *124 rue St-Raphael, Cap-à-l'Aigle (3 km, or 2 mi, north of La Malbaie), G0T 1B0,* ☎ *418/665–4431,* FAX *418/665–7156. 26 rooms, 1 suite. 2 restaurants, 3 lounges, indoor pool, sauna, tennis court, beach. MAP. AE, MC, V.*

$$$ 🏨 **Hôtel Manoir Richelieu.** The Manoir Richelieu, an imposing castle nestled amid trees on a cliff overlooking the St. Lawrence River, has been offering first-class accommodations for a hundred years. This hotel was constructed in 1929 on the site of an earlier property, but the Manoir Richelieu retains the air of a turn-of-the-century hostelry. Still, it has kept up with the times: A recent addition is Relaxarium Manoir Richelieu, a health spa with treatments from lymphatic drainage to hydrotherapy. The links-style golf course, similar to those in Scotland, overlooks the St. Lawrence. The casino here is owned by the Québec government. ✉ *181 rue Richelieu, Pointe-au-Pic (3 km, or 2 mi, south of La Malbaie), G0T 1M0,* ☎ *418/665–3703 or 800/463–2613,* FAX *418/665–3093. 380 rooms. Restaurant, indoor and outdoor pools, sauna, spa, 18-hole golf course, tennis courts, cross-country skiing, snowmobiling, casino. AE, DC, MC, V.*

Nightlife and the Arts

Domaine Forget, a music and dance academy, presents concerts on summer evenings by fine musicians from around the world, many of whom are teaching or learning at the school. The Domaine also functions as a stopover for traveling musicians, who take advantage of its rental studios. A 600-seat concert hall has recently been added. ✉ *Ste-Irenée (15 km, or 9 mi, south of La Malbaie),* ☎ *418/452–8111 or 418/452–2535,* FAX *418/452–3503.* ⏲ *Concerts May–Aug.*

Outdoor Activities and Sports

GOLF

Club de Golf de Manoir Richelieu (✉ 181 rue Richelieu, Pointe-au-Pic, ☎ 418/665–2526 or 800/463–2613) is a par-72,18-hole course.

SKIING

Mont-Grand Fonds (✉ 1000 chemin des Loisirs, ☎ 418/665–0095), 10 km (6 mi) north of La Malbaie, has 14 downhill slopes, a 1,105-ft vertical drop, and two lifts. It also has 135 km (84 mi) of cross-country trails. Two trails meet the standards of the International Ski Federation, and the resort hosts major ski competitions occasionally. Other sports are dogsledding, sleigh riding, skating, and tobogganing.

Tadoussac

27 *71 km (44 mi) north of La Malbaie.*

The small town of Tadoussac shares the view up the magnificent Saguenay Fjord with Baie-Ste-Catherine across the river. The drive here from La Malbaie, along Route 138, leads past a lovely series of villages and views along the St. Lawrence. Jacques Cartier made a stop at this point in 1535, and it became an important meeting site for fur traders until the mid-19th century. Whale-watching excursions and cruises of the fjord now depart from Tadoussac, as well as from Chicoutimi, farther up the deep fjord.

As the Saguenay River flows from Lac St-Jean south toward the St. Lawrence, it has a dual character: Between Alma and Chicoutimi, the once rapidly flowing river has been turned into hydroelectric power; in its lower section, it becomes wider and deeper and flows by steep mountains and cliffs, en route to the St. Lawrence. The white beluga whale breeds in the lower portion of the Saguenay in summer, and in the confluence of the fjord and the seaway are many marine species, which attract other whales, such as pilot, finback, humpback, and blues.

Sadly, the beluga is an endangered species; the whales, along with 27 other species of mammals and birds and 17 species of fish, are being threatened by pollution in the St. Lawrence River. This has inspired a $100 million project funded by both the federal and provincial governments. The 800-square-km (496-square-mi) **Parc Marine du Saguenay–St-Laurent** (✉ 182 rue de l'Église for park office, ☎ 418/235–4703), a marine park at the confluence of the Saguenay and St. Lawrence rivers, has been created to protect its fragile ecosystem. Exhibits at La Maison des Dunes (☎ 514/235–4238), an interpretive center 5 km (3 mi) northwest of the village, explain the tides and the flora and fauna, including sand dunes.

Outdoor Activities and Sports

Croisières Navimex Canada, Inc. (✉ 124 rue St-Pierre, Bureau 300, Québec City G1K 4A7, ☎ 418/692–4643, 800/463–1292 in season) has three-hour whale-watching cruises ($30) and 4½-hour dinner cruises on the Saguenay Fjord ($40). Cruises depart from Baie-Ste-Catherine, Tadoussac, and Rivière du Loup (the departure from Rivière du Loup costs an additional $5). The best months for seeing whales are July, August, and September, although some operators extend the season at either end if whales are around.

THE GASPÉ PENINSULA

Jutting into the stormy Gulf of St. Lawrence like the battered prow of a ship, the Gaspé Peninsula (Gaspésie in French) remains an isolated region of unsurpassed wild beauty. Sheer cliffs tower above broad beaches, and tiny coastal fishing communities cling to the shoreline. Inland rise the Chic-Choc Mountains, eastern Canada's highest, the realm of woodland caribou, black bear, and moose. Townspeople in some Gaspé areas speak mainly English.

The Gaspé was on Jacques Cartier's itinerary—he first stepped ashore in North America in the town of Gaspé in 1534—but Vikings, Basques, and Portuguese fishermen had come before. The area's history is told in countless towns en route. Acadians, displaced by the British from New Brunswick in 1755, settled Bonaventure; Paspébiac still has a gunpowder shed built in the 1770s to help defend the peninsula from American ships; and United Empire Loyalists settled New Carlisle in 1784.

Today the area still seems unspoiled and timeless, a blessing for anyone dipping and soaring along the spectacular coastal highways or venturing on river-valley roads to the interior. Geographically, the peninsula is among the oldest lands on earth. A vast, mainly uninhabited forest covers the hilly hinterland. Local tourist officials can be helpful in locating outfitters and guides for fishing. The Gaspé has many parks, nature trails, and wildlife sanctuaries. The most accessible include Parc de l'Ile-Bonaventure-et-du-Rocher-Percé, which embraces Bonaventure Island, a sanctuary for 250,000 birds; Forillon National Park at the tip of the peninsula, with 50 km (31 mi) of trails and an interesting boardwalk; and the Parc Provincial de la Gaspésie. The provincial park embraces the Chic-Choc Mountains and has terrain ranging from tundra to subalpine forest.

Carleton

28 *201 km (125 mi) southeast of Mont-Joli.*

The Notre Dame Oratory on Mont-St-Joseph dominates this French-speaking city. There are lookout points and hiking trails around the site. The views, almost 2,000 ft above Baie des Chaleurs, are lovely.

Dining and Lodging

$$ **Motel Hostelerie Baie-Bleue.** This motel is snuggled up against a mountain beside the Baie des Chaleurs and has great views. Daily guided bus tours leave from the hotel June–September. The large restaurant, La Seignerie, has been recognized for excellence. Chef Simon Bernard prepares regional dishes, especially seafood. The table d'hôte won't break your budget, and the wine list is extensive and well chosen. ✉ *482 blvd. Perron, Rte. 132, G0C 1J0,* ☎ *418/364–3355 or 800/463–9099,* FAX *418/364–6165. 95 rooms. Restaurant, pool, tennis court, beach. AE, MC, V.*

Outdoor Activities and Sports

Windsurfers and sailors enjoy the breezes around the Gaspé; there are windsurfing marathons in Baie des Chaleurs each summer.

Percé

29 *193 km (120 mi) east of Carleton.*

A pretty fishing village, Percé has a number of attractions and can get busy in summer. The most famous sight in the region is the huge fossil-embedded rock offshore that the sea "pierced" thousands of years ago. There are many pleasant places to walk and hike near town, and it's also possible to do some fishing or take a whale-watching cruise.

The largest colony of gannets in the world summers off Percé on
★ 30 **Bonaventure Island.** From the wharf at Percé, you can take a scenic boat ride to the island and walk the trails here. Trips are offered by Croisières

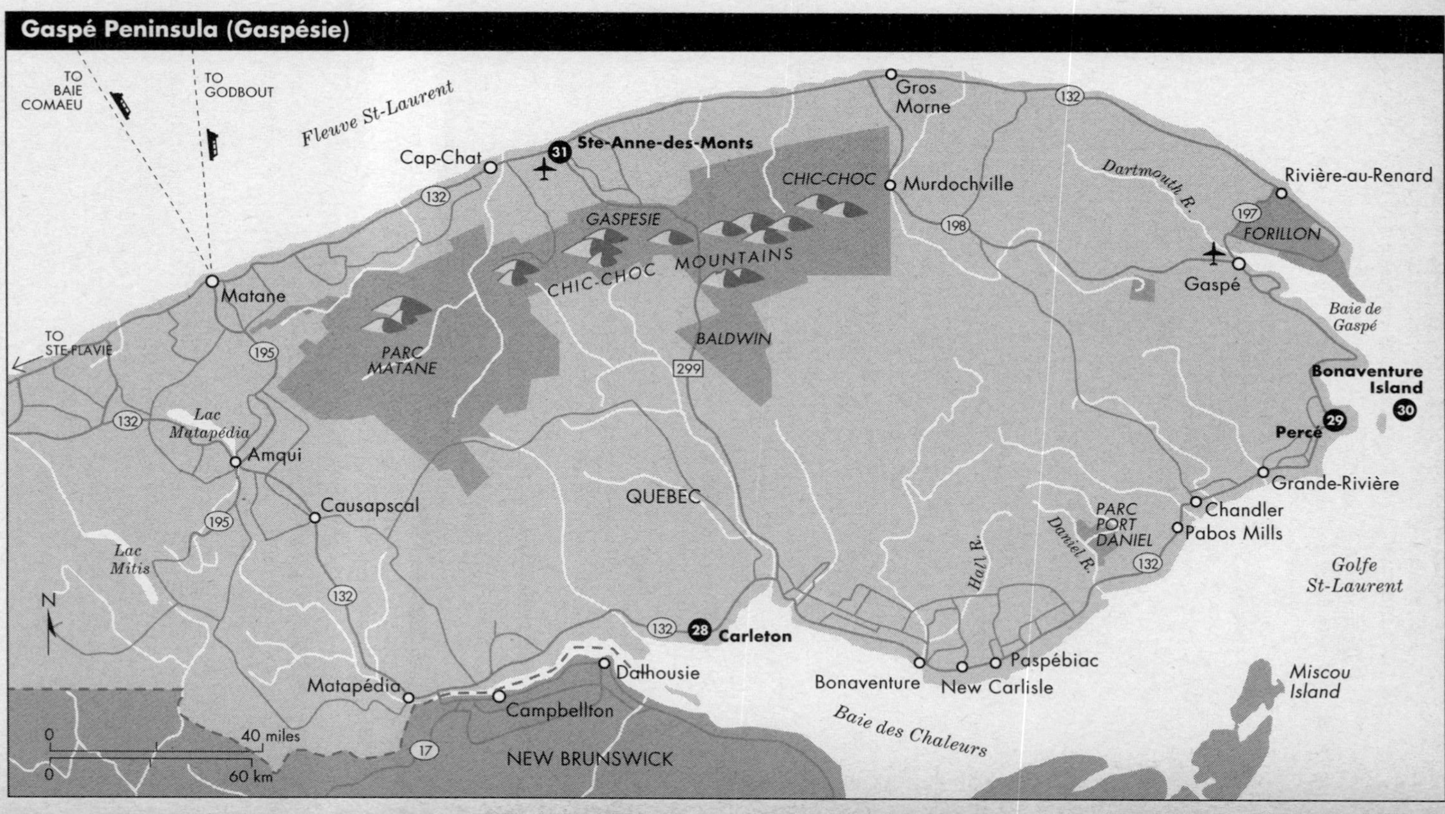
Gaspé Peninsula (Gaspésie)
TO BAIE COMAEU
TO GODBOUT
Fleuve St-Laurent
Cap-Chat
Ste-Anne-des-Monts
Gros Morne
Murdochville
Rivière-au-Renard
Dartmouth R.
FORILLON
Gaspé
Baie de Gaspé
Bonaventure Island
Percé
Grande-Rivière
Chandler
Pabos Mills
PARC PORT DANIEL
Daniel R.
Hall R.
Golfe St-Laurent
Miscou Island
Paspébiac
New Carlisle
Bonaventure
Baie des Chaleurs
Carleton
Dalhousie
Campbellton
NEW BRUNSWICK
Matapédia
Matane
TO STE-FLAVIE
GASPESIE
CHIC-CHOC
CHIC-CHOC
MOUNTAINS
BALDWIN
PARC MATANE
QUEBEC
Lac Matapédia
Amqui
Causapscal
Lac Mitis
N
132
195
197
198
299
17
28
29
30
31
0
40 miles
0
60 km

Baie de Gaspé (☎ 418/892–5500), Agences Touristiques de Gaspé (☎ 418/892–5629), and Les Bateliers de Percé (☎ 418/782–2974. Take binoculars and a camera; there are many kinds of birds here.

Dining and Lodging

$–$$ ✕ **La Sieur de Pabos.** Serving some of the best seafood in the province, this rustic restaurant overlooks Pabos Bay, south of Chandler, about 40 km (25 mi) south of Percé. The chef suggests *crêpe de la seigneurie,* a seafood crepe with a delicately seasoned white sauce. ✉ *325 Rte. 132, Pabos Mills,* ☎ *418/689–2281. AE, MC, V.*

$$$ 🏨 **La Normandie Hotel/Motel.** All but four rooms of this split-level motel face the ocean, with views of Percé Rock and Bonaventure Island. The location in the center of town puts shops and restaurants within walking distance; a beach and a municipal pool are also nearby. Third-floor rooms are more spacious. ✉ *221 Rte. 132 Ouest, C.P. 129, G0C 2L0,* ☎ *418/782–2112 or 800/463–0820. 45 rooms. Restaurant, lounge, sauna, exercise room. EP, MAP. AE, DC, MC, V. Closed Nov.–Apr.*

$$–$$$ 🏨 **La Bonaventure-sur-Mer Hotel.** The waterfront location with views of Percé Rock and Bonaventure Island makes up for the motel-standard decor. Some motel units have kitchenettes. The restaurant serves mainly beef and seafood dishes. ✉ *Rte. 132, C.P. 339, G0C 2L0,* ☎ *418/782–2166. 90 rooms. Restaurant, beach. AE, DC, MC, V. Closed Nov.–May.*

$$ 🏨 **La Côte Surprise Motor Hotel.** Most of the rooms of this motel have views of Percé Rock and the village. Decor is standard in both motel and second-floor hotel units, but the private balconies and terraces are a plus. ✉ *Rte. 132, C.P. 339, G0C 2L0,* ☎ *418/782–2166,* FAX *418/782–5323. 36 rooms. Dining room, lounge, snack bar. AE, D, DC, MC, V. Closed Oct.–May.*

$ 🏨 **Hôtel-Motel Rocher Percé.** Owned by Madeleine Pidgeon and Marc Bourdages, this hostelry is a 10-minute walk from the beach. Picnic tables and chairs have views over the Percé Rock and the sea. Some motel units have kitchenettes. ✉ *111 Rte. 132 Ouest, C.P. 34, G0C 2L0,* ☎ *418/782–2330,* FAX *418/782–5136. 4 rooms in hotel, 14 in motel. Closed in winter.*

Ste-Anne-des-Monts

31 *282 km (175 mi) northwest of Percé.*

The area south of this coastal town has Québec's highest peaks, the Chic-Choc Mountains. **Parc de la Gaspésie** (Gaspé Peninsula Park) ✉ Rte. 299, ☎ 418/763–3301) has climbing, telemark skiing, mountain hiking, and nature interpretation programs such as moose watching.

There's telemark skiing at **Club du Grand Yétis** (✉ 85 blvd. Ste-Anne Ouest, ☎ 418/763–7782 or 800/665–6527), where overnight accommodation is in cabins heated by wood-burning stoves. Hardier types can opt for camping out.

Dining and Lodging

$–$$ ✕ **Restaurant Monaco.** The Monaco's eclectic menu includes grilled meat as well as fish, seafood, pastas, and Chinese dishes. The air-conditioned dining room, near the entrance to the Parc de la Gaspésie, is open 24 hours a day. ✉ *90 blvd. Ste-Anne,* ☎ *418/763–3321 or 800/463–7468. AE, DC, MC, V.*

$$ 🏨 **Gite du Mont-Albert.** Nestled in the middle of the Chic-Choc Mountains, this property is 40 km (25 mi) south of Ste-Anne, in the Parc de la Gaspésie. It's a perfect retreat for hiking, bicycling, horseback riding, or salmon fishing on the Ste-Anne River. ✉ *Rte. 299, C.P. 1150, G0E 2G0,* ☎ *418/763–2288 or 888/270–4483. 48 rooms. Restaurant, bar, dining room. AE, MC, V.*

QUÉBEC A TO Z

Arriving and Departing

By Bus

Most major bus lines in the province connect with **Voyageur** (☎ 514/842–2281).

By Car

Major entry points are Ottawa/Hull, U.S. 87 from New York State south of Montréal, U.S. 91 from Vermont into the Eastern Townships area, and the Trans-Canada Highway (Highway 1) just west of Montréal.

By Plane

Most airlines fly into Montréal or Québec City (☞ Montréal A to Z *in* Chapter 2 *and* Québec City A to Z *in* Chapter 3).

By Train

Regular **VIA Rail** (☎ 800/835–3032) passenger service connects many towns in the province with Montréal and Québec City and offers limited service to the Gaspé Peninsula.

Getting Around

Québec

BY BUS

Most bus traffic to the outer reaches of the province begins at the **bus terminal** in Québec City (✉ 320 rue Abraham-Martin, ☎ 418/525–3000).

BY CAR

Québec has fine roads, along which drivers insist on speeding. The major highways are Autoroute des Laurentides 15, a six-lane highway from Montréal to the Laurentians; Autoroute 10 East from Montréal to the Eastern Townships; U.S. 91 from New England, which becomes Autoroute 55 as it crosses the border to the Eastern Townships; and Route 138, which runs from Montréal along the north shore of the St. Lawrence River. Road maps are available at seasonal or permanent Québec **tourist offices** (call 800/363–7777 for locations).

The Laurentians

BY BUS

Frequent bus service is available from the **Terminus Voyageur** (✉ 505 blvd. de Maisonneuve Est, ☎ 514/842–2281) in downtown Montréal. **Limocar Laurentides** service (☎ 514/435–8899) departs regularly for L'Annonciation, Mont-Laurier, Ste-Adèle, Ste-Agathe-des-Monts, and St-Jovite, among other stops en route. Limocar also has a service to the Lower Laurentians region, departing from the Laval bus terminal at the Métro Henri-Bourassa stop in north Montréal, stopping in many towns and ending in St-Jérôme.

BY CAR

Autoroute des Laurentides 15 and Route 117, a slower but more scenic secondary road, lead to this resort country. Try to avoid traveling to and from the region on Friday evening or Sunday afternoon, as you're likely to sit for hours in traffic.

The Eastern Townships

BY BUS

Buses depart daily from the **Terminus Voyageur** in Montréal (✉ 505 blvd. de Maisonneuve Est, ☎ 514/842–2281) to Granby, Lac-Mégantic, Magog, and Sherbrooke.

BY CAR

Autoroute 10 East heads from Montréal through the Townships; from New England, U.S. 91 becomes Autoroute 55, a major road.

Charlevoix

BY CAR

The main roads through the region are the scenic Route 362 and the faster Route 138.

Gaspé Peninsula

BY CAR

The Trans-Canada Highway (Highway 1) runs northeast along the southern shore of the St. Lawrence River to just south of Rivière-du-Loup, where the 270-km (167-mi) Route 132 hugs the dramatic coastline. At Ste-Flavie, follow the southern leg of Route 132. The entire distance around the peninsula is 848 km (526 mi).

Contacts and Resources

Camping

Inquiries about camping in Québec's national parks should be directed to **Canadian Heritage Parks Canada** (✉ Passage du Chien d'Or, Box 6060, Québec City, G1R 4V7, ☎ 418/648–4177). For information on camping in the province's private trailer parks and campgrounds, write for the free publication "Québec Camping," available from **Tourisme Québec** (✉ Box 979, Montréal H3C 2W3, ☎ 514/873–2015 or 800/363–7777).

Emergencies

Ambulance, fire, police (☎ 911).

Fishing

Nineteen outfitters are members of the Laurentian tourist association; several recommendations follow. **Pourvoirie Baroux** (✉ St-Jovite, ☎ 819/425–7882). **Pourvoirie Boismenu** (✉ Lac-du-Cerf, ☎ 819/597–2619). **Pourvoiries Mekoos** (✉ Mont-Laurier, ☎ 819/623–2336).

The **Fédération des Pourvoyeurs du Québec** (✉ Québec Outfitters Federation, 5237 blvd. Hamel, Bureau 270, Québec City G2P 2H2, ☎ 418/877–5191) has a list of of outfitters, which is also available through tourist offices. Fishing requires a permit, available from the regional offices of the **Ministère de l'Environnement et de la Faune** (✉ Ministry of the Environment and Wildlife, 150 blvd. René-Lévesque Est, Québec City G1R 4Y1, ☎ 418/643–3127 or 800/561–1616), or at regional sporting-goods stores displaying an "authorized agent" sticker.

Guest Farms

Agricotours (✉ 4545 av. Pierre-de-Coubertin, C.P. 1000, Succursale M, Montréal H1V 3R2, ☎ 514/252–3138), the Québec farm-vacation association, can provide lists of guest farms in the province.

Mountain Climbing

The **Fédération Québécoise de la Montagne** (✉ Québec Mountain-Climbing Federation, 4545 rue Pierre-de-Coubertin, C.P. 1000, Succursale M, Montréal H1V 3R2, ☎ 514/252–3004) has information about this sport, as do the province's tourist offices.

Nature Tours

The **Montréal Zoological Society** (✉ 2055 rue Peel, Montréal H3A 1V4, ☎ 514/845–8317) is a nature-oriented group that offers lectures, field trips, and weekend excursions. Tours include whale-watching in the St. Lawrence estuary and hiking and bird-watching in national parks throughout Québec, Canada, and the northern United States.

River Rafting

Four companies specializing in white-water rafting at Rivière Rouge are on-site at the trip's departure point near Calumet. (To get here, take Route 148 past Calumet; turn onto chemin de la Rivière Rouge until you see the signs for the access road to each rafter's headquarters.) **Aventures en Eau Vive** (☎ 819/242-6084 or 800/567-6881), **Nouveau Monde** (☎ 819/242-7238 or 800/361-5033), **Propulsion** (☎ 514/229-6620 or 800/461-3300), and **W-3 Rafting** (☎ 514/334-0889) all offer four- to five-hour rafting trips and provide transportation to and from the river site, as well as guides, helmets, life jackets, and, at the end of the trip, a much-anticipated meal. Most have facilities on-site or nearby for dining, drinking, camping, bathing, swimming, hiking, and horseback riding.

Skiing

For information about ski conditions, call **Tourisme Québec** (☎ 800/363-7777) and ask for the ski report.

Snowmobiling

Regional tourist offices (☞ Visitor Information, *below*) have information about snowmobiling in their area, including snowmobile maps and lists of essential services. Snowmobilers who use trails in Québec must obtain an access pass or day user's pass for the trails. The sport is regulated by the **Québec Federation of Snowmobiling Clubs** (✉ 4545 av. Pierre-de-Coubertin, Box 1000, Montréal, Québec H1V 3R2, ☎ 514/252-3076).

Jonview Canada (✉ 1227 av. St-Hubert, Suite 200, Montréal H2L 3Y8, ☎ 514/843-8161) offers snowmobile tours in the Laurentians, in Charlevoix, and as far north as the James Bay region. Other weeklong packages may include dogsledding and ice fishing.

Visitor Information

QUÉBEC

Tourisme Québec (✉ C.P. 979, Montréal H3C 2W3, ☎ 800/363-7777) can provide information on provincial tourist bureaus throughout the province.

THE LAURENTIANS

The major tourist office is the **Maison du Tourisme des Laurentides** (✉ 14142 rue de Lachapelle, R.R. 1, St-Jérôme J7Z 5T4, ☎ 514/436-8532 or 800/561-6673), just off the Autoroute des Laurentides 15 at Exit 39. The office is open mid-June–August, daily 8:30–8; September–mid-June, Saturday–Thursday 9–5, Friday 9–7.

Year-round regional tourist offices are in the towns of Labelle, Mont-Laurier, Mont-Tremblant, Piedmont, St-Jovite, Ste-Adèle, Ste-Agathe-des-Monts, St-Sauveur-des-Monts, and Val David. **Seasonal tourist offices** (mid-June–Labor Day) are in Grenville, Lachute, L'Annonciation, Ste-Marguerite-du-Lac-Masson, St-Eustache, Oka, Notre-Dame-du-Laus, and St-Adolphe-d'Howard.

THE EASTERN TOWNSHIPS

Year-round regional provincial tourist offices are in Bromont, Eastman, Granby, Lac-Brome (Foster), Lac Mégantic, Magog, Sherbrooke, Sutton, Mansonville, and Waterloo. **Seasonal tourist offices** (June–Labor Day) are in Coaticook, Pike River, Frelighsburg, and Granby. Seasonal bureaus' schedules are irregular, so it's a good idea to contact the **Association Touristique des Cantons de l'Est** (✉ 20 rue Don Bosco Sud, Sherbrooke J1L 1W4, ☎ 819/820-2020 or 800/455-5527) before visiting. This association also provides lodging information.

CHARLEVOIX

The regional tourist office is **Association Touristique Régionale de Charlevoix** (✉ 630 blvd. de Comporté, C.P. 275, La Malbaie G5A 1T8, ☎ 418/665–4454).

GASPÉ PENINSULA

The regional tourist office is **Association Touristique de la Gaspésie** (✉ 357 Rte. de la Mer, Ste-Flavie G0J 2L0, ☎ 418/775–2223 or 800/463–0323).

FRENCH VOCABULARY

One of the trickiest French sounds to pronounce is the nasal final *n* sound (whether or not the *n* is actually the last letter of the word). You should try to pronounce it as a sort of nasal grunt—as in "huh." The vowel that precedes the *n* will govern the vowel sound of the word, and in this list we precede the final *n* with an *h* to remind you to be nasal.

Another problem sound is the ubiquitous but untransliterable *eu,* as in *bleu* (blue) or *deux* (two), and the very similar sound in *je* (I), *ce* (this), and *de* (of). The closest equivalent might be the vowel sound in "put," but rounded.

Words and Phrases

Basics

English	French	Pronunciation
Yes/no	Oui/non	wee/nohn
Please	S'il vous plaît	seel voo **play**
Thank you	Merci	mair-**see**
You're welcome	De rien	deh ree-**ehn**
That's all right	Il n'y a pas de quoi	eel nee ah pah de **kwah**
Excuse me, sorry	Pardon	pahr-**dohn**
Sorry!	Désolé(e)	day-zoh-**lay**
Good morning/ afternoon	Bonjour	bohn-**zhoor**
Good evening	Bonsoir	bohn-**swahr**
Goodbye	Au revoir	o ruh-**vwahr**
Mr. (Sir)	Monsieur	muh-**syuh**
Mrs. (Ma'am)	Madame	ma-**dam**
Miss	Mademoiselle	mad-mwa-**zel**
Pleased to meet you	Enchanté(e)	ohn-shahn-**tay**
How are you?	Comment ça va?	kuh-mahn-sa-**va**
Very well, thanks	Très bien, merci	tray bee-ehn, mair-**see**
And you?	Et vous?	ay **voo**?

Numbers

English	French	Pronunciation
one	un	uhn
two	deux	deuh
three	trois	twah
four	quatre	**kaht**-ruh
five	cinq	sank
six	six	seess
seven	sept	set
eight	huit	wheat
nine	neuf	nuff
ten	dix	deess
eleven	onze	ohnz
twelve	douze	dooz

thirteen	treize	trehz
fourteen	quatorze	kah-**torz**
fifteen	quinze	kanz
sixteen	seize	sez
seventeen	dix-sept	deez-**set**
eighteen	dix-huit	deez-**wheat**
nineteen	dix-neuf	deez-**nuff**
twenty	vingt	vehn
twenty-one	vingt-et-un	vehnt-ay-**uhn**
thirty	trente	trahnt
forty	quarante	ka-**rahnt**
fifty	cinquante	sang-**kahnt**
sixty	soixante	swa-**sahnt**
seventy	soixante-dix	swa-sahnt-**deess**
eighty	quatre-vingts	kaht-ruh-**vehn**
ninety	quatre-vingt-dix	kaht-ruh-vehn-**deess**
one-hundred	cent	sahn
one-thousand	mille	meel

Colors

black	noir	nwahr
blue	bleu	bleuh
brown	brun/marron	bruhn/mar-**rohn**
green	vert	vair
orange	orange	o-**rahnj**
pink	rose	rose
red	rouge	rooje
violet	violette	vee-o-**let**
white	blanc	blahnk
yellow	jaune	zhone

Days of the Week

Sunday	dimanche	**dee**-mahnsh
Monday	lundi	**luhn**-dee
Tuesday	mardi	**mahr**-dee
Wednesday	mercredi	**mair**-kruh-dee
Thursday	jeudi	**zhuh**-dee
Friday	vendredi	**vawn**-druh-dee
Saturday	samedi	**sahm**-dee

Months

January	janvier	**zhahn**-vee-ay
February	février	**feh**-vree-ay
March	mars	marce
April	avril	a-**vreel**
May	mai	meh
June	juin	zhwehn
July	juillet	**zhwee**-ay
August	août	oot
September	septembre	sep-**tahm**-bruh
October	octobre	awk-**to**-bruh
November	novembre	no-**vahm**-bruh
December	décembre	day-**sahm**-bruh

Useful Phrases

Do you speak . . . English?	Parlez-vous . . . anglais?	par-lay **voo** **ahn**-glay
I don't speak . . . French	Je ne parle pas . . . français	zhuh nuh parl **pah** frahn-**say**
I don't understand	Je ne comprends pas	zhuh nuh kohm-prahn **pah**
I understand	Je comprends	zhuh kohm-**prahn**
I don't know	Je ne sais pas	zhuh nuh say **pah**
I'm American/ British	Je suis américain/ anglais	zhuh sweez a-may-ree-**kehn**/ahn-**glay**
What's your name?	Comment vous appelez-vous?	ko-mahn voo za-pell-ay-**voo**
My name is . . .	Je m'appelle . . .	zhuh ma-**pell** . . .
What time is it?	Quelle heure est-il?	kel air eh-**teel**
How?	Comment?	ko-**mahn**
When?	Quand?	kahn
Yesterday	Hier	yair
Today	Aujourd'hui	o-zhoor-**dwee**
Tomorrow	Demain	duh-**mehn**
This morning/ afternoon	Ce matin/cet après-midi	suh ma-**tehn**/set ah-pray-mee-**dee**
Tonight	Ce soir	suh **swahr**
What?	Quoi?	kwah
What is it?	Qu'est-ce que c'est?	kess-kuh-**say**
Why?	Pourquoi?	**poor**-kwa
Who?	Qui?	kee
Where is . . .	Où se trouve . . .	oo suh **troov**
the train station?	la gare?	la gar
the subway?	la station de?	la sta-**syon** duh
station?	métro?	may-**tro**
the bus stop?	l'arrêt de bus?	la-**ray** duh **booss**
the airport?	l'aérogare?	lay-ro-**gar**
the post office?	la poste?	la post
the bank?	la banque?	la bahnk
the hotel?	l'hôtel?	lo-**tel**
the store?	le magasin?	luh ma-ga-**zehn**
the cashier?	la caisse?	la **kess**
the museum?	le musée?	luh mew-**zay**
the hospital?	l'hôpital?	lo-pee-**tahl**
the elevator?	l'ascenseur?	la-sahn-**seuhr**
the telephone?	le téléphone?	luh tay-lay-**phone**
Where are the rest rooms?	Où sont les toilettes?	oo sohn lay twah-**let**
Here/there	Ici/là	ee-**see**/la
Left/right	A gauche/à droite	a goash/a drwaht
Straight ahead	Tout droit	too drwah

Is it near/far?	C'est près/loin?	say pray/lwehn
I'd like . . .	Je voudrais . . .	zhuh voo-**dray**
a room	une chambre	ewn **shahm**-bruh
the key	la clé	la clay
a newspaper	un journal	uhn zhoor-**nahl**
a stamp	un timbre	uhn **tam**-bruh
I'd like to buy . . .	Je voudrais acheter . . .	zhuh voo-**dray ahsh**-tay
a cigar	un cigare	uhn see-**gar**
cigarettes	des cigarettes	day see-ga-**ret**
matches	des allumettes	days a-loo-**met**
dictionary	un dictionnaire	uhn deek-see-oh-**nare**
soap	du savon	dew sah-**vohn**
city map	un plan de ville	uhn plahn de **veel**
road map	une carte routière	ewn cart roo-tee-**air**
magazine	une revue	ewn reh-**vu**
envelopes	des enveloppes	dayz ahn-veh-**lope**
writing paper	du papier à lettres	dew pa-pee-**ay** a **let**-ruh
airmail writing paper	du papier avion	dew pa-pee-**ay** a-vee-**ohn**
postcard	une carte postale	ewn cart pos-**tal**
How much is it?	C'est combien?	say comb-bee-**ehn**
It's expensive/ cheap	C'est cher/pas cher	say share/pa share
A little/a lot	Un peu/beaucoup	uhn peuh/bo-**koo**
More/less	Plus/moins	plu/mwehn
Enough/too (much)	Assez/trop	a-say/tro
I am ill/sick	Je suis malade	zhuh swee ma-**lahd**
Call a . . . doctor	Appelez un . . . médecin	a-play uhn mayd-**sehn**
Help!	Au secours!	o suh-**koor**
Stop!	Arrêtez!	a-reh-**tay**
Fire!	Au feu!	o fuh
Caution!/Look out!	Attention!	a-tahn-see-**ohn**

Dining Out

A bottle of . . .	une bouteille de . . .	ewn boo-**tay** duh
A cup of . . .	une tasse de . . .	ewn **tass** duh
A glass of . . .	un verre de . . .	uhn **vair** duh
Ashtray	un cendrier	uhn sahn-dree-**ay**
Bill/check	l'addition	la-dee-see-**ohn**
Bread	du pain	dew pan
Breakfast	le petit-déjeuner	luh puh-**tee** day-zhuh-**nay**
Butter	du beurre	dew burr
Cheers!	A votre santé!	ah vo-truh sahn-**tay**
Cocktail/aperitif	un apéritif	uhn ah-pay-ree-**teef**

Dinner	le dîner	luh dee-**nay**
Special of the day	le plat du jour	luh plah dew **zhoor**
Enjoy!	Bon appétit!	bohn a-pay-**tee**
Fixed-price menu	le menu	luh may-**new**
Fork	une fourchette	ewn four-**shet**
I am diabetic	Je suis diabétique	zhuh swee dee-ah-bay-**teek**
I am on a diet	Je suis au régime	zhuh sweez oray-**jeem**
I am vegetarian	Je suis végé-tarien(ne)	zhuh swee vay-zhay-ta-ree-**en**
I cannot eat . . .	Je ne peux pas manger de . . .	zhuh nuh **puh** pah mahn-**jay** deh
I'd like to order	Je voudrais commander	zhuh voo-**dray** ko-mahn-**day**
I'm hungry/thirsty	J'ai faim/soif	zhay fahm/swahf
Is service/the tip included?	Le service est-il compris?	luh sair-**veess** ay-teel com-**pree**
It's good/bad	C'est bon/mauvais	say bohn/mo-**vay**
It's hot/cold	C'est chaud/froid	say sho/frwah
Knife	un couteau	uhn koo-**toe**
Lunch	le déjeuner	luh day-zhuh-**nay**
Menu	la carte	la cart
Napkin	une serviette	ewn sair-vee-**et**
Pepper	du poivre	dew **pwah**-vruh
Plate	une assiette	ewn a-see-**et**
Please give me . . .	Merci de me donner . . .	Mair-**see** deh meh doe-**nay**
Salt	du sel	dew sell
Spoon	une cuillère	ewn kwee-**air**
Sugar	du sucre	dew **sook**-ruh
Waiter!/Waitress!	Monsieur!/ Mademoiselle!	muh-**syuh**/ mad-mwa-**zel**
Wine list	la carte des vins	la **cart** day van

MENU GUIDE

French	English

General Dining

French	English
Entrée	Appetizer/Starter
Garniture au choix	Choice of vegetable side
Selon arrivage	When available
Supplément/En sus	Extra charge
Sur commande	Made to order

Breakfast

French	English
Confiture	Jam
Miel	Honey
Oeuf à la coque	Boiled egg
Oeufs au bacon	Bacon and eggs
Oeufs sur le plat	Fried eggs
Oeufs brouillés	Scrambled eggs
Tartine	Bread with butter or jam

Appetizers/Starters

French	English
Anchois	Anchovies
Andouille(tte)	Chitterling sausage
Assiette de charcuterie	Assorted pork products
Crudités	Mixed raw vegetable salad
Escargots	Snails
Jambon	Ham
Jambonneau	Cured pig's knuckle
Pâté	Liver puree blended with meat
Quenelles	Light dumplings
Saucisson	Dried sausage
Terrine	Pâté in an earthenware pot

Soups

French	English
Bisque	Shellfish soup
Bouillabaisse	Fish and seafood stew
Julienne	Vegetable soup
Potage/Soupe	Soup
Potage parmentier	Thick potato soup
Pot-au-feu	Stew of meat and vegetables
Soupe du jour	Soup of the day
Soupe à l'oignon gratinée	French onion soup
Soupe au pistou	Provençal vegetable soup
Velouté de . . .	Cream of . . .
Vichyssoise	Cold leek and potato cream soup

Fish and Seafood

French	English
Bar	Bass
Bourride	Fish stew from Marseilles
Brandade de morue	Creamed salt cod
Brochet	Pike
Cabillaud/Morue	Fresh cod
Calmar	Squid
Coquilles St-Jacques	Scallops
Crabe	Crab
Crevettes	Shrimp
Daurade	Sea bream

Écrevisses	Prawns/crayfish
Harengs	Herring
Homard	Lobster
Huîtres	Oysters
Langouste	Spiny lobster
Langoustine	Prawn/lobster
Lotte	Monkfish
Lotte de mer	Angler
Loup	Catfish
Maquereau	Mackerel
Matelote	Fish stew in wine
Moules	Mussels
Palourdes	Clams
Perche	Perch
Poulpe	Octopus
Raie	Skate
Rascasse	Scorpion-fish
Rouget	Red mullet
Saumon	Salmon
Thon	Tuna
Truite	Trout

Meat

Agneau	Lamb
Ballotine	Boned, stuffed, and rolled
Blanquette de veau	Veal stew with a white-sauce base
Boeuf	Beef
Boeuf à la Bourguignonne	Beef stew
Boudin blanc	Sausage made with white meat
Boudin noir	Sausage made with pig's blood
Boulettes de viande	Meatballs
Brochette	Kabob
Cassoulet	Casserole of white beans, meat
Cervelle	Brains
Châteaubriand	Double fillet steak
Côtelettes	Chops
Choucroute garnie	Sausages and cured pork served with sauerkraut
Côte de boeuf	T-bone steak
Côte	Rib
Cuisses de grenouilles	Frogs' legs
Entrecôte	Rib or rib-eye steak
Épaule	Shoulder
Escalope	Cutlet
Foie	Liver
Gigot	Leg
Langue	Tongue
Médaillon	Tenderloin steak
Pavé	Thick slice of boned beef
Pieds de cochon	Pig's feet
Porc	Pork
Ragoût	Stew
Ris de veau	Veal sweetbreads
Rognons	Kidneys
Saucisses	Sausages
Selle	Saddle

Tournedos	Tenderloin of T-bone steak
Veau	Veal
Viande	Meat

Methods of Preparation

À point	Medium
À l'étouffée	Stewed
Au four	Baked
Bien cuit	Well-done
Bleu	Very rare
Bouilli	Boiled
Braisé	Braised
Frit	Fried
Grillé	Grilled
Rôti	Roast
Saignant	Rare
Sauté/poêlée	Sautéed

Game and Poultry

Blanc de volaille	Chicken breast
Caille	Quail
Canard/caneton	Duck/duckling
Cerf/chevreuil	Venison (red/roe)
Coq au vin	Chicken stewed in red wine
Dinde/dindonneau	Turkey/young turkey
Faisan	Pheasant
Lapin	Rabbit
Lièvre	Wild hare
Oie	Goose
Pigeon/pigeonneau	Pigeon/squab
Pintade/pintadeau	Guinea fowl/young guinea fowl
Poularde	Fattened pullet
Poulet/Pouissin	Chicken/Spring chicken
Sanglier/marcassin	Wild boar/young wild boar
Volaille	Fowl

Vegetables

Artichaut	Artichoke
Asperge	Asparagus
Aubergine	Eggplant
Carottes	Carrots
Champignons	Mushrooms
Chou-fleur	Cauliflower
Chou (rouge)	Cabbage (red)
Choux de Bruxelles	Brussels sprouts
Courgette	Zucchini
Cresson	Watercress
Épinard	Spinach
Haricots blancs/verts	White kidney/green beans
Laitue	Lettuce
Lentilles	Lentils
Maïs	Corn
Oignons	Onions
Petits pois	Peas
Poireaux	Leeks
Poivrons	Peppers

Pomme de terre	Potato
Pommes frites	French fries
Tomates	Tomatoes

Sauces and Preparations

Béarnaise	Vinegar, egg yolks, white wine, shallots, tarragon
Béchamel	White sauce
Bordelaise	Mushrooms, red wine, shallots, beef marrow
Bourguignon	Red wine, herbs
Chasseur	Wine, mushrooms, shallots
Diable	Hot pepper
Forestière	Mushrooms
Hollandaise	Egg yolks, butter, vinegar
Indienne	Curry
Madère	With Madeira wine
Marinière	White wine, mussel broth, egg yolks
Meunière	Brown butter, parsley, lemon juice
Périgueux	With goose or duck liver puree and truffles
Poivrade	Pepper sauce
Provençale	Onions, tomatoes, garlic

Fruits and Nuts

Abricot	Apricot
Amandes	Almonds
Ananas	Pineapple
Cacahouètes	Peanuts
Cassis	Black currants
Cerises	Cherries
Citron/citron vert	Lemon/lime
Figues	Figs
Fraises	Strawberries
Framboises	Raspberries
Fruits secs	Dried fruit
Groseilles	Red currants
Marrons	Chestnuts
Melon	Melon
Mûres	Blackberries
Noisettes	Hazelnuts
Noix de coco	Coconut
Noix	Walnuts
Pamplemousse	Grapefruit
Pêche	Peach
Poire	Pear
Pomme	Apple
Pruneaux	Prunes
Prunes	Plums
Raisins blancs/noirs	Grapes green/purple
Raisins secs	Raisins

Desserts

Coupe (glacée)	Sundae
Crêpe	Thin pancake
Crème brûlée	Custard with caramelized topping

Crème caramel	Caramel-coated custard
Crème Chantilly	Whipped cream
Gâteau au chocolat	Chocolate cake
Glace	Ice cream
Mousse au chocolat	Chocolate mousse
Sabayon	Egg-and-wine-based custard
Tarte aux pommes	Apple pie
Tarte tatin	Caramelized apple tart
Tourte	Layer cake

Alcoholic Drinks

À l'eau	With water
Avec des glaçons	On the rocks
Kir	Chilled white wine mixed with black-currant syrup
Bière	Beer
blonde/brune	Light/dark
Calvados	Apple brandy from Normandy
Eau-de-vie	Brandy
Liqueur	Cordial
Poire William	Pear brandy
Porto	Port
Vin	Wine
sec	*dry/neat*
brut	*very dry*
léger	*light*
doux	*sweet*
rouge	*red*
rosé	*rosé*
mousseux	*sparkling*
blanc	*white*

Nonalcoholic Drinks

Café	Coffee
noir	*black*
crème	*with steamed milk/cream*
au lait	*with steamed milk*
décaféiné	*caffeine-free*
express	espresso
Chocolat chaud	Hot chocolate
Eau minérale	Mineral water
gazeuse/non gazeuse	*carbonated/still*
Jus de . . .	. . . juice
Lait	Milk
Limonade	Lemonade
Thé	Tea
au lait/au citron	*with milk/lemon*
glacé	*Iced tea*
Tisane	Herb tea

INDEX

✕ = *restaurant*, 🏨 = *hotel*

M

Fodor's Travel Publications

Available at bookstores everywhere. For descriptions of all our titles and a key to Fodor's guidebook series, visit http://www.fodors.com/books/

Gold Guides

U.S.

Alaska
Arizona
Boston
California
Cape Cod, Martha's Vineyard, Nantucket
The Carolinas & Georgia
Chicago
Colorado
Florida
Hawai'i
Las Vegas, Reno, Tahoe
Los Angeles
Maine, Vermont, New Hampshire
Maui & Lāna'i
Miami & the Keys
New England
New Orleans
New York City
Oregon
Pacific North Coast
Philadelphia & the Pennsylvania Dutch Country
The Rockies
San Diego
San Francisco
Santa Fe, Taos, Albuquerque
Seattle & Vancouver
The South
U.S. & British Virgin Islands
USA
Virginia & Maryland
Washington, D.C.

Foreign

Australia
Austria
The Bahamas
Belize & Guatemala
Bermuda
Canada
Cancún, Cozumel, Yucatán Peninsula
Caribbean
China
Costa Rica
Cuba
The Czech Republic & Slovakia
Denmark
Eastern & Central Europe
Europe
Florence, Tuscany & Umbria
France
Germany
Great Britain
Greece
Hong Kong
India
Ireland
Israel
Italy
Japan
London
Madrid & Barcelona
Mexico
Montréal & Québec City
Moscow, St. Petersburg, Kiev
The Netherlands, Belgium & Luxembourg
New Zealand
Norway
Nova Scotia, New Brunswick, Prince Edward Island
Paris
Portugal
Provence & the Riviera
Scandinavia
Scotland
Singapore
South Africa
South America
Southeast Asia
Spain
Sweden
Switzerland
Thailand
Toronto
Turkey
Vienna & the Danube Valley
Vietnam

Special-Interest Guides

Adventures to Imagine
Alaska Ports of Call
Ballpark Vacations
The Best Cruises
Caribbean Ports of Call
The Complete Guide to America's National Parks
Europe Ports of Call
Family Adventures
Fodor's Gay Guide to the USA
Fodor's How to Pack
Great American Learning Vacations
Great American Sports & Adventure Vacations
Great American Vacations
Great American Vacations for Travelers with Disabilities
Halliday's New Orleans Food Explorer
Healthy Escapes
Kodak Guide to Shooting Great Travel Pictures
National Parks and Seashores of the East
National Parks of the West
Nights to Imagine
Orlando Like a Pro
Rock & Roll Traveler Great Britain and Ireland
Rock & Roll Traveler USA
Sunday in San Francisco
Walt Disney World for Adults
Weekends in New York
Wendy Perrin's Secrets Every Smart Traveler Should Know
Worlds to Imagine

Fodor's Special Series

Fodor's Best Bed & Breakfasts

America

California

The Mid-Atlantic

New England

The Pacific Northwest

The South

The Southwest

The Upper Great Lakes

Compass American Guides

Alaska

Arizona

Boston

Chicago

Coastal California

Colorado

Florida

Hawai'i

Hollywood

Idaho

Las Vegas

Maine

Manhattan

Minnesota

Montana

New Mexico

New Orleans

Oregon

Pacific Northwest

San Francisco

Santa Fe

outh Carolina

outh Dakota

outhwest

exas

nderwater Wonders
f the National Parks

tah

irginia

Vashington

Vine Country

Visconsin

Vyoming

itypacks

msterdam

tlanta

erlin

oston

hicago

orence

ong Kong

ndon

s Angeles

iami

ontréal

ew York City

ris

Prague

Rome

San Francisco

Sydney

Tokyo

Toronto

Venice

Washington, D.C.

Exploring Guides

Australia

Boston & New England

Britain

California

Canada

Caribbean

China

Costa Rica

Cuba

Egypt

Florence & Tuscany

Florida

France

Germany

Greek Islands

Hawai'i

India

Ireland

Israel

Italy

Japan

London

Mexico

Moscow & St. Petersburg

New York City

Paris

Portugal

Prague

Provence

Rome

San Francisco

Scotland

Singapore & Malaysia

South Africa

Spain

Thailand

Turkey

Venice

Vietnam

Flashmaps

Boston

New York

San Francisco

Washington, D.C.

Fodor's Cityguides

Boston

New York

San Francisco

Fodor's Gay Guides

Amsterdam

Los Angeles & Southern California

New York City

Pacific Northwest

San Francisco and the Bay Area

South Florida

USA

Karen Brown Guides

Austria

California

England B&Bs

England, Wales & Scotland

France B&Bs

France Inns

Germany

Ireland

Italy B&Bs

Italy Inns

Portugal

Spain

Switzerland

Pocket Guides

Acapulco

Aruba

Atlanta

Barbados

Beijing

Berlin

Budapest

Dublin

Honolulu

Jamaica

London

Mexico City

New York City

Paris

Prague

Puerto Rico

Rome

San Francisco

Savannah & Charleston

Shanghai

Sydney

Washington, D.C.

Languages for Travelers (Cassette & Phrasebook)

French

German

Italian

Spanish

Mobil Travel Guides

America's Best Hotels & Restaurants

Arizona

California and the West

Florida

Great Lakes

Major Cities

Mid-Atlantic

Northeast

Northwest and Great Plains

Southeast

Southern California

Southwest and South Central

Rivages Guides

Bed and Breakfasts of Character and Charm in France

Hotels and Country Inns of Character and Charm in France

Hotels and Country Inns of Character and Charm in Italy

Hotels of Character and Charm in Paris

Hotels of Character and Charm in Portugal

Hotels of Character and Charm in Spain

Wines & Vineyards of Character and Charm in France

Short Escapes

Britain

France

Near New York City

New England

Fodor's Sports

Golf Digest's Places to Play (USA)

Golf Digest's Places to Play in the Southeast

Golf Digest's Places to Play in the Southwest

Skiing USA

USA Today The Complete Four Sport Stadium Guide

Fodor's upCLOSE Guides

California

Europe

France

Great Britain

Ireland

Italy

London

Los Angeles

Mexico

New York City

Paris

San Francisco